BACK IN THE SADDLE AGAIN

New Essays on the Western

Edited by
Edward Buscombe and Roberta E. Pearson

 Publishing

First published in 1998 by the
British Film Institute
21 Stephen Street, London W1P 2LN

The British Film Institute exists to promote appreciation, enjoyment, protection and
development of moving image culture in and throughout the whole of the United
Kingdom. Its activities include the National Film and Television Archive; the National
Film Theatre; the Museum of the Moving Image; the London Film Festival; the
production and distribution of film and video; funding and support for regional
activities; Library and Information Services; Stills, Posters and Designs; Research,
Publishing and Education; and the monthly *Sight and Sound* magazine.

British Library Cataloguing-in-Publication Data
A catalogue record for this book is available from the British Library

ISBN 0–85170–6606 (hbk)
       0–85170–6614 (pbk)

Cover design: Swerlybird Art & Design

Typeset by Fakenham Photosetting Limited, Fakenham, Norfolk
Printed in Great Britain by St Edmundsbury Press, Suffolk

Contents

List of Contributors

Richard Abel is Center for the Humanities Director and Professor of English at Drake University, where he teaches cinema studies and cultural studies. His most recent books are *The Ciné Goes to Town: French Cinema, 1869–1914* (1994), *Silent Film* (1996), and *The 'Red Rooster' Scare, or Making Cinema American* (1998).

William Boddy is a professor at Baruch College and the Graduate Center of the City University of New York and the author of *Fifties Television: The Industry and Its Critics* (1992).

Edward Buscombe was until 1996 Head of Publishing at the British Film Institute. He has taught film at a number of American universities and colleges, most recently at Middlebury College, Vermont. Together with Manuel Alvarado and Richard Collins he is the editor of *The Screen Education Reader* (1993). He has published a number of articles on American cinema in *Screen*, and is the editor of *The BFI Companion to the Western* (1988) and a volume on *Stagecoach* in the BFI Film Classics series.

Noël Carroll is Monroe C. Beardsley Professor of Philosophy at the University of Wisconsin-Madison and the president-elect of the American Society for Aesthetics. His most recent books include: *Theorizing the Moving Image* (1996), *Interpreting the Moving Image* (1998), and *A Philosophy of Mass Art* (1997).

Edward Countryman teaches history at Southern Methodist University. He was a consulting editor for the *BFI Companion to the Western* and is finishing a BFI Film Classics volume on *Shane* together with Evonne von Heussen-Countryman. He also has written extensively on the American Revolution and American social history.

Jane Marie Gaines teaches film and literature at Duke University in Durham, North Carolina. **Charlotte Cornelia Herzog** teaches art history and film at William Rainey Harper College in Palatine, Illinois. Together they co-edited *Fabrications: Costume and the Female Body* (1991) and have written together on Joan Crawford's fans and the history of the man-tailored suit.

Jean-Louis Leutrat teaches cinema history and aesthetics at the University of Paris III – Sorbonne Nouvelle. He has written books on Jean-Luc Godard, Alain Resnais, John Ford, Jean Renoir, the Western, the Fantastic of Cinema and Julien Gracq.

Suzanne Liandrat-Guigues teaches cinema history and aesthetics at the University of Paris VII – Denis Diderot. She has written books on Visconti, Godard, the Western and *Red River*. She contributes to the French magazine, *Positiv* and has edited a book on Jacques Rivette.

Steve Neale is Research Professor in Film, Media and Communication Studies at Sheffield Hallam University. He is the author of *Genre* (BFI, 1987) and *Cinema and Technology* (1985), and co-author of *Popular Film and Television Comedy* (1990). He is currently completing *Hollywood and Genre* for Routledge.

Roberta E. Pearson is a senior lecturer in the School of Journalism, Media and Cultural Studies at Cardiff University of Wales. She has authored, edited and co-authored numerous books and articles. Among them are: *Eloquent Gestures: The Transformation of Performance Style in the Griffith Biography Films* (1992), *Reframing Culture: The Case of the Vitagraph Quality Films* (co-authored with William Uricchio, 1993), and *The Many Lives of the Batman: Critical Approaches to a Superhero and his Media* (1991).

Tassilo Schneider received his Doctorate in Film and Literature from the University of Southern California with a dissertation on the popular German cinema of the 1950s and 1960s. He is currently working for a publishing house in Freiburg, Germany.

Peter Stanfield is a senior lecturer in the Media Arts Faculty, Southampton Institute. His essay in this volume is a condensed version of chapters from *Dixie Cowboys: Hollywood and the 1930s Western* (forthcoming, 1999). He is currently working on a study of Hollywood and American popular song.

Gaylyn Studlar is Director of the Program in Film and Video Studies at the University of Michigan, Ann Arbor, where she is Professor of Film Studies and English Language and Literature. She has published widely on gender issues in the cinema and, with Matthew Bernstein, is in the final stages of co-editing an anthology on John Ford's Westerns.

Rick Worland received his M.A. and Ph.D. in Motion Picture/Television Critical Studies from UCLA. He is Associate Professor of Cinema in the Center for Communication Arts at Southern Methodist University where his teaching includes silent film, popular genres, and film theory. His research has concentrated on popular film and television in the Cold War period.

Introduction
Edward Buscombe and Roberta E. Pearson

By 1960, the production of Westerns in Hollywood had entered a decline from which it has never recovered. Although for a time in the mid-60s the supply was augmented from an unexpected source, as the Italians found new ways to inject life into a dying genre, that proved to be a short-lived phenomenon, and by the early 70s Hollywood was struggling to produce a bare score of Westerns per year. In the 80s, with production declining still further, the death of the genre was pronounced on all sides. In the 90s the Western girded itself for one last stand, like a wounded gunfighter – Joel McCrea in *Ride the High Country*, perhaps. Director-stars like Kevin Costner and the stoically resilient Clint Eastwood attempted by a sheer effort of will to get the genre back on its feet. But the predicted full-scale revival obstinately refused to arrive.

We can speculate on the reasons for this decline. The decline of the studio system meant the disappearance of the staple Western form, the B film, during the 1950s. More recently, production patterns cater for the changing demographics of the cinema audience, the majority of whom are now too young for a genre that always venerated age; recent discussions on the bulletin board H-Film about why 'students hate Westerns', as well as personal experience, would seem to confirm this. This younger audience is attracted to other genres – horror, science fiction – that offer many of the traditional satisfactions of the Western without a dated historical baggage that seems increasingly irrelevant near the turn of the 21st century. Changing cultural attitudes, especially in terms of sexuality and ethnic difference, have left the 'classical' Western marooned in its essentially nineteenth-century ideology, while 'revisionist' Westerns that acknowledge identity politics – *Bad Girls, Posse, The Quick and the Dead* – seem to be trying too hard. All these factors, and doubtless others too, have played a part.

It is tempting to take the long view on this. The Western has many times been pronounced dead, only to renew itself. As far back as 1911 the film trade journal *Nickelodeon* declared that the Western was 'a gold mine that had been worked to the limit'. In 1929 the spectacular exploits of Charles Lindberg seemed to usher in a new age of adventure which would decisively outstrip such an old-fashioned type as the cowboy; as *Photoplay* then put it: 'The Western novel and motion picture heroes have slunk away into the brush, never to return.' And indeed for a time in the 1930s it did seem as if the Western was in terminal decline, or at least reduced to the marginal status of the second feature. Yet at the end of the decade Westerns made a spectacular comeback, with *Stagecoach, Jesse James* and *Dodge City* all appearing to great acclaim in 1939. The 40s and the 50s then saw the

Western's greatest years. Yet by the 60s and the 70s the Western film, as if anticipating its own demise, took up the theme of the vanishing West. A series of nobly elegiac works such as *The Wild Bunch*, *Monte Walsh* and *The Shootist* told stories of heroes who seemingly had outlived their time but who refused to go quietly into the night.

Not only the Western genre, but the American West itself has always seemed in a state of imminent decay, yet always renewing itself. If part of the value of the West was that it refused to be what the East had become – civilised, industrialised, domesticated, tamed – then the mere fact of observation, the intrusion of even the most respectful and self-effacing outsider, threatened its pristine perfection. As early as the 1830s, George Catlin, the first person to make pictures of the trans-Mississippi West, lamented the fate of the Indians, doomed as he saw it to inevitable decline, leaving behind no trace but the pictures he had painted of them: 'If I should live to accomplish my design, the result of my labours will doubtless be interesting to future ages; who will have little else left from which to judge of the original inhabitants of this simple race of beings, who require but a few more years of the march of civilization and death, to deprive them of all their native customs and character.'[1] Fifty years later, on his first visit to the West in 1881, the painter Frederic Remington mourned the encroachment of commerce and industrialisation upon the free and open vistas: 'I knew the railroad was coming. I saw the men already swarming into the land. I knew the derby hat, the smoking chimney, the cord-binder and the thirty-day note were upon us in a restless surge. I knew the wild riders and the vacant land were about to vanish for ever.'[2]

But as Remington lamented the passing of the 'real', geographical West, the imaginary West that most Americans (and Europeans) believed in flourished within popular culture. Publishers such as Beadle and Adams turned out hundreds of Western dime novels. Writers such as Zane Grey and Owen Wister took up where the dime novels left off while in Germany Karl May made a career of writing about a place he had never visited. Even today bookstores reserve special sections for Westerns by Louis L'Amour and others. Buffalo Bill's Wild West Show and its countless imitators brought cowboys, Indians, buffalo and other Western icons to eager audiences in the East and in Europe. Buffalo Bill's appearance in an early Edison film presaged the advent of the Western film on thousands of cinema screens over several decades.

But the decline in Western film production that set in during the 60s has lasted nearly forty years now, almost one-third of the entire life span of the cinema. Even in an industry as notorious as Hollywood for repeating its past successes, the return of the Western to the pre-eminent position it once occupied in production schedules looks very unlikely. So why at this moment write a book about the Western?

There are two compelling reasons. The first is that, even though the Western movie has ceased to occupy the commanding position it once had in popular cinema, the idea of the West and the Western within the wider popular culture is as alive as ever. In the field of country music, Western visual and aural motifs are pervasive. In fashion, both through the designer-Western clothes of Ralph Lauren and his imitators, and in street fashion, Western clothing has never lost its appeal.

The West as a mecca for tourists is booming. Western painting fetches higher prices than ever, whether for the classic canvases of Frederic Remington and Charlie Russell or for their contemporary followers. While the output of Western pulp fiction may, like the movies, have declined, writers such as Larry McMurtry and Cormac McCarthy have demonstrated that as a form in which to create serious literature the Western is by no means exhausted. And while the Western no longer dominates the large screen it remains important on the small one. Mini-series such as *Lonesome Dove* and series such as *Dr Quinn, Medicine Woman* per-form well in the ratings. Numerous documentaries and documentary series have aired recently on the US terrestrial and cable networks; for example, the Arts and Entertainment Network's series *The Real West* and the multi-part PBS documen-tary *The Way West*. Anyone who wishes to understand popular cinema needs to look at its wider cultural context, and the persistence of the West as an idea is a fascinating case study in how meanings may migrate from one medium to another.

The persistence of the West in various cultural forms also attests to the central role it continues to play in conceptions of national identity. Turner may famously have declared the frontier closed in 1893 but more than a hundred years later debates over the frontier retain the capacity to engender controversy precisely because of their imbrication with the very idea of 'America' and 'Americanness'. The work of the 'new' Western historians such as Patricia Nelson Limerick and Richard White affronts many within the academy and even more outside it by substituting a narrative of genocide and environmental destruction for the more traditional one of the triumphal progress of white American civilisation. The dis-semination of these perceptions to a larger public through the Smithsonian's exhibit 'The West As America' led to outrage in the halls of Congress and articles in *The New York Times*. The West of hardy pioneers, brave cavalry troopers and virginal school-marms that existed nowhere but on cinema and television screens still exercises a powerful hold on the American imaginary.

Another reason why the Western still repays our interest is that the articulations between the genre and the concerns of contemporary film studies are more com-plex and more surprising than we might think. The conventional view is that the Western is sexist and racist, that it purveys a white male, indeed a middle-aged white Anglo-Saxon Protestant male view of the world. The most recent exponent of this dismissive view is Jane Tompkins in her book *West of Everything*, who argues that 'the western struggles and strains to cast out everything feminine.'[3] But the great Westerns are a good deal more subtle than that. It would be instructive, perhaps, to produce a series of readings of particular films each of which set out to challenge easy assumptions about the genre's dealings with issues of sexuality, ethnicity, national identity and so forth. To some extent this is the intention of the recent *Movie Book of the Western*.[4] This collection, however, adopts a different approach. Instead of looking in detail at a small number of individual films, we have set out to explore a number of topics, themes and approaches which seem to us neglected by traditional film history but which bring into play many of the cen-tral concerns of contemporary film studies.

The first two essays are about Indians/Native Americans. Steve Neale counters the assumption that many Westerns about Indians are but thinly disguised treatments of race relations between blacks and whites. Instead, he argues, the actual history of white–Indian relations, in particular the conflicting models of assimilation and separation, is quite significant enough to provide the social and political points of reference for the films he discusses. Moving away from the reductionism of so much commentary on films about Indians, in which points are awarded for 'progressive' attitudes, Neale's essay is a model of how to deal with connections between films and history; the history in question being not only the period in which the film is set, but also the time in which it was made.

Edward Buscombe's essay on Indians and photography relates certain modes of white representation of Indians to fundamental conceptions of the Indians' place in a white-dominated society. Like Neale, he sees the notion of 'the vanishing American', the idea that Indians are ultimately doomed to extinction, as central. The conflict-model of the Western narrative can only deal with those Indians whose defeat has confined them to history. Living Indian societies, such as the Pueblo Indians of the South-west, find virtually no place in the Western movie.

Noël Carroll, like Neale, relates films to the politics of the time in which they are set. In his essay on four Westerns set south of the border he takes issue with Will Wright's classification, in his book *Sixguns and Society*, of these films as 'professional' Westerns in which the heroes are motivated solely by the desire to practise their own élite skills. Carroll argues that this classification ignores the films' representation of Mexican society, in particular their treatment of the theme of revolution, with which the heroes identify. But in siding with the revolutionaries these films are also justifications of American foreign policy in its proclaimed purpose of supporting 'democracy'. Though he differs in many points of detail, Carroll's approach has something in common with Richard Slotkin's recent book *Gunfighter Nation: The Myth of the Frontier in Twentieth-Century America*.

The theme of masculinity is at the heart of the Western, and Gaylyn Studlar's essay on the little-known Westerns of Douglas Fairbanks shows how, as far back as the late teens, the Western was capable of producing complex negotiations of the conflicts engendered between the civilising, even 'feminising', effects of modern life and the essentially nineteenth-century notions of masculinity which ideologues such as Teddy Roosevelt identified as specifically Western. This theme of masculinity resurfaces in essays later in the book.

From the earliest days of the story film, the Western established itself as the most popular narrative form. But considering the vast output between 1903 and 1927, the silent Western has been little explored. Richard Abel shows how the earliest Westerns functioned both as a means whereby the American film industry could fight back against foreign competition, and as sites on which an authentic American national identity, often based on racial difference, could be constructed. In focusing on the pre-sound Western Abel, like Studlar, points the way forward for more detailed explorations of a rich and so far largely unsurveyed terrain.

Another area of Western production which has so far been largely ignored is that of the B feature, especially during the 30s, the heyday of the singing cowboy. Peter Stanfield's essay takes a close look at the key role played by Gene Autry in this generic development, which he relates to the strategy, dictated by commercial forces, of grafting Western elements on to the traditions of southern country music. Stanfield is alert to the close connections between film and other media, especially radio and the recording industry, and he also appreciates the importance of the female audience in this shift to a new kind of Western hero.

Another medium in which the Western was to play a crucial role, albeit only for a brief period, was television. The late 50s saw a boom in the number of Western series on prime-time television, with no less than forty-eight shows on in 1959. Yet very little of any significance has ever been written about this outpouring of material. William Boddy shows how the Western focused a whole range of social and political issues to do with television's role in national, even international affairs, as well as being a site on which were played out anxieties over violence, masculinity and family life.

Such anxieties also, according to Tassilo Schneider, played a part in the rise of an even more short-lived, but rather extraordinary phenomenon, the West German Western of the 1960s. The considerable output of European Westerns, from the earliest years (the National Film and Television Archive has identified over thirty British Westerns before 1920), has received scant attention, with the notable exception of Christopher Frayling's pioneering work *Spaghetti Westerns*,[5] first published in 1981. Schneider shows that the German Westerns based on the works of Karl May, the hugely popular author of Western fiction in the late 19th century, offered 60s audiences troubled by an oppressive past and an uncertain present the promise of a world of total escape. In this respect he sees the German films as fundamentally different both from the Hollywood Western, with its traditional concern with issues of community, and from the Italian Western and its highly political ideological agendas.

The appearance of a recent book on the East German Western[6] is an indication that the involvement of the European film industry in the production of Westerns is even more extensive than might have been supposed. Not only European cinema, but European scholarship too has contributed much to the Western. André Bazin's suggestive essays 'The Western, or the American Film par excellence' and 'The Evolution of the Western' are well known. Jean-Louis Leutrat has written widely on the genre, including a study of the silent Western (*L'alliance brisée*), a short but highly original work on *The Searchers*, and a more wide-ranging book entitled *Les Cartes de l'Ouest*.[7] His essay on Monument Valley, written with Suzanne Liandrat-Guigues, is included in this volume not only for its intrinsic merits but also as a representative of a tradition of work that does not often find its way into Anglo-American scholarship.

The last four contributions return to the exploration of relations between the Western movie and its wider context. Colin McArthur, who has been concerned with genre issues since his widely praised book on film noir, *Underworld USA*, was first published in 1972, provides a commentary on a selection of advertising images from American magazines from the 30s to the 50s. He shows both the pervasiveness of such images, and their consonance with the narrative modes and ideological concerns of the cinema during its classic years.

Given its importance in establishing a distinctive generic world, it is surprising how little attention has been paid to the way in which costume functions in the Western. The cowboy's hat, boots, gunbelt are powerful signifiers, with their roots deep in American social history, but with a specific generic history too. Movie fashion has its own dynamic. Mainstream film studies has largely ignored the role of fashion designers such as Nudie Cohn, who perhaps did more than any other single person to influence the physical look of Western stars. The detailed work on the influence upon Westerns of such fashion centres as Nashville and rodeo remains to be done, but Jane Gaines and Charlotte Herzog have provided the essential methodological preliminaries in their discussion of the fundamental antinomies of authenticity and fantasy.

This collection ends where it began, with history. Much useless effort has been expended on telling audiences what they already know, that Western movies do not provide a reliable record of America's Western past. History, nevertheless, is at the heart of the genre. Over the past few years the history of the West itself has been changing, as scholars bring to bear the methodologies and politics developed in other historical spheres. Western history has become more conscious of the roles played by women and minorities, by social class and ethnicity, by economics and technology. Rick Worland and Edward Countryman, both professional historians, assess the importance of these developments to our understanding of Western movies.

Finally, Roberta E. Pearson provides a case study of one of the most famous episodes in Western history, dissected in scores of historical studies, encrusted with myth from as many media representations, in fiction and painting, film and television. General George Armstrong Custer is probably the most famous Westerner of all. As views of the West change, over time and from differing social and political perspectives, so he offers a different face, a perfect example of the gnomic truth of every Western movie historian's favourite quotation: 'This is the West, sir. When the legend becomes fact, print the legend.'

What we have tried to do with this volume is to suggest some directions in which future studies of the Western might progress. Considering its key role within the American film industry, the Western is still a critically neglected genre, still, one suspects, the victim of academic snobbery. Yet, as these essays show, there are many lines of enquiry which can lead to productive results. Nor, indeed, does this volume exhaust them. Consider, for example, the importance to the Western of the Hispanic presence in the West. John Ford's Westerns are packed with Hispanic references. *My Darling Clementine* is a film about Wyatt Earp, a quintessential WASP figure, at least as portrayed in the movies. But the entire town of Tombstone is pervaded by Hispanics. Not only is the Mexican woman Chihuahua central to the film's symbolic structure (East/West, garden/desert, respectability/open sexuality). At the town theatre a Mexican woman sells enchiladas, the musicians in the saloon where the Earps drink are Mexicans, the actor Thorndike is tormented by the Clantons in a Mexican cantina, even the man who holds Wyatt Earp's horse as he mounts to ride off after Doc Holliday is a Mexican. The Spanish language and Mexican music are woven in and out of the soundtrack. Nor is this Ford's only film with such a strong Hispanic influence. *3 Godfathers*, *The Searchers*, *Two Rode Together* have equally strong Hispanic elements. Indeed, there is a long essay if not a whole book to be written on what might be called 'the South-western', the Western as expressive of Hispanic cultural survival. The title of this volume, *Back in the Saddle Again*, is a reference to Gene Autry's theme song, first recorded in 1939. The following year Autry had another hit with 'El Rancho Grande'. This song had previously been featured in the Mexican film of 1936, *Allà en el Rancho Grande*, which inaugurated the Mexican sub-genre of the Western, the *comedia ranchera*. Half of the words of the song Autry sings in the original Spanish, a fact not much noticed in all that has been written on the theme of multiculturalism in the cinema.

Notes

1 George Catlin, *Letters and Notes on the Manners, Customs, and Conditions of the North American Indians* [1844] (New York: Dover, 1973), p. 16.
2 Quoted in Lonn Taylor and Ingrid Maar, *The American Cowboy* (Washington: Library of Congress, 1983), p. 19.
3 Jane Tompkins, *West of Everything* (New York and Oxford: Oxford University Press, 1992), p. 127.
4 Ian Cameron and Douglas Pye (eds), *The Movie Book of the Western* (London: Studio Vista, 1996).
5 Christopher Frayling, *Spaghetti Westerns: Cowboys and Europeans from Karl May to Sergio Leone* (London: Routledge & Kegan Paul, 1981).
6 Frank-Burkhard Habel, *Gojko Mitic, Mustangs, Marterpfähle: Die DEFA-Indianerfilme* (Berlin: Schwarzkopf & Schwarzkopf, 1997).
7 Jean-Louis Leutrat, *L'alliance brisée: Le Western des années 1920* (Lyon: Presses universitaires de Lyon, 1985); Jean-Louis Leutrat, *John Ford: La prisonnière du désert, une tapisserie navajo* (Paris: Editions Adam Biro, 1990); Jean-Louis Leutrat and Suzanne Liandrat-Guigues, *Les Cartes de l'Ouest: un genre cinématographique: le western* (Paris: Armand Colin, 1990).

1 Vanishing Americans: Racial and Ethnic Issues in the Interpretation and Context of Post-war 'Pro-Indian' Westerns
Steve Neale

Among other things, the appearance of a recent cycle of 'Indian' and 'pro-Indian' Westerns, of films like *Black Robe* (Bruce Beresford, 1993), *The Last of the Mohicans* (Michael Mann, 1992), *Dances with Wolves* (Kevin Costner, 1990) and *Geronimo: An American Legend* (Walter Hill, 1993), prompts identification, consideration and reconsideration of previous cycles of films of this kind.[1] For instance, many hundreds of Indian Westerns were made in the late teens and early 20s. Although they have been discussed – and often dismissed – *en bloc*, they still await detailed analysis. Clearly of industrial and cultural significance, the contours of the cycle and the different elements, trends and films within it have hardly been explored at all.[2] The cycle that appeared in the late 60s and early 70s is much better known, and has been subject to much more analysis. Films like *Tell Them Willie Boy Is Here* (Abraham Polonsky, 1969), *Soldier Blue* (Ralph Nelson, 1970), *Little Big Man* (Arthur Penn, 1970) and *Ulzana's Raid* (Robert Aldrich, 1972) have often been discussed, and have generally been seen as vehicles for 60s radicalism and counter-cultural values, and, more specifically, as coded commentaries on America's involvement in the Vietnam War, and hence on Euro-American militarism, racism and imperialism.[3]

Also well known is the cycle of liberal pro-Indian Westerns made in the 50s and early 60s, a cycle that includes such films as *Broken Arrow* (Delmer Daves, 1950), *Apache* (Robert Aldrich, 1954), *White Feather* (Jesse Hibbs, 1956) and *Geronimo* (Arnold Laven, 1962). The ideological significance of this particular cycle has been discussed at some length by John H. Lenihan and Richard Slotkin, and also in passing by Thomas Cripps.[4] During the course of these discussions a consensus has emerged regarding the ways in which the preoccupation with racial conflict, racial tolerance and race relations as a whole should be read. Broadly speaking, Lenihan, Slotkin and Cripps all argue that this preoccupation was motivated by the struggles over black civil rights in the late 40s, the 50s and the early 60s, and thus that the cycle as a whole should be interpreted allegorically in at least two ways. On the one hand, the films should be seen as allegories – set in the past – about contemporary racial issues, struggles and debates. On the other, the ethnic group with which they are ostensibly concerned – Native Americans – should be treated, to use Cripps's term, as a 'stand-in' for African-Americans.[5] A similar approach can be found in Brian Henderson's essay, '*The Searchers*: An American

Dilemma.'[6] While *The Searchers* (John Ford, 1956) cannot itself be easily labelled as either liberal or pro-Indian, and thus cannot easily be slotted into the liberal, pro-Indian cycle, Henderson sees the film's obsessive meditations upon racism, race, ethnic allegiance and, in particular, the opposition between 'kinship by blood *versus* kinship by adoption'[7] as motivated in general by contemporary struggles over black civil rights and in particular by the struggles and debates surrounding the Supreme Court's ruling in May 1954 (in the case of *Brown* v. *Board of Education of Topeka, Kansas*) against segregation in public schools.[8]

Henderson argues that his reading of *The Searchers* is 'non-reductive – the Indian–white ideological theme remains'.[9] However, he also argues that 'The emotional impact of *The Searchers* can hardly come from the issue of the kinship status and marriageability of an Indian in white society in 1956. ... It becomes explicable only if we substitute black for red and read a film about red–white relations in 1868–1873 as a film about black–white relations in 1956.'[10] In a similar manner, Lenihan argues that 'in its repeated dramatisation since 1950 of Indian–white relations on the frontier, the Western contained implications relevant to the contemporary racial issue', and that while generic specificities vis-à-vis the depiction of Native Americans and the staging of stories that involve them are not to be ignored, 'the racial issue' he is referring to here is one that centres, not on Indians, but on blacks: 'In 1973 the militant demonstration at Wounded Knee and Marlon Brando's refusal of the Academy Award drew public attention to the Indian, but for audiences of the fifties and sixties the racial question chiefly involved black America. The contemporary relevance of the Indian theme in Westerns of the fifties and sixties must be viewed accordingly.'[11]

There does exist evidence and there do exist grounds for readings and for statements of this kind, as we shall see. However, as we shall also see, 'public attention', however defined, was drawn to Indians, to Indian affairs, to Indian policy and the question of the relationship between Indians and Euro-American society in the 50s and the 60s as well as in the early 70s. At the moment, though, the main point I should like to make is as follows. For several centuries, Indians have been constructed, represented and imagined as 'vanishing Americans', as on the point of final disappearance as a 'race', as a culture, or as a people.[12] In the accounts I have cited above, they once again come close to disappearance, not just from the films that seem to be about them, but also from post-war America, and from post-war struggles, debates and concerns over racial prejudice, civil rights, and America's ethnic make-up, and hence from the discourse of which the accounts themselves are an instance, a discourse that rather ironically perhaps seems to pride itself on its sensitivity to issues of this kind. As Richard Maltby has pointed out, Native Americans have often functioned, in films and in film criticism, as 'empty signifiers', as 'stand-ins', to repeat Cripps's phrase, for some other topic, group or concern.[13] What seems so striking in this case is that they are made to function as signifiers of a preoccupation with racism, race and ethnicity in such a way as to exclude them from this same preoccupation, on the one hand, and thus to preclude any analysis of their position within it on the other. Hollywood, like America, was in the late 40s, the 50s and the early 60s full of discussions, debates and representations of these issues as they affected not just blacks, not even just Native Americans, but also the Japanese, in films like *Japanese War Bride* (King

Vidor, 1952), *House of Bamboo* (Samuel Fuller, 1955), *Sayonara* (Joshua Logan, 1957), *The Barbarian and the Geisha* (John Huston, 1958), as well, of course, as numerous war films; Jews, in *Gentleman's Agreement* (Elia Kazan, 1947), *Crossfire* (Edward Dmytryk, 1947), and *Ivanhoe* (Richard Thorpe, 1952), and also numerous biblical epics; Mexicans, in *Border Incident* (Anthony Mann, 1948), *Giant* (George Stevens, 1956); and Puerto Ricans in *Cry Tough* (Paul Stanley, 1959) and *West Side Story* (Robert Wise, 1961). These films (and the ethnic groups they represent) have largely been ignored in commentary on the Indian Western, and this is a problem, I think, when it comes to understanding both its cinematic and its cultural contexts. But the main point to make at this juncture is that no one has yet suggested that the ethnic groups in these films are really stand-ins for other groups, that the Japanese in *Sayonara* and *House of Bamboo* are stand-ins for blacks, or, for that matter, that the blacks in, say, *Intruder in the Dust* (Clarence Brown, 1949) or *Bright Road* (Gerald Mayer, 1952) or *A Raisin in the Sun* (Daniel Petrie, 1961) – all of them contributions to two distinct cycles of films that overtly concerned themselves with African-Americans – are really stand-ins for Jews or Puerto Ricans or Mexicans.[14] There do exist examples of films in which, in the process of adaptation from a novel or a play, one ethnic group or minority is substituted for another. *Crossfire*, for instance, substitutes a Jew for a male homosexual, and *Home of the Brave* (Mark Robson, 1949) substitutes an African-American for a Jew. In discussing these films, commentators have to my knowledge never argued that they do not in some way really deal with anti-Semitism on the one hand, and with the case of a paralysed black soldier on the other. However, in discussing *Reprisal* (George Sherman, 1956), an adaptation in Western guise of a novel about the lynching of a black in contemporary Georgia, it is axiomatic that the film, ostensibly about a half-breed Indian, is really about an African-American.[15] I have no quarrel with this view of *Reprisal*. It seems to me to be at least one unequivocal instance where the allegorical reading of 'black for red' is empirically as well as logically warranted. What I want to highlight is the extent to which the propensity for allegorical readings and for the location of ethnic stand-ins tends to be limited to Westerns and to Native Americans.

A partial explanation for this may be that most of the films I have cited above are set, unlike most Westerns, in the recent past or in the present. But this explanation is indeed only partial. For both *The Barbarian and the Geisha* and *Ivanhoe* are set in the more distant past, and no one has yet suggested that the Japanese and the Jews in these films are stand-ins for other ethnic groups. Moreover, Hollywood did make at least one film in the 50s about a twentieth-century Indian, *Jim Thorpe – All American* (Michael Curtiz, 1951), one of a cycle of biopics about non-Anglo-Americans (often sporting figures, as here, or figures from the world of show business) whose appearance also testifies to Hollywood's preoccupation with race and race relations at this time.[16] However, *Jim Thorpe – All American* is ignored by Henderson, Slotkin, Lenihan and Cripps. Ignored also, therefore, is the liberal, assimilationist stance implicit in its very title, and the implications of this stance vis-à-vis contemporary Native Americans, and this brings me on to the principal point I wish to make here, and to the principal topic of this essay. What is occluded in the substitution of 'red for black' in the reading of 50s and 60s pro-Indian and Indian Westerns is not just the possibility of any discussion of contemporary Native Americans and of contemporary relations between Native Americans, Euro-Americans and the Euro-American government, but the possibility of any address to the particular, indeed unique position of Native Americans vis-à-vis Euro-American liberalism, vis-à-vis segregation, vis-à-vis integration and vis-à-vis civil rights in the late 40s, the 50s and the early 60s. My argument is not that post-war pro-Indian and Indian Westerns are all always 'really about' contemporary Native Americans. (I would deny neither the potential for allegory nor the potential for stand-ins or for the substitution of red for black in the case of certain Westerns – like *Reprisal* at least.) It is rather that the elements and issues outlined above need to be taken more fully into account in attempting to understand the ideological context and in attempting to assess the ideological significance and impact of this particular cycle of films. In order to pursue this argument, I want firstly to outline in more detail the contours of this cycle, its place in relation to other post-war Westerns, and its place in relation to other cycles of post-war Hollywood films that concern themselves overtly with issues of ethnicity, race and racial prejudice.[17]

Of the commentators I have cited on the post-war pro-Indian and Indian Western, John Lenihan provides the most comprehensive account, both in terms of the number of films discussed and in terms of an attempt to locate them in relation to a variety of cycles and trends. (Richard Slotkin uses the framework provided by Lenihan's account, though he tends to discuss fewer films in greater detail. Henderson focuses on one particular film. And Cripps's comments are made in passing.) Lenihan identifies two principal strands of ideological concern at work in post-war Westerns that involve or centre on Indians: the Cold War, international relations, American imperialism and the role of the military; and racism, race and race relations. These strands of concern tend to interweave with one another, and aside from the years of the Korean War in the early 50s, they tend also to be linked by a liberalism that favours negotiation, co-existence and mutual respect, on the one hand, and tolerance and integration on the other. The principal location of both of these strands is a cycle of post-war films about the cavalry and the Indian wars set mainly in the mid- to late 19th century. Inaugurated by *Fort Apache* (John Ford, 1948) and *She Wore a Yellow Ribbon* (John Ford, 1949), this cycle continued on into the early 70s. By then, though, post-war liberalism had foundered on the rocks of the Vietnam War, anti-war protest, ethnic militancy, race riots, ghetto violence and the collapse of 'hopes for a peacefully integrated "Great Society" '.[18] *A Distant Trumpet* (Raoul Walsh, 1964) and *Cheyenne Autumn* (John Ford, 1964) can be seen as marking the end of the liberal strand, with *Major Dundee* (Sam Peckinpah, 1965) the first in a series of increasingly cynical and increasingly violent 'post-liberal' cavalry films.

The cavalry film (a vehicle not only for what Slotkin calls the 'Cult of the Cavalry' but also, as he himself points out, for the cult of the military and military activity in general that pervades so much of Hollywood's output – and of Euro-American society and culture as a whole – in the 50s) is by no means the only vehicle, though, for the 'Cult of the Indian'.[19] Largely as a matter of historical verisimilitude, the cavalry occasionally makes an appearance in some of the following films, but all the same neither *Buffalo Bill* (William Wellman, 1944), which Lenihan cites as among the first to display the new, more liberal attitude to

11

Indians at this time, nor *Broken Arrow, Across the Wide Missouri* (William Wellman, 1951), *The Big Sky* (Howard Hawks, 1952), *Hiawatha* (Kurt Neumann, 1952), *Navajo* (Norman Foster, 1952), *Broken Lance* (Edward Dmytryk, 1954), *The Vanishing American* (Joseph Kane, 1955), *The White Squaw* (Ray Nazarro, 1956), *Flaming Star* (Don Siegel, 1960) and *Oklahoma Territory* (Edward L. Cahn, 1960), among others, can be considered cavalry Westerns, and the same is arguably true of films like *The Half-Breed* (Stuart Gilmore, 1952) and *Walk the Proud Land* (Jesse Hibbs, 1956), in which the cavalry plays a much more prominent role.

Hiawatha, Navajo, White Squaw, The Vanishing American and *Oklahoma Territory* were all made, by Monogram, Lippert, Columbia, Republic and Premium/UA respectively, as B films and/or as independently produced second features, and this is itself indicative of the widespread nature of liberal attitudes and the Cult of the Indian. (They are by no means the only examples. Other instances include *Apache Chief* (Fred MacDonald, Lippert, 1949), *Daughter of the West* (Harold Daniels, Film Classics, 1949), *Rose of Cimarron* (Harry Keller, Fox, 1952), *Apache Woman* (Roger Corman, Golden State/ARC, 1955) and *Daniel Boone, Trail Blazer* (Albert Gannaway, Republic, 1957).)[20] Indicative, too, is the extent to which lip service is paid to the Cult and to liberal attitudes in films which are otherwise governed not only by racist, imperialist and conflict-oriented conventions (which is the case, of course, with most Westerns), but also by an overt and apparently self-conscious racist, imperialist and conflict-oriented ideological agenda. In *Dakota Incident* (Lewis R. Foster, 1956, another Republic film), for instance, we witness the 'savage' consequences of an Indian raid on a stagecoach; we hear the heroine, Amy Clarke (Linda Darnell) ask a peace-preaching politician from the East, 'How do you feel about the Indians now? Why don't you get on your soapbox and tell us how misunderstood they are?'; and we later hear the film's hero, John Banner (Dale Robertson) tell this self-same politician, by now a figure of contempt, 'to send an army out here. Tell 'em to dig every Indian out from every rock and wipe the warpaint off his face with a bullet.' Towards the end, in a classic last-stand scenario (itself, as Slotkin in particular has shown, a quintessentially racist and imperialist narrative trope),[21] the politician is killed by the Indians as he steps towards them appealing for an end to violence and mutual hatred, and, aside from one mortally wounded secondary character, Amy and John are the only whites left alive. There is a final attack, and hand-to-hand combat ensues. John is about to strangle his Indian assailant when suddenly, and for no internally logical or motivated reason, he stops. 'It's no use,' he says. 'I can't kill a man with my bare hands.' He lets the Indian go. The following morning, the Indian returns with other braves from his village and with a horse for Amy and John. He rides away. 'The language of friendship,' says Amy. 'The senator tried to sow the seeds. All it needed was good ground to fall on.'

Dakota Incident was filmed from an original script by Frederick Louis Fox. However, a number of other pro-Indian and Indian films were adapted from novels and short stories, and it is worth mentioning here that liberal attitudes and the Cult of the Indian (and often the Cult of the Cavalry) found articulation in all kinds of Western fiction at this time – including comic books like *Indians, Indian Braves, Indian Warrior* and *Indian Chief* – whether it functioned as source material for Western films or not. A range of attitudes can be found across the spectrum of

Western fiction as a whole, from the straightforward racism of Burt Arthur's *Bugles in the Night* (first published in 1960) to novels like *Buffalo Soldiers* (John Prebble, 1959), and *Santa Fe Passage* (1952), *Yellow Hair* (1953), *Yellowstone Kelly* (1957) and *River of Decision* (1958) (all of them written under the pen-name 'Clay Fisher' by Henry Wilson Allen), which display not just an awareness – and a dis-approval – of racism, but often also a positive interest in the ethnic diversity of the American south-west in the 19th century, to 'serious' Indian-oriented novelised histories like *Blood Brother* (Elliot Arnold, 1947) and *Cheyenne Autumn* (Marie Sandoz, 1953). *Santa Fe Passage, Yellowstone Kelly* and *Cheyenne Autumn* were all made into films (*Santa Fe Passage* by William Witney for Republic in 1955, and *Yellowstone Kelly* by Gordon Douglas for Warner Bros. in 1959). *Blood Brother*, meanwhile, seems to have been the source not just for *Broken Arrow*, but also in part at least for *Drum Beat* (Delmer Daves, 1954). Other source novels and stories vary, too, in their attitudes to racism, race and to Indians. What is striking, though, is the extent to which, in the process of adaptation, a number of the more openly racist (or ethnically pessimistic) of these novels and stories are toned down, rendered more complex, rendered more liberal or more optimistic. Howard Hawks's adaptation of A. B. Guthrie's *The Big Sky* (novel 1947, film 1952) is much more upbeat than the novel in its treatment and in particular in its res-olution of the inter-ethnic romance between Teal Eye (Elizabeth Threatt in the film) and Boone (Dewey Martin).[22] John Ford's adaptation (as *Fort Apache*) of James Warner Bellah's short story, 'Massacre' (1947), is much more complex than its source – and much more critical of its central protagonist (Colonel Thursday – Henry Fonda in the film) and of his contemptuous attitude to Indians.[23] And the same is true of Ford's adaptation of *The Searchers* (Alan Le May, 1954).[24]

Finally, it is also worth mentioning that liberal attitudes and the Cult of the Indian found a place in the television Western as well as in films of the 50s. A CBS series called *Brave Eagle*, which according to Richard West 'presented the encroachment of the white man on to Indians' lands from the Indians' point of view', ran from September 1955 through to June 1956,[25] and *Broken Arrow*, cen-tred on Cochise and inspired by the film, ran on ABC from September 1956 through to September 1958. In addition, *Law of the Plainsman* (NBC) featured an Apache marshal, and of course an Indian, Tonto, featured prominently as the companion of the *Lone Ranger* (ABC).[26] Individual episodes of other Western series (like the 'Incident of the Valley in Shadow' episode of *Rawhide* (CBS) and the episode of *Bonanza* (NBC) entitled 'The Honor of Cochise') are strongly marked by 50s liberalism too.

Noting the initial wave of post-war social problem films about African-Americans, Lenihan charts the subsequent relationship between pro-Indian Westerns, post-war liberalism and the issues of racism, race and race relations as follows:

> During the early and mid-fifties when production of modern black-problem dramas declined, Hollywood Westerns exhibited a more liberal racial perspective through stories about frontier intolerance toward the Indian. During the critical period of legal desegregation by the federal judiciary, the Western became a more prolific and pointed commentary on the issue of racial equality than were the few films about blacks. It was only with *Edge of the City* (1957) and especially *The Defiant Ones* (1958) that

Hollywood again significantly probed the racial question with respect to black Americans.[27]

However, while it is true that there were two quite distinct cycles of social-problem films about African-Americans, one in the late 40s and the early 50s, the other in the late 50s and early 60s, and while it is also true that the proportion of liberal, pro-Indian Westerns increased in the early to mid-50s, Lenihan's analysis takes no account of the fact that Westerns of this kind continued to be made in great numbers in the late 50s and early 60s, at a time when the second cycle of social-problem films about African-Americans and anti-black prejudice was well under way. Thus it does not seem as though Indian Westerns operated simply as substitutes for films about the African-American 'problem'. More importantly, it takes no account either of the cycle of films featuring Japanese (and other Asian and 'Oriental') characters mentioned above, or indeed of the general trend towards the representation of ethnic diversity, inter-ethnic relations and ethnocentric prejudice evident in Hollywood's output as a whole in the 50s.

One of the reasons, perhaps, for the lack of attention to this trend and to this cycle is the fact that few of the films are social-problem 'dramas' as such. A striking feature of the Japanese and Asian cycle, in particular, is the extent to which it deals with inter-ethnic relations and ethnocentric prejudice through stories of love and romance: aside from *Japanese War Bride*, *Sayonara*, *The Barbarian and the Geisha* and *A Bridge to the Sun*, all mentioned above, the cycle also includes *Love is a Many Splendored Thing* (Henry King, 1955), *China Doll* (Frank Borzage, 1958), *The World of Suzie Wong* (Richard Quine, 1960) and *Bhowani Junction* (George Cukor, 1956), and the story-line centred on Joseph Cable (John Kerr) and Liat (France Nuyen) in *South Pacific* (Joshua Logan, 1958), as well.[28] *Bhowani Junction* was set in India, and can be related to a series of films dealing either specifically with the British Empire, or more generally with European or American colonies or colonial rule. Others include *Kim* (Victor Saville, 1950), *Thunder in the East* (Charles Vidor, 1953), *King of the Khyber Rifles* (Henry King, 1953), *His Majesty O'Keefe* (Byron Haskin, 1953), *Something of Value* (Richard Brooks, 1957) and *Donovan's Reef* (John Ford, 1963). *South Pacific*, of course, was a Rodgers and Hammerstein musical, as was another pertinent film, *The King and I* (Walter Lang, 1956). Hammerstein's liberal views with regard to race and racial prejudice found articulation in songs like 'You've Got to be Carefully Taught' (in *South Pacific*) and the narrative ballet sequence, 'The Small House of Uncle Thomas' in *The King and I*. Such views had been expressed much earlier in Hammerstein's career, in *Showboat* (which was originally staged in 1927), and it is worth pointing out in this context that *Showboat* was revived on Broadway in the immediate post-war period (in 1946), and that a second film version, directed by George Sidney, was released by MGM in 1951.

Two further points are worth making here. The first is that musicals about blacks were also produced as films in the 50s, for example *Carmen Jones* (Otto Preminger, 1954) and *Porgy and Bess* (Otto Preminger, 1959).[29] The second is that the source novels, stories, plays and shows for the films mentioned here – and for others – were themselves important vehicles for debates, discussions and representations of ethnic diversity, ethnic interaction and ethnocentric prejudice. Aside from Hammerstein (and Rodgers), it is worth citing Han Suyin's *A Many Splendored Thing* (1952), Edna Ferber's *Giant* (1952), *Tales of the South Pacific* (1947) (the source for *South Pacific*) and *Sayonara* (1954) by James A. Michener, and John Patrick's play, *The Teahouse of the August Moon* (1952), filmed in 1956, and the novel by Vern Sneider on which it is based.

Nearly all these novels, plays, stories, shows and films adopt an identifiably liberal point of view. The roots of this liberalism lay, for the most part, in the Depression, in the New Deal, and in the anti-Fascist campaigns of the 30s. Its more immediate source and context, however, was the Second World War, and the struggles, contradictions and debates inevitably engendered by a war waged in the name of tolerance and freedom by a country riven by institutionalised racism, against an avowedly white supremacist regime on the one hand, and on the other an 'Oriental' country claiming to free Asia from Anglo-American imperial rule.[30] Of particular importance as far as writers, directors, actors, musicians and the practitioners of art, entertainment and culture in general were concerned were the liberal policies and views of the agencies of government propaganda, especially the Office of War Information.[31] Although the OWI – and New Deal liberalism in general – came under increasing attack from conservatives in the later stages of the war, it served to legitimise left–liberal opinions and to cement left–liberal alliances in a number of spheres of cultural activity, including the cinema.[32]

The precise nature and extent of any gains made by minority ethnic groups in America and by Anglo-American liberal opinion with regard to matters of race during the Second World War itself is open to some dispute. Nevertheless, most commentators argue that the war and the circumstances and conditions of war created a framework for subsequent change and improvement as well as for subsequent struggle.[33] And it is certainly the case that the period towards the end of the Second World War and the immediate post-war period itself witnessed a plethora of statements, promises and plans for change in the field of entertainment that bespeaks a determination on the part of a number of hitherto subordinate ethnic groups and their organisations, on the one hand, and a degree of confidence on the part of Euro-American liberals and leftists on the other. In 1945 and 1946 *Variety*, for instance, is simply full of reports of activity on this front – reports of plans for shows, films and broadcasts, reviews of shows, films and broadcasts, and a number of reports connected with a study made of racial stereotyping in show business by Columbia University's Office of Communication Research.[34]

As far as Hollywood was concerned, few of the plans and promises came to fruition until the end of the decade. *Crossfire* and *Gentleman's Agreement* were released in 1947, but it was not until 1949 that a discernible cycle took shape with the release of *Home of the Brave*, *Lost Boundaries* (Alfred L. Werker), *Pinky* (Elia Kazan) and *Intruder in the Dust*. The delay is usually attributed to declining cinema attendances, box-office worries and an initial reluctance to experiment – and hence possibly to alienate audiences further – on the part of the industry.[35] However, it is likely that the advent of the Cold War, the initial post-war activities of HUAC, and the consequent attack on liberal values also played a part, especially in view of the fact that *Variety* explicitly cited the re-election of Harry S. Truman, and the return to liberal values that this event was perceived to signal, as a major factor in the cycle that emerged in 1949.[36]

Certainly liberals and leftists were prominent in all the films cited above. Darryl Zanuck produced *Pinky* and *Gentleman's Agreement*,[37] Carl Foreman wrote and Stanley Kramer directed *Home of the Brave*, Edward Dmytryk directed *Crossfire*, Ben Maddow scripted *Intruder in the Dust*, and Dudley Nichols scripted *Pinky*. Liberals and leftists can also be found among the credits for films about prejudice and race made during the course of the 50s. Dore Schary produced *Bad Day at Black Rock* (John Sturges, 1955), John Huston directed *The Barbarian and the Geisha* and Richard Brooks co-scripted *Storm Warning* (Stuart Heisler, 1951). And Samuel Fuller, whose liberalism was, of course, anything but orthodox, wrote and directed *House of Bamboo*, and wrote, produced and directed *China Gate* (1957) and *The Crimson Kimono*, while Douglas Sirk, an exile from Nazi Germany in the late 30s, directed the remake of *Imitation of Life* (1959). The key point, though, is that liberals and leftists can be found in abundance among the credits for Indian and pro-Indian Westerns as well. Dudley Nichols scripted *The Big Sky*, Edward Dmytryk directed *Broken Lance*, Ben Maddow scripted, John Huston directed, and Burt Lancaster starred in and co-produced *The Unforgiven* (1960). Lancaster also starred in and co-produced *Apache*, which was directed by Robert Aldrich, Dore Schary produced and Richard Brooks directed *The Last Hunt* (1956), Samuel Fuller wrote, produced and directed *Run of the Arrow* (1957), Douglas Sirk directed *Taza, Son of Cochise* (1954), and it has recently emerged that Albert Maltz, who was blacklisted at the time, wrote the script for *Broken Arrow* fronted by a friend, Michael Blankfort.[38]

The point is key because it suggests that the same strand of liberalism can be found in Indian and pro-Indian Westerns as in black social-problem films and other films and cycles made about racism, race and race relations in the late 40s and 50s, and because, as we shall see, some of the tenets, assumptions and aims of this liberalism interacted in particularly paradoxical ways with other strands of discourse about Native Americans, with the status of Native Americans vis-à-vis the American government, with post-war government policy, and hence with the lives and struggles of Native Americans themselves.

The pro-Indian and Indian cycle emerged at more or less the same time as the cycle of social-problem films mentioned above. Following the release of *Fort Apache* in 1948, the cycle took shape with the release of *Apache Chief, The Cowboy and the Indians* (John English), *Daughter of the West* and *Ranger of Cherokee Strip* (Philip Ford) in 1949, and of *Broken Arrow, North of the Great Divide* and *Devil's Doorway* (Anthony Mann) among others in 1950. *Devil's Doorway* in particular highlights the importance of the Second World War, not only in the shaping of Euro-American liberalism, but also in the shaping of the lives of Native Americans. *Devil's Doorway* is the story of Lance Poole (Robert Taylor), a Shoshone Indian who returns home as a highly decorated veteran of the American Civil War only to find himself the victim of prejudice, government regulations and the machinations of a white racist businessman. As Lenihan indicates, there is more than a hint of reference here to contemporary post-war situations and events, as well as a mobilisation of 'the commonly used argument that Americans, regardless of their race, deserved equitable treatment in civilian life because of their service in World War II'. He goes on to add, though, that '*Devil's Doorway* . . . clearly evokes this rationale in its story of a decorated Civil War hero who loses his

Robert Taylor (left) in Devil's Doorway.

land because he is an Indian. He, like the *black* veteran of the 40s and 50s, has earned recognition as a first-class citizen and should be treated as such.'[39] Thus, in illustration both of the general and of the specific arguments I am seeking to pursue here, Lenihan's reading not only displaces and ignores the potential pertinence to *Devil's Doorway* of contemporary Native Americans, but also the contribution made by Native Americans to the conduct of the Second World War, and hence the fact that they too may have 'earned recognition'.[40] Ironically, earning recognition as citizens, especially when coupled with the assimilationist ideology implicit in such a phrase, was to prove not only a major topic of debate and legislation at the end of the war, but also a major source of the difficulties – as well as the opportunities – faced by Native Americans during the post-war period as a whole.[41]

In an extremely interesting discussion of *Devil's Doorway*, Richard Slotkin sums up the film's ideological and narrative movement in the following terms:

> At the beginning of the film Poole indicates his willingness to play by White Men's rules: he has fought in their army for their flag, dresses like a White Man, insists that his people speak English, and is a successful businessman. It is White bigotry, not racial atavism, that drives him to define himself more and more as *Indian* rather than American. Nonetheless, the change in his ideological stance is signalled by racial imagery. As he refuses Orv's penultimate plea for compromise, he moves out of the shadows that have hidden him and we see that he now wears his hair long, with a band across his forehead, Indian style. If we begin by identifying with Poole as a White/Indian, by the end we are clearly asked to accept him as a distinctly Indian hero.[42]

Devil's Doorway is a highly unusual film. On the one hand it articulates a wish on behalf of its hero that he be treated as an equal by white society, while on the other it allows him to retain an attachment to his people and their traditions. It recognises that the source of Poole's problems lies in white racism, in white law, and in white greed – and need – for land. The failure of Poole's wish is seen as poignant and tragic because it forces him, Slotkin points out, to become an 'Indian' in the traditional sense – a warrior whose future as such is doomed when confronted by the superior firepower and numbers of the Euro-American cavalry. The alternative, though, the aim that Poole himself restates at the end of the film, is not to be an American in any straightforward sense. This is where I disagree with Slotkin, or at any rate feel that the term he uses here requires further specification. Poole wants to be, not an American, but an Indian-American. These are the terms in which he asks for recognition from the society that eventually destroys him. And this, I think, is the significance of his wearing his Union army uniform and his Congressional Medal of Honor *and* his Indian head-band when he dies at the end of the film.

What is unusual about this can, I think, be made clear if we compare and contrast the role of Poole's army uniform with the role of the army uniform worn by Taza (Rock Hudson) in *Taza, Son of Cochise*. Taza's uniform, which he wears as head of the Apache police on the San Carlos reservation, is a sign that he has accepted the identity proposed by Euro-American society and is thus an American in so far as he conforms to this society's rules, regulations and norms. Where Poole fights these rules, regulations and norms as and when they are unjust, where he wants to determine his own identity and is eventually killed by the cavalry for doing so, Taza accepts them as just, and fights on behalf of the cavalry against the renegade Apache, Geronimo. Taza achieves the recognition that Poole fails to achieve, but precisely in so far as the basis of that recognition is fundamentally different.

One way of encapsulating the difference between the two films would be to say that *Taza* is assimilationist whereas *Devil's Doorway* is not. What is significant about this, and what is significant, therefore, about both films is that assimilationism tended to mark most liberal, pro-Indian Westerns in the late 40s and 50s, and that assimilationism had a specific resonance and meaning for Native Americans at this time, posing them particular difficulties and particular threats.

As Kenneth R. Philp points out, 'The assimilation of Indians into the dominant society has been the overriding concern of the federal government since the Washington and Jefferson administrations.'[43] This was at least putatively as true of the policies pursued by John Collier as head of the Bureau of Indian Affairs in the 30s and early 40s as it was of the policies that preceded them.[44] However, whatever the shortcomings in practice of the Indian New Deal, as it came to be called, however guided it may have been by Collier's primitivist idealisation of what he perceived to be the essence of Indian philosophy, life and society, it was founded upon a respect for Indians, a wish to improve their economic condition, and a wish to revive and foster their culture. The forces, events and conditions of the Second World War came, though, to pose a series of threats both to Collier's philosophy and to the power and the status of the BIA.

In 1941 the BIA was moved from Washington to Chicago, thereby losing direct, everyday contact with central government. A number of New Deal relief programmes geared to help Indians, among others, were ended. Partly in consequence, Indians left their reservations in great numbers to serve in the armed forces and to work in war-related industries. 'After becoming better acquainted with the outside world,' notes Philp, 'many of these individuals no longer wanted to return to the poverty and segregation associated with reservation life.'[45] In addition, as Philp goes on to point out, 'The Second World War ... encouraged a sense of national unity and consensus that led to integrating minority groups in mainstream society.'[46] As we have seen, Euro-American liberals were among those actively promoting integration. But at least as far as Indians were concerned, they were by no means the only ones. Both towards the end of the war and in the post-war period through to the early 60s, conservatives promoted the integration of Indians too. They did so initially and specifically in order to undermine Collier's position and views and in order to attack the BIA. They did so more generally as part of an attack on New Deal policies of government aid and intervention, and no doubt also to make reservation lands available for commercial exploitation by Euro-American businessmen. The result was a three-pronged policy of compensation, relocation, and what came to be enshrined in Congressional resolutions and in law as termination: Indians were to be compensated for past wrongs, once and for all, through the setting up of an Indian Claims Commission; Indians were to be encouraged to leave reservations and relocate to cities; and in general federal services to Indian peoples, groups and tribes were to be terminated. Eventually terminated too, perhaps, would be the special status of Indians in Euro-American law as 'domestic dependent nations'.[47]

There are four key points here. The first is that termination, as the policy as a whole came to be called, was an extreme form of assimilation, and the second is that in promoting assimilation there was a remarkable and ironic coincidence as between both the rhetoric and to a considerable extent also the ideology and policy of liberals and conservatives. Liberals, for instance, supported the Indian Claims Commission Act of 1946, which they saw as a means of redressing past injustices and wrongs. Conservatives saw it, in the words of Arthur V. Watkins, one of the main architects of termination, as a means of finally settling the government's 'obligations'.[48] And as Clayton R. Koppes points out, 'It was the Truman administration that reversed the Indian New Deal as liberalism changed from supporting traditional community to finding community in the nation.'[49] James S. Olson and Raymond Wilson elaborate:

> To most liberals, racial discrimination of any kind was a violation of the natural rights philosophy. So while President Truman was desegregating the armed forces and the Supreme Court was preparing for its historic assault on Jim Crow, some liberals were taking another look at the reservations, seeing them not as havens preserving tribal values but as anachronistic relics of a racist past. To them, reservations seemed another variety of *de jure* segregation – one more monument to prejudice and separatism. Caught up as they were in celebrating individualism and integration, these liberals were uneasy with ideas of tribal sovereignty, reservation autonomy, ethnic identity, and cultural pluralism; thus they resorted to the 'melting pot' ideology as the ultimate answer to American ethnicity. Assimilation would solve the 'Indian problem' after all.[50]

For conservatives, assimilation would ensure conformity and the ultimate superiority of Euro-American rules, norms and laws.

19

As far as rhetoric was concerned, the key term, of course, was 'freedom':

> For many Americans, the Indian war record had prompted concern that Indians be treated fairly. O. K. Armstrong's article in the August 1945 *Reader's Digest* urged Americans to 'Set the American Indians Free!' House of Representatives Majority Leader John. W. McCormack read Armstrong's piece advocating the removal of 'restrictions' from Indians and wrote to his colleague, W. G. Stigler, that he was 'interested in seeing justice done for all – and this applies with great force to our fine American Indians.'[51]

Senator Watkins was to write in passionate and grandiose defence of termination that 'Following in the footsteps of the Emancipation Proclamation of ninety-four years ago, I see the following words emblazoned in letters of fire above the heads of the Indians – These people shall be free!'[52]

There are clear echoes and references here to the situation of African-Americans, references and echoes which Watkins himself made explicit in hearings on termination in 1954 for the purposes not just of comparison but also of contrast. 'The Indians have made some progress, yes,' he said.

> But it is deplorable, on many of the reservations, the way they are standing still, not going ahead as other people have done in this country. ... But see what the colored people have done without reservations, without properties that came to them. ... No one would think, I am sure, of getting around to the point of saying the colored people should be put under some sort of trusteeship, or guardianship, or whatever you want to call it.[53]

This brings me to my third and most crucial point. Viewed from a multi-culturalist perspective, from the standpoint of a particular politics of cultural identity, post-war assimilation can be perceived as just as much a threat to African-Americans, Japanese-Americans, Chicanos and other ethnic minorities in America as it was to Native Americans, especially given the context of Cold War conformity within which assimilationism developed in the late 40s and 50s.[54] This is precisely the basis for the numerous complaints and critiques that exist of so many of the assimilationist films made at this time.[55] However, in its liberal guise at least, assimilationism also meant desegregation, civil rights and equal rights in Euro-American law, things for which most ethnic minorities, organisations and groups, as well as most Euro-American liberals, were themselves campaigning at the time. For Native Americans things were different precisely because their status in Euro-American law was different. The threat was greater precisely because that status was under threat.

As David Murray has pointed out, 'Indians are unique in being the only group specifically identified in the Constitution, and this has meant that they have been regarded not as a racial or ethnic group like others, but as a distinct political entity or series of entities.'[56] There has thus always been what Richard White describes as a 'tension between the attraction of separate rights and equal rights' for Indians.[57] Because of this tension and because of their unique 'sovereign status', 'the efforts of Indians to secure their rights as both citizens and tribal members obviously stood apart from the struggles of other minorities'.[58] For this reason, 'the experience and the goals of southern blacks and western Indians' has been 'different indeed'.[59] And for this reason, Vine Deloria Jr would note apropos of termination that

The argument of 'freeing' the Indians was as phony as could be. The act did nothing but dissipate tribal capital and destroy the rights of Indian tribes to have their own communities. But termination fitted exactly into the integrationist thought-world of the period, and the expanding Civil Rights movement of the black community, which had been given impetus by the decision of *Brown* v. *Topeka Board of Education*, the famous school desegregation case of 1954.[60]

Hence the particular and conservative strategic purpose inherent in Watkins's references to African-Americans. Hence the ironies inherent in post-war liberalism and in the fledgling civil rights movements as far as Indians were concerned. And hence the ironies inherent in treating Indians as stand-ins for African-Americans in post-war pro-Indian and Indian Westerns, whether at the point of contemporary production or reception, or at the point of subsequent analysis. Only further research can determine which films were intended or read as allegories about African-Americans, as allegories about other ethnic minorities (or about ethnic minorities in general), as statements about America's past or about Euro-American racism, or as allegories about contemporary Native Americans.[61] But it is worth pointing out that the plight of Native Americans and the adverse consequences of government policy in the late 40s and the 50s was (along with the nature and rationale of the policy itself) given at least some contemporary publicity, and that subsequent commentators like Brian Dippie and Alvin Josephy argue that this publicity, and the Indians' own 'resistance to termination', 'caused many whites to recognise the right of Indians to be Indians'.[62] To cite just one telling instance of the former, in 1957 *Time* magazine published an article on the plight of relocated Indians in Minneapolis. The article was entitled 'Broken Arrow'. It summarised the findings of a series of articles written for *Tribune* by Carl Rowan, an African-American.[63]

Two final comments. The first is that distinctions need to be made among the films of the post-war pro-Indian and Indian cycle between those, like *Taza, Son of Cochise* and *Walk the Proud Land*, which advocate assimilation or which draw on assimilation principles, those, like *Geronimo*, which at the cost of combining historical distortion with historical amnesia appear to advocate a position akin to 'separate but equal',[64] those, like *Devil's Doorway*, which advocate such a position but which acknowledge the obstacles to it, and those, like *The Searchers* and *The Last Hunt*, which either focus on white racism, as is the case with *The Last Hunt*, or which seek to interrogate ethnocentrism and racism and indeed the ethnocentric and racist tropes of the Western itself from within the limits of its ethnocentric framework, as is the case with *The Searchers*.[65]

Secondly, as the most recent cycle of pro-Indian films – liberal and otherwise – continues to testify, as far as the Western in general is concerned, Native Americans are still poignantly but relentlessly vanishing before our very eyes.[66] Twentieth-century Indians remain more or less invisible, not only to Hollywood film-makers and their audiences, but also, it seems, to film commentators, critics and historians.

I should like to thank Ed Buscombe for commissioning this piece and for allowing me to change its topic from the one I originally proposed, Richard Maltby for letting me have a manuscript copy of 'A Better Sense of History' and for providing me with video copies of *Geronimo* and *The Unforgiven*, and Roberta Pearson whose comments and queries helped me to clarify my argument.

Notes

1 The terms 'Indian' and 'pro-Indian' are, of course, fraught with problems, as are all terms, including 'Native American', which are used with respect to the indigenous peoples of America and which are English or European in origin. Here I use either terms employed by contemporary reviews or by subsequent writers on the Western, particularly when referring to films or to Western fiction, or the term 'Indian' or 'Native American', particularly when referring to the peoples themselves.

2 On the early Western, see in particular Angela Aleiss, 'Native Americans: The Surprising Silents', *Cineaste* 21:3, 1995; Eileen Bowser, *The Transformation of Cinema, 1907–1915* (Berkeley: University of California Press, 1990); Kevin Brownlow, *The War, The West and the Wilderness* (London: Secker & Warburg, 1978) and Ralph E. Friar and Natasha A. Friar, *The Only Good Indian ... The Hollywood Gospel* (New York: Drama Book Specialists, 1972), pp. 69–147.

3 See, for instance, Phil Hardy, *The Encyclopedia of Western Movies* (London: Octopus Books, 1985), p. 322, John H. Lenihan, *Showdown: Confronting Modern America in the Western Film* (Urbana and Chicago: University of Illinois Press, 1980), pp. 47–51, and Richard Slotkin, *Gunfighter Nation: The Myth of the Frontier in Twentieth-Century America* (New York: Atheneum, 1992), pp. 628–32.

4 Lenihan, pp. 23–81, Slotkin, pp. 347–78, and Thomas Cripps, *Making Movies Black: The Hollywood Message Movie from World War II to the Civil Rights Era* (New York: Oxford University Press, 1993), pp. 281–3.

5 Cripps, p. 281.

6 Brian Henderson, '*The Searchers*: An American Dilemma,' *Film Quarterly* 34:2 (Winter 1980–1).

7 Henderson, p. 19.

8 Henderson, pp. 20–3. For an interesting discussion of the representation of Indians in *The Searchers*, and a pertinent argument against standard liberal modes of representing non-white ethnic groups and ethnic difference, see Tag Gallagher, 'Angels Gambol Where They Will: John Ford's Indians', *Film Comment* 29:5 (September/October, 1993).

9 Henderson, p. 23.

10 Henderson, p. 19.

11 Lenihan, pp. 57–8.

12 See Brian Dippie, *The Vanishing American: White Attitudes and US Indian Policy* (Middletown: Weslyan University Press, 1982).

13 Richard Maltby, 'A Better Sense of History: John Ford and the Indians', in Ian Cameron and Douglas Pye (eds), *The Movie Book of the Western* (London: Studio Vista, 1996), p. 36.

14 For commentary on some or all of the cycles and films see Donald Bogle, *Toms, Coons, Mulattoes, Mammies and Bucks: An Interpretive History of Blacks in American Films* (New York: Continuum, 1991 edition), pp. 143–93; Thomas Cripps, *Black Film as Genre* (Bloomington: Indiana University Press, 1979), pp. 45, 47; Cripps, *Making Movies Black*; Patricia Erens, *The Jew in American Cinema* (Bloomington: Indiana University Press, 1984), pp. 173–87, 223–5; Daniel J. Leab, *From Sambo to SUPERSPADE: The Black Experience in Motion Pictures* (London: Secker & Warburg, 1975), pp. 145–68; Gina Marchetti, *Romance and the 'Yellow Peril': Race, Sex and Discursive Strategies in Hollywood Films* (Berkeley: University of California Press, 1993), pp. 78–201; James R. Nesteby, *Black Images in American Films: The Interplay Between Civil Rights and Film Culture* (Lanham: University Press of America, 1982), pp. 235–56; Jim Pines, *Blacks in Film: A Survey of Racial Themes and Images in the American Film* (London: Studio Vista,

1979), pp. 63–88; and Peter Roffman and Jim Purdey, *The Hollywood Social Problem Film: Madness, Despair and Politics from the Depression to the Fifties* (Bloomington: Indiana University Press, 1981), pp. 235–56. For comments on *Ivanhoe* see John H. Lenihan, 'English Classics for Cold War America: MGM's *Kim* (1950), *Ivanhoe* (1952), *Julius Caesar* (1953)', *Journal of Popular Film and Television* 20:3 (Fall, 1992), pp. 45–8.

15 On *Reprisal*, see Lenihan, *Showdown*, pp. 68–9.

16 Other instances include *The Jolson Story* (Alfred E. Green, 1946), *Jolson Sings Again* (Henry Levin, 1949), *The Jackie Robinson Story* (Alfred E. Green, 1950), *The Joe Louis Story* (Robert Gordon, 1953), *The Eddie Cantor Story* (Alfred E. Green, 1953) and *St Louis Blues* (Allen Reisner, 1958).

17 It should, of course, be borne in mind that 'ethnicity and race inhere in virtually all films, not only those where ethnic issues appear on the "epidermic" surface of the text. ... The disciplinary assumption that some films are "ethnic" where others are not is ultimately based on the view that certain groups are ethnic whereas others are not' (Ella Shohat, 'Ethnicities in Relation: Toward a Multicultural Reading of American Cinema', in Lester D. Friedman (ed), *Unspeakable Images: Ethnicity and the American Cinema* (Urbana and Chicago: University of Illinois Press, 1991), p. 215.

18 Lenihan, *Showdown*, p. 81.

19 The 'Cult of the Indian' is also Slotkin's term. See *Gunfighter Nation*, pp. 357–65 for the 'Cult of the Cavalry', and pp. 366–78 for the 'Cult of the Indian'.

20 This is neither to privilege the A film nor to denigrate the B film. B films were among the first to articulate liberal attitudes in the post-war period. (*Apache Chief* and *Daughter of the West* both preceded *Broken Arrow*.) And *Navajo*, which I have not yet been able to see, sounds like a truly radical film.

21 Slotkin, pp. 316–19.

22 For a discussion of the novel, see James K. Folsom, *The American Western Novel* (New Haven: College and University Press, 1966), pp. 64–70.

23 For a comparison, see Jim Hitt, *The American West from Fiction (1823–1976) into Film (1909–1986)* (Jefferson and London: McFarland & Company, 1990), pp. 38–40.

24 For a comparison, see Henderson, pp. 20–1 and Hitt, pp. 75–7. For a discussion of the novel, see Folsom, pp. 163–6.

25 Richard West, *Television Westerns: Major and Minor Series, 1946–1978* (Jefferson and London: McFarland & Company, 1987), p. 23.

26 Of course, as J. Fred MacDonald points out, a point of significance in regard to the rest of my argument, 'Tonto was an assimilated Indian, a partner who embraced the white man's dominion and now rode to enforce its laws.' J. Fred MacDonald, *Who Shot the Sheriff? The Rise and Fall of the Television Western* (New York: Praeger, 1987), p. 31. As he also points out, *The Lone Ranger* was among the early wave of TV Western series, one which drew heavily on – and sometimes consisted of – B films and series. Most commentators on the television Western in the 40s and the 50s, including MacDonald, argue that this early wave was displaced – or complemented – in the mid-50s by programmes and series that drew on the image of the 'adult' A Western promoted by Hollywood in relation to films like *High Noon* (1952), *Shane* (1953) and a number of liberal pro-Indian Westerns like *Broken Arrow*. (See MacDonald, pp. 51–116 and Christopher Anderson, *Hollywood TV: The Studio System in the 1950s* (Austin: University of Texas Press, 1994), pp. 203–5.) The suggestion is that on the one hand the liberalism of the TV Western with regard to Indians, ethnicity and race was very much a borrowed, second-hand phenomenon, and on the other that it was a phenomenon confined to the adult Western series of the mid- to late 50s. Most of the examples I have cited here bear this out. But it is worth bearing in mind both the example of the *Lone Ranger* and my point about the B film in note 20 above. It may be that a number of liberal B films were shown on American television prior to the mid-50s. A final point to note here is MacDonald's observation that Asians and African-Americans rarely figured in television Westerns at this time, and that in 1960 the Organization of Oklahoma Indians Tribes and the Association on American Indian Affairs approved of the representation of native Americans in *Law of the*

Plainsman, The Lone Ranger, Gunsmoke and *Have Gun Will Travel*, but disapproved of *Wagon Train, Laramie* and *The Overland Trail* (MacDonald, pp. 114–15).

27 Lenihan, *Showdown,* pp. 56–7.

28 For a number of brief but interesting comments on *South Pacific* in this context, see Robert J. C. Young, *Colonial Desire; Hybridity in Theory, Culture and Race* (London: Routledge, 1995), pp. xi–xii.

29 For discussions of *Carmen Jones* in this context, see Bogle, pp. 168–71, and Cripps, *Making Movies Black,* pp. 262–3. For a discussion of *Porgy and Bess,* see Bogle, pp. 174 and 183.

30 For discussions of racial issues and ethnic struggles in America in the Second World War, and some of the contradictions involved, see Michael C. C. Adana, *The Best War Ever: America and World War II* (Baltimore and London: The Johns Hopkins University Press, 1994), pp. 82–3, 119–20, 145–6; William H. Chafe, *The Unfinished Journey: America Since World War II* (New York and Oxford: Oxford University Press, 1991 edition), pp. 17–25; John W. Dower, *War Without Mercy: Race and Power in the Pacific War* (New York: Pantheon Books, 1986); and Richard Polenberg, *One Nation Divisible: Class, Race and Ethnicity in the United States since 1938* (Harmondsworth: Penguin Books, 1980), pp. 69–85.

31 For a general history and study of the OWI, see Allan M. Winkler, *The Politics of Propaganda: The Office of War Information, 1942–1945* (New Haven: Yale University Press, 1978).

32 For studies of the OWI and Hollywood, see Clayton R. Koppes and Gregory D. Black, *Hollywood Goes to War: How Politics, Profits and Propaganda Shaped World War II Movies* (New York: The Free Press, 1987).

33 Aside from the books cited in note 30 above, see Roger Daniels, *Asian Americans, Chinese and Japanese in the United States since 1850* (Washington: University of Washington Press, 1988), pp. 186–99, 299–316; Manning Marable, *Race, Reform and Rebellion: The Second Reconstruction in Black America, 1945–1990* (Jackson and London: University Press of Mississippi, 1991 edn), pp. 13–25; John Modell, Marc Goulden and Sigurdur Magnusson, 'World War II in the Lives of Black Americans: Some Findings and an Interpretation', *The Journal of American History* 76:3 (December, 1989); Ronald Takaki, *Strangers from a Different Shore: A History of Asian-Americans* (Harmondsworth: Penguin Books, 1989), pp. 362–79; and Neil A. Wynn, *The Afro-American and the Second World War* (New York: Holmes & Meier, 1975). This appears to be true even for Japanese-Americans, many of whom were interned during the war. See Daniels, pp. 199–299; Kevin Allen Leonard, ' "Is This What We Fought For?" ' Japanese-Americans and Racism in California: The Impact of World War II', *The Western Historical Quarterly* 21:4 (November 1990); David J. O'Brien and Stephen S. Fugita, *The Japanese-American Experience* (Bloomington and Indianapolis: Indiana University Press, 1991), pp. 60–100; and Takaki, pp. 379–420. Japan's role in the Cold War is clearly of importance here.

34 See, in particular, 'Gear Show Biz Vs. Race Bias', 157:5, 10 Jan. 1945, pp. 1, 18; 'Diverse Intellectuals Use Showmanship to Break Down Race Prejudice', 157:7, 17 Jan. 1945, p. 2; 'Another All-Negro Serial in Web Bid', 157:13, 17 March 1945, p. 31; 'Stage "Most Liberal" of Show World In Treatment of Minority Groups', 158:2, 21 March 1945, p. 11; 'Ethel Waters Heads All-Negro Vauder', 158:3, 28 March 1945, p. 1; 'Show Biz Rates Bows in Inter-Racial Bouquets Handed Out by Negro Daily', 164:4, 2 Jan. 1946, p. 2; 'Race Problem Too Rich For War Dept. Blood Gets V.A. Okay', 162:11, 5 May 1946, p. 31. See also reviews of radio programmes, plays and shows such as *The Negro in the War* (WABC–CBS), 157:13, 7 March 1945, p. 38; *Too Long America* (WJZ–Blue), 158:2, 21 March 1945, p. 36; *Racial Discrimination* (WEVD), 159:7, 25 July 1945; *Deep Are the Roots,* 160:1, 12 Sep. 1945, p. 54; *American Negro Theater* (WNEW), 160:3, 26 Sep. 1945, p. 36; *Strange Fruit,* 160:13, 5 Dec. 1945; *The Bulge* (WOV), 161:11, 20 Feb. 1946, p. 26; *Jeb,* 161:12, 27 Feb. 1946, p. 60 and *On Whitman Avenue,* 162:10, 15 May 1946, p. 68.

35 Neve, p. 91.

36 'Truman "Rewrites" H'wood Scripting as Pix Lean to Social Significance', *Variety* 173:6, 19 Jan. 1949, pp. 1, 32. See also Neve, pp. 91–2.

37 On Zanuck see Russell Campbell, 'The Ideology of the Social Consciousness Movie: Three Films of Darryl F. Zanuck', *Quarterly Review of Film Studies* 3:1 (Winter, 1978) and Neve, pp. 102–7.

38 See Neve, p. 121.

39 Lenihan, *Showdown*, p. 64.

40 According to Philip J. Deloria, 'Native people may have participated in the War more completely than any other group on American society. Almost one-third of the pool of able-bodied Indian men joined the military. Another one-fourth found work in war industry and related services. Indian women participated both in military auxiliaries and in war-related work' ('The Twentieth Century and Beyond', in Betty Ballantine and Ian Ballantine, eds, *The Native Americans: An Illustrated History* (London: Virgin Books, 1994), pp. 422–3). For further details and a full discussion of the Indians' role in the War and of the War's impact on Indians, see Alison R. Bernstein, *American Indians and World War II: Toward a New Era in Indian Affairs* (Norman and London: University of Oklahoma Press, 1991).

41 An interesting point of comparison here is between *Devil's Doorway* and *The Vanishing American* (1925), and between the cultural and political contexts and effects of Indian participation in the First and Second World Wars and of subsequent government 'recognition', legislation and action. American citizenship was awarded to Indian veterans in 1919 and to all Native Americans in 1924. On the one hand this can be viewed as an act of liberal gratitude for the Indian contribution to the war effort, and as a modification of the extreme assimilationism inaugurated by the passing of the Dawes Act in 1887, which tied the acquisition of citizenship to the acquisition of individual allotments of land and to the abandonment of traditional tribal loyalties, customs and ways of life. On the other hand, it can be seen as an extension of assimilationism at a time when assimilationist policies and previous attitudes to Indians were coming under threat. (The policies associated with the Dawes Act were heavily criticised by the Meriam report on *The Problem of Indian Administration* in 1928, while John Collier's tribalist views were being put forward in various campaigns on behalf of the Pueblo.) As Anglela Aleiss points out, *The Vanishing American* was made precisely at the point at which these new views were coming to the fore and at which both sets of views were coming into conflict. As she also points out, it is a film riven with contradiction and ambiguity:

> The film's importance lies not so much in its accurate depiction of the misguided reservation system as in its ability to reveal the frustration of a society unable to resolve its 'Indian problem.' *The Vanishing American* was one of Hollywood's first feature films to fault white agents for the Indians' plight; it tried to appease both reactionary and liberal groups who sought to reform the country's deteriorating reservations. As the film underscores the cultural loss within Indian society, its appeal to Christianity, however, emerges as an empty gesture that points to racial assimilation as the ultimate solution.

(Angela Aleiss, '*The Vanishing American*: Hollywood's Compromise to Indian Reform', *Journal of American Studies* 25:3 (December 1991), pp. 467–8.) For further discussion of the film and its context see Brownlow, pp. 344–8 and Dippie, pp. 209–21. Herein lie the differences between *The Vanishing American* and *Devil's Doorway*, and between the contexts in which they were made. Where the former advocates assimilation while lamenting the passing of a race, the latter reveals the limits of assimilation, and the racism that surrounds both its adoption and its refusal; where the 20s was a period in which assimilationism began to give way to tribalism (or at least to a greater respect for traditional values and ways of life), the late 40s and the 50s were to witness a sustained attack on tribalism and a resurrection of assimilationism, as we shall see.

42 Slotkin, p. 333.

43 Kenneth R. Philp, 'Termination: A Legacy of the New Deal', *The Western Historical Quarterly*, vol. 14, no. 2, April 1983, p. 166.

44 The literature on Collier and the Indian New Deal is extensive. See, among others,

Lawrence C. Kelly, 'The Indian Reorganization Act: The Dream and the Reality', *Pacific Historical Review*, vol. 44, 1975; James S. Olson and Raymond Wilson, *Native Americans in the Twentieth Century* (Urbana and Chicago: University of Illinois Press, 1984), pp. 107–30; Donald L. Parman, *Indians and the American West in the Twentieth Century* (Bloomington and Indianapolis: Indiana University Press, 1994), p. 89–106; Kenneth R. Philp, *John Collier's Crusade for Indian Reform* (Tucson: University of Arizona Press, 1977); and Graham D. Taylor, *The New Deal and American Indian Tribalism* (Lincoln and London: University of Nebraska Press, 1980).

45 Philp, p. 167.

46 Philp, p. 167.

47 On termination see, in particular, Larry W. Burt, *Tribalism in Crisis: Federal Indian Policy, 1953–1961* (Albuquerque: University of New Mexico Press, 1982); Clayton R. Koppes, 'From New Deal to Termination: Liberalism and Indian Policy, 1933–1953', *Pacific Historical Review*, vol. 46, 1977; Parman, pp. 123–47; Philp, 'Termination: A Legacy of the New Deal'; Olson and Wilson, pp. 131–56; and Frederick J. Stefon, 'The Irony of Termination: 1943–1958', *The Indian Historian*, 11:3 (Summer, 1978). The phrase 'domestic dependent nations' derives from Chief Justice John Marshall's judgment in the case of the *Cherokee Nation* v. *Georgia* in 1831. For discussion of some of the general implications of this status vis-à-vis Native Americans and their struggles, see Joyotpaul Chaudhuri, 'American Indian Policy: An Overview', and Vine Deloria Jr, 'The Evolution of Federal Indian Policy Making', in Vine Deloria Jr (ed.), *American Indian Policy in the Twentieth Century* (Norman and London: University of Oklahoma Press, 1985), and William T. Hagan, *American Indians* (Chicago and London: University of Chicago Press, 1993 edn), pp. 195–210.

48 Arthur V. Watkins, 'Termination of Federal Supervision: The Removal of Restrictions over Indian Property and Person', *Annals of the American Academy of Political and Social Science*, vol. 311, May 1957, p. 50.

49 Koppes, p. 544. It was during Truman's second term of office that the Hoover Commission on Indian Affairs recommended 'complete integration' of Indians 'into the mass of the population as full, tax-paying citizens' (quoted in Charles F. Wilkinson and Eric R. Biggs, 'The Evolution of the Termination Policy', *American Indian Law Review*, vol. 5, 197, p. 147).

50 Olson and Wilson, p. 133.

51 Perter Iverson, 'Building toward Self-Determination: Plains and Southwestern Indians in the 1940s and 1950s', *The Western Historical Quarterly* 16:2, April, 1988, p. 106.

52 Watkins, p. 55.

53 Arthur V. Watkins, contribution to the debate on Joint House and Senate Hearings on the Menominee Termination Bill, March, 1954, quoted in Stefon, p. 8.

54 On the Cold War, ethnicity, assimilation and civil rights, see Polenberg, pp. 108–26. On the Cold War, conformity and identity politics, see David Campbell, *Writing Security: United States Foreign Policy and the Politics of Identity* (Manchester: Manchester University Press, 1992), pp. 156–79. On Cold War conformity, assimilation, termination and Native Americans, see Burt, pp. 4, 19, Olson and Wilson, pp. 142–3 and Philp, p. 168. It is worth noting in this context that Koppes cites Republican Senator George 'Molly' Malone, as follows: 'While we are spending billions of dollars fighting Communism ... we are at the same time ... perpetuating the systems of Indian reservations and tribal government, which are natural Socialist environments' (Koppes, p. 556).

55 Most of those cited in note 14 above are fairly scathing about the assimilationist and Euro-oriented nature of most late 40s and 50s films, though Cripps, in *Making Movies Black*, re-evaluates some of the films about blacks and some of the contributions of stars like Sidney Poitier.

56 David Murray, *Modern Indians: Native Americans in the Twentieth Century* (British Association of American Studies, 1982), p. 39.

57 Richard White, *It's Your Misfortune and None of My Own: A New History of the American West* (Norman and London: University of Oklahoma Press, 1991), p. 585.

58 Murray, p. 588.

59 Murray, p. 582.

60 Vine Deloria Jr, 'The War Between the Redskins and the Feds', in Francis Paul Prucha (ed.), *The Indian in American History* (New York: Holt, Rhinehart and Winston, 1971), p. 121. Similar points are made by Donald Parman in 'Indians of the Modern West', in Gerald D. Nash and Richard W. Etualain (eds), *The Twentieth Century West: Historical Interpretations* (Albuquerque: University of New Mexico Press, 1973), p. 16, and by Darcy McNickle in *Native American Tribalism: Indian Survivals and Renewals* (New York and Oxford: Oxford University Press, 1973). McNickel writes that 'Some of the issues involved in the civil rights struggle were not Indian issues. Segregation, which the black man protested so bitterly, was not seen as a denial of social status by Indians. They had never aspired to a place in the white man's society, except as individuals might make that choice for themselves' (p. 122).

61 John E. O'Connor's book *The Hollywood Indian: Stereotypes of Native Americans in Films* (Jersey City: New Jersey State Museum, 1980) contains useful information on the production of *Devil's Doorway* (pp. 45–8), *Broken Arrow* (pp. 49–57) and *Cheyenne Autumn* (pp. 57–61). He indicates the extent to which the original story upon which *Devil's Doorway* was based was radically changed to emphasise racial issues and the extent to which both *Devil's Doorway* and *Broken Arrow* came to be conceived of as social-problem films with a contemporary resonance, though he remains equivocal as to the specificity of the racial issues both films address. It is worth pointing out that, while Samuel Fuller states in one of his interviews that he made *Run of the Arrow* 'because I was very angry with what was happening in the South' ('Samuel Fuller talking to Jean-Louis Noames' (Edinburgh: Edinburgh Film Festival, 1969), p. 109), Burt Lancaster's most recent biographer claims that he and Ben Hecht made *Apache* because they were 'frustrated by their failure to examine civil rights and the Indian problem in *Jim Thorpe, All-American*' (Michael Munn, *Burt Lancaster: The Terrible-Tempered Charmer* (London: Robson Books, 1995), p. 83). Delmer Daves argues that as a consequence of *Broken Arrow*, 'I think we ended up with the public understanding the Apaches and all the American Indians. . . . It created a whole new attitude' (Christopher Wicking, 'Interview with Delmer Daves', *Screen*, 10:4/5 (July–October, 1969, p. 63). A propos of *Broken Arrow*, it is worth pointing out too that in summing up what he sees as the film's significance, Frank Manchel refers to an unpublished MA thesis by Angela Aleiss ('Hollywood's Ideal of Postwar Assimilation: Indian/White Attitudes in *Broken Arrow*', Columbia University, 1985) whose views he endorses, and whose arguments vis-à-vis assimilation and termination appear to echo my own: 'If *Broken Arrow* is remembered by many today as a well-intentioned film, it may because they are willing to say that in 1950, people didn't know any better, that this was a significant step forward, compared to what had come earlier. [But] reasonable people will have no difficulty accepting Aleiss' position that the film reflects the controversial policies of 'termination' that Congress pursued in the 1950s, when they wanted to jettison any federal responsibility for Indian laws, treaties and individuals' (Frank Manchel, 'A Cultural Confusion: A Look Back at Delmar (*sic*) Daves' *Broken Arrow*', *Film and History* 23:1–4 (1993), p. 66). These views have been recently echoed by Terry Wilson in 'Celluloid Sovereignty: Hollywood's 'History' of Native Americans', in John Denvir (ed.), *Legal Reelism: Movies as Legal Texts* (Urbana: University of Illinois Press, 1996) esp. pp. 208-15, which was published while this piece was in press. Finally, it is worth noting that in its review of *The Half-Breed* (Herman Schlom, 1952), the *New York Times* wrote that 'while *The Half-Breed* is immensely dull, it does possess concern for the Indians of 1867, which is commendable but hardly timely. Perhaps it will give someone the idea for a motion picture about the plight of the contemporary Indian, the Navajos of the Southwest for instance (5 July, 1952).

62 Alvin M. Josephy Jr, 'Modern America and the Indian', in Frederick E. Hoxie (ed), *Indians In American History* (Arlington Heights: Harlan Davidson, 1988), p. 262. Dippie testifies to the 'flurry of public interest in the Indian' on p. 340 of *The Vanishing American*. Influential essays, articles and reports on the plight of Indians in the wake of post-war assimilationist policies and termination include: John Collier, 'Beleaguered

Indians', *Nation*, 17 Sept. 1949, and 'Hour of Crisis for American Indians', *New York Herald Tribune*, 4 Oct. 1948; Harold L. Ickes, 'The Indian Loses Again', *New Republic*, 24 Sept. 1951; John Collier, 'Indian Takeaway: Betrayal of a Trust', *New York Times*, 8 Aug. 1953; Dorothy Bohn, ' "Liberating" the Indian: Euphemism for Land Grab', *Nation*, 20 Feb. 1954; Ruth Mulvey Harmer, 'Uprooting the Indians', *Atlantic Monthly*, March 1956; Dorothy Van De Mark, 'The Raid on the Reservations', *Harper's Magazine*, March 1956; and, following what Burt describes as a concerted campaign by Church groups to inform their members about contemporary Indian affairs, a whole series of articles in *Christian Century*, particularly from 1955 on, written by John Collier, Harold Fey, Lawrence Lindley and others (see *Tribalism in Crisis*, pp. 66–7).

63 *Time*, March 4, 1957, pp. 30–1.

64 *Geronimo* manages to represent Geronimo's surrender as implying an honourable recognition of Apache grievances and rights on the part of the US government. It manages, therefore, to 'forget' that Geronimo's surrender was followed not by a return to the local reservation as promised, and as implied in the film, but by banishment first to Florida then to Oklahoma. Walter Hill's version is in this respect much more accurate, though in part, one suspects, because historical accuracy here serves the film's fantasy of Geronimo as an exemplary – and vanishing – warrior.

65 This aspect of *The Searchers* is dealt with by Slotkin, pp. 461–73. Very little has been written about *The Last Hunt*, but see Julian Petley's entry on the film in Edward Buscombe (ed.), *The BFI Companion to the Western* (London: Andre Deutsch/BFI, 1988), p. 279.

66 For an excellent review of a number of recent Westerns, see Pat Dowell, 'The Mythology of The Western: Hollywood Perspectives on Race and Gender in the Nineties', *Cinéaste* 21:1–2 (1995).

2 Photographing the Indian
Edward Buscombe

I Photography and the Vanishing American

In the classic Western *High Noon* (1952) there is a scene early in the film when Ben, one of the three men waiting at the station for the noon train, rides back into town for a drink. He dismounts from his horse outside the Ramirez saloon. As he enters, he passes two Indian men standing by the door. One is wearing a shirt with a diamond pattern, over which he wears braces (suspenders) supporting his trousers. The other man wears a shirt with a spotted pattern. Each has on a dark hat with a tall crown and straight brim, decorated with a single large white feather.

These characters exist only on the periphery of the frame. They are still there when Ben comes out, but our attention is drawn not to the Indians but to Marshall Will Kane, Ben's antagonist, with whom he has a brief confrontation. The Indians are not seen again and have no narrative function in the story.

So what are they doing in the film? The clothes the Indians are wearing identify them as being from one of the South-western tribes who encountered whites early and who by the 1880s (assuming this to be the approximate date of the action) had assimilated elements of European dress. We can presume the function of the Indians is merely to identify the South-west setting, to act as markers of the diegetic location, somewhere in Arizona or New Mexico, presumably.

In *The Harvey Girls* (1946), an MGM musical starring Judy Garland, we already know we are in the South-west because the film is about the Fred Harvey Company, which ran hotels and restaurants for the Santa Fe railroad throughout the region dating from the 1880s. Near the beginning of the film there is a spectacular musical number ('The Atcheson, Topeka and the Santa Fe') in which a Santa Fe train arrives, bringing with it a posse of Harvey girls to work in the town's newly opened restaurant. As they descend from the train, we notice a couple of Indians. One is wearing a yellow headband round his long black hair, a red shirt, a bear-claw necklace and a silver conch belt over black trousers. The other has a pink headband, an orange shirt over blue trousers, and a bead necklace. These two Indians neither speak nor sing, but simply stand in the background. Elsewhere in the crowded scene we can see other Indians, similarly garbed (a woman has a blue dress and a silver headband), but they are unobtrusive. They have no narrative role. Their function is to provide local colour; they are part of the décor.

Indians in the Western do not usually loiter unobtrusively in the background. Commonly they have a more active role, as antagonists of the white heroes. Drawing on a tradition well established by graphic artists and others throughout

William S. Hart (centre left) and Thomas Ince (centre right) with the Inceville Sioux.

Custer's Last Fight *(1912)*.

the 19th century, the earliest years of the Western film saw the Sioux and other mounted warriors of the plains firmly fixed as the dominant type of Indian, with feathered head-dress, decorations of porcupine quill and bear-claw, and a war-bow or tomahawk at the ready. The 101 Bison studio at Santa Ynez, often referred to as Inceville after its most famous producer, Thomas Ince, kept a group of Indians who had previously been employed by the Miller Brothers 101 Ranch Wild West show. These Indians, popularly known as the Inceville Sioux, were kept busy in a stream of pictures the studio turned out from 1911, and which was continued by Universal when it acquired the 101 Bison brand name from the original owners, the New York Motion Picture Company.[1]

A popular subject was the Custer massacre, an event still fresh in the minds of many at this time, not much more distant to film-makers of the day than the Vietnam War is to contemporary Hollywood. A successful example was *Custer's Last Fight* (1912), directed by Francis Ford, the older brother of John Ford. The Battle of the Little Big Horn in Montana in 1876 between the 7th Cavalry under Custer and a combined force of Sioux and Cheyenne was only the most spectacular engagement of the many battles of the Indians wars of the period between the end of the Civil War and the Massacre of Wounded Knee in 1890. These events and others generated a vast outpouring of printed and visual material in the later years of the 19th century, aimed at the huge markets developing in the East, and spurred by the technological and commercial innovations in printing, photography and reproduction techniques within the communications industries. Indians in feathered war bonnets rode across the pages of mass-circulation magazines such as *Harper's Weekly*, whooped their war cries in hundreds of dime novels, and on the stage and in the arena courtesy of the entertainments devised by Buffalo Bill Cody. Indians in action were dramatised in the paintings of Frederic Remington and Charles Schreyvogel (many of them specially commissioned for reproduction by *Harper's* and other magazines), and decorated the walls of a thousand saloons and hotel lobbies in the highly coloured chromolithographs reproduced in their millions by firms such as Currier and Ives. By the early 1900s, when the movies began to draw on this material, the befeathered and mounted warriors of the plains had become the dominant Indian stereotype within popular culture, and the movies imported them wholesale.

In this explosion of images, photography played a major role. Though the first photograph of a North American Indian was taken in England by David Octavius Hill and Robert Adamson as early as 1845, photography did not come into its own out West until after the Civil War. From then until the end of the century and the development of the cinema, many thousands of photographs of Indians were taken. Until the introduction of the Kodak camera by Eastman in 1888, which hugely simplified the technical process, the photographers taking the pictures were professionals, and most photographs had a semi-official status. Some photographers were working directly for the government, attached to official government explorations, such as John K. Hillers, who was part of John Wesley Powell's expedition down the Colorado River in 1871 and who became photographer for the Bureau of Ethnography founded by Powell in 1879. Other photographers made visual records of the numerous delegations of Indians who visited Washington through the 19th century. There were also photographers attached,

Red Cloud, photographed by Charles M. Bell in 1880.

often very informally, to army forts and Indian agencies throughout the West. Many of these were running a commercial business, making pictures that could be sold to locals or tourists.[2]

The slowness of the exposure times required by the processes in use, and the cumbersomeness of the bulky equipment, meant that until some time after the appearance of the portable Kodak the photography of Indians, as indeed of whites, was largely confined to portraiture, for which the subject was carefully posed, often in the studio, his head held in an iron clamp to ensure a steady image, or else in his 'natural' setting, in front of or occasionally inside his abode, or on horseback in the great outdoors.

The combination of official or semi-official status and the degree of stiffness imposed by the technology of the time meant that the Indians in these pictures appear guarded, reserved, lacking any obvious emotion. A portrait of Red Cloud, taken in Washington DC in 1880 by Charles M. Bell, shows him gazing into the distance with an expression the very blankness of which invites the viewer to supply an interpretation of the subject's thoughts.[3] Certain signifiers added by the photographer supply some pointers. The studio backdrop of painted clouds and sky, and the rock to the subject's right, we may no doubt read as elements of the natural world in which the Indian was presumed to be uniquely at home. Red Cloud wears the formal regalia of single eagle feather, porcupine-quill breastplate, fringed and beaded buckskin; he is therefore the official representative of his race. All these elements suggest that Red Cloud stands for an essence, for Indianness as a certain discourse of nineteenth-century white society defined it: dignified, stoical, noble (as in 'noble savage'). But what Red Cloud himself is really thinking we cannot tell. Very few of the pictures of Indians at this time display what the 20th century has seen as one of the defining elements of photography – its seeming ability to capture subjects off guard, unprepared for or even unaware of the camera, registering emotion direct and uncensored. Instead, Red Cloud gazes out at us with an expression which we are forced to interpret according to preconceived ideas of what he signifies.[4]

Whether official or independent, the photographers of this time were invariably white, and they were making their photographs for a white audience. Beyond offering the minimum consent necessary for the picture to be posed, the Indian did not control either the manner in which the image was taken, or the use to which it was put. Instead, he was inserted into a discourse which had already determined its meaning. What were the meanings likely to be attributed? From the earliest days, the documentation and recording of the West had been suffused with a sense of melancholy, shot through with a pang of imminent loss. For the European, no sooner had America been discovered in all its glory than his own presence began the process of spoliation. The very act of being there to observe was in itself the first step in the process whereby change and decay set in. As European settlement advanced westwards, on each frontier the same pattern was re-enacted. The West was always already being spoilt. Those who depicted the West were constantly asserting that their mission was to capture what would soon be gone for ever. As early as the 1830s George Catlin, the first painter to picture the Indians west of the Mississippi, wrote:

> I have, for many years past, contemplated the noble races of red men who are now spread over these trackless forests and boundless prairies, melting away at the approach of civilization. Their rights invaded, their morals corrupted, their lands wrested from them, their customs changed, and therefore lost to the world; and they at last sunk into the earth, and the ploughshare turning the sod over their graves, and I have flown to their rescue – not of their lives or of their race (for they are *'doomed'* and must perish), but to the rescue of their looks and their modes, at which the acquisitive world may hurl their poison and every besom of destruction, and trample them down and crush them to death; yet, phoenix-like, they may rise from the 'stain on a painter's palette,' and live again upon canvass, and stand forth for centuries to come, the living monuments of a noble race.[5]

This theme, of the so-called Vanishing American, was to inform almost every aspect of thought about the Native American during the century and a half from the Revolution to the Second World War.[6] Both progressives and reactionaries on the 'Indian question' believed that the Indian peoples had already greatly declined, both in numbers and in every other way, since the arrival of Columbus, and that they were destined eventually to pass away. Whether the passing of the savage Indian was to be mourned or celebrated, it was generally assumed to be inevitable, so much so that a series of natural metaphors seemed irresistibly to suggest themselves, such as the melting of snow, the falling of leaves or the setting of the sun. As one writer put it in 1825:

> As a race they have withered from the land. Their arrows are broken, their springs are dried up, their cabins are in the dust. Their council fire has long since gone out on the shore, and their war cry is fast dying away to the untrodden west. Slowly and sadly they climb the distant mountains, and read their doom in the setting sun. They are shrinking away before the mighty tide which is pressing them away; they must soon hear the roar of the last wave, which will settle over them for ever.[7]

The long-drawn out and often bitter arguments over government Indian policy centred on whether this inevitable demise should be hastened through the encouragement of assimilation, whereby through a combination of force and persuasion the Indian be turned loose in white society and rapidly transformed into a white man; or whether by isolation in the reservation system this eventual dissolving of Indian identity into white society could be postponed until the Indian was better equipped. The notion that the Indians might be able to carve out a separate, permanently sustainable identity for themselves seemed all but unthinkable.

Red Cloud's gaze out beyond the camera would therefore have been interpreted by a white audience in the 1880s as an expression of a sad but noble, dignified but resigned stoicism in the face of inevitable extinction. This was the tradition of Indian photography that had become established by the beginning of the 20th century, when the movies were looking for an image of the Indian which they could dramatise. Just at this point, the concept of the Vanishing American was to be refined and aestheticised in the work of the greatest of all Indian photographers, Edward Sheriff Curtis (1868–1952), whose twenty huge volumes of photographs entitled *The North American Indian* were published between 1907 and 1930. Curtis was influenced by the Pictorialists, a photography movement which began in England and moved to America, where it had an effect on the theories of Alfred Stieglitz and the group he founded in 1902, known as the Photo-Secession. As technical developments made photography more readily usable as a recording device, either to the amateur for the recording of informal images of everyday life, or as a tool of journalism, so there was a counter-tendency towards the pursuit of aesthetic effect, which resisted the notion that photography should merely reproduce reality, and instead emphasised the means whereby it could transform and even manipulate it. Though Stieglitz himself was averse to some of the more extreme manipulations of the image practised by others such as Edward Steichen and Gertrude Käsebier, preferring what he called 'straight' photography, his ultimate objective was to advance the cause of photography as art. This essentially required the abandonment of any naïve belief that photography was a documentary medium which could guarantee to register objective truth.[8]

Though he claimed that his pictures of Indians were 'directly from Nature' Curtis clearly had an aesthetic intent which drew inspiration from the ideas of Stieglitz. As he remarks in the introduction to his work, 'the fact that the Indian and his surroundings lend themselves to artistic treatment has not been lost sight of'.[9] Curtis employed a whole variety of methods to ensure he got the pictures he wanted. In the first place, he frequently altered the costumes and other objects in the possession of his subjects, on the grounds that they were not authentically Indian. Curtis, along with the prevailing doctrine of ethnography at the time, believed in an essence of the Indian, separate from the whites. To the extent that Indians showed evidence of contact with whites, they were no longer Indians. The Indian, then, was outside history; if he was inside it, his Indianness was inevitably diluted. Yet Curtis was inconsistent in his attitude to what was essentially Indian. Horses and rifles had after all been introduced by whites, but had become part of the iconography of the plains Indian, and so acceptable.

This selective manipulation of objects in order to inject extra authenticity into the picture sometimes led Curtis to supply costumes for his subjects, posing members of entirely separate tribes in the same head-dress or necklace. Curtis's ability to get from his subjects exactly the effect he wanted was further aided by paying his sitters, a common enough practice at the time, but one which could all too easily affect the documentary purity of what was recorded. Then once the image had been constructed, Curtis retouched to achieve the desired aesthetic effect. He drew objects on to the frame (as for example an Indian pot, in order to be able to title a picture of Indian women round a fire 'Firing pottery') or he took them out (for example removing from a picture of Indian tepees the labels that

Edward S. Curtis, 'Ogalala War Party' (1907).

35

would have indicated they were made from feed sacks, not the traditional buffalo hide).[10]

Curtis's project led him eventually to produce a photographic record of Indians in virtually every state in the trans-Mississippi West, a work unparalleled for its scope and depth. But though he had a genuine interest in virtually every manifestation of Indian life, his work on the plains Indians seemed especially to rely on the stereotypes already made familiar by nineteenth-century popular culture. His work of aesthetic transformation was dedicated to showing the plains Indian not as he was when Curtis was taking his photographs, but as Curtis imagined he had been when in his prime. A picture dated 1907 is entitled 'Ogalala War Party'. It shows a group of mounted Indians in war bonnets, outlined against the sky, carrying rifles and spears. By the time Curtis took this picture the Indian wars had been over for a quarter of a century. Yet in his photographs of the Sioux and the Cheyenne he consistently refers to the men as warriors, and what he frequently shows are reconstructions of scenes of warfare. And over it all he casts a spell of nostalgia for a people he assumed were fading fast. A 1904 picture shows a band of mounted Navajo riding away from the camera into the desert twilight. Curtis placed it at the beginning of the first folio supplement, and entitled it 'The Vanishing Race'. In his caption Curtis wrote: 'The thought which this picture is meant to convey is that the Indians as a race, already shorn of their tribal strength and stripped of their primitive dress, are passing into the darkness of an unknown future.'[11]

Curtis was only the best known of many photographers who saw their work as a deliberate and sustained attempt to preserve a visual record of Indian life before it was too late. In 1898 representatives from every cultural area were invited to the Trans-Mississippi Exposition in Omaha, Nebraska. A local photographer, Frank Rinehart (c. 1862–1928), was hired by the Exposition to commission pictures of them. Rinehart, who later worked for Curtis, had a definite view of his mission:

> The camera ... was ever busy recording scenes and securing types of these interesting people who with their savage finery are rapidly passing away. In a remarkably short time, education and civilization will stamp out the feathers, beads and paint – the sign language, the dancing – and the Indian of the past will live but in memory and pictures.[12]

Roland Reed (1864–1934) produced a series of photographs executed in the first fifteen years or so of the 20th century which were elaborately posed tableaux, composed with meticulous attention to detail. His Indians were cast in their roles according to the degree to which they conformed to Reed's preconceptions. Thus his picture 'The Wooing' (1908) shows two Indians in a romantic pose, each of whom in fact was married to someone else and who lived thirty miles apart. Reed took weeks finding his cast and days shooting the picture exactly as he wanted it. Many of his photographs have an elegiac tinge. One, of a lone Indian standing on a rock holding in his hand an arrow snapped in two, is titled 'Broken Arrow'. Another, of two Indians contemplating some ruined cliff dwellings, is called 'Alone with the Past'. Some of Reed's photographs leave behind any pretence at recording actual Indian life, and are entirely fictional creations. One image of two Indians standing by their canoes pointing over a lake and entitled 'Coming of the

White Man' depicts a scene set several centuries before the invention of photography, and is as much a fictional reconstruction as anything in the movies.

The most single-minded of all the attempts at preserving the record of a dying race was a series of expeditions west between 1909 and 1913, financed by Rodman Wanamaker, a wealthy philanthropist. Their purpose was to record for posterity an Indian life assumed to be rapidly disappearing. In all some 11,000 photographs were taken and no less than 50 miles of moving film, including a movie version of *Hiawatha* shot on the Crow reservation in Montana. The second expedition resulted in a book, *The Vanishing Race*, written by Joseph Kossuth Dixon. It contained a series of highly sententious photographs with titles such as 'The Final Trail', 'Vanishing into the Mists' and 'The Sunset of a Dying Race', which are intended to illustrate the theme of the inevitable decline of the Indian. As Dixon wrote in his bombastic prose, 'Ninety millions, with suffused eye, watch this vanishing remnant of a race, whose regnant majesty inspires at the very moment it succumbs to the iconoclasm of civilization.'[13] Two years later, in 1915, James E. Fraser displayed his famous statue *The End of the Trai'* at the Panama-Pacific International Exposition in San Francisco. It shows a mounted Indian, his head, his lance and his horse's head all tipped towards the ground in an attitude of resignation. Nothing could be more starkly emblematic of the perceived condition of the Indian, and his presumed fate.

Once the cinema discovered narrative, in the early years of the 20th century, it soon became apparent that the West offered an almost inexhaustible source of exciting stories. Among the most compelling were tales of conflict between white men and red. Not all the earliest movie stories of Indians are about violent conflict, but a significant proportion are. And the fledgling Western movie, in selecting the plains Indian wars as the focus for its treatment of the Indian, was bound to draw heavily on established stereotypes and attitudes. Since the first twenty years of movie history were the period in which the notion of the Vanishing American reached its apogee, it was inevitable that the nascent form of the Western should import it as a principal influence upon its dramaturgy. Set in the past as most Westerns were, they were able to partake of the romantic appeal of the Sioux and the Cheyenne in their prime while leaving their audience secure in the knowledge that the threat of the Indian was gone. The Western reconstructed a past whose outcome was known, preordained, and of no conceivable danger to the present. The effect was much the same as the studiously composed images of Curtis and the other Pictorialists, which had similarly preferred to reconstruct a glorious past rather than record a more problematic present. The cinema audience could indulge its nostalgia for the wildness of a people whose threat had been conclusively neutralised.

Just occasionally a film about Indians was set in the present. Paramount's *The Vanishing American* (1925), based upon Zane Grey's novel of the same title published in that year, is the story of a Navajo who falls in love with a white schoolteacher, goes off to fight in the First World War and who dies at the end lamenting the passing of his race. Yet despite the contemporary setting, the title situates the story squarely within the tradition which Curtis and others were working in. Grey's conclusion is emphatically valedictory: 'It is symbolic. ... They are vanishing, vanishing. ... At last only one Indian was left on the darkening horizon...

bent in his saddle, a melancholy figure, unreal and strange against that dying sun-set, moving on, diminishing, fading, vanishing – vanishing.'[14] While both the film and the book are sympathetic to the Navajo, and scathingly critical of the whites who exploit them, they are working within a concept of history which sees the Indian as inevitably a victim of progress. In the film there is a kind of pseudo-his-torical prologue, set in Monument Valley, which traces how the present-day Navajo themselves ousted the original occupants of their south-western lands. The narrative of the film then demonstrates how they too are destined to be replaced by the encroaching whites.

II The Southwest, the Taos School and the Harvey Company

Yet by 1925, unnoticed by the movies, a remarkable transformation in the image of the Indian had come about in painting and photography, which directly chal-lenged both the stereotype of the plains Indian warrior, and the concept of the vanishing race.[15] Up to the 1870s the south-western United States, not absorbed into the Union until after the war with Mexico in 1848, were little known. Inhabited largely by Indians and Hispanics, it was an inhospitable region of deserts and inaccessible mountains. In 1871 Major John Wesley Powell's expedi-tion down the Colorado River brought back the first photographs of the Grand Canyon. John Hillers's pictures of the region were used as illustrations for gov-ernment publications, were sold as stereographs and exhibited at international expositions. Another expedition to the South-west in 1871 was led by Lieutenant George Wheeler of the US Army. His photographer was Timothy O'Sullivan, who took many extraordinary pictures both of the desert landscapes they journeyed through and of their Indian inhabitants.

These photographs helped to bring about a profound change in the aesthetics of the Western landscape, which previously had valorised only the Rockies as worthy of artistic attention. The artist Thomas Moran joined Powell and Hillers on a further expedition to the Colorado in 1873, after which he began a series of paintings of the Grand Canyon and other scenic sights of the region. Many of these paintings appeared as engravings in *Scribner's* and other magazines. In the 90s Moran began an association with the Santa Fe railroad, which was anxious to publicise the scenic wonders of the South-west in order to encourage tourism. In 1901 the railroad built a spur line to the Grand Canyon. Moran was given free travel and other facilities while producing pictures that were then used in the Santa Fe's publicity literature and guidebooks, and were also hung in the company's Chicago office and in the El Tovar hotel at the Canyon.[16]

At the same time that Moran was helping to transform the aesthetics of the Western landscape, a group of artists based in Taos, New Mexico, were taking a fresh look at the Indian. The so-called Taos School of Artists resulted from an expedition west in 1898 by Ernest Blumenschein and Bert Philips, both of whom had trained in Paris but who were looking for something authentically American to paint. They formally founded the Taos Society of Artists in 1915, together with Joseph Sharp, Oscar Berninghaus, E. Irving Couse and W. Herbert Dunton. What the Taos School artists saw in the Pueblo Indians whom they took as their subjects was a combination of primitive innocence, an antidote to modern urban life, and at the same time an ancient and successful civilisation. Whereas the nomad Indian societies of the plains appeared to be fast disappearing, the Pueblo Indians in their adobe villages followed a way of life whose successful adaptation to its environment ensured permanence. One of the most influential propagators of this view of the South-western Indians was Edgar L. Hewett, anthropologist and creator of the Museum of New Mexico in Santa Fe. In *Ancient Life in the American Southwest* (1930) Hewett wrote:

> A Pueblo Indian at an afternoon tea in New York is out of place. In his own Southwest he is a harmonious element in a landscape that is incomparable in its nobility of color and mass and feeling of the Unchangeable. He never dominates it, as does the European his environment, but belongs there like the mesas, skies, sunshine, spaces and the other living creatures. He takes his part in it with the clouds, winds, rocks, plants, birds and beasts: with the drum beat and chant and symbolic gesture keeping time with the seasons, moving in orderly procession with nature, holding to the unity of life in all things, seeking no superior place for himself but merely a state of harmony with all created things – the most rhythmic life, so far as I know, that is lived among the races of men.[17]

Reinforcing this view of the South-western Indians as a solid and settled society, the Taos School artists depicted Indians engaged not in warfare but in the arts of peace, making pottery, weaving baskets, cooking, playing musical instruments. Their work gained a wide circulation. From 1914 paintings of Indians by E. Irving Couse, the most commercially minded of the Taos artists, were frequently used by the Santa Fe railroad in its annual calendars (twenty-three in all by 1938). In pictures such as *The Pueblo Weaver* (1916) and *Turquoise Bead Maker* (1925) Couse's Indians are posed near-naked, squatting intently over their task. There is something solid, permanent, self-sufficient about them; they have no intention of vanishing.

The representation of Indian artisans in paintings of the Taos School helped to bring about a revival of Indian arts and crafts from the 1920s. A major exhibition was held in 1931 in New York at the Grand Central Galleries. Items from the South-west were in the great majority. 'The American Indian race possesses an innate talent in the fine and applied arts,' said the catalogue.[18] But if white society's taste for Indian arts and crafts was given cultural legitimacy by the Taos artists, it was the Fred Harvey Company which did most to turn it into a business. In 1876 Harvey had formed an agreement with the Atcheson, Topeka and Santa Fe Railroad to develop restaurants and hotels along its tracks. The company joined enthusiastically in the Santa Fe's project of selling the South-west as a tourist experience. Besides providing excellent food and lodging, its premises offered a range of Indian goods for sale in craft shops. Adjoining the Alvarado hotel in Albuquerque (the company's hotels were usually named after early Spanish explorers or missionaries) was the Indian Building, in which guests could not only buy Indian artefacts but watch Indian craftsmen at work. Antonio Apache, who had appeared in the Indian exhibit at the World's Columbian Exposition in Chicago in 1893, was hired to purchase goods for sale from local Indian workers: silverware from the Navajo, baskets from the Pimas and Papagos of Arizona, pottery from the Pueblo Indians.[19]

In 1910 the Harvey Company hired Mary Colter, a former art teacher, to supervise its design concepts. At the Grand Canyon, next to the El Tovar hotel, she built the Hopi House, constructed like a multi-storey pueblo building, in which Hopi Indians did craftwork and performed a daily dance at 5 p.m. for the benefit of tourists. Visitors to the Grand Canyon increased from 44,000 in 1919 to 300,000 in 1937. The El Navajo hotel in Gallup, New Mexico, opened by the Harvey Company in 1923, was decorated with Indian sand-paintings. For the Harvey Company dining cars of the luxurious Super Chief, which ran between Chicago and Los Angeles, and which had been christened by Hollywood luminaries Mrs Eddie Cantor and Eleanor Powell, special crockery was manufactured, based on the pottery of Mimbreño Indians. In 1940 Colter designed the Harvey luncheon room in the new Union Station in Los Angeles, combining an Indian blanket zigzag pattern in red, black and buff for the floor tiles with art deco wall vents and light fittings.

Indian design motifs were used extensively by the Harvey Company in its promotional literature. And in 1926 the Harvey Company began its famous Indian Detours, offering transcontinental travellers on the Santa Fe the chance to break their journey at Albuquerque or Las Vegas, New Mexico, and take a trip by luxury motor coach to the Indian pueblos, and to Santa Fe and other local sights. Young women were trained as couriers and provided with uniforms which incorporated an Indian velvet shirt, silver conch belt and leather boots.[20] Some of the Detours got as far off the beaten track as Monument Valley. They were highly successful, attracting such notables as Albert Einstein and Douglas Fairbanks.

By the Second World War the South-west had become a highly marketable commodity, in which both the Hispanic and the Indian heritage were essential components. As far as the Indian elements were concerned, there was a carefully managed balance between the exoticism of racial and cultural difference, and the reassurance of a civilised infrastructure that successful commercial tourism required. A Harvey Company brochure of 1928 stated that 'Motorists crossing the southwestern states are nearer to the primitive than anywhere else on the continent.'[21] But if part of the appeal of the South-west was the lure of the Indian as primitive, the potentially threatening qualities of this needed to be neutralised before Harvey customers could sleep easily in the company's beds. Thus a postcard issued by the company titled 'In Apache Land, Arizona' depicts two tepees in open country with the caption:

> The Apache Indians were until recently the most warlike of all the Southwestern Indians and have caused the government of the United States, as well as early settlers, no end of trouble. Today, with their numbers fast diminishing and with several forts on or near their scattered reservations, with the railroad as an ally the government has no trouble with them and the Indian has turned his talents to the weaving of baskets and plaques and is at last enjoying the fruits of his labors in peace.[22]

Photography played a major role in the construction of a tourist-friendly image of the South-west as a land of ancient and picturesque buildings, rich in artistic and religious traditions, inhabited by exotic but essentially placid Indians industriously engaged in the production of basketwork, jewellery and other desirable souvenir crafts. The Harvey Company produced a large number of postcards of South-western scenes, many of them depicting Indians. Among the most promi-

Adam Clark Vroman, 'Hopi woman weaving coiled plaques' (1901). This photograph, colour-tinted, appeared as a Harvey Company postcard.

nent of the photographers who supplied pictures for Harvey postcards was Carl Moon, whose pictures had been exhibited at the Smithsonian in Washington and, by invitation of Theodore Roosevelt, at the White House. From 1907 Moon worked for the Harvey Company, moving his studio to the Grand Canyon in order to be near to the South-west tribes he photographed. Moon's pictures are mostly studied genre pieces, carefully posed shots of Indians engaged in everyday pursuits such as weaving or making pottery, very much in the style of the Taos School. In 1914 Moon left the Harvey Company and moved to Pasadena, California, where he became one of the so-called Pasadena Eight, a loosely knit group of artists dedicated to reviving and developing the Indian and Hispanic traditions of California and the South-west generally. Other members included Charles Lummis, an energetic journalist, the founder of the Southwest Museum and a campaigner for Indian rights, and Adam Clark Vroman, George Wharton James, Frederick Monsen, all photographers. Vroman (1856–1916) produced a series of pictures of Indian pueblos, particularly Hopi, where he photographed the Snake Dance. James (1858–1923) was a prolific writer, who produced numerous photographs, also including the Snake Dance. Monsen began experimenting with the new Kodak camera around the end of the century, and some of the results were included in his book *With a Kodak in the Land of the Navajo* (1909).

Exploiting the portability of the new camera, Monsen's pictures eschew the studied formality of most earlier Indian photography:

This new order of things proved to be a great blessing for before I had found this new way – the Kodak way – I had never made the kind of Indian picture I wanted. The stiff, posed time-exposed attempt at dramatic effect I could not recognise as either truth or art, but now there opened the new method, and I began to photograph the Indian *instantaneously*, without previous warning, posing or preparation, securing the most charming pictures and actually getting the very spirit of their life.[23]

The book was published by Eastman Kodak of Rochester, which may explain some of the hype, but Monsen's pictures are indeed altogether more relaxed than most of what had gone before. Many of them show happy, laughing children. The children are frequently naked and for a modern viewer it is perhaps not easy to read them as innocently as the photographer may have wished to intend. But Monsen's pictures are clearly an attempt to portray the Indians as members of a thriving society rather than members of a doomed race.

Yet so pervasive and powerful was the notion of the Vanishing American that neither Moon nor Monsen were immune to its influence. Monsen wrote:

I ... have seen many changes. Entire tribes have been destroyed by disease, and others have been scattered by encroaching civilization. The Indian, as an Indian, is rapidly disappearing. He is adopting the white man's ways and losing his tribal characteristics. He is gradually giving up his deeply significant nature-lore, his religions and his ceremonies, ancestral manners and customs will have passed from his life.

Realizing these conditions, I have devoted many years to the making of an ethnographic record of the Indians, photographing their life, manners and habitat, and thus preserving for future generations, a picture-history which will show what these most interesting early Americans were like, before they were disturbed by the influences of the white man.[24]

Moon produced some pictures imbued with all the nostalgic aura of the Vanishing American, with titles such as 'Last of Their Tribe' and 'The Last of his People'. Even so, both the studiously composed images of Moon and the informal snapshots of Monsen, together with other photographs of South-western Indians by the Pasadena Eight and the popularised versions disseminated by the Harvey Company, are notable for their emphasis on the domestic, everyday rhythms of Indian life, and on the continuing vitality of its rituals. In the pictures of the Taos School as well as in the postcards of the Harvey Company, men are often depicted in their customary domestic activities such as weaving or making jewellery and pots. There is little interest in fixed poses of warlike nobility, contemplating the lost splendours of the past, and rather more in Indians doing things here and now. Most strikingly, perhaps, is the way in which the image of the Indian is feminised. Women and children appear frequently in their pictures, whereas in the tradition of Curtis, and Reed especially, they are more marginalised, apart from occasional pictures of sexualised young Indian women in the tradition of Pocahontas, Minnehaha and Ramona.

The image of Indians produced by the Taos artists and the Fred Harvey Company was no less idealised than that produced by Curtis and the Pictorialists. The Taos painters largely ignored the squalor in which many Indians were obliged to live, and the lack of educational and medical provision. Indian culture assumed a decorative function that did not always connect with the social realities of Indian life. As a 1919 catalogue to an exhibition of Oscar Berninghaus's work had put it, 'in much of our Western landscape we need the Indian in the same way that a finely wrought piece of gold needs a jewel to set off its beauty in a piece of jewelry'.[25] The Indian was constantly in danger of being reduced to no more than an element of décor. But at their best the Taos School, and even in its way the Fred Harvey Company, tried to make some connection between the Indian and contemporary life. There were, after all, real Indians living in real pueblos – and still are to this day. Whereas when Curtis took a picture entitled 'War Party's Farewell – Atsina' he knew that no war parties had set out on the northern plains for a generation.

For the Western, however, the image of a feminised and domesticated Indian offered nothing it could use. Frederic Remington, in so many ways the spiritual precursor of the Western movie, remarked in a telling phrase that as a subject for painting he thought pueblos 'too tame . . . they don't appeal to me – too decorative – and too easily in reach of every tenderfoot'.[26] Pueblo life did not offer the stirring narratives the movies required; above all, the sedentary societies of farmers and weavers could not deliver the violent action that the Plains nomads could. The only role the movies could find for the Pueblo Indian was at the margins, as a decorated fringe of local colour.

The strong light of the South-western landscape, the picturesque adobe villages and their inhabitants, the bright colours and intricate designs of Pueblo art, all offered ideal subjects for painting and photography. But for the movies these static tableaux provided only a backdrop. They lacked the dynamism, the raw conflict and violence upon which the Hollywood Western depended for its thrills. A handful of films attempted to find drama in stories of contemporary Indian life, such as *Redskin* (1929), *Massacre* (1934), and much more recently *The Dark Wind* (1991) and *Thunderheart* (1992). But in the early years of Hollywood such narratives were too controversial for mainstream film-making, and they lacked the promise of a happy ending. Locked into a certain kind of narrative in which 'action' is primary, the Western, unlike painting and photography, has been unable to interest itself in Indian culture. It has as a result been largely cut off from the regeneration of the Indian which began in the 1920s and 30s and continues to this day. Indians in the movies still whoop their war cries, but the Western is essentially a museum piece, a reconstruction of the past, not a re-creation of the present.

The Grapes of Wrath was directed in 1940 by John Ford, whose name is practically synonymous with the Hollywood Western. As the Joad family, refugees from the Oklahoma dustbowl, cross Arizona on their way to the promised land of California, there is a shot of their jalopy trundling along Route 66. They drive by an adobe pueblo. Beside the road is an Indian man fashioning something out of metal; possibly a Navajo making jewellery. Next to the man is a baby in a cradle that is an exact copy of a popular Harvey card entitled 'A Navajo Papoose, Arizona'. We don't see the Indians close up, nor do they speak. For Hollywood, it seems, Pueblo Indians are marginal even to the displaced Oakies.

Some of the work on which this essay is based was carried out while I was a Mayer Fund Fellow at the Huntington Library, San Marino, California. I am grateful to the Library for its hospitality, and especially to Jennifer Watts and Peter Blodgett for their assistance. I would also like to thank Mick Gidley for helpful comments and corrections.

Notes

1 See Kevin Brownlow, *The War, the West and the Wilderness* (London: Secker & Warburg, 1979), pp. 253f.
2 There are several useful compilations of photographs of Indians, including: Paula Richardson Fleming and Judith Luskey, *The North American Indian in Early Photographs* (Oxford: Phaidon Press, 1988); Nancy Hathaway, *Native American Portraits 1862–1918* (San Francisco: Chronicle Books, 1990); William H. Goetzmann, *The First Americans: Photographs from the Library of Congress* (Washington DC: Starwood Publishing Co., 1991); Lucy R. Lippard, *Partial Recall* (New York: The New Press, 1992); Paula Richardson Fleming and Judith Lynn Luskey, *The Shadow Catchers: Images of the American Indian* (London: Lawrence King Publishing, 1993); Alfred L. Bush and Lee Clark, *The Photograph and the American Indian* (Princeton: Princeton University Press, 1994); Ulrich W. Hiesinger, *Indian Lives: A Photographic Record from the Civil War to Wounded Knee* (Munich, New York: Prestel, 1994).
3 This photograph has been used on a 10 cent stamp issued by the US Post Office, but Red Cloud's feather has been cropped. The picture must have had a very wide currency. In an English junk shop a friend found me the same picture, hand-painted on silk in full colour; in this version Red Cloud wears *two* feathers.
4 In *The Indian Fighter* (1955) Elisha Cook Jr plays a photographer. He shows some of his pictures to Kirk Douglas. 'How do you like this one of Red Cloud?' he enquires. 'He looks like he swallowed a stick,' Douglas replies.
5 George Catlin, *Letters and Notes on the Manners, Customs, and Conditions of the North American Indians* (London: 1844; reprinted New York: Dover, 1973), vol. I, p. 16.
6 The most comprehensive treatment of this topic is Brian W. Dippie, *The Vanishing American* (Lawrence: University of Kansas Press, 1982).
7 Quoted in Dippie, p. 15.
8 See Mick Gidley, 'Pictorialist Elements in Edward S. Curtis's Photographic Representations of American Indians', *The Yearbook of English Studies*, vol. 24, 1994.
9 See Christopher M. Lyman, *The Vanishing Race and Other Illusions: Photographs of Indians by Edward S. Curtis* (New York: Pantheon Books, 1982), p. 62.
10 See Lyman, pp. 63f.
11 Quoted in Lyman, p. 79.
12 Quoted in Fleming and Luskey, p. 82.
13 Joseph K. Dixon, *The Vanishing Race: The Last Great Indian Council* (Garden City, NY: Doubleday, Page & Co., 1913), p. 222.
14 Zane Grey, *The Vanishing American* (New York: Harper Paperbacks, 1991), p. 329. Mick Gidley suggests that Grey was here actually describing Curtis's image 'The Vanishing Race'. See Mick Gidley, 'Repeated Return of the Vanishing American' in Brian Holden Reid and John White (eds), *American Studies: Essays in Honour of Marcus Cunliffe* (London: Macmillan, 1991).
15 It is also worth noting that Zane Grey picked the wrong tribe when he chose the Navajo as the Vanishing Americans, since they are now the most populous of all Native American groups.
16 For more detail on this shift in the aesthetics of the Western landscape, see Edward Buscombe, 'Inventing Monument Valley: Nineteenth-Century Landscape Photography and the Western Film', in Patrice Petro (ed.), *Fugitive Images: From Photography to Video* (Bloomington: Indiana University Press, 1995).
17 Quoted in Charles C. Eldredge, Julie Schimmel and William H. Truettner, *Art in New Mexico 1900–1945: Paths to Taos and Santa Fe* (New York; Abbeville Press, 1986), p. 70.
18 Quoted in Eldredge, Schimmel, and Truettner, p. 81.

19 See, for example, Marta Weigle, 'On Coyotes and Crosses: That Which is Wild and Wooden of the Twentieth-Century Southwest', in Richard Francaviglia and David Narrett (eds), *Essays on the Changing Images of the Southwest* (College Station: Texas A & M University Press, 1994).

20 Lesley Poling-Kempes, *The Harvey Girls* (New York: Paragon House, 1989), p. 151.

21 Quoted in Eldredge, Schimmel, and Truettner, p. 81.

22 This postcard is in the Huntington Library, San Marino, California.

23 Frederick I. Monsen, *With a Kodak in the Land of the Navajo* (Rochester, NY: Eastman Kodak Co., n.d. [1909]), p. 20.

24 Quoted in Fleming and Luskey, pp. 12–13.

25 Sandra D'Emilio and Suzan Cambell, *Visions and Visionaries: The Art and Artists of the Santa Fe Railway* (Salt Lake City: Peregrine Smith Books, 1991), p. 85.

26 Peggy and Harold Samuels, *Frederic Remington: A Biography* (Garden City, NY: Doubleday & Co., 1982), pp. 306–7.

Since this was written, three useful books have come my way: James C. Faris, *Navajo and Photography* (Albuquerque: University of New Mexico Press, 1996); Kathleen L. Howard and Diana F. Pardue, *Inventing the Southwest: The Fred Harvey Company and Native American Art* (Flagstaff: Northland Publishing, 1996); Marta Weigle and Barbara A. Babcock, *The Great Southwest of the Fred Harvey Company and the Santa Fe Railway* (Phoenix: Heard Museum, 1996).

3   The Professional Western: South of the Border
Noël Carroll

Introduction

The topic of this essay is a series of four thematically related American Westerns: *Vera Cruz* (1954), *The Magnificent Seven* (1960), *The Professionals* (1966), and *The Wild Bunch* (1969). In each, a group of American mercenaries finds itself south of the border and becomes involved in what may be described as various Mexican revolutions. Because these Westerns involve a paramilitary group of expert warriors, they are apt to be categorised as members of the sub-genre called the professional Western. The professional Western, in turn, has been theorised as a celebration of expertise that reflects the ethos of an emerging social class in America which has been alternatively referred to as the managerial class, the technocracy, the professional managerial class or, more recently, the overclass. However, this interpretation of these particular Westerns does not strike me as adequate, especially because it pays scant attention to the recurring theme of indigenous revolution that runs through the films in this cycle.[1] The purpose of this essay is to develop an interpretation that takes account of the significance of the appearance of Mexican revolutions in these Westerns.

The notion of the professional Western is explored in depth in an ambitious book by Will Wright entitled *Six Guns and Society: A Structural Study of the Western*.[2] According to Wright, the American Western (from 1931 to 1972) can be divided into four major types: the classical plot, the vengeance variation, the transition theme and the professional plot. These groups are not exhaustive, nor are they necessarily exclusive. The typology was derived from the study of best-selling Westerns, defined as those that were among the highest grossing films of the year in which they appeared.

Wright's analyses are not only aimed at identifying the plot structures of these Westerns, but also at correlating these Westerns with developments in American society. In addition, Wright notices a change in the incidence of Westerns of different sorts. Whereas from the 30s to the late 50s the classical plot is preponderant, from the 60s onwards the professional plot becomes the dominant form.

Of the films that interest me here, *The Professionals* and *The Wild Bunch* are identified by Wright as examples of the professional plot and are discussed at length by him. He does not address *The Magnificent Seven*, since, presumably, it did not meet the criterion of being one of the highest grossing films of 1960. Nevertheless, I think that it is pretty uncontroversially what he calls a professional

Western. On the other hand, he categorises *Vera Cruz* as an exemplar of the classical plot, but, for reasons to be discussed, I think that at best it is a mixture of classical and professional elements, if not a professional Western outright.

In characterising the professional plot, Wright says:

> All these films are about a group of heroes working for money. They are not wandering adventurers who decide to fight for a lost cause because it is right, or for the love of a girl. They are professionals, men doing a job. They are specialists who possess the unique skills used in their profession. No longer is the fighting ability of the hero the lucky attribute of a man who happens to be in the right place at the right time [a mark of the classical Western plot, exemplified by a film such as *Shane*]. Now it is a profitable skill that the heroes utilise professionally, and this profitable skill *explains* why they are in that particular place at that particular time.[3]

In the classical plot, the hero, often a lone gunfighter like Shane, is an outsider. He comes upon a situation where positive social forces are in conflict with a group of antagonists, noteworthy for their superior talent for violence. Initially, the hero avoids involvement in the conflict, but eventually enters it on the side of society, defeating assorted villains, to the advantage of whatever the film regards as positive social forces. The hero is marked by special abilities, especially martial ones. And, persuaded by reasons of justice, he comes to pit his virtually mythic prowess against the forces of oppression. Often, but not always, he then becomes incorporated in society and thus is no longer an outsider.

In contrast, the professional plot presents viewers with a group of heroes, each remarkable for his special abilities. Furthermore, this group is co-ordinated; they function as a unit. Specifically, the imagery is of a military unit. The actions they undertake against this or that villain are putatively not motivated by reasons of justice, but rather by the promise of money. They are mercenaries, or soldiers of fortune. But if at times they seem willing to take risks unjustifiable solely in terms of dollar value, it is because of their professionalism – which is not only a matter of their guild-like fidelity to abiding by their contracts, but also involves the pride and emotional satisfaction that they derive from exercising their special skills as warriors.

The professionals in these films have their own code of conduct. This code distinguishes them from the members of ordinary society. Unlike the hero in the classical Western, in Wright's view, the professional hero is not motivated by claims of justice, but by the code of the professional. Wright argues:

> In many ways, the professional plot is similar to the classical plot: the hero is a gunfighter, outside of society, whose main task is to fight the villains who are threatening parts of society. But the relations between the different characters of the story have changed significantly. The heroes are now professional fighters, men willing to defend society only as a job they accept for pay or love of fighting, not from commitment to ideas of law and justice. As in the classical plot, society is portrayed as weak, but it is no longer seen as particularly good or desirable. The members of society are not unfair and cruel, as in the transition theme; in the professional plot they are simply irrelevant. The social value of love, marriage, family, peace, and business are things to be avoided, not goals to be won. As a result, the relations of the heroes, or of the villains with society are minimal. Society exists as a ground for the conflict, an excuse for fighting, rather than as a serious option as a way of life. The focus of the professional plot is on the conflict

between the heroes and the villains. Typically, both are professionals and their fight becomes a contest of ability for its own sake. A concern with a fight between equal men of special ability is an aspect of all Westerns, yet only in this particular version of the myth does the fight itself, divorced from all its social and ethical implications, become of such central importance. The final gunfight that climaxes such films as *Shane* or *Stagecoach* has become a battle extending throughout the film with skirmishes, strategies, and commanders. How the fight is fought is now the crucial issue, since the fight itself generates the values that replace the values of society in the myth.[4]

The disappearance of society from the value nexus of the narrative and its substitution by the professional ethos of martial skill provides a central element in Wright's characterisation of the ideological work that the professional Western performs. According to Wright, among others, the recent development of capitalist economies has placed more and more emphasis on, to use Habermas's terminology, 'sets of leaders of administrative personnel', or as Wright glosses that, a 'technical elite'.[5] Perhaps this group is also what others have called the 'professional-managerial class', or the 'overclass'. Of this class, Wright remarks:

> Membership in the technostructure provides great social satisfaction for the individual. He works closely with a group that depends on him and on whom he depends; he is close to a source of power and receives social prestige accordingly. He is a professional; he identifies with the group and the corporation, and they in turn recognise and reward his contribution.[6]

Moreover, 'The individual in the technostructure identifies his goals with those of the corporation, and these goals become social goals. Though the individual seems to be working for the newly defined social goals, he is in fact working to maintain his group.'[7] In Wright's view, decision by the technostructure is replacing democratic decision-making with management in terms of expertise. Society is allegedly being run by experts – by professionals – for whom 'the social group [i.e. the professional cadre] satisfies every requirement for meaningful social relationships, except commitment to social values'.[8]

This characterisation of the technocrat, furthermore, is reflected in the heroes of the professional Western.[9] These figures reflect the ethos of the managerial élite. The professional Western, in this regard, is a celebration of the ideology of the managerial élite. And, in addition, it addresses not only fellow celebrants in the managerial élite but the rest of society as well, promoting a view of the professional ethos as heroic. Through the iconography of the Western, professionalism is represented as a worthy ideal. Its anti-democratic bias is obscured by the colourful apotheosis of perfectionism. In short, the professional Western performs a suspect legitimating function for managerialism.

Whether this interpretation is successful for the professional Western in general is a question too large for this paper. Instead, I want to focus on what I take to be a subset of the professional Western, namely those that take place south of the border. In these cases, I think that the relationships of the professional heroes to representatives of the Mexican people force us to reconsider the ideological themes that are in play in films like *Vera Cruz*, *The Magnificent Seven*, *The Professionals*, and *The Wild Bunch*.

In Wright's theory of the professional Western, the professional group becomes the centre of value, and ordinary society becomes, as Wright says, 'simply irrelevant'. It more or less disappears, or functions only as the backdrop against which professional competitions are staged. However, this is not the case in the professional Westerns set in Mexico. For though *American* society may recede from view in these films, *Mexican* society, generally in the form of some sort of indigenous revolution, does not. Nor is the relation of the professional heroes to the representatives of what we might call the Mexican resistance either incidental or merely instrumental (i.e., merely financial). The professional heroes become emotionally and/or existentially involved with these resistance movements and they are willing to stake their very lives on their outcome.

Wright, of course, is interested in a general theory of the professional Western. Thus, it is perhaps no surprise that he ignores certain details that only recur in a small number of the films that he considers. However, I think that, by overlooking the role of Mexican society in the professional Westerns set south of the border, he misses the ideological wish that these films sustain. But before elucidating the ideological operation of these films, we need to analyse them each in turn.

Vera Cruz

Vera Cruz is set in Mexico during the reign of Maximilian in the aftermath of the American Civil War. A rolling title informs us that it is a time when the Mexican people were struggling for their freedom. A lone horseman, Ben Trane (played by Gary Cooper), dismounts his limping horse. Later, we learn that the horse has a broken leg. Ben walks to a churchyard, where he meets Joe Erin (played by Burt Lancaster) who sells him another horse for the exorbitant price of $100. As they ride off, they are attacked by a group of Maximilian's imperial lancers. Joe explains to Ben that the horse that he is riding is stolen. There is a rousing chase in which they evade the lancers. Ben then tricks Joe, riding off on Joe's horse and leaving him with the stolen one.

Several important themes are established in the opening scene. There is the three-way conflict between Ben, Joe and the imperial government that continues both above and below ground throughout the film. And there is the somewhat complex relationship between Ben and Joe. Joe admires Ben's skill and gumption even as Ben outdoes him. They are competitors, but they also respect each other's martial skill – a mark of the professional Western, according to Wright.

The opening scenes also establish that Ben has a strict sense of justice and what Joe calls a 'soft spot', exemplified by the care he shows for his injured horse, which will come to mark the central difference between Ben and Joe throughout the story.

Ben rides into town and when members of Joe's gang realise that he has Joe's horse, they prepare to slice him to pieces with a broken bottle. However, Joe arrives, saves Ben from his gang and invites him to join up. Presumably Joe admires the way that Ben handles himself. Ben is a refugee from the Civil War. He suggests at times that he may have done something that caused him to flee the States. He says that the war cost him everything but the shirt on his back and he implies that he is in Mexico for the sole purpose of getting money.

Joe's gang, along with Ben, travels to another village in order to find an employer. After an episode in which Ben, showing his ethical uprightness, rescues a woman named Nina from some slavering gringos, an agent of Maximilian's, the marquis (played by Cesar Romero), shows up with an offer of work. But the proceedings are interrupted by General Ramirez and his peasant army of freedom fighters who attempt to take both the imperial troops and the Americans prisoner. Ben, showing his 'soft spot' once again, points out that there are children in the line of fire, an insight Joe exploits by taking them hostage. The freedom fighters retreat, and the marquis is pleased by the performance of his newly acquired mercenaries. This scene is especially important because it introduces another important force – the Mexican revolutionaries – into the narrative equation.

Ben consistently talks the part of the mercenary cynic but, given his concern for his injured horse, Nina and the children, the audience suspects that his cynicism is ultimately a pose. Joe, on the other hand, is a rascal, one whose big smile may make him appear loveable, but who, as the film progresses, is revealed to be an irredeemable egoist and sadist.

Ben, Joe and the gang, along with the marquis and his lancers, arrive at Maximilian's palace in Mexico City in the midst of a ball. Energy is spent contrasting the barbarism of the Americans with the behaviour of the French (and the Austrians?). It is the old opposition of the uncouth but vital Americans against the artificial, false pretensions of Europe. When Maximilian arrives, the Americans display their skills in a round of bravura sharp-shooting, and Maximilian offers them fifty thousand dollars to accompany the carriage of a countess to Vera Cruz.

In this scene, we learn more about Ben; it is suggested that he has come to Mexico to earn money in order to rebuild his plantation, especially in terms of securing the welfare of its former inhabitants (the film is not explicit about who these people are, but one assumes it is probably his family and perhaps his former slaves). To Joe, this is more evidence of Ben's soft spot. The scene is also an occasion for Ben and Joe to display their awesome professional skill with weaponry – semi-competitively and with mutual admiration. Joe also admires, as he will later in the film as well, Ben's bargaining ability, as Ben raises Maximilian's bid from $25,000 to $50,000.

The entourage sets out. Ben and Joe come to realise that the countess's carriage has a false bottom that contains $3 million in gold, which is supposed to go to Paris in order to buy more troops for Maximilian. They also learn that the countess has made plans to abscond with the money. The three of them form a compact, though each of the thieves distrusts the others. Joe and the countess are outright, merciless cut-throats; the audience is less certain about Ben. One has the feeling that he would like to trust Joe, even if in some sense he knows that that is inadvisable.

The caravan is subject to guerrilla warfare. At one point, it is ambushed by Ramirez's troops and nearly captured. Nina, the woman Ben had rescued earlier, leaps on one of the wagons and drives it to safety. Though she appears to be on the side of the caravan, in reality she is a freedom fighter, as we eventually learn. At the same time, the marquis is aware of the countess's machinations and he plans to remove the gold before Joe, Ben and the countess can steal it. So, there evolves an intricate five-way fabric of deception between Ben, Joe, the countess, the marquis and Nina, each with his or her own agenda. In such a context, it is not surprising that the theme of trust emerges with Joe as the ideologue of the 'you can't trust anyone' point of view, and Ben talking about money but acting with palpable care and concern for others, including Joe.

Ben falls in love with Nina, a figure perhaps for his final 'seduction' to the cause of the freedom fighters. But the marquis successfully spirits the gold to Vera Cruz. The professionals set out after the carriage, but the carriage, now empty, is a diversionary tactic. The empty coach and the professionals are surrounded by Ramirez's army. Ben strikes a deal with Ramirez, and the freedom fighters, along with the professionals, lay siege to Vera Cruz.

It is a brutal battle. Ben remarks that if the freedom fighters get the gold they will have deserved it; Joe says he wouldn't give them the sweat off his brow. Ben, we divine, has been won over to the revolution, his Confederate idealism (in terms of the point of view of the film) rekindled by the rebel sacrifices (along with prodding from Nina). Joe remains the selfish egoist. The wagon laden with gold falls into Joe's hands. But Ben steps in and the two men shoot it out. Ben wins, but his face in victory is etched with frustration and disappointment. One feels that he liked Joe and that he had hoped that Joe's egoism would melt away when the chips were down. But in the end, he had to destroy the only person equal to him in ability in the world of the film.

Despite his harsh talk of mercenary interests and the suggestion that he may be wanted by the law stateside, Ben's actions consistently point to his decency. He shows ethical concern for animals, children, women, the displaced folks back on his plantations, and, ultimately, for the Mexican revolutionaries. He is trustworthy and clean. Joe is his *doppelgänger* – vicious to one and all, untrustworthy as a matter of principle, and cursed with a virtually perpetually dirty face throughout the film (perhaps the better to show off Burt Lancaster's glowing ivories). Joe's gang, for the most part, is made up of the dregs of humanity. The French are equally untrustworthy (marked by being insincere and overcivilised), as well as being tyrannical bullies. A score of lancers tortures a captured freedom fighter like cats playing with a mouse.

In this matrix the only other locus of decency, apart from Ben, are the Mexican revolutionaries, represented primarily by Ramirez and Nina. Like Ben, the Mexicans are clean, as opposed to the French who are too clean, and Joe and his gang who are too dirty. Ramirez speaks in a deliberate, judicious manner about freedom – indeed, he has the diction often reserved for saints in Hollywood films – and Nina fiercely speaks in favour of justice. The trajectory of the plot pulses towards bringing the forces of decency together.

There is also a subplot of racial tolerance. One of the members of the professional gang is an African-American named Ballard. Like Ben, he too appears to have a 'soft spot' and a sense of justice. Like Ben, he saves Nina from potential rapists. Thus, unsurprisingly perhaps, he is Ben's one genuine ally in the gang. Decency bonds across racial differences – white, black and mestizo. Moreover, Ben's ultimate support of the Mexican revolutionaries is not represented as a corollary of his love for Nina. He is converted, against his cynical wariness, to their cause. In a world of deception, as represented by Joe, the countess and the rest of the French, he has found something to believe in again.

Perhaps because of the theme of Ben's reintegration into society, Wright felt justified in categorising *Vera Cruz* as an example of the classical plot. But it also accords with his characterisation of the professional Western, especially in terms of the relationship between Ben and Joe, who themselves are contrasted to the professional French soldiery. Joe is in it for the money unequivocally and Ben equivocally. Both are fantastically skilled, and they form a mutual admiration society on that basis. The rest of the gang is not highly individuated in terms of their abilities, but they are very effective in their business (indeed, they are more effective than the French), which business is killing. However, *Vera Cruz* is not marked by the absence of society as an active force of positive value, once one realises that the relevant society is Mexican society as represented by the revolutionaries.

If Wright responds that it is for this very reason that *Vera Cruz* should not be considered as an example of the professional Western, I would begin to suspect, given the elements I've cited, that he may be begging the question. Moreover, this same oversight shows up in cases where the status of the films as professional Westerns is uncontroversial.[10]

The Magnificent Seven

In *The Magnificent Seven*, which was adapted from *The Seven Samurai*, the presence of Mexican society is more pronounced than it is in *Vera Cruz*. Set somewhere vaguely in the late 19th century, the film begins as thirty or forty bandits, led by Calvera (Eli Wallach), ride into a Mexican farming village to exact tribute. Calvera speaks civilly, as if he were a good friend of the villagers, but this makes their situation all the more humiliating. One of the villagers resists, and is shot down. When the bandits leave, the farmers discuss their plight, and, following the advice of an old wise man, they head for the border to buy guns in order to fight back when the bandits return. What is perhaps most notable here is that the decision-making is roughly democratic, in the sense that the men of the town (though not the women) evolve their plan communally.

Across the border, the farmers witness a display of nerve, verve and firepower when Chris (played by Yul Brynner) and Vin (played by Steve McQueen) escort a hearse, carrying a dead Native American, to the graveyard. This introduces the theme of racial tolerance, since the local townspeople have denied the Indian burial rights because he is not white. Called 'Injun Lovers', Chris and Vin blast their way to Boot Hill. The scene also establishes their martial expertise, coolheadedness under fire, and mutual admiration for one another's skill.

The Mexicans approach Chris to help them buy guns. But he says that nowadays men are cheaper than guns and suggests that they commission some hired gunmen. They offer him the job, and after he delivers a speech about how hard such a war would be (in order to test their commitment), he agrees. Next ensues a series of scenes in which the rest of the Magnificent Seven are enlisted.

Vin is first. Though the pay is a measly $25, plus room and board, he agrees because his only alternative is to work in a grocery store. The mere prospect of an opportunity to exercise his warrior skills outweighs the option of productive citizenship. A man called Reilly (played by Charles Bronson) is next. Chris and Vin appeal to him by flattery, talking about his legendary exploits in Travis County and Salina (which also informs the audience of his professional prowess). He is down on his luck, and also agrees to join. Next they approach Reb (played by James Coburn), who displays his special ability, knife-throwing, in a showdown with a cowboy. Having heard of the venture, Harry (played by Brad Dexter) and Lee (played by Robert Vaughn) approach Chris, and the professionals are ready to head south.

Along the way, they are followed by Chico (played by Horst Buchholz), a journeyman gunman, who has appeared in earlier scenes, but who had been rejected by Chris for being unseasoned. His persistence wins them over, and now the professionals number seven. They ride into the Mexican village and, auspiciously enough, their first full day there is on the occasion of the anniversary of the founding of the town. It is hard not to read this as an Independence Day celebration, replete with native dancing and fireworks. It is a way of analogising the resistance of this Mexican village to the American Revolution.

The professionals prepare the town's defences, training the farmers in a montage of rudimentary boot camp exercises and rigging all manner of traps – walls, moats and so on. In all this, the growing confidence of the farmers is a major theme, since, to a great extent, the autonomy of the villagers is what this film is about. When the bandits return, there is an extended shoot-out; not only the professionals, but the farmers fight splendidly, and the bandits beat a disorderly retreat. However, they have not left the field entirely. They head for the hills to regroup and to launch their next attack.

The interlude between battles provides breathing space for a number of important developments. Bernardo Reilly's interactions with some of the children of the village lead him to rediscover, as they say, his Mexican roots. Gradually his commitment to the farmers is transformed from mercenary to emotional. He tells the children that they should honour their fathers for their everyday courage. Chris and some of the other gunmen philosophise about the lonely life of the professional, their tone signalling that it contrasts unfavourably with the life of ordinary folks who have people and a place that means something to them and to which they mean something. A love interest blossoms between Chico and one of the young women of the village. Love, here, stands as another of the values that mundane society proffers in contrast to professionalism. Thus, though this film fits the professional formula, its underlying argument is that social life in a community, as represented by the Mexicans, is superior to the professional alternative. Professionalism for its own sake is not celebrated, but rather it is justified in the service of defending the ordinary social values evinced by the farmers.

Moreover, it turns out that both Bernardo Reilly and Chico are of Mexican heritage. This establishes a commonality between the professionals and the community. When each, in turn, acknowledges this, the argument for society is advanced. Of all the professionals, only Harry appears to remain completely mercenary in his relation to the village, and even this may be ambiguous. The rest of the professionals, it seems, become committed to the village because of the social value it represents.

While the town awaits the next attack, dissension begins to erupt among the villagers. They fear that they have got more than they bargained for. While the professionals attempt to deliver a surprise attack on the bandit camp, some of the villagers turn the town over to the marauders. When the professionals return home they are surrounded and forced to abandon the village. Rather than returning north, however, they stage a counter-attack, in which they are woefully outnumbered, until the farmers, their courage regained, join the battle and the bandits are decisively vanquished.

Of the professionals left standing, Chico decides to remain in the village with his new-found love, a choice that rhetorically stands for the superiority of the social life over the professional life. A old man suggests that Chris and Vin also stay, but it is conceded that the villagers really won't care one way or the other. The village is something permanent – the farmers are the land and the gunmen merely the wind that blows over it. Chris and Vin leave, looking back at the village wistfully, with a tangible sense of loss. 'Only the farmers won. We lost. We always lose.'

The overt theme of the film is that the gunslinger's life is inferior to that of ordinary society. With its professional motif, it is rather like *The Gunfighter* writ large. Martial prowess is celebrated, but ultimately it must be integrated with society, as it is when the farmers are turned into warriors. Society must acquire the military capacity to defend itself if it is to remain autonomous. Skill at arms is not valuable for its own sake, but only as an instrument in the service of autonomy. The film is about resisting tyranny in defence of the values of ordinary society.

One might say that even if that is the major narrative theme, it is not the major visual theme. The major visual theme is violence and martial prowess. But however much truth there is in that observation (and there is a great deal), it is important to remember that the final defeat of the bandits is achieved by the farmers wielding chairs, machetes and hoes and not by the gunfighters. The triumphal feelings that the battle engenders in the audience have as their objects the Mexican farmers fighting for their own freedom.

Wright does not consider *The Magnificent Seven* in his book. However, I would contend that it is clearly a professional Western. In some regards, it may even be a prototype. But it does not accord with the notion that society recedes in this type of film. For in this film, social values, in the shape of Mexican resistance to tyranny, are not just the pretext of the film, but its emotional fulcrum as well.

The Professionals

The Professionals is one of Wright's paradigms of the sub-genre that, in fact, takes its name from the title and the language of this film (wherein terms like 'professional code' and 'specialists' appear). For my own part, I think this film shows the influence of *The Magnificent Seven*. Under the titles, we see the professional team assembled in vignettes that recall the enlistment of several of the Magnificent Seven. Rico Fardan (played by Lee Marvin) is shown demonstrating a .30 calibre Browning water-cooled machine-gun; Ehrengard (played by Robert Ryan) is involved in horse training; Jake (played by Woody Strode) is delivering a fugitive from justice to the law. Each of these vignettes give us a sense of the professional's special abilities. Bill Dolworth (played by Burt Lancaster) is discovered in an adulterous tryst, which associates him with the erotic life, a characteristic which will ultimately figure in the major plot reversal of the film.

Set somewhere in the early teens, the film shows how the professionals are assembled by Mr Grant (played by Ralph Bellamy). As he introduces them to each other, he elaborates on their extraordinary skills, thus giving the audience a glimpse of their professional prowess. Rico, wearing clothes that are highly suggestive of military attire, is a tactician. Ehrengard is an expert horse trainer. Jake is a scout and an archer. The theme of racial tolerance is made explicit when Grant asks Rico and Ehrengard if they object to working with a Negro (Jake). Rico looks at him as if the question were beneath contempt. For professionals, at least, skill is the criterion, not skin pigmentation.

Grant explains that he has brought them together to rescue his wife Maria (played by Claudia Cardinale) who has been kidnapped by Raza (played by Jack Palance). Rico, who, along with Dolworth, has ridden with Pancho Villa and Raza, talks of the impossibility of such a rescue operation. He argues that Dolworth, a demolitions expert, must be added to the group as an 'equaliser'. Grant agrees, Dolworth is enlisted, and the professionals are briefed. They are ready to head south.

The journey provides the opportunity for Rico and Dolworth to extol Raza's martial prowess. They are perplexed that Raza would stoop to kidnapping. It does not correspond to the Raza they knew. The professionals ride on, and they are attacked twice, which enables them to display their own skills to great advantage. There is some dissension in the ranks. Ehrengard, introduced to us under the credits as a horse lover, resents what he takes to be Dolworth's cold-heartedness, although every time that he opposes what he thinks is Dolworth's ruthlessness, his judgements (about not killing the horses, and about the goat herder) turn out to be wrong.

The professionals enter Raza's territory and they witness Raza and his troops attack a federal army train. Raza and his men execute the federal troops, which leads Ehrengard to express his disgust. Dolworth tells him to shut up and then explains that the troops in question are guilty of numerous atrocities against the Mexican people, including the savage murder of Rico's Mexican wife whom they stripped and ran into a cactus. This reduces Ehrengard to asking, somewhat dismissively, why Americans would be involved in the Mexican revolution anyway, to which Dolworth replies, 'Maybe there's only been one revolution since the beginning. The good guys against the bad guys. The question is who are the good guys.'

This exchange introduces a hint of something upon which the plot will ultimately hinge. Who are the good guys and the bad guys here? Is Raza really the bad guy? It also endorses revolutionary activity in the abstract. Combined with the previous question, it suggests the possibility that Raza is a genuine revolutionary. After all, consider his name; 'la raza' means 'the people'.

Reaching Raza's domain, the professionals reconnoitre, plan their attack against outlandish odds and begin their assault at dawn, exploiting Dolworth's expertise with dynamite to simulate the effect of an artillery barrage. The deployment for the attack and the battle itself are veritable miracles of split-second timing and applied technique – a fantasy of military professionalism. Rico and Dolworth sneak into Mrs Grant's dwelling in order to carry her off, but a complication develops. Raza arrives apparently to rape her, but she responds more in the manner of a consort than a captive. Rico and Dolworth conk Raza on the head and abduct Mrs Grant. But they know that something is not quite right about their assignment.

Raza and his men take off in hot pursuit of the professionals, who now possess Mrs Grant. Several ingenious action scenes ensue. As the escape continues, the professionals learn that Mrs Grant was not kidnapped. She has always been Raza's lover. Her father had unconscionably forced her to marry Mr Grant. But her love for Raza and the Mexican revolution has never flagged. She conspired with Raza to send Mr Grant the ransom note in order to buy guns and bullets for the revolution. In effect, it is the professionals who are the kidnappers, and Mrs Grant is not a compliant damsel in distress.

Mrs Grant tries to rekindle Rico's commitment to the revolution. The theme of the superiority of fighting for what one believes in over fighting for money is repeated several times. Furthermore, Dolworth admires Mrs Grant and tells Rico that her spiritedness reminds him of Rico's dead wife. This intimates that Dolworth's sympathies may be shifting and, sensing this, Rico says, implicitly invoking the professional credo, that he'll deliver Mrs Grant to her husband if he has to do it himself.

Raza and his men are fast on the heels of the professionals. In order to slow the Mexicans down, Dolworth stays behind to ambush them in a ravine. Dolworth's performance is spectacular. He kills all of Raza's men and severely wounds Raza himself. Lastly, he kills Lieutenant Chiquita, a former lover of his from his days with Villa. While kissing her lips as she dies, Dolworth recognises, as he puts it, that he's a sucker for love.

Meanwhile, the professionals arrive for their rendezvous with Mr Grant. In short order Dolworth arrives with Raza in tow, followed by Grant and his men. Will the professionals turn Mrs Grant over or not? Rico reverses the situation, noting that they were hired to rescue a kidnapped woman and that, in fact, Mr Grant is the kidnapper. So they turn a willing Mrs Grant over to Raza. Raza and Mrs Grant head south in a buckboard and the professionals ride off, leaving an enraged Mr Grant empty-handed. Perhaps the viewer recalls Dolworth's speech about knowing who the good guys are. We thought Mr Grant represented righteousness, but all along Raza was the good guy, and therefore, in the terms of Dolworth's argument, the genuine revolutionary article.

The Professionals does not present us with ordinary society in the manner of *The Magnificent Seven*. Indeed, if one thinks that Mr Grant represents (American) society, then it surely seems fallen. However, that is the wrong place to look for society in *The Professionals*. The Mexican revolution, represented by Raza and his men, stand for the values of society against the tyrannical federal troops. As is often the case, love here (the relation between Raza and Mrs Grant) symbolises social value but, as in *Vera Cruz* and *The Magnificent Seven*, love is also associated with resistance to tyranny.

Society figures in *The Professionals* as social revolution. And as in *Vera Cruz* and *The Magnificent Seven*, the professionals commit themselves to the cause of justice, rather than to their code. Indeed, Rico sophistically interprets their contract so that it works out in terms of the authentic lovers and the cause they represent.

Once again, professionalism appears justified in the service of society. It is not divorced from society, construed as a Mexican revolution.

The Wild Bunch

From the point of film history, *The Wild Bunch* is probably the most important film in the group under discussion. Along with *Bonnie and Clyde* it initiated a new style of cinematic violence, employing accelerated montage and slow motion. Made during the Vietnam War, its massacres were compared at the time to fire-fights on the Mekong Delta. Set in roughly the same period as *The Professionals*, it begins as a group of bandits, the Wild Bunch, led by Pike (played by William Holden) and Dutch (played by Ernest Borgnine) ride into town disguised as horse soldiers. Their arrival is intercut with a group of sadistic children torturing scorpions by pushing them into hordes of furious red ants. One supposes that the scorpions stand for the professionals.

As the gang enters the railway office that they intend to rob, we learn that it is a trap. Bounty hunters led by Thornton (played by Robert Ryan), who was formerly Pike's partner, have them surrounded. To complicate matters, a crack-brained temperance parade is marching into the line of fire. This doesn't deter the bounty hunters. They open fire on the robbers, who shoot their way out of town, sustaining heavy losses, though in all it seems that the town has taken more casualties than either the bounty hunters or the gang. As the robbers ride past the children, the kids burn up the scorpions, a gesture that seems to refer symbolically to the conflagration we have just witnessed as well as to the ultimate fate of the Wild Bunch.

The depiction of the town in terms of sadistic children and evangelical temperance nuts gives a poor picture of settled society but, as in other films in this cycle, American society is not the relevant locus of social value here: Mexican society is. The Wild Bunch head for the border, intending to recuperate in the village of their Mexican member, Angel. A posse led by Thornton and composed, it seems, of mental defectives is hot on their trail.

After the raid, the Wild Bunch learn that they have been duped. The money bags they stole contain nothing but worthless metal washers. This disappointment is occasioned by several of them saying that they had hoped this would be their last job. Pike, for example, emphasises the theme that they are getting too old for this business. They know that their way of life is on the way out. There are several conflicts in the group. At one point, Tector Gorch (played by Ben Johnson) seems ready to kill Old Sykes (played by Edmond O'Brien). This prompts Pike to make a speech: 'We're gonna stick together just like it used to be. When you side with a man you stay with him. And if you can't do that you're like some animal. You're finished. We're finished. *All* of us.' This conception of commitment becomes especially important at the end of the film.

Arriving at Angel's village provides a kind of idyll amid all the violence and depravity in the film. We learn that in Angel's absence, federal troops led by General Mapache raped the village and killed Angel's father. Angel's girlfriend left the village to become Mapache's mistress. Angel wants revenge. His anguish is contrasted with the festivities and warm social life in the village. It seems to reduce Tector and Lyle Gotch (played by Warren Oates), the most degenerate members of the Wild Bunch, to engaging in chaste playfulness. There is a celebratory dance, and goodwill is shared all around. When the Wild Bunch finally leave the village, they parade out to lilting guitar music and singing. Swathed in a mist, they ride past the townspeople who regard them lovingly, bestowing gifts and flowers on them. One senses that they bond with this community and that their experiences dispose them against Mapache and towards the Mexican people and the guerrilla resistance, since it is this special moment that closes the film by means of a flashback.

The Wild Bunch approach Mapache in the hope of selling him their extra horses. When Pike suggests that Mapache is a bandit just like they are, Dutch objects: 'We ain't nothing like him. We don't hang nobody. I hope these people here kick him and the rest of the scum like him into their graves.' Angel responds, 'We will if it takes for ever.'

When Angel sees his former girlfriend in Mapache's arms, he shoots her. But Mapache doesn't kill the Wild Bunch. Instead he offers them a job – to rob a US Army train and seize the guns and ammunition on it. The Wild Bunch agree; one of their conditions is that Angel be released. Angel, on the other hand, refuses to work for Mapache and against his own people until Pike and Dutch promise to give him some of the guns for the Mexican guerrillas. The highjacking of the train is a breathtaking exercise in timing. But unbeknownst to the Wild Bunch, Thornton has anticipated their attack and no sooner are the Wild Bunch on their way than Thornton and his band of subhumans are after them. The Wild Bunch elude them by blowing a bridge out from under the bounty hunters. But when the gang settle down for the night, they are surrounded by the guerrillas who have come for the guns Angel has promised them. Perhaps surprisingly, most of the Wild Bunch hardly resent this. Instead, they express their admiration for the guerrillas. Dutch says, 'I'd say those fellas know how to handle themselves.' Pike adds, 'If they ever get armed, with good leaders, this country will go up in smoke.' 'That it will, son, that it will,' Old Sykes concludes.

After a series of pretty dicey negotiations with Mapache and his men, the Wild Bunch begin a complicated transfer of the arms to the federal troops who have just been dealt a defeat by Pancho Villa. However, as the last transaction is under way, Mapache seizes Angel who he has learnt has given rifles and ammunition to the guerrillas.

As the Wild Bunch discuss what to do about this, they realise that Thornton's posse is still after them. They decide to go to Mapache's stronghold, since that is one place where Thornton will not follow them. Arriving there, they see Angel being tortured – he is being dragged by a Model T while children burn him with flares, rather as the scorpions were torched in the opening of the film. They try to buy Angel from Mapache, but they fail. Mapache's troops, roughly two hundred men, drink themselves into a stupor, and members of the Wild Bunch spend the night with whores.

The next morning, Pike approaches Lyle and Tector Gorch and says, 'Let's go.' 'Why not?' Lyle agrees. Nothing about what they intend to do is stated, but the men all seem to understand each other. Dutch just has to look at a fellow professional and he knows. They get their rifles and go to Mapache to demand Angel's release. Mapache feigns compliance, but instead slits Angel's throat. Pike shoots Mapache and there is a pause, as if no one knows what to do. Then the Wild Bunch start shooting Mapache's staff and a battle royal is joined. As is well known, it is quite a sustained gunfight for its period in film history, and by the end Pike, Dutch and the Gorch brothers are dead, but not before they have seemingly wiped out Mapache's entire army.

When Thornton's posse arrives, almost everyone is dead. Then the posse, *sans* Thornton, ride offscreen where they are killed by the guerrillas, led by Old Sykes. The guerrillas return to the killing field to strip Mapache's men of their guns and their ammunition. The Wild Bunch's last stand is a *de facto* victory for the revolution, supplying the rebels with a large store of arms while also decimating the federal army. Old Sykes invites Thornton to join the guerrillas. Thus, in effect, what is left of the Wild Bunch – recall that Thornton was once Pike's partner – becomes part of the Mexican revolution. And then the whole story is rounded off with flashbacks of the members of the Wild Bunch celebrating their camaraderie, and culminating, significantly enough, in their best moment, their bonding with the people in Angel's village.

Since the members of the Wild Bunch never say why they decide to confront Mapache, one cannot be certain of their motives. But the film does make clear that the significance of their last battle is to be understood in terms of advancing the cause of the revolution towards which they had expressed their sympathies. Part of the reason for their showdown with Mapache surely has to do with Pike's earlier speech about commitment to one's partners. The Wild Bunch had to rescue Angel as part of the code of the professional. But Angel is also the leading representative of the Mexican revolution, and in standing by him they also advanced the revolution and the cause of the people they admired.

The Wild Bunch presents a cankered vision of an American society made up of religious temperance fanatics, nasty children, lunatic lawmen, unscrupulous, vicious railroad representatives, and an incompetent army. But the Mexican people, represented by Angel's village, are portrayed in an affirmative light and their revolution (the head of Angel's village is one of the guerrillas) is endorsed throughout the film. Whether or not it is the express intention of the Wild Bunch to forward the revolution (and there is some evidence in this direction) as a matter of fact (in the world of the fiction), they die fighting for it.

Conclusion

In my descriptions of these four films, I have tried to show that, *pace* Will Wright, the professional Westerns situated south of the border do not accord, in significant respects, with his model. Most importantly, I have wanted to emphasise that society is not irrelevant in these films, once one realises that the society in question is Mexican society, which, in turn, is closely associated with various Mexican resistance movements. I do not think that Wright failed to note this because he was ethnically blinkered, but because he aspired to create a general model of the professional Western, and Mexican society only figures in a subset of them.

However, I do think that, in ignoring this feature of films like *The Professionals* and *The Wild Bunch*, he missed a key dimension of their ideological operation.

Wright's story about the ideological operation of the professional Western in general is that it is an expression and/or celebration of the technocratic ethos. Thus, from his viewpoint, the professional Western reflects and reinforces attitudes that we might say are significant internally to contemporary American society. However, the professional Westerns that travel south of the border cross national boundaries, and therefore it is natural to suppose that they have something to do with prevailing ideological attitudes concerning international affairs.[11]

As I hope I have established, a major recurring motif in these films is that of professionals who devote their energies in support of certain social values, namely, freedom and resistance to tyranny. Although certain of the professional attitudes that Wright describes appear in these films, they coexist with and are often outweighed by sympathy for the struggles of the Mexican people. The professionals in these films are hardly as oblivious of society as Wright contends. In each of these films, the heroes, professionals though they be, wind up on the side of social revolutions for the sake of justice, not money. They may fight for their love of battle and because of their fidelity to the group. But, equally, they are motivated by a hatred of tyranny, an attraction to the social value of freedom, and/or an admiration for the Mexican people.

Quite clearly, from a political point of view these films are about an opposition to oppression and the support of social liberation. Underlying these films is the presupposition of a principle that the justification of professional prowess rests in its service for freedom and against tyranny. At the same time, there is a pretty clear-cut association of the professionals in these films with the military. They either have military backgrounds (Ben Trane, Rico Fardan, Bill Dolworth), or they wear military regalia (Rico Fardan, the Wild Bunch), or they exhibit military behaviour (the Magnificent Seven training the peasants). Putting this together with the previous principle, we see that these films rest on the view that the justification of the military is its promotion of freedom.

Moreover, if these professionals represent the military, they are the American military operating outside their national boundaries. Thus, we may hypothesise that what these films are about is what Americans want to believe, namely, that American military operations abroad are undertaken in the defence of freedom.

I am not saying that these films accurately represent American intervention abroad. They express a wish; they show how a great many Americans wished to conceive American foreign policy throughout the period of the *Pax Americana*. Like the professionals in these films, America may appear mercenary, driven by commercial interest, but finally it turns out that they are freedom fighters allied to indigenous, authentic social revolutions. These films express that ideological conviction at the same time that they reinforce it. That is the central ideological function of the south-of-the-border, professional Western.

To some readers, it may seem strange that the professional Western takes such a favourable view of the Mexican revolution, on the one hand, and the Mexican people on the other. Surely, there is a history of American antipathy and prejudice regarding both. However, it is important to remember that from the Second World War onwards, in part due to the war (and the need for a reliable ally to the south), American attitudes towards both the revolution and its vicissitudes, and towards Mexicans, became increasingly more positive than they had been.[12] This is perhaps reflected somewhat in the themes of racial tolerance and acceptance that run through all of these films, which, of course, also correlate with an important phase of the American civil rights movement.

Given the way in which American society appears to be represented in these films – the suggested injustice of the Union in *Vera Cruz*, the prejudiced town in *The Magnificent Seven*, Mr Grant in *The Professionals*, and the pervasive degeneracy in *The Wild Bunch* – a superficial reading of these films might propose that they are involved in social criticism. However, this overlooks the fact that it is the professionals who mobilise the audience's allegiance and that those professionals cater to an American self-conception of itself as a nation committed to freedom. This self-conception, abetted in part by these professional Westerns, had important ideological work to do in the throes of the Cold War.

The Western genre, along with the crime film, addresses American politics in a particularly straightforward way. They are forums for the expression of political anxieties, beliefs, desires, sentiments, and convictions. Films like *Posse* and *Bad Girls* attempt to serve as vehicles for contemporary identity politics. The south-of-the-border professional Western presupposed, as a condition of narrative intelligibility, audiences that would easily accept the plausibility of these paramilitary, American professionals risking everything for the cause of freedom. Since this was a sentiment, albeit idealised, that Americans already embraced about themselves as a nation, these films activated it reliably and, in the process of activating it, reinforced it.[13] Nor, as the Gulf War indicates, is this sentiment merely an artefact of the past.

The films I have been discussing span a period of fifteen years, years in which public attitudes towards American intervention abroad changed, often momentously. Some of those changes are reflected in these films. However, in this essay I have been less concerned with year-to-year fluctuations in opinions about American foreign policy than with what I contend is an underlying, unvarying conviction, shared by American conservatives and radicals alike, regarding intervention, namely, that it is justified in the name of abetting freedom. Virtually everyone in the debate avails themselves of this rhetoric no matter what the situation. Thus, what I have found to be of note in these professional Westerns is not that they reflect contemporary American opinions about specific foreign policy issues, but that they reveal something about the enduring framework in which Americans regard such issues. Americans want to believe that intervention is justified in support of social justice. They are predisposed emotionally to respond favourably to situations depicted in this light. This is one of the reasons that the professional Westerns we have examined are successful. And it is also a perennial disposition that can be readily exploited for ideological purposes.

Notes

1 There are other films in this cycle. I have focused on these four because I think that they are the best known. *A Fistful of Dynamite* (1972) is also an important example, but I

shall not dwell on it because it is an Italian production and, for reasons that will become obvious when I discuss the ideological operation of these films, I am concerned with American productions.

    I call this series of films a cycle for a number of reasons. Not only do they share settings, themes and plot motifs. They also share actors, a number of whom appear in two of the films under discussion. And, more importantly, the earlier films in this series seem to have influenced the later films in a multiplicity of ways from dramatic development to costumes to props. For two examples, consider the ways in which the professionals are introduced in *The Magnificent Seven* and *The Professionals*, and the similar weaponry in *The Professionals* and *The Wild Bunch*. Moreover, I am not the first person to note the importance of Mexican revolutions to these films. Richard Slotkin regards *Vera Cruz* and *The Magnificent Seven*, among other films, as part of a series concerned with Mexican revolutions which he calls 'the counterinsurgency scenario'. See Richard Slotkin, *Gunfighter Nation: The Myth of the Frontier in Twentieth-Century America* (New York: Atheneum, 1992), pp. 435–40.

2 Will Wright, *Six Guns and Society: A Structural Study of the Western* (Berkeley: University of California Press, 1975).

3 Wright, p. 97 (bracketed remarks added).

4 Wright, pp. 85–6.

5 Wright, p. 177.

6 Wright, p. 178.

7 Wright, p. 179.

8 Wright, p. 179 (bracketed remarks added).

9 Of course, the theme of the professional is not restricted to the Western. It is often important in caper films. War films, such as The *Guns of Navarone*, also celebrate the theme. Parenthetically, it is interesting to note that several of these sorts of films have numbers in their titles – not only *The Magnificent Seven*, but *Ocean's Eleven* and *The Dirty Dozen*. The integer usually refers to the number of professional heroes in the film.

10 On p. 41 of *Six Guns and Society*, Wright categorises *Vera Cruz* as a classical Western on the grounds that the hero (Ben Trane) is accepted by the arbiters of respectable society after he saved it from destruction. This is not exactly accurate descriptively, since he has not saved the Mexican revolutionaries from destruction, but rather aided them. However, it is true that Wright does somewhat abstractly acknowledge the importance of a society, which happens to be Mexican, in this film. Nevertheless, he surprisingly fails to discuss the degree to which the film also coincides with his characterisation of the professional Western. So, despite what he says, I think that on his own terms he should consider it at least a mixed case. Moreover, this has repercussions for his accounts of other professional Westerns, since, as I hope to show, in both *The Professionals* and *The Wild Bunch*, the gunfighters manifest a sympathy for Mexican revolutionaries rather like Ben Trane's. Thus, his distinction between the classical Western and the professional Western is unstable throughout his theory. Moreover, with respect to *Vera Cruz*, I think that the film shares more elements with Wright's characterisation of the professional Western than it does with the classical Western and, therefore, merits the criticism advanced above. But, apart from questions of categorisation, I also think that Wright ignores the importance of the *Mexican* people in the film and this is ultimately the crux of my criticism.

11 Indeed, Richard Slotkin regards them as thought experiments concerning counterinsurgency. See Slotkin, pp. 439–40.

12 For information on attitudes towards the Mexican Revolution, see John A. Brittan, *Revolution and Ideology: Images of the Mexican Revolution in the United States* (Lexington: University of Kentucky Press, 1995). For information on changing American attitudes towards Mexicans, especially along the border, see David Montejano, *Anglos and Mexicans in the Making of Texas, 1836–1986* (Austin: University of Texas Press, 1987) and Arnoldo De Leon, *They Called Them Greasers* (Austin: University of Texas Press, 1983).

13 For a more general account of the operation of ideology in narrative film, see Noël Carroll, 'Film, Rhetoric and Ideology', in Salim Kemal and Ivan Gaskell (eds) *Explanation and Value in the Arts* (Cambridge: Cambridge University Press, 1993).

4 Wider Horizons: Douglas Fairbanks and Nostalgic Primitivism

Gaylyn Studlar

In 1916, social commentator George Creel declared Douglas Fairbanks to be 'what every American might be, ought to be, and frequently is *not*. ... And let no one quarrel with this popularity. It is a good sign, a healthful sign, a token that the blood of America still runs warm and red, and that chalk has not yet softened our bones.'[1] The next year, *Photoplay* called Fairbanks '*the* representative American actor' whose roles 'represent America and the biff-bang Americanism for which we are, justly and unjustly, renowned'.[2] These comments give some indication of why, in the years 1915–20, Douglas Fairbanks became not only a movie star but a cultural icon. He evoked widespread and zealous praise for his youthfulness, his 'spirit', his personality, his amazing athleticism, in short, his personification of everything little boys dreamed of becoming and everything men wished they might have retained of an idealised youth.[3]

The trademark Fairbanksian hero was a young man of a certain patrician quality and privileged Eastern upbringing who ran, jumped, punched, and smiled his way into a vigorous, 'red-blooded' manhood. Frederick James Smith described 'Doug' (a.k.a. 'Old Doc Cheerful', 'Mr Pep', 'Mr Electricity', and 'Dr Smile') in a 1917 interview: 'He is athletically rugged and distinctly masculine. When he talks you get the impression of a boy who hasn't grown up. He seems to be charged with a sort of restless energy.'[4] The actor who represented 'what every American ... ought to be' began his career by starring in that most American of all genres, the Western, from his smash-hit début film, *The Lamb* (1915)[5] to *The Half-Breed* (1916), *The Good Bad Man* (1916), *The Man from Painted Post* (1917), *Wild and Woolly* (1917), *A Modern Musketeer* (1917), *Arizona* (1918), *The Knickerbocker Buckaroo* (1919), *The Mollycoddle* (1920). Fairbanks's Westerns of these years were enormously popular attractions, perhaps because they resonated with the cultural concerns of a rapidly urbanising nation. Changes in economic, ethnic and demographic structures were perceived as threatening American masculinity and manly virtues. With Social Darwinism providing even more fuel for an ethnocentric Americanism focused on matters of nationality conflated with race, much anxiety centred around the preservation of traditional white, Anglo-Saxon-identified, Protestant, middle-class-identified masculinity.[6]

As a result, many popular cultural discourses, including Fairbanks's films, attempted to redefine the nature of masculine identity in a society increasingly regarded as 'overcivilised' and 'feminised'.[7] Thus Fairbanks's Westerns demand to be considered in the context of a widespread effort to redefine

American male identity in response to perceived threats associated with modernity.

With the notable exception of *The Half-Breed* (1916), a serious and sensitive examination of racial prejudice in the Old West, Fairbanks's Westerns usually came under the rubric of 'comedy-melodrama', 'thrillers' or 'the athletic straight comedy'.[8] No matter how his films were labelled, they foregrounded the actor's performance in some of the most spectacular athletic feats ever shown on the screen. The film industry craved the kind of commodity Fairbanks exemplified: a respectable Broadway talent whose body seemed made for movement. As Fairbanks's movie publicity would soon note at every opportunity, no mere stage seemed capable of holding his movement, which demanded a wider horizon. 'His "joyous personality" was "cramped, cabined and confined" in the narrow limits of the playhouse. He needed, not knowing it, the wide sweep of mountain and plain. Fairbanks was already popular, though the stage never gave him the elbow-room he needed.'[9]

Fairbanks's expansive, energetic style of masculinity seemed to cut across class differences to suggest the symbolic reconciliation of modern American dilemmas and the mythic restoration of American masculinity, accomplished most often within the athletic-centred comedy formula of the Fairbanks Western. Fairbanks's films depicted him as an adult who none the less remained, in the words of Adele Rogers St Johns, 'a boy of boundless energy and irrepressible enthusiasm'.[10] Who else but Fairbanks would, as in *A Modern Musketeer,* attempt a handstand on the edge of the Grand Canyon, then, as if in sudden realisation of his audacity, crawl away on hands and knees while grinning at the camera? No wonder the chain of antics inevitably set into play in any Fairbanks vehicle was thought to appeal strongly to children and to make a particular impression on boys. They were diving off roofs and falling out of trees in unprecedented numbers in their attempt to emulate their cinematic hero.[11]

Even when his films were 'melodramas' with serious-minded elements, Fairbanks's exuberant personality and bouncing body turned them into a celebration of athletic daring and sheer movement. For example, *The Man from Painted Post* is ostensibly the story of a Western detective in pursuit of a vicious cattle rustler who murdered his sister. However, it is dominated by Fairbanks's easy humour and athletic stunts. An advertisement for the film said it had 'everything that is typically Fairbanks; the "pep" the good-natured "rough stuff", the thrills, and *the* smiles'.[12] A review noted of the film: 'Fairbanks is once more the superman who can – and does – scramble up the side of a barn, shoot unerringly with both hands at once, mount a mustang with a fifteen-foot leap, vanquish a whole army of villains, and ride away with the girl for a fadeaway.'[13] Thus, even at their most thematically serious, Fairbanks's Westerns present themselves as a world of amusing play, as fanciful concoctions far removed from the verisimilitude sought by Western star William S. Hart. A review of *The Good Bad Man* suggests the primary reason for the consistent tone of Fairbanks's Westerns: 'The ordinary type of wanderer . . . is usually very serious. Mr Fairbanks's presence does away with any possibility of an entirely serious hero, for his humour is such that it cannot be suppressed no matter what role he assumes.'[14]

Fairbanks's roles must be understood within the cultural framework of a boy-centred reform movement that sought to build character in American boys and ensure the proper development of a 'strenuous' masculinity. Despite their light-hearted tenor, Fairbanks's films were amazingly convergent with the ideals of 'character building' that believed that 'manhood not scholarship is the first aim of education'.[15] As Jeffrey Hantover has observed of the founding of the Boy Scouts of America: 'Men believed they faced diminishing opportunities for masculine validation in the workplace, but adolescents faced immense barriers, it was thought, to the very development of masculinity.'[16] Reforming the lives of boys and recapturing the romance of America's lost boyhood became an Anglo-American growth industry. At the forefront of this movement to build character in boys were scouting advocates Robert Baden-Powell (founder of the Boy Scouts of Britain) and Ernest Thompson Seton (founder of the Woodcraft Indians and Boy Scouts of America Chief of Scouts), Daniel Carter Beard (the Sons of Daniel Boone and a Boy Scouts of America founder), as well as Edgar M. Robinson and Luther Gulick of the Young Men's Christian Association and psychologists William Forbush and G. Stanley Hall.[17] All these reformers and organisations shared a common purpose stated succinctly by Seton: 'To make a man.'[18]

Character-builders embraced a nostalgia for a primitive masculine past. The strongest evidence of that past in contemporary life was the instinct-driven 'savagery' of boys. Among the most socially radical of the character-builders, Seton believed a return to the principles of living in harmony with nature was an antidote to 'city rot' and the 'degeneracy' of modern life.[19] With the distribution of millions of copies of his *Woodcraft Handbook,* Seton's nostalgic obsession with the woods, woodlore and woodcraft skills became a central feature of the Boy Scouts of America's attempt to develop manly boys who would become manly men. Anticipating descriptions of Fairbanks as an all-around athlete, Seton declared that the ideal American boy should have all the skills associated with rural boyhood and frontier life. The boys of the past could 'ride, shoot, skate, run, swim; [they were] handy with tools ... physically strong, self-reliant, resourceful' and 'altogether the best material of which a nation could be made'.[20]

Most boy reformers agreed with Seton that the current generation of boys had to recapture those mythic qualities of masculine character that had been taken for granted as a natural part of the vigorous boy culture of America's rural past. Those qualities were based on those 'ancient virtues of savagery' that boys possessed instinctively but which had become the 'vices of civilisation'.[21] They were skills easily acquired in the more savage past, but now they had to be taught as 'play' by reformers to boys whose primitive, manly instincts were being smothered by the 'pink cotton wool' of mothers who thought of them 'as only a rougher and more troublesome sort of girl'.[22] Boys' sudden impulses and vital activity, the very evidence of the necessary savage instincts that created manly men, were being repressed at every opportunity by mothers and female teachers who were ignorant of male developmental processes.[23]

Like Seton, G. Stanley Hall had immense impact on those concerned with male development in the 1900s. He believed that each boy repeated the 'history of his own race-life from savagery unto civilisation'.[24] As George Fiske described it: 'The whole process of child development like race development is a climb upward from savagery through barbarism to civilisation.'[25] Primitive heartiness and childlike simplicity were valorised. In childhood and extended adolescence, the ideal male type was still subject to savage impulses, to 'boy instincts'.[26] The nostalgic primitivism theorised by Hall and Seton was advanced by 'boy reformers' and 'boys' workers' on numerous political, social, artistic, and even religious fronts. Boy reformers believed that manly instincts were rooted in physicality, which was primarily served by physical exertion in an outdoor setting. The great outdoors was idealised as the natural habitat of boys and the best site for the development of manly self-reliance: it was where the moral strength of an adult individuality might be made compatible with a vision of communally minded, hardy male citizenship.

Character-builders' view of the West was convergent with a 'wilderness cult', which, as scholars such as Roderick Nash have noted, was enthusiastically promoted by urbane easterners such as Theodore Roosevelt, artist and journalist Frederic Remington, and novelist Owen Wister.[27] This cult exalted what was left of the American wilderness, especially in the West, as the best place for the development of manhood. Even in the modern form of tourist destination and temporary campground, the West could rebuild the values of the individual man as it had been the original crucible for the fundamental American values.[28] Character-builders saw the West as the place of wildness that demanded the skills and qualities regarded as an antidote to 'overcivilisation' or 'coddling'.

Praised as being 'almost as strenuous as ex-President Teddy',[29] Fairbanks most vigorously embodied the ideal of perpetual youthfulness and uninhibited, playful physicality. A fan magazine article of 1917 noted that: 'The Fairbanks' hobby is the out-of-doors and everything that goes with it. . . . The strength which the popular "Duggie" [sic] so frequently and picturesquely displays in most of his pictures is his by rights; it is his diploma from the school of strenuous life.'[30] Like Roosevelt, Fairbanks appeared to be a man in whom the primitive urges and instincts of boyhood had not died and who, as a result, reflected ideal masculine goodness through physical regeneration and optimistic moral action. As a counter to anxieties surrounding masculinity in an overcivilised, urban society, Fairbanks's optimistic, performative masculinity had a capacity to make audiences feel as if they were encountering something absolutely innocent and indisputably encouraging.[31]

Just as Roosevelt made himself over from a sickly child into a robust advocate for the strenuous life, in many of his Westerns Fairbanks's characters are transformed into vigorous, manly men. The 'Wild West' as tourist destination still sufficed to provide many Fairbanks heroes with a regenerating encounter with wilderness adventure. *Knickerbocker Buckaroo* offers the most literal embodiment of character-building's middle-class ideals for boyhood. Kicked out of his Manhattan men's club for practical jokes (a habit attributed also to Remington), Teddy Drake (Fairbanks) realises the selfishness of his existence and goes off to the Great American Desert to do 'something for somebody'. During his travels, Teddy helps an old lady, doing a 'good turn' worthy of a Boy Scout which enmeshes him in a series of unexpected adventures involving Mexican bandits and a crooked sheriff.

Teddy Drake suffered from selfishness, but Fairbanks's protagonists most often are depicted as 'mollycoddles', men who are soft, squeamish 'sissies', overcivilised, morally passive, physically weak, and, at their worst, thoroughly 'effeminate'.[32] These character defects related to a man's privileged social position, since it was believed that wealth and aristocratic privilege added a serious obstacle to the attainment of proper masculinity. In the beginning of *The Lamb,* Gerald fits the mollycoddle stereotype of failed, upper-class masculinity; he is passive, squeamish, inept and without a profession. The film ascribes these failings not only to his effete, upper-class Eastern upbringing, but to his having been brought up by his socialite mother. As the introductory intertitle tells us: 'This is the story of a Lovesick Lamb, whose Dad, an Old War Horse, had died. Clinching his Teeth in a Wall Street Bear, leaving The Lamb to gambol around on The Long Green.'

Gerald's situation is not unusual for a Fairbanks protagonist, many of whom are not only fatherless but very self-conscious about the fact. In *The Good Bad Man,* Passin' Through (Fairbanks) so obsesses about his unknown father that he becomes a kind of juvenile delinquent, staging hold-ups to steal trinkets. When asked why he steals, he says: 'To forget there's no decent way I can make a living 'cause I never had no father.' Only by discovering the key to his past can he start a new life. In *The Man from Painted Post,* the Eastern-educated cowboy-detective 'Fancy Jim' Sherwood (Fairbanks) befriends the mixed-blood son of the villain, Bull Madden (Frank Campeau). Madden is attempting to intimidate the school-marm into marrying him, in spite of his living with a 'squaw'. Like a proto-scout-master, Fancy Jim gives Bull's neglected young son proper guidance. He teaches his 'pal' to do rope tricks and wrestle steers to the ground. In turn, the boy warns Jim of his father's plan to ambush the detective. After sending the villain off to jail, Sherwood declares that the boy has a 'new' father – him.

These two films, together with the many others of the 1910s and 20s populated by fatherless heroes, point to the contemporary anxiety surrounding boys, who were seen as dangerously lacking in masculine influence. Writing in *The Forum* in 1914, Michael Monahan declared that children were being abandoned to women and, as a result, 'we are producing a generation of feminised men ("sissies" in the dialect of real boys) who will be fit only to escort women to poll or public office and to render such other puppy attentions as may be demanded by the Superior Sex!'[33] Economics and custom had reduced fathers to being minor influences in their sons' lives. The new capitalism forced fathers to be 'chained to business through the hours when their boys were free of the restraint of school, which is just the time when they most need wise guidance in finding a proper outlet for their accumulated energy and surcharged spirits'.[34] As a result, character-builders believed, it was becoming more difficult for boys to identify with manliness.

The Lamb offers a comic representation of the anxieties surrounding manliness and masculine influence. Gerald has been shaped by the watchfulness of women that has repressed his natural manly instincts for male companionship, physical exertion, and impulsive, playful risk-taking. Exhibiting properly masculine instincts, Gerald attempts to tip-toe away from his society mama's tea party, but he is too awkward to quietly navigate the stairs. He cannot leap over a low hedge-row unless he is lost in the throes of romantic bliss. When he does jump over, he looks back, unable to figure out how he managed to get to the other side. If he gets his hands dirty, he is at a loss as to what to do. In a moment of pique, Gerald's girl Mary (Seena Owens), inspects his hands and berates him for their shocking softness. It is no wonder that she finds him wanting when she compares him with a burly visitor, a Westerner whom the intertitles dub 'The Cactus-fed Goat' (Alfred Paget).

Not long afterwards, Gerald and his friends are at the beach. He sees a woman in the ocean in need of rescue. Boy Scouts were trained to always 'be prepared' through the acquisition of the skills of swimming and first aid. Gerald, however, is totally unprepared. Before he can do anything, the Westerner dives in for the rescue. Gerald collapses in a heap of self-loathing and fury. The intertitle notes the obvious: 'The Lamb was Horrified that in the Crisis he had proved himself the Weakling.' Gerald has been unable to fulfil the scout maxim that, for American popular culture in the 1910s, defined the ideal relationship between masculinity and goodness: 'Be Prepared in body by making yourself strong and active and able to do the right thing at the right moment.'[35] Goaded by his lack of preparedness for basic lifesaving and stung by his fiancée's earlier display of contempt, Gerald goes on a physical training programme. To the horror of his watchful mother, he boxes and takes ju-jitsu lessons – two of Teddy Roosevelt's strenuous interests. He has the desire to be something more than his mama's repressiveness and his untrained body allow him to be.

Although Gerald starts the physical process of becoming a man, he has yet to achieve the graceful, athletic male body of the character-building masculine ideal when he receives a telegram inviting him to join the 'Cactus-fed Goat' and the vacation party of Mary's family in Arizona. As oblivious to the demands of geography as he has formerly been to those of proper masculinity, Gerald gets 'all dolled up in Alpine Togs', to follow Mary to the 'Bad Lands'. Although Gerald does not know it, the telegram provides him with the opportunity to make the era's classic journey of masculine regeneration.

'Fleeced' and knocked senseless by Native Americans selling curios, Gerald is left behind by the train and falls in among 'Crooks from the East'. Next he is kidnapped by rebellious Yaqui Indians. The innate strength of Gerald's pioneer stock, together with his own efforts, has helped him overcome his beginnings as a laughable 'mollycoddle'. He discovers the roots of the masculine primitive on which he can establish a truly manly, uniquely American identity.[36] Left to his own devices, without money or companionship, he learns the resources of his own body. By the end of the film, he bounds across the Arizona landscape by horse, by car, and his own athletic propulsion. Once incapable of resisting his society mama's domestic control, he now wards off a band of Yaqui warriors with a Gatling gun. This transformation occurs because, as the intertitles inform us: 'Blood will speak – though society drowns the conversation.'

In The Lamb, the Western wilderness is still the free place where character-builders believed man's 'natural' primitive urges could find expression and where Americans, if of the proper Anglo-Saxon ancestry, could find their instinctual, 'racial' heritage confirmed and renewed.[37] Often quoted, George S. Evans's 'The Wilderness' in Overland Monthly (1904) still stands as a classic statement of this kind of writing:

> Dull business routine, the fierce passions of the market-place, the perils of envious cities become but a memory. ... And now you have become like your environment. ... The

wilderness will take hold on you. It will give you good red blood; it will turn you from a weakling into a man.[38]

The character-reformers made a key distinction, however. The West or the wilderness was not the place to become uncivilised, but the place to become self-reliant, strong, and manly. If its way of life was obsolete, the West was not obsolete in its importance to the character of the nation. In keeping with these sentiments, Fairbanks's Westerns frequently set their action at sites conventionally associated with the extremes of masculine imperilment or redemption: the comfortable Eastern vacation haunts of the old and *nouveau riche* and the regenerative semi-wilderness of the contemporary West. Fairbanks's protagonists go from civilisation not into a pioneer confrontation with pure savagery, but into a tourist playground that requires a playful interweaving of primitive skills with civilised gentility. Following in the famous footsteps of Wister, Roosevelt and Remington, Fairbanks's heroes are often urbane Easterners with an exaggerated love of the West. In *Manhattan Madness,* the aptly named hero Steve O'Dare (Fairbanks) returns to civilisation after a regenerating encounter with the West. Steve regales his Manhattan men's club with tales of masculine daring and castigates Eastern softness. He starts arguments with declarations such as: 'New York is all wrong, superficial, un-American, overcrowded. I can't breathe – can't sleep – can't eat.' In spite of his conviviality with his old college chums, his dismissal of the East is so irritating that his friends finally decide to teach him a lesson by enticing him into a fake adventure involving a foreign count and a damsel in distress.

Another key Fairbanks film that plays with the contrast between masculinity East and West, *Wild and Woolly* begins with a visual thumbnail sketch contrasting the old West and the modern one, then shifts to the Manhattan mansion of a millionaire railroad tycoon. The tycoon's son, Jeff (Fairbanks), like Roosevelt and Seton, has been stricken with 'Western fever', which drives him to emulate the more primitive life of cowboys. But, as the confined son of the privileged urban upper class, he ends up looking more like a Boy Scout than a buckaroo. The film shows the boyish Jeff sitting cross-legged in front of his tent in what might be taken to be an outdoors setting. Only when the camera pulls back is it revealed that Jeff has transformed his bedroom into the indoor equivalent of a Boy Scout camp where he builds fires and hangs out in a tepee. Jeff's homelife in Manhattan bears an uncanny resemblance to J. Adams Puffer's descriptions of how the instinct-driven boy with the 'migratory impulse' compensates when in civilised confinement:

> The son of a good home is usually made too comfortable, and unconsciously he feels the need of some more invigorating substitute for warm room and soft bed. When, therefore, nothing better offers itself, it often does a boy good to sleep out in his own back-yard, with a dismantled revolver in his belt, and a lasso hung beside him on the clothes pole. He will probably not get much sleep, and he may catch cold; but the experience will be a powerful stimulus to his imagination, and at the same time will help, at small risk, to gratify a wholesome instinct.[39]

In spite of his confinement, Jeff tries to hone his wilderness skills, including bronco riding, which he practises on saw-horse-mounted saddles as well as on the ageing butler. To his chagrin, Jeff knows the cowboy life only through representations: photographs, sculpture, and, of course, Remington's paintings. He stares at what appears to be Remington's *His First Lesson* (1903) and imagines himself as the painting's fearless (though novice) bronco-buster. Like an overly imaginative film spectator, he identifies so strongly that he is able to literally insert himself into the painting, which becomes animated as if it were a movie. Jeff's fantasy emulation of cowboys is also played out in his wild rides on horseback through Central Park. These cause him to be dismissed as a 'nut' by city dwellers. Even his feminine ideal is derived from Western movies. He exits a movie theatre to admire the display of the Western serial's horse-back riding heroine: 'That's the kind of mate I'm going to have!' he enthuses.

Jeff's frustrated father entertains the hope that his son, 'the Comanche Indian', will be cured of his primitive behaviour by an encounter with the real West. He sends him on a business assignment to Bitter Creek, Arizona, to attend to the matter of extending a rail line to a promising mine. The townspeople, forewarned of Jeff's fanatical love for the West of the 1880s, remake themselves and their town into the equivalent of a Western movie set to give the unsuspecting young man what he wants. However, currying the little capitalist's favour proves dangerous play. Like a boy of pure savage instincts, Jeff is ready to shoot at almost anyone. The town fathers covertly confiscate his live ammo and send him off on long walks with Nell (Eileen Percy), the unsophisticated prairie flower who is really the city accountant's rather sophisticated daughter. But, of course, their plans go awry, a real crisis is instigated by a crooked Indian agent and the situation demands Jeff's carefully cultivated frontier skills.

Wild and Woolly and *Manhattan Madness* ultimately endorse the ideal of masculinity which the films also kid, as indeed did Doug himself in the extratextual construction of his 'star personality'.[40] Contemporary reviewers noticed this paradox. The *New York Times* remarked of *Wild and Woolly*: 'the depiction of a young man still carried away with dime novel ideas must be overlooked. . . . [T]hen it is redeemed by the farce developing into the real thing . . . the young easterner becomes a genuine hero.'[41] As the *Variety* reviewer noted of *Wild and Woolly*:

> You've got to laugh when the hero rides into the midst of a bunch of drunken Indians, swings the girl on the back of his horse and makes a getaway without being shot. . . . It is all so utterly absurd that you must laugh in spite of yourself. And then, having done so. . . . [you] come to the realisation that you 'fell for it'.[42]

The excesses of Fairbanks's heroes spoke to what Jackson Lears characterises as the era's antimodernist yearning for intensified experience and masculine regeneration.[43] In the wake of threatening trends in immigration, America's destiny – linked to its wilderness – was increasingly regarded as distinct from an Old World equated with effeminacy, degeneracy, and overcivilisation.[44] While, in *The Lamb*, Gerald is a weakling who is toughened up through his isolating wilderness experience, Jeff in *Wild and Woolly* already has the spirit of the strenuous life, but has to enter the West to have it properly channelled. In their treks west, Fairbanks's heroes, whether mollycoddle or frustrated buckaroo, do not go in search of the roots of their European cultural heritage. They go west to search, consciously or not, for the regenerative roots of masculine Americanness conceived in primitive terms. The value of such a search was contrasted to the Grand Tour of the idle rich that would inevitably end in Europeanisation and, therefore, feminisation. Washington Irving noted in 1835: 'We send our youth abroad to grow luxurious and effeminate in Europe. ... [I]t appears to me that a previous tour of the prairies would be more likely to produce that ... simplicity and self-dependence most in union with our political institutions.'[45]

The contrast between these two destinations and their influence on American masculinity is demonstrated most forcefully in Fairbanks's *The Mollycoddle* (1920). Reiterating the era's conflation of civilisation and femininity, *The Mollycoddle* defines its unlikely hero as 'a man surrounded by supercivilisation'. The over-civilising mother bemoaned in character-building discourse is replaced by an over-civilising Europe. The result is 'the mollycoddle', Richard Marshall V (Fairbanks), who has lost touch with the pioneer instincts of his ancestors, those American heroes of the past who were 'leather-necked shaggutted buckaroos(s) ... such as Remington knew'. 'What forefathers!' the intertitles proclaim as the film shows his grandfather fighting off Indians. This scene restages Remington's classic Western painting, *Fight for the Water Hole* (1901) and, in doing so, invokes the mythic, character-building West valorised by Roosevelt and painted by Remington.[46]

Brought to England at the age of four, Marshall has been made into a morning-coated, monocled 'mollycoddle' by his European upbringing. He is so effete and, therefore, un-American that he is mistaken for an Englishman by vacationing Americans in Monte Carlo. These vigorously youthful tourists are depicted as middle-class, melting-pot Americans (Patrick O'Flannigan, Ole Olsen, and Samuel Levinski). They are shocked by the discovery of Marshall's true nationality: 'That fellow is contrary to the Constitution of the United States. Something ought to be done about it!' The trio serve as his boys' gang, helping him to regain a robust masculinity and leading him back to 'the fold' of America. Virginia Warren (Ruth Renick), a young woman touring with a chaperone, is sympathetic: 'I like him. I think he had the makings of a man,' she says to her companion. However, Mrs Warren (Adele Farrington), remains unconvinced, throwing up her hands in disgust and flapping her wrists back down in imitation of him as she sputters: 'Bah! That mollycoddle!'

The All-American gang's plans for their new friend are sidetracked when Richard is shanghaied by German spies. His friends wait to rescue him because, as they remark, 'Work won't hurt him – it will help make a man of him.' Richard emerges from the heat, the roll and the filth of the stokehole 'a different man', outfitted in the archetypal Fairbanksian (and Rooseveltian) tweeds. These have been provided by pooling the gang's extra clothing: 'Suit by O'Flannigan – Cap by Olsen – Shoes by Levinski.'

But the ship is still populated by German smugglers/spies, and Richard's amateur counter-spying lands him in chains and then overboard. He is rescued again and is off to Arizona, the destination of both smugglers and vacationers. It is also his birthplace, the site where generations of ancestral Richard Marshalls were 'found in the vanguard of civilisation – God-fearing, hell-bustin', fighting adventurers and two-fisted pioneers'. On the rim of the Painted Desert, Richard V emerges from the Holbrook Mercantile Co. in cowboy clothes, with his great-grandfather's medal for bravery pinned to his chest. An intertitle declares: 'A western breeze, born on the snow-capped tips of the Apache range ... swept straight to the heart of young Marshall – and the blood of his forefathers seemed to respond.'

The film promotes the wilderness cult as a regenerative release of manliness linked to the genetic, race-specific compendium of qualities Roosevelt and Remington associated with Anglo-Saxon/American adventure and the fight against 'race suicide'.[47] In Richard's regeneration of instinct through environment, he runs around disguised as a Hopi, rescues his friends from capture, leaps through roofs, and rolls down mountains. As Marshall slides down from a ridge on his belly in the process of rescuing his friends, an intertitle echoes character-building discourse: 'Primitive cunning, born of instinct, now guides his every move.' In the end, Marshall rescues Virginia (who, it turns out, is really a US government agent!), foils the spies, and even has time to check out the aches and pains he has acquired with his new physical ferocity. The film ends with Richard and Virginia sitting on a ledge in front of a beautiful sunset. With manly, cowboy ease, he shows her how to roll a cigarette with one hand, but his masculine prowess is counterpointed by the humorous visual effect of the innumerable bandages dotting his neck and face.

Fairbanks's films offered appealing fantasy versions of the transformative power of the West as the last romantic place in America. As one of many figurative 'sons of Roosevelt', Fairbanks acknowledged the farcical excesses in the stereotype of the westernised Easterner all too familiar by 1920. Nevertheless, the textual inscription of Fairbanks's vigorous childishness and athletic antics was perfectly convergent with the valorisation of a regenerating 'wilderness cult'. The contrived Rooseveltian-brand solution to making a man sought to restore the essential, instinctual nature of the American male through contact with the 'wilderness' even as it was also compatible with a twentieth-century world-view of a Utopian merger of technology and the pastoral.[48] Although officially closed, the supposedly uncivilised, largely uninhabited frontier is made romantically congruent with technology, especially through the modern iconology of twentieth-century tourism. As the film audience enjoys the films' location shooting (of the Grand Canyon, Canyon de Chelly, the Painted Desert and the Hopi mesas), Fairbanks performs like a 100-horse-power machine. He runs, rolls, batters through walls or leaps over ledges. He takes off in fast cars, railway locomotives or aeroplanes. This is in keeping with character-builders' rhetoric, in blending apparently divergent iconographies in an attempt to forge a new (and widely accepted) masculinity, dynamically modern and transformative and yet naturally instinctive and nostalgically rooted in the small-town, agrarian values of America's past.

Fairbanks served as an appealing mediator between America's nineteenth-century past and its twentieth-century future, between the body and the machine, wilderness and urbanisation, intensified social control and a nostalgic desire for a mythically free, childlike past. In his films, without literally becoming a child, Douglas Fairbanks seemed to achieve a change that many American men in routine-driven, sedentary, bureaucratised jobs yearned for. The onerous psychic and physical demands of masculinity could be held in abeyance by a hero who embodied qualities of intensity, vitality, and instinctual liberation which seemed, to many, to be increasingly difficult to acquire and retain among the complacency, compromise, and consumerist comfort of modern bourgeois life.[49]

The nostalgia for the American past as well as the anxiety attached to its future figure significantly in the end of *Wild and Woolly*, which offers Jeff a fantasy escape from the East, from his father and from modern capitalism. The intertitles pose a dilemma: 'For Nell likes the East. Jeff likes the West. So where are the twain to meet?' The solution is a fabulous mansion on the range. Bewigged footmen open its doors so Jeff and Nell can greet the cowboys gathered to celebrate the couple's marriage with six-shooters and wild whoops. In this Utopic reconciliation of East and West, primitive and sophisticated, male and female, Jeff, like so many other Fairbanks protagonists, is saved from restricting urban environs and middle-class adult norms. It is as if the film does not trust that the hero's boyish instincts can be accommodated by modern American industrial society.

East and West, Modern Society and the Manly Past – 'So where are the twain to meet?' Perhaps the secret, fearsome answer ('Nowhere'), so dreaded by character-builders, could only be avoided for a little while longer. In 1919, Teddy Roosevelt died. Soon, complex personal and professional reasons motivated Fairbanks's shift to swashbucklers and fantasy films. While Fairbanks's films of the 1920s still constituted a proving ground for normative masculinity, they would not as literally reflect American social life and its mythically charged solution to imperilled masculinity. No longer would the screen offer 'Douggie' as the contemporary ideal of manhood gracefully balancing moral gentility and primitive instincts, wilderness skills and genteel urbanity against the landscape of the American West. *The Mollycoddle* would mark the final fade-out over the Fairbanksian Western sky. Recapturing the romance of America's lost boyhood would require more extreme measures than Fairbanks could provide in the reconciliation of modernity with 'Western fever'.

Notes

1 George Creel, 'A "Close-Up" of Douglas Fairbanks', *Everybody's Magazine* 25, no. 6 (December 1916), pp. 730, 738.

2 'The Shadow Stage', *Photoplay* 11 (March 1917), p. 116.

3 In a reappraisal of Fairbanks in The *New York Times* in 1939 after the actor's unexpected death from a heart attack, Frank Nugent recalled: 'Doug Fairbanks was make-believe at its best, a game we youngsters never tired of playing, a game ... our fathers secretly shared. He was complete fantasy ... unabashed and joyous.' Quoted in Gary Carey, *Doug and Mary* (New York: Dutton, 1977), p. 224.

4 Frederick James Smith, 'Roping Doug Fairbanks into an Interview', *Motion Picture Classic* (September 1917), p. 46.

5 On its impression on audiences, see 'Triangle's Auspicious Opening', *Moving Picture World* 26 (9 October 1915), p. 233. In an unusual move, the *New York Times* reported on the film's special screening as a news event. 'Triangle Debut', *New York Times* 24 September 1915, 2: 2.

6 Three culturally influential Easterners obsessed with the West, Theodore Roosevelt, Frederic Remington and Owen Wister, all, in varying degrees, subscribed to the idea of the cowboy as the last pure representative of Anglo-Saxon virility and primitive individualism. Remington's diatribe against strikers is infamous: 'I've got some Winchesters

and when the massacreing begins which you speak of, I can get my share of 'em and what's more I will. Jews – Injuns – Chinamen – Italians – Huns – the rubbish of the earth I hate': Remington, letter to Poultney Bigelow (May 1893) in Allen Splete and Marilyn Splete (eds), *Frederic Remington, Selected Letters* (New York: Abbeville, 1988), p. 171. Remington's friend, playwright August Thomas, was also into racial consciousness. See Augustus Thomas, *The Witching Hour* (New York: Grosset and Dunlap, 1980), p. 100. Thomas's play *Arizona* was turned into a Fairbanks screen vehicle in 1917. I have not been able to locate a print of it. There is high irony in Fairbanks's personification of heroes who represent the revitalisation of this Anglo-Saxon spirit, since Fairbanks was half Jewish. His biological father (who deserted the family) was a lawyer, Hezekiah Charles Ulman. See Booton Herndon, *Mary Pickford and Douglas Fairbanks* (New York: Norton, 1977), pp. 12–23.

7 On the overcivilised man who has 'lost the great fighting, masterful virtues', see Theodore Roosevelt, *The Strenuous Life* (New York: The Century Co., 1901), pp. 1–7.

8 This phrase was often used. See, for example, the caption for an illustration of Fairbanks's imitator William Russell, *Motion Picture Classic* (November 1917): n.p. *The Half-Breed*, adapted from a Bret Harte short story, is an anomaly in Fairbanks's work because of its seriousness and the quality of Fairbanks's extremely restrained performance. I do not discuss it since it does not focus on masculine transformation.

9 Marjorie Gleyre Lachmund, 'Douglas Fairbanks Discourses on Work and Play', *Motion Picture Classic* (December 1917): p. 54.

10 Adele Rogers St Johns, 'The Married Life of Doug and Mary', *Photoplay* 31 (February 1927): p. 35.

11 For a personal account of such antics see Robert Parrish, *Growing Up in Hollywood* (Boston: Little, Brown, 1976), pp. 3–8. See also Herbert Blumer, *Movies and Conduct* (New York: Arno Press, 1978 [*c.* 1933]), pp. 243, 254. Blumer relates an account by an adolescent girl who recalled identifying strongly with the star's screen adventures even though, as one says, 'you know, ethics (and now I am sarcastic) state that little ladies must not handle dangerous weapons, must not even dream of acting so tomboyish' (p. 254).

12 Advertisement for *The Man from Painted Post*, *Exhibitor's Trade Review* 2, no. 18 (6 October 1917): p. 1376.

13 'Douglas Fairbanks Plays in Another Wild West Film', *New York Times* (1 October 1917), 14:2, reprinted in the *New York Times Film Reviews* (*New York Times*, 1969): p. 30.

14 'The Good Bad Man,' *Exhibitors Herald* 2, no. 43 (15 March 1916): p. 12.

15 Ernest Thompson Seton, letter to Robert Baden-Powell, 24 June 1910, in collection of Mrs Dee Seton Barber, quoted by Michael Rosenthal, *The Character Factory: Baden-Powell and the Origins of the Boy Scout Movement* (New York: Pantheon Books, 1986), p. 80.

16 Jeffrey P. Hantover, 'Sex role, sexuality, and social status: The early years of the Boy Scouts of America', unpublished doctoral dissertation (University of Chicago, 1976), p. 288.

17 The most balanced and broadly defined discussion of the role of all these men in boy reform is David I. Macleod's excellent study, *Building Character in the American Boy* (Madison: University of Wisconsin Press, 1983).

18 Seton, quoted from 'History of the Boy Scouts', cited in Rosenthal, *The Character Factory*, p. 65.

19 City life, in particular, was creating citizens who were 'strained and broken by the grind of the over-busy world'. Ernest Thompson Seton, *Boy Scouts of America: A Handbook of Woodcraft, Scouting, and Lifecraft* (New York: BSA, 1944): pp. xi, xii, 1, 2.

20 Seton, 'The Boy Scouts in America', p. 630. Seton blamed urban growth, the industrialisation of work and spectator sports for the weakness in and perversion of masculinity.

21 J. Adams Puffer, *The Boy and His Gang* (Boston: Houghton Mifflin, 1912), p. 84.

22 Quote from Puffer, *The Boy and His Gang*, p. 177. For a typical assessment of the middle-class situation in which the mother manages the boy, 'blindly, and often with poor success', see Carl Werner, *Bringing up the Boy: A Message to Fathers and Mothers*

from a Boy of Yesterday concerning the Man of Tomorrow (New York: Dodd, Mead & Co., 1913 [1911]), pp. 8–9.

23 See Carl Werner, *Bringing up the Boy*, pp. 7–8.

24 Norman Richardson and Ormond Loomis offer a partial rebuttal to the recapitulation theory, and in the process suggest the dominance of Hall's theories over boy-reform thought. See *The Boy Scout Movement as Applied by the Church* (New York: Scribner's, 1915), pp. 66–75.

25 Fiske, quoted in James Frankin Page, *Socializing for the New Order* (Rock Island, Ill.: Augustana College, 1919), pp. 30–1. Ernest Thompson Seton refers to the 'well-known stages of race development' in the introduction to John L. Alexander's *Boy Training* (New York: Association Press, 1911, 1912), p. 2.

26 As Russell suggests in *Stories of Boy Life*, 'Healthy, manly boys become manly men.' Thomas H. Russell, *Stories of Boy Life: A Book of Stories about Boys for Boys* (n.p.: Fireside Edition, 1914), p. 56. For another statement on how the 'manly boy' should act, see also Theodore Roosevelt, 'What We Can Expect of the American Boy', *St. Nicholas* 27 (May 1900): pp. 570–4.

27 Roderick Nash, *Wilderness and the American Mind* (New Haven: Yale University Press, rev. edn [1975] 1967), pp. 46–54.

28 Nash, *Wilderness and the American Mind*, p. 202.

29 [Review] '*The Good Bad Man*', *Motion Picture World* 28 (22 April 1916): p. 643.

30 Arthur Hornblow, Jr, 'Douglas Fairbanks, Dramatic Dynamo', *Motion Picture Classic* (March 1917): p. 48.

31 On Roosevelt's virtuous, child-like primitivism, see William Allen White, 'Roosevelt: A Force for Righteousness', *McClure's* 28, no. 4 (February 1907): p. 389. An advertisement for Fairbanks's *The Man from Painted Post* calls the star: 'just a big-hearted citizen who will tickle your sense of humor and make you glad you're alive'. *Exhibitor's Trade Review* 2 (22 September 1917): p. 1201.

32 As Nelson W. Aldrich, Jr, has noted,, 'the men of Old Money were seen as passive and pretty, with soft, slender bodies, pettish temperaments, frivolous tastes, and squeamish sensibilities'. Aldrich, *Old Money: The Mythology of America's Upper Class* (New York: Vintage Books, 1988), p. 113.

33 Michael Monahan, 'The American Peril', *The Forum* 52 (June 1914): p. 878. Roosevelt noted that something had to be done 'to stave off effeminacy that is one of the dangers of nations that grow old and soft and unwilling to endure hardships'. Theodore Roosevelt, quoted in Michael T. Isenberg, *John L. Sullivan and His America* (Urbana: University of Illinois Press, 1988), p. 63.

34 Thornton W. Burgess, 'Making Men of Them', *Good Housekeeping* (9 September 1914), p. 5.

35 Quoted in Rosenthal, *The Character Factory*, p. 164. That American boys and men had to 'Be Prepared' at all times to do the right thing was embraced by boy culture reformers as ideological and political necessity within a world marked by deteriorating behaviour in the leadership classes as well as newly emergent eugenic dangers: the rise of non-Anglo-Saxon, 'inferior' peoples.

36 See G. Edward White, *The Eastern Establishment and the Western Experience* (New Haven: Yale University Press, 1968), p. 108.

37 See White, *The Eastern Establishment and the Western Experience*, p. 109. On Remington's reaction to immigration and for Roosevelt's Anglo-Saxon élitism, see White, pp. 174–5, 190, 197.

38 George S. Evans, 'The Wilderness', *Overland Monthly* 43 (1904): p. 33.

39 Puffer, *The Boy and His Gang*, p. 117.

40 Fairbanks produced many articles in general interest magazines and almost a dozen (ghost-written) books that preached character-building maxims including *Live and Let Live* (1917), *Taking Stock of Ourselves* (1918), *Making Life Worth While* (1918), and *Youth Points the Way* (1924). It should also be mentioned that Fairbanks's popularity caused him to be imitated by other actors, some of whom, like William Russell, starred in unabashed rip-offs of Fairbanks vehicles: *Snap Judgment* (1917) and *Leave it to Me*

(1920). Even established stars such as J. Warren Kerrigan and William Hart were promoted to exhibitors with Fairbanks-like monikers.

41 [Review] *New York Times,* 22 July 1917, reprinted in the *New York Times Film Reviews,* n.p.

42 Walter Bytell, [Review of *Wild and Woolly*] *Variety* (22 June 1917), reprinted in *Variety Film Reviews 1907–1980,* Vol. 1 (New York: Garland, 1983): n.p.

43 T. J. Jackson Lears, *No Place of Grace: Antimodernism and the Transformation of American Culture 1880–1920* (New York: Pantheon Books, 1981), p. 117.

44 On the degeneracy of American cities because of 'hordes of encroaching alien vermin' and the Anglo-Saxon's unique claim to the West's demand for a 'spirit of adventure, courage, and self-sufficiency' see Owen Wister, 'The Evolution of the Cow-Puncher', in Ben Merchant Vorpahl, *My Dear Wister: The Frederic Remington–Owen Wister Letters* (Palo Alto: American West Publishing, 1972), p. 80.

45 Washington Irving, *Tales of a Traveller: A Tour on the Prairies* (New York: Century Co., 1909), p. 43.

46 For a discussion of this painting within the context of a well-researched account of the race views of the artist, see Alexander Nemerov, *Frederic Remington & Turn-of-the-Century America* (New Haven: Yale University Press, 1995), especially pp. 12–15, 73–5.

47 See Nemerov, *Frederic Remington,* and also White, *The Eastern Establishment.*

48 See Cecelia Tichi, *Shifting Gears: Technology, Literature, Culture in Modernist America* (Chapel Hill: University of North Carolina Press, 1987), p. 34.

49 Jackson Lears, *No Place of Grace,* pp. 144–5. See also Nemerov, *Frederic Remington,* pp. 8–43, 103–14.

5 'Our Country'/Whose Country? The 'Americanisation' Project of Early Westerns
Richard Abel

In June 1908, the *New York Dramatic Mirror* had this to say about Pathé's *Justice of a Redskin*, together with Gaumont's *The Red Man's Revenge*:

> As both of these films are identical in story and almost identical in treatment ... they will be treated together. Evidently one is borrowed from the other, but which film maker is guilty of the piracy it is impossible for THE MIRROR to determine, although it may be pertinent to state that the Gaumont film was advertised in America first.[1]

One week later, the *Mirror* returned to this 'Alleged Pirating':

> THE MIRROR is now informed, however, that a similar film was produced nearly two years ago by the American Vitagraph company of New York under the title, 'The Indian's Revenge', so that if Pathé pirated from Gaumont, Gaumont had previously pirated from the Vitagraph.[2]

Manufacturers, of course, had been selling duped, pirated, and remade film titles on the American market for years, and the practice had not ended with the formation of the Film Service Association (FSA) six months earlier. So why would the *Mirror* make such a big deal about this one instance of piracy? The question may seem trivial, but this issue of the *Mirror* claimed to be printing, not simply 'press notices or advertisements', but 'reviews of films'– that is, 'unprejudiced criticisms of the pictures and the story they tell'. At least two things are significant about this allegedly 'unprejudiced criticism' of 'identical' films. First of all, the *Mirror* was marking the boundary not between 'licensed' and 'unlicensed' manufacturers, as one might expect (given its tacit support of the 'independents' led by Biograph and George Kleine), but between American and foreign (and unmistakably French) film products – a boundary the trade paper would draw even more sharply the following November.[3] Second, that boundary was being drawn according to which titles were more 'original' or 'authentic' among the 'Western pictures' for which, *Moving Picture World* claimed, 'everybody [was] clamoring' by the winter of 1908–9.[4]

The *Mirror*'s review of these two French films points to a question that was beginning to preoccupy the trade press of the new industry: what was distinctive, and of special value, about American films compared with foreign films? The question, of course, arose out of a specific historical conjuncture of conditions which I shall only allude to here. Within the cinema industry itself, for instance, there was the mass audience of 'moviegoers' attracted to the nickelodeons and new larger cinemas, where 'foreign film product' (largely French Pathé titles) too often dominated the programmes.[5] More generally, there was the rising tide of immigrants into the United States, whose numbers and origins – 'the least desirable part' of Europe, in the words of *The World's Work* – threatened to jeopardise (for some) the concept of a uniquely 'American character' or national identity.[6] These conditions fostered various practices of excluding 'foreign film product' on the American cinema market, whether institutional (through the FSA, Motion Picture Patents Company (MPPC), and National Board of Censorship) or discursive (through the trade press and national magazines), but simultaneously they provoked efforts to create, promote, and exploit a distinctively American film product.[7] Here, I would argue, the production and circulation of Westerns played such a crucial role that, by 1909, the genre would become what the *World* described as the quintessential 'American subject'.[8] In this essay, I want to sketch out several explanations for the early Western's rise to popularity, drawing on descriptions and commentaries in the trade press as well as viewings of the few extant film prints. More important, I want to suggest how early Westerns functioned within a rejuvenated discourse of Americanisation at the turn of the last century, an overtly racist discourse which sought to privilege the 'Anglo-Saxon' (and the masculine) as dominant in any conception of American national identity.

'National Wealth' in Story and Spectacle

First of all, early Westerns played a significant role in securing the new industry's transition from a 'cinema of attractions' to a cinema dominated by fiction films.[9] They offered, I would argue, an exemplary model of negotiation between what Tom Gunning has called 'the desire to tell a story' and 'the desire to display', between narrative engagement and spectacle attraction.[10] That is, Westerns told a certain kind of story within the context of displaying particular, picturesque American landscapes. As the 1991 Smithsonian exhibition, 'The West as America', made clear, those landscapes had coalesced into an iconographic tradition already quite widespread in American popular culture by the turn of the last century.[11] Several generations of painters and photographers had produced a palimpsest of images in which the Great Plains from Texas to the Dakotas and Montana, the mountain ranges of Colorado and California, and the desert regions of the Southwest had turned, in Alan Trachtenberg's apt phrase, into a myth of 'unimaginable natural wealth'.[12] These images were broadly disseminated throughout the East and Midwest in magic lantern slide lectures, stereographs and chromolithographs. Such works as Albert Bierstadt's *Sunset: California Scenery*, Fanny Palmer's *The Rocky Mountains – Emigrants Crossing the Plains* or *Across the Continent*, and Andrew Putnam Hill's *George Hoag's Record Wheat Harvest*, for instance, all circulated as inexpensive 'chromo' reproductions for decorating the walls of urban lower- and middle-class homes.[13] Most of this iconography, Martha Sandweiss reminds us, served the interests of railroad and mining companies, land speculators, and local business enterprises (see the chromo, *California Powder Works*) as a way to attract cheap labour and immigrant settlers to the Western states.[14] But it also served the interests of another kind of exploitation and consumption, that of tourism: by means of the railroads, William Cullen Bryant wrote, 'we now have easy access to scenery of a most remarkable character ... [to] Nature in her grandest forms'.[15]

The Selig company of Chicago, as Robert Anderson has pointed out, was probably the first to systematically exploit the attraction of these landscapes and their 'natural wealth' with its location shooting in Colorado.[16] In advertising *Western Justice*, in June 1907, the company crowed that Edison, Vitagraph, and Kalem could never match the 'magnificent scenic effects' of the film's Western mountains and plains (already made familiar by earlier *actualités*) because they were confined to 'some backyard in the East'.[17] By early 1908, Selig could be even more explicit. The story of *The Squawman's Daughter*, for instance, 'was re-enacted on the same ground' where it was said to have occurred, in a prairie landscape 'that reache[d] as far as the eye [could] see'.[18] That summer, outside Denver, the company used local cowboys to shoot several films that would 'boost the State and create ... [a] desire to visit the places where the pictures were made'.[19] In its reviews of Selig films, the *Mirror* took up the spirit of these claims. Due to the 'magnificently picturesque mountain[s]' in *An Indian's Gratitude*, the *Mirror* wrote, 'no film, foreign or American, that has been produced in a long time can approach [it] in scenic splendor'.[20] The spectacle attraction produced by such location shooting is still visible in a surviving print of *The Cattle Rustlers*, which includes an *actualité* sequence of rounding up and branding cattle in a mountain valley, repeated scenes of the rustlers' camp beside a swiftly flowing stream, and a climactic shoot-out at a log cabin, isolated on a treeless hilltop and backed by high, distant mountains.[21] Both the *Mirror* and the *World* took special note of the unusual popularity of Selig Westerns in New York City the following winter and spring: *On the Warpath* (probably inspired by a well-known 1872 chromo), *The Bad Lands*, and *The Indian Trailer*, for instance, all were loudly applauded at the Manhattan and Union Square cinemas.[22] And in Chicago, as *Show World* suggested, the 'authenticity' of the Selig Westerns functioned much the same as the railroad-sponsored travelogues boosting the Southwestern states as a prime site for new settlements.[23]

In their display of distinctive American landscapes, then, some early Westerns appropriated the iconographic tradition of the chromo and the travelogue, offering short, inexpensive tours of the Far West, which were especially appealing for urban audiences in the East and Midwest. Others, however, offered models of narrative construction, formulas for standardising the production of one-reel fiction films. Here, it was Biograph and Vitagraph titles (most of them made in the East) that the *Mirror* frequently lauded for their 'clear, well-told' stories, perhaps in imitation of the 'vivid and clear-cut prose' that *Munsey's* saw as so characteristic of American magazine fiction.[24] In August, for instance, Biograph's *The Redman and the Child* was rated 'best film of the week' (and was 'held over two days by special request' at the Manhattan) chiefly because 'the story is original and consistent, and the scenes follow each other consecutively and naturally. Interest is aroused from the start, and is held with increasing power to the very end.'[25] That autumn, other Biograph Westerns such as *The Red Girl* and *The Call of the Wild* served to point up 'the particular elements that go to make up a successful moving picture story'.[26]

Within several months, the *Mirror* also was praising Selig's *On the Warpath* for a plot which was easy to follow and ended in a 'big logical climax' as well as Essanay's *The Road Agents* for a 'straight story' uncomplicated by side issues or 'maudlin sentiment'.[27] The Western, in other words, was coming to exemplify, at least for the *Mirror*, the kind of 'simple story' that 'all good film stories should be'.[28] That French Pathé films were still often cited by the *Mirror* as models of clear, coherent storytelling, comprehensible to any kind of audience, suggests just how significant these early Westerns were as a 'repeatable' American subject distinctively different from the 'foreign film product'.[29]

As the genre developed and grew ever more popular during 1909, however, an important difference began to emerge in the trade press discourse between one 'school' of films that valued action above all else and another that valued acting and logical plotting. In October, the *World* marked this as a difference between Selig and Biograph, between one 'class' of fiction aimed at the 'masses' and another aimed at a 'discriminating' audience.[30] The 'school of action' undoubtedly formed the basis for the Western's 'immense popularity with the people', but Selig was not its undisputed leader. As early as May, for instance, the *World* described *Why the Mail Was Late*, a 'Western melodrama from Lubin', as having 'all the snap and go for which these pictures have become known'.[31] Once used to distinguish American from foreign films, the slang phrase now marked the Westerns most filled with thrilling action, those involved in a rejuvenation of the dime novel tradition. It was precisely this kind of Western that the new independents, Bison and Centaur, exploited in order to secure a niche in the American market.[32] In September, the *World* wrote that Bison's *The Paymaster* had 'all the dash and go of the usual melodrama and [held] the attention of the audience from the opening until the close'.[33] In November, it headlined Essanay's formation of a new production unit, headed by G. M. Anderson, to specialise in Westerns 'in which the wild and woolly plays the leading part'.[34] By the year's end, the *World* was comparing Bison's *The Ranchman's Wife* to Selig's 'wild and woolly' *On the Border* for thrills and applause.[35] Now, too, Bison films like *Romany Bob's Revenge* and *Government Relations* could be consistently categorised, without approbation, as 'dime novel subjects'.[36] The resurgent dime novel Western thrived in this moving picture 'school of action', and was neatly epitomised in Essanay's *The Heart of a Cowboy*, which beat, wrote the *World*, with 'much of the true Western snap and go'.[37]

One thing remained constant, however, in this process of product differentiation which cut across 'licensed' and 'unlicensed' manufacturers: the 'foreignisation' of Pathé. In May 1909, the *World* remarked on how New York audiences at a Keith Bijou Dream much preferred the 'threadbare story' of Essanay's *The Indian Trailer* to Pathé's 'more finished' *film d'art*, *Père Milon*.[38] In July, it even reprinted a letter from an exhibitor excoriating the company for factual errors in *A Western Hero*, as if it were an act of piracy for Pathé to even try mining the genre. 'The denizens of the far West are ... jealous of their customs and characteristics,' warned the *World*, 'and telling a picture story at long range is treading on dangerous ground.'[39] No matter how 'beautifully colored' or 'romantic and artistic' its scenes, the *Mirror* chimed in, they were not authentic – 'they were not American'.[40] That Pathé released *A Western Hero* in stencil colour reveals its 'foreignness' in another way. Here, the trade press was unanimous: stencil colour was perfectly appropriate for certain *films d'art* and 'exotic' scenics, but not for American subjects, especially Westerns.[41] For the latter, the 'realist' aesthetic promoted by the *Mirror* and the *World* dictated a concern for the 'orthochromatic', the accuracy of tonal values in 'the black and white picture', which by 1909–10, so went the claim, the public preferred, from whatever 'school' it came.[42] The *World* singled out Biograph in particular as a model for other manufacturers to imitate, for its films' 'fine, rich deposit in the shadows and clear, delicate lights'.[43] The chiaroscuro of black and white could be enhanced by tinting and/or toning effects, but, as Frank Woods argued, those had to serve the purpose of 'approximating reality and at the same time making the story clear'.[44] If *colour* were to be invoked in the American cinema, it would be yoked to an aesthetic of 'impressive realism' (to cite a Biograph ad), one imbued with a distinctive, historically specific, American ideology.[45]

The Western as White Supremacist Entertainment

The formulaic stories the Westerns told, however, were even more significant for their inscription within the prevailing discourse of 'Americanisation'. The history of that discourse, especially its construction of national identity, has been charted by Trachtenberg and others through a variety of written texts and visual images in the late 19th century.[46] Josiah Strong's widely reprinted tract, *Our Country: Its Possible Future and Its Present Crisis* (1885), for instance, makes 'race' its foundational concept: 'the world [is entering] upon a new stage of its history – the final competition of races, for which the Anglo-Saxon is being schooled . . . the mighty centrifugal tendency, inherent in this stock, and strengthened in the United States, will assert itself'.[47] So does John Fiske's infamous 'Manifest Destiny' (1885), which envisioned that 'every land on the earth's surface . . . shall become English in its language, in its political habits and traditions, and to a predominant extent in the blood of its people'.[48] The same goes for Theodore Roosevelt's popular *The Winning of the West* (1889), which celebrated the appearance of the 'American' (a new breed of Anglo-Saxon) as a culminating moment in 'race-history'.[49] This was nothing less than 'ancestor worship' with a double function, argues Michael Kammen: that is, 'to enhance the prestige of the living more than to honor the dead' and 'to marginalize or exclude the country's "less desirable" inhabitants'.[50]

This racist conception of an 'American character' coincided with, and was partly determined by, white middle-class fears of all the 'undesirable' immigrants from eastern and southern Europe, who were settling in already densely populated cities like New York, Philadelphia and Chicago.[51] Yet, in a tradition that went back at least to Thomas Jefferson, it was projected most forcefully upon the mythic (and now closed) frontier of 'The West'.[52] In that projection process, perhaps best articulated by Frederick Jackson Turner (in his 1893 Chicago Exposition lecture), the West served to produce and entitle specifically 'masculine' traits in this new breed of the 'Anglo-Saxon'.[53] Or as Roosevelt put it in 'The Strenuous Life' (1897), the frontier became an imaginary space for testing and renewing the 'virility' of the race and its 'fighting spirit'.[54] Whereas the civilising figure of a white woman once had represented 'American Progress' (1873) in popular chromos, according to Ronald Takaki, now Western heroes like General George Custer and even Buffalo Bill Cody were coming to personify 'the masculine advance guard of civilization'.[55] In 1896, for instance, Anheuser-Busch began shipping free chromos of Cassily Adams's *Custer's Last Fight* to promote Budweiser beer, and the huge painting ended up on the walls of most American bars and saloons.[56] In short, as Robert Rydell argues, the discourse of Americanisation defused and deflected all kinds of perceived threats (chief among them class conflict) by asserting white male supremacy as the basis for constructing a new national identity.[57]

For early Westerns, more specifically, the parameters of this discourse are starkly, and usefully, exposed in Owen Wister's 1895 *Harper's Monthly* essay, 'The Evolution of the Cow-Puncher'.[58] Only the 'Anglo-Saxon' (male) supposedly had 'the spirit of adventure, courage, and self-sufficiency' needed for survival 'in the clean cattle country' of the American West. Unlike those *others*, those 'hordes of encroaching alien vermin that [were turning] our cities to Babels and our citizenship to a hybrid farce', wrote Wister, the *cow-puncher* was a 'direct lineal offspring' of the knights of Camelot: 'in personal daring and in skill as to the horse, the knight and the cowboy are nothing but the same Saxon of different environments.' The cowboy's 'inveterate enemies', however, were the Mexican and the Indian, who had to be vanquished in order for Wister to imagine a 'clean cattle country'. Acknowledging and even celebrating 'the Saxon contempt for the foreigner', Wister praised the cowboy for supplanting the Mexican, 'this small, deceitful alien', and simply erased the Indian as one 'whose hand was against all races but his own immediate tribe'. This openly racist, covertly masculinised, discourse framed Wister's own best-seller fiction, as in *The Virginian* (1902), but was widespread at the time.[59] It fuelled what Richard Slotkin has called the '*virilist* realism' or 'red-blooded fiction' of Wister's friends, Frank Norris and Frederic Remington.[60] Norris said he drew inspiration from the 'tremendous tales' of the Frontier, where 'there was action and fighting, and ... men held each others' lives in the crook of a forefinger'; Remington was ready to blur any and all distinctions between fiction and life: 'I've got some Winchesters and when the massacring begins, I can get my share of 'em ['the rubbish of the Earth'] and what's more I will.'[61] However mollified, this discourse penetrated nearly every level of mass-market writing, from *Saturday Evening Post* stories like 'A Round-Up in Central Park' (August 1905)[62] to the 'moralistic adventure stories about clean-cut boys' in Frank Tousey's *Wild West Weekly* (first published in 1902) or Street and Smith's *Rough Rider Weekly* (first published in 1904).[63]

Western films made up a small, but increasingly influential component of what Rydell has described as this 'universe of white supremacist entertainments'.[64] In June 1907, for instance, the ads for an early Kalem title, *The Pony Express*, heralded the express rider as one of the great figures in the history of the West, 'harassed on every side by Indians and Highwaymen', but in this particular story waylaid by 'Mexican vaqueros' or 'Greasers'.[65] The following year, similar stories cropped up in films from most MPPC manufacturers. In Edison's *Pioneers Crossing the Plains in '49*, Indians massacre a wagon train of settlers and carry off 'the [white] heroine' who has to be rescued.[66] In Kalem's *The Renegade*, a falsely accused soldier restores his honour by freeing a little white girl from hostile Indians.[67] In Lubin's *The White Chief*, an 'American' saves an 'Indian girl' from an abusive Mexican and ends up being named chief of her tribe.[68] In Selig's *Cowboy's Baby*, the white child of the title survives a wagon train attack by Sioux Indians, is adopted by the cowboy hero, Joe Dayton, and then (to top things off) has to be rescued from the clutches of a wealthy Mexican, who wanted revenge on Dayton and his new wife (whom he had once wooed).[69] In the already cited *Cattle Rustlers* (at least according to the narrative summary provided by *Views and Films Index*), the leader of the rustlers is a half-breed named Cherokee, their camp cook a Mexican, and the log cabin site of the climactic shoot-out is home to Cherokee's 'Indian sweetheart, Wahnita'.[70] By the end of the year, the *World* was prompted to write, 'theater managers [were] clamoring after' these kinds of 'Wild West subjects'.[71]

An important variant on Wister's 'knight errant' appeared in early 1909, the horse soldier of the US cavalry, a figure cloaked even more overtly in the mantle of national identity. Selig films developed the figure extensively, beginning with *In Old Arizona*, 'a story of the plains, true to life', where soldiers come to the aid of white settlers against a jealous Mexican who has induced a band of Indians to attack them.[72] Such cavalry films culminated aptly in Selig's *On the Little Big Horn*, which made Custer's martial masculine heroics unabashedly emblematic of 'the advance guard of [American] civilization'.[73] Yet throughout 1909, the 'purer' strain of Wister's formulaic offspring was far more legion. Mexicans continued to act as villains, as in Essanay's *The Road Agents* or Lubin's *Mexican Bill*.[74] Indians went on harassing white settlers, as in Vitagraph's *Children of the Plains* which complicated a massacre and rescue by separating two sisters, who only recognise one another years later by means of matching lockets.[75] As the independents gradually won a foothold in the American market, the Bison films that the *World* argued soon matched those of Selig for 'dime novel action and heroics' – assuring 'licensed' and 'unlicensed' exhibitors of one Western (and probably more) per week – often worked within this racist conception of 'American character' as well. In late October, for instance, in *Iona, the White Squaw*, a white girl raised by Indians becomes the object of a search and reward, is retrieved by a cowboy, and 'safely secured among her [white] friends'.[76] Singled out as a top film by the *World* two weeks later, *Mexican's Crime* was said to have 'all the dash and go of the usual Western drama', with cowboys, Mexicans [as the bad guys], careening horses [and] gun play'.[77] In all these films, the *World* glibly noted, violence and 'lively gun play' was neither 'out of place' nor 'create[d] unfavorable impressions'.[78] What made it 'seem proper and right'? These were American not foreign (and especially not French) subjects, and their action was predicated on American assumptions about race. One *World* reviewer even staked a claim of authenticity: in Selig's *The Indian Wife's Devotion*, he found the representation of a 'despicable ... half-breed' fitted perfectly with his personal experience of 'many such cowardly characters'.[79]

When, in late 1909, the *World* proposed 'Wild West subjects' as 'the foundation of an American moving picture drama', they were envisioned as an extension of the country's 'national literature'.[80] However ambivalent even the *World* may have been about many films' resemblance to dime novels, it recognised their educational (that is, ideological) potential: the Westerns of thrilling action aimed at the masses were usually popular with the young, and especially boys.[81] Here, Michael Kimmel provides a significant historical context: the new masculinity advocated by Roosevelt, Norris, Wister and others arose partly in response to a perceived threat of 'cultural feminisation', through 'the predominance of women in the lives of young boys', in the social institutions of family, school, and religion.[82] Among the new public spaces of mass consumption, I would argue, nickelodeons (where women comprised a large part of the audience) exacerbated that sense of threat. Westerns may well have offered boys – particularly 'white boys' of whatever class, including some immigrants – a counterpoint to this 'feminisation', something like a genre of their own to go along with the separate spheres of play, toys and clothing that were becoming part of their training for manhood.[83] Westerns also had the advantage of being 'distinctly American in characterization, scenery, and surroundings' and having, in the *World*'s strikingly revealing phrase, given this era of aggressive Americanisation 'themes "racy of the soil" '.[84] Their nostalgic backward glance served as a form of national memory, securing, in the midst of rapid social change a fixed, exclusionary sense of identity – however false – for the 'young and vigorous group of men of intellect, will and ceaseless activity' whose testing ground was the American city.[85] In short, Westerns perfectly embodied the 'good, clean, wholesome, national, patriotic, educational films' that the *World* insisted American manufacturers should be offering the American public to compete with, subjugate, and assimilate anything that was 'alien'.[86]

The Not So 'Vanishing Indian'

Not all Westerns, however, were inscribed so unproblematically within the discourse of Americanisation, and it is these others which demand to be considered more fully, and in some detail. As certain titles like *The Redman and the Child* or *The Red Girl* should already suggest, the previous pages have deliberately been constructed according to the principles of exclusion and co-optation defining the USA as 'our country'. For the term designating such films in the trade press during this early period was not 'Westerns' but 'Indian and Western subjects', a point the *World* made clear in its polemic for American subjects and 'an American school of moving picture drama'. In fact, at least half of the so-called Westerns produced between 1907 and 1910 were actually Indian stories or had an Indian (or Mexican) as the central character or hero.[87] Nearly every manufacturer became involved in their production at some point, but there were differences. Edison and Essanay were least committed to Indian subjects; Selig and Vitagraph released a number of titles at crucial moments; Kalem, Biograph and Bison came close to specialising in them. Once again, the boundary between competing MPPC and independent factions seemed less important than one distinguishing an American 'school' of acting and logical plotting from an American 'school' of action. In conjunction with that, significant differences arose in terms of what kinds of stories the films told and how they functioned for certain audiences.

Early Indian subjects tended to follow one of two narrative trajectories. Beginning with Kalem's *Red Man's Way*, whose 'Indian rites' were to be accompanied by specific 'incidental music',[88] a few worked out melodramatic stories of good versus bad characters (both usually played by white actors) within an Indian community. The attraction here, as in the same company's *Red Cloud*, according to the *Mirror*, was 'the careful research' and 'attention to detail' that went into depicting 'Indian pastimes and costumes'.[89] In other words, these were promoted as 'realistic' spectacles, meant to educate as well as entertain, much like the ethnographic displays or tableaux vivants mounted in museums and world's fairs. But *Red Cloud* did something especially devious: it transposed the name of the famous Oglala Sioux leader to an Indian addicted to gambling who, after being rejected by a chief's daughter, murders him and is hunted down and killed by another Indian who loves her and replaces her father as chief. Biograph's *The Mended Lute*, whose 'familiar love story' of generational conflict is resolved when an Indian brave 'exhibits [unusual] fortitude' under tribal torture, extended this ethnographic impulse by using a Winnebago Indian, James Young Deer, to play its Sioux hero.[90] The film blended 'so much poetry and romance', according to the *World*, that it offered an unfamiliar view of Sioux life for 'discriminating' spectators' contemplation.[91] As Bison began producing Indian subjects in 1909, with Young Deer and his wife Red Wing an integral part of its new California production unit, such contemplative spectacle (but not the attention to detail) began to dissipate, at least within this kind of story.[92] Instead, Bison films like *The Love of a Savage*, *A Redman's Devotion*, *Young Deer's Bravery* and *Young Deer's Gratitude* all exhibited the 'dime novel action and heroics' for which the company was now so noted.[93]

Most Indian subjects, however, told stories of Indian characters defined in relation to whites, with the hero/heroine demonstrating a sense of honour, justice, or self-sacrifice equal to or even surpassing that of his/her American 'masters'. Selig's 1908 film, *An Indian's Gratitude*, provides one basis for this: because the lead character has been taught by a young white woman 'that it is wrong to kill', he tracks a 'white bully' who has insulted her and injured her lover and keeps a group of white vigilantes from hanging him.[94] Something similar happens in Biograph's *The Call of the Wild*: an Indian football hero (much like Jim Thorpe) and cavalry soldier 'abandons his ways of civilisation' after being rejected by a 'well-born white girl'; kidnapping her in anger, he then 'abandon[s] his revenge when she appeals to his higher nature'.[95] Biograph's *The Redman and the Child* varies this slightly, perhaps out of gender difference: an Indian brave takes revenge on two outlaws who, in stealing a cache of gold, have killed a young white boy's grandfather and kidnapped the boy himself (whom the brave has befriended).[96] The same company's *Red Girl*, by contrast, has the title's heroine help capture, but not kill, a Mexican woman and a half-breed who have robbed white miners of their gold.[97] At least one film, Vitagraph's *An Indian's Honor*, however, defines its heroism as distinctive.[98] Here, an Indian falsely condemned to death for murder has a friend take his place as a prisoner (until the day of execution) while he visits his home one last time, but he is robbed en route by friends of the gambler he killed in self-defence. In order to honour his vow to return, he travels fifty miles on foot, reaching the hangman's tree just in time to fall dead from exhaustion. In this film, the 'noble savage' re-emerges to die, transformed into an enduring sign of a 'natural' sense of morality that could even serve as a model for white American civilisation.

Throughout 1909, all but a few films tracing the relations between Indians (or Mexicans) and whites defined their heroes in terms of 'natural' or learned goodness. Those that did not, from Kalem's *The Trail of the White Man* to an early Imp effort, *Destiny*, usually drew harsh words from the trade press for 'sensationalism', whether for a gruesome revenge exacted outside 'the law' or for an overall sense of 'death and depression and gloom'.[99] When revenge killing was acceptable, as in Biograph's *The Indian Runner's Romance*, it was because the story was historical (justifying a Sioux brave's vengeance on a cowboy who has kidnapped his wife), because Young Deer and Red Wing played the Sioux characters, and because the film was American-made.[100] It certainly was not acceptable if French-made, as in Pathé's otherwise absorbing *The Justice of a Redskin*, where an Indian not only kills a white man 'before the dead body of the [white] girl he murdered' but 'hurls the [man's] body into a stream and watches it sink from view'.[101] In most films, how-ever, the Indians (both men and women) who rescued or saved white Americans did so out of a sense of 'innate' goodness – as in Essanay's *The Indian Trailer*, Bison's *The Cowboy's Narrow Escape*, or Selig's *The Indian* – or out of indebtedness to benevolent whites – as in Edison's *A Child of the Forest*, Bison's *Dove Eye's Gratitude*, or Vitagraph's *Red Wing's Gratitude*.[102] In a variant of this, Essanay's *A Mexican's Gratitude*, a Mexican recognises a sheriff who had once saved him from hanging and rescues the white lawman (and his fiancée) from a 'treacherous rival', who just happens to be his own Mexican employer.[103] Only rarely did relations between whites and Indians (or Mexicans) become permanent: as a rule the races were kept separate. Interracial marriage was carefully avoided, usually through an Indian woman's tragic death, as in Selig's *A Daughter of the Sioux*; when it did occur, as in Bison's *Red Girl's Romance* or Essanay's *The Cowboy and the Squaw*, the couple remained isolated, but well within the boundaries of the white man's law.[104]

The Fictions of Assimilation

That Indian subjects were unusually popular with moving picture audiences dur-ing this period demands an explanation.[105] And that demand is especially acute because such stories were no longer appearing as often as they had previously in the regular press, from dime novels and story weeklies to middle-class magazines. As early as 1904, *The Bookman* asserted that 'the Indian as a factor had dropped out' of the dime novel 'about twenty years before'.[106] That seems to have been true as well of the story weeklies which had replaced the dime novel by then, especially for juvenile readers. In *Wild West Weekly*, for instance, after the boy hero, Young Wild West, saves his 'sweetheart' Arietta from Indian captivity, the stories celebrate his 'manly virtues' in adventures (financed by his gold mine and other properties) which pit him and his friends against outlaws and Eastern criminals more often than Indians.[107] In *Rough Rider Weekly*, Ted Strong and Stella, his 'Queen of the Range', are involved even less frequently with Indians.[108] In other words, the prin-cipal, if not exclusive, venue for Indian subjects at this historical moment seems to have been moving pictures. In trying to explain this phenomenon, moreover, one has to ask whether Indian subjects functioned differently than did the Westerns young boys so loved. One also has to ask whether it mattered if the cen-tral character was an Indian brave or an Indian maiden, and if he or she were played by an Indian or a white in disguise. Here, Bison's chief film-maker, Fred

Balshofer, offers a point of entry by attributing the success of some films to the spectacle of the nearly naked male body: 'the ladies simply went gaga over' Charles Inslee in 'his naked Indian hero roles'.[109] However smugly put, his remark deserves some consideration, given that women (both single and married) frequented the shows in large numbers at the time and that efforts to regulate the behaviour of bodies, both in the audience and on the screen, were still being contested.

Yet there are several other explanations that seem even more historically specific. First of all, Indian subjects have to be situated within the iconographic tradition of the West. By the turn of the century, the Indian once represented as opposing 'civilisation' (whether 'nobly' or 'savagely') in chromos such as 'American Progress' had been transformed into the 'Vanishing American', or what might be called, after Renato Rosaldo, a figure of 'imperialist nostalgia'.[110] The 'thanatological tenderness' of that figure was captured perhaps most tellingly in James Earle Fraser's sculpture of a defeated brave on horseback, *The End of the Trail*.[111] But the 'Vanishing American' also circulated in all sorts of commercial attractions prior to moving pictures like *An Indian's Honor* or *The Red Man's View*, from Buffalo Bill's Wild West to the 'exotic' villages so popular at world's fairs from Chicago (1893) and Omaha (1898) to St Louis (1904) or Portland (1905). Here, as Brian Dippie puts it, 'Americans were invited to look with tenderness on the few living remnants of their own beginnings ... "the Alpha of the alphabet of American history"'[112] Whatever the attraction, including moving pictures, however, the Indian was presented as visual spectacle, commodified for mass consumption, within a nationalistic ideology of 'racial progress'. Accordingly, a hierarchy of types, from the highest (or closest to the 'Anglo-Saxon' American) to the lowest, framed the distribution of Indian (or Mexican) characters in these films, just as it did, for example, the peoples inhabiting the Philippine Reservation at the St Louis Exposition.[113] Put simply, the 'good' film Indian (or Mexican) could also serve as a model of 'assimilation' (encouraged by the Dawes Severalty Act of 1887), especially when that figure abandoned his or her culture and gratefully adopted the values and behaviour of the more 'advanced' white American culture, predicated on private property and a male-dominated nuclear family, which assumed a paternalistic attitude towards women and children.[114]

As a model of 'assimilation', then, the Indian's appeal exceeded that of an elegiac nostalgia. For, as Richard Slotkin has argued, throughout the last two decades of the 19th century, Indians often were conceived as a displaced figure of the 'working class [or] alien mob' and its threat of 'savage war'.[115] After the 1886 Haymarket 'riots' in Chicago, for instance, one New York newspaper called for ending further immigration on the (confused geographical) grounds that 'such foreign savages ... [were] as much apart from the rest of the people of this country as the Apaches of the plains are'.[116] Nearly twenty years later, David Perry (then president of the National Association of Manufacturers) made a similar claim that 'organized labor know[s] one law, and that is ... the law of the savage'.[117] As Alex Nemerov suggests, the equation of 'savage tribes' and 'urban mobs' also can be traced in the paintings of Remington, Charles Schreyvogel, and others.[118] The 'good' film Indian, consequently, must have had a special appeal for the working-class immigrants who made up a significant mass of the moving picture audience in metropolitan centres from New York and Philadelphia to Chicago. Mary Heaton Vorse gives evidence of that, particularly for women, in her sharply etched account of an East Side nickelodeon: one young Jewish woman she observed in some detail was thoroughly 'rapt and entranced' by an Indian film.[119] Surely such films would have appealed to the progressive reformers interested in the 'assimilation' of those immigrants.[120] For, if the Indian (or Mexican), despite the alleged savagery or deceitful nature of his or her 'racial type', could acquire, embody, and enact the values of an 'American' (being a white actor like Charles Inslee in disguise, of course, helped immeasurably), so too could the newly arrived immigrants from eastern and southern Europe, who were even closer to the 'Anglo-Saxon' ideal. The 'good' Indian (or Mexican), therefore, may well have been a more potent mirror image of cultural transformation (and managed social struggle) than the 'clean, good-looking actor' who played the more conventional Western hero.[121]

The increasingly popular Westerns of 1907–10,[122] I would argue, served not only as models of negotiation in the construction of the single-reel fiction film but as models of exclusion and inclusion, defined sharply according to 'race' and gender differences, in the construction of national identity. As quintessentially 'American' subjects, they also staked out a territorial claim against 'foreign' incursions, at least according to the trade press – which returns me to my beginning. Prior to 1910, the few Westerns Pathé released were often criticised for their inauthentic landscapes or their 'savage torture[s]' and other 'cold-blooded act[s]' deemed far too gruesome for American tastes.[123] Not unexpectedly, that criticism did not cease when the French company assigned Louis Gasnier to produce American films in New Jersey, beginning with *The Girl from Arizona*, and even after he had the audacity to hire Young Deer and Red Wing away from Bison.[124] For one thing, the kinds of Westerns Gasnier chose to make were supposed money-makers, 'full of snap and go', and that meant, the *Mirror* sniffed, they were 'only too clearly of dime-novel origin'.[125] For another, and on this the *Mirror* and the *World* agreed, however well staged and photographed and whatever their 'thrilling interest', the Wild West scenes in these Pathé films looked woefully out of place in 'unmistakable New Jersey rocks and woods'.[126] Finally, Pathé consistently used 'burly' Indians, rather than 'clean, good-looking [that is, white] actors', to play its Indian heroes, a casting practice already evident in *Justice of a Redskin* and one that Young Deer would continue in the Westerns produced at the company's new West Coast studio beginning in late 1910.[127] However commendable, this practice could never fully embody the requisite magic – or racist sleight of hand – of *American* assimilation.

This essay was first presented as a paper at the Society for Cinema Studies Conference, New York, 5 March 1995. For its revision and expansion, I had the support of a grant from the Drake University Center for the Humanities and the benefit of excellent suggestions from Tom Gunning, Barbara Hodgdon, Roberta Pearson, Vanessa Schwartz and Dan Streible. An even longer version appears in *The 'Red Rooster' Scare, or Making Cinema American*, forthcoming from University of California Press, 1998.

Notes

1 'Reviews of Late Films', *NYDM* (13 June 1908), p. 10.

2 'Alleged Pirating of Films', *NYDM* (20 June 1908), p. 6.

3 'Earmarks of Makers', *NYDM* (14 November 1908), p. 10.

4 See, for instance, 'Some Coming Headliners and a New Religious Subject', *MPW* (24 October 1908), p. 318; 'Latest Films: Selig's *A Montana Schoolmarm*', *MPW* (19 December 1908), p. 512; John Bradlet, 'A Tour Amongst Country Exhibitors', *MPW* (13 February 1909), p. 169; and 'Motion Pictures in New Jersey', *MPW* (6 March 1909), p. 277.

5 For an analysis of how Pathé achieved its pre-eminence in the United States, see Abel, 'Pathé Goes to Town: French Films Create a Market for the Nickelodeon', *Cinema Journal* 35,1 (Fall 1995), pp. 3–26.

6 See 'The Burden of the New Immigration', *The World's Work*, 6,3 (July 1903), p. 3603. For a good sense of the response to the 'threat' of immigration at this peak period, in 1907, see Herbert N. Casson, 'The Americans in America', *Munsey's Magazine* 36 (January 1907), pp. 432–6; Brander Matthews, 'The American of the Future', *Century Illustrated* 74 (July 1907), pp. 474–80; and Josiah Strong, *The Challenge of the City* (New York: Eaton & Mains, 1907), pp. 73–89, 131–66.

7 For institutional and discursive analyses of this exclusion, respectively, see Kristin Thompson, *Exporting Entertainment: America in the World Film Market, 1907–1934* (London: BFI, 1985), pp. 1–27; and Abel, 'The Perils of Pathé, or the Americanization of Early American Cinema', in Leo Charney and Vanessa Schwartz (eds), *Cinema and the Invention of Modern Life* (Berkeley: University of California Press, 1995), pp. 183–223.

8 Robert Anderson first sketched out some of the lines of this argument in 'The Role of the Western Film Genre in Industry Competition, 1907–1911', *Journal of the University Film Association* 31,2 (Spring 1979), pp. 19–26. Here, I disagree with Miriam Hansen who writes, 'Actually, the "Americanization" of the cinema seems to have been less a question of treating nationally specific themes (like Indian and Western films) than of developing a particular *type* of film' – see Hansen, *Babel & Babylon: Spectatorship in American Silent Film* (Cambridge, Mass.: Harvard University Press, 1991), p. 79.

9 The term 'cinema of attractions' was developed by André Gaudreault and Tom Gunning to distinguish the first decade of cinema history from that which followed – see, for instance, Tom Gunning, 'The Cinema of Attraction: Early Film, Its Spectator and the Avant-Garde', *Wide Angle* 8.3/4 (1986), pp. 63–70.

10 See, for instance, Tom Gunning, ' "Now You See It, Now You Don't": The Temporality of the Cinema of Attractions', *Velvet Light Trap* 32 (Fall 1993), pp. 3–12.

11 The catalogue edited by William Truettner, *The West as America: Reinterpreting Images of the Frontier, 1820–1920* (Washington: Smithsonian Institution Press, 1991), is an extraordinary source of images from that iconographic tradition as well as of essays rethinking that tradition.

12 Alan Trachtenberg, *The Incorporation of America: Culture and Society in the Gilded Age* (New York: Hill & Wang, 1982), pp. 17–18.

13 See Truettner, *The West as America*, pp. 123, 131, 231, and Peter Marzio, *The Democratic Art: Pictures for a 19th-Century America* (Boston: David Godine, 1979), pp. 116–28, 312. See also Neil Harris, *Cultural Excursions: Marketing Appetites and Cultural Tastes in Modern America* (Chicago: University of Chicago Press, 1990), p. 322.

14 Martha Sandweiss, 'Views and Reviews: Western Art and Western History', in William Cronon, George Miles, and Jay Gitlin (eds), *Under an Open Sky: Rethinking America's Western Past* (New York: Norton, 1992), pp. 193–4. See also Marzio, *The Democratic Art*, p. 339.

15 William Cullen Bryant, *Picturesque America* (1874), quoted in Trachtenberg, *The Incorporation of America*, pp. 18–19.

16 Anderson, 'The Role of the Western Film Genre', pp. 22–4.

17 See the Selig ad for *Western Justice* in *MPW* (22 June 1907), p. 251, and 'Comments on Film Subjects', *MPW* (7 March 1908), p. 195.

18 'Comments on Film Subjects', *MPW* (7 March 1908), p. 195.

19 'Pictures of Real Western Life Coming', *MPW* (27 June 1908), p. 541. H. H. Buckwalter headed up Selig's Western film-making unit in Colorado, but Francis Boggs did the writing and directing.

20 'Reviews of Late Films', *NYDM* (18 July 1908), p. 7.

21 'This is an ambitious out-door production' – see 'Reviews of New Films', *NYDM* (19 September 1908), p. 9. The 35mm print of *The Cattle Rustlers* at the National Film and Television Archive runs 862 feet.

22 'Reviews of New Films', *NYDM* (27 February 1909), p. 13; and '*The Indian Trailer*', *MPW* (22 May 1909), p. 672. See also Sime's review of Selig's *A Montana Schoolmarm* in 'Moving Picture Notes', *Variety* (6 February 1909), p. 13. The 1872 chromo, *On the Warpath*, is reprinted in Marzio, *The Democratic Art*, p. 329.

23 'Motion Pictures to Boost Immigration', *Show World* (19 December 1908), p. 22. See also 'Immigration and the Purity of the American Race', *The World's Work*, 6,4 (August 1903), p. 3716.

24 See, for instance, the reviews of Biograph's *The Stage Rustlers* and Vitagraph's *Twixt Love and Duty* as well as *An Indian's Honor*, in 'Reviews of Late Films', *NYDM* (18 July 1908), p. 7, (25 July 1908), p. 7, and (15 August 1908), p. 7. See also Casson, 'The Americans in America', p. 435.

25 'Reviews of New Films', *NYDM* (8 August 1908), p. 7. See also 'Moving Picture Reviews', *Variety* (1 August 1908), p. 13. Tom Gunning cites this film as 'show[ing] the first stirrings of the narrator system' which Griffith developed throughout 1908 and 1909 – see Gunning, *D.W. Griffith and the Origins of American Narrative Film* (Urbana: University of Illinois Press, 1991), pp. 69–74.

26 'Reviews of New Films', *NYDM* (26 September 1908), p. 9, and (7 November 1908), p. 8. *The Call of the Wild* 'was liberally applauded' at Keith's Fourteenth Street Bijou Dream. See also the analysis of *Call of the Wild*'s concluding tableau in Gunning, *D.W. Griffith*, pp. 108–9.

27 'Reviews of New Films', *NYDM* (27 February 1909), p. 13, and (27 March 1909), p. 13.

28 'Reviews of New Films', *NYDM* (26 September 1908), p. 9.

29 See, for instance, Pathé's *L'Arlesienne*, which 'sets a new standard of excellence' as 'a model object lesson for every American manufacturer', and *The Assassination of the Duke de Guise*, in 'Reviews of New Films', *NYDM* (5 December 1908), p. 8; and Thomas Bedding, 'The Modern Way in Moving Picture Making', *MPW* (13 March 1909), p. 294.

30 See Hans Leigh, 'Acting and Action', *MPW* (2 October 1909), p. 443. Frank Woods responded to Leigh by arguing that Biograph, at its best, succeeded at acting and action equally well – see 'Spectator's' Comments', *NYDM* (2 October 1909), p. 32.

31 'Comments on Film Subjects', *MPW* (1 May 1909), p. 554. See also the review of Lubin's *The Falling Arrow*, in 'Comments on Film Subjects', *MPW* (8 May 1909), p. 592; and that of Lubin's *A Nugget of Gold*, in 'Comments on the Week's Films', *MPW* (24 July 1909), p. 125.

32 The first Bison film to get the *World*'s attention was *The Cowboy's Narrow Escape* – see 'Comments on the Week's Films', *MPW* (26 June 1909), p. 871. Bison was releasing one Western per week by late summer. Centaur's Westerns appeared much more infrequently.

33 See 'Comments on the Week's Films', *MPW* (25 September 1909), p. 416. The *Mirror* was more critical of Bison Westerns, finally granting some praise to *Iona, the White Squaw*, in 'Reviews of New Films', *NYDM* (30 October 1909), p. 15.

34 See 'Essanay Will Release Two Reels', *MPW* (6 November 1909), p. 638. Two weeks later, the *Mirror* used much more circumspect language in its announcement, revealing a clear bias in favour of the other 'school' – see 'Essanay Two Reels', *NYDM* (20 November 1909), p. 16.

35 See 'Comments on the Week's Films', *MPW* (20 November 1909), p. 722, and (4 December 1909), p. 799. One of Selig's more popular Westerns, *The Cowboy Millionaire*, imports the 'wild and woolly' directly into the city, where the 'roughhouse' action quickly loses its allure for the film's hero – see 'Comments on the Week's

Films', *MPW* (6 November 1909), p. 643. *The Cowboy Millionaire* survives in a 35mm print at the Nederlands Filmmuseum.

36 See 'Comments on the Films', *MPW* (5 February 1910), p. 169, and (26 February 1910), p. 300. The company announced its own 'phenomenal success', in 'Bison Notes', *MPW* (12 March 1910), p. 387; this is supported by Fred Balshofer and Arthur Miller, *One Reel a Week* (Berkeley: University of California Press, 1967), p. 67.

37 See 'Comments on the Films', *MPW* (8 January 1910), p. 17. For the *Mirror*, this Essanay film was 'frankly a Western melodrama' – see 'Reviews of Licensed Films', *NYDM* (1 January 1910), p. 17. In its year-end wrap-up of the moving picture industry, *Film Index* praised Selig and Essanay for their 'realistic Western subjects' – see 'Reviewing the Year', *FI* (1 January 1910), p. 2.

38 See '*The Indian Trailer*', *MPW* (22 May 1909), p. 672.

39 See 'The Producer's Art', *MPW* (31 July 1909), p. 151. This editorial excoriation is significant because the *World* frequently criticised American Westerns for inaccuracies, but never so harshly as in this case. From July through to September, the *World* also published letters purportedly from 'Wild West' singling out Eastern locations falsely representing Western landscapes – see, for instance, Wild West, 'Accuracy in Indian Subjects' and 'Wild West in the East', *MPW* (10 July 1909), pp. 48 and 57.

40 See 'Reviews of New Films', *NYDM* (10 July 1909), p. 15.

41 See, for instance, 'On the Screen', *MPW* (25 December 1909), p. 919. One boy, interviewed for the San Francisco *Sunday Call* (15 May 1910), singled out coloured French films as the best scenics, and other kids referred to specific Pathé titles – see 'A Little Child Shall Lead Them', *MPW* (4 June 1910), p. 936.

42 See 'Black and White Pictures. Do the Public Prefer Them?' *MPW* (19 February 1910), p. 245. See also 'The Pictures of the Future', *MPW* (18 December 1910), pp. 1398–9. By 1911, once the American cinema was no longer threatened by the 'foreign', the *World* could return to the issue of colour and praise 'toned pictures' – see 'Toning and Tinting as an Adjunct to the Picture', *MPW* (18 March 1911), p. 574.

43 Interestingly, the foreign manufacturer now cited as a model was Gaumont – see 'Orthochromatic Moving Pictures', *MPW* (12 February 1910), p. 202, and 'The Qualitative Picture: The Influence of the French School of Picture Making', *MPW* (25 June 1910), pp. 1089–90. This was another clear signal of Pathé's exclusion, for one year earlier the *World* had cited Pathé as a model for such pictorial qualities – see Thomas Bedding, 'The Modern Way in Moving Picture Making', *MPW* (15 May 1909), pp. 626–7.

44 See 'Spectator's' Comments', *NYDM* (13 November 1909), p. 15. See also the *World's* review of *The Indian Runner's Romance*, in which 'the reproduction of outdoor scenery is so good that it seems as though one were actually in the woods and fields' – 'Comments on the Week's Films', *MPW* (4 September 1909), pp. 315–16.

45 See the Biograph ad for *The Country Doctor* in *NYDM* (10 July 1909), p. 16.

46 See, for instance, Trachtenberg, *The Incorporation of America*, pp. 12–13.

47 Josiah Strong, *Our Country: Its Possible Future and Its Present Crisis* (New York: 1885), pp. 174–5. See also Trachtenberg, *The Incorporation of America*, pp. 78–9, 102–4, and Alexander Saxton, *The Rise and Fall of the White Republic: Class Politics and Mass Culture in Nineteenth-Century America* (London: Verso, 1990), pp. 343–4.

48 Fiske's 'Manifest Destiny' was given as a lecture first in London, in 1880, and then some fifty times throughout England and the United States, until its publication in *Harper's Monthly* (March 1885), pp. 578–90, and in Fiske, *American Political Ideas Viewed from the Standpoint of Universal History* (Boston: Houghton Mifflin, 1885). This passage is quoted in Richard Drinnon, *Facing West: The Metaphysics of Indian-Hating and Empire-Building* (Minneapolis: University of Minnesota Press, 1980), p. 240.

49 See, especially, Richard Slotkin, *Gunfighter Nation: The Myth of the Frontier in Twentieth-Century America* (New York: Atheneum, 1992), pp. 29–62.

50 Michael Kammen, *Mystic Chords of Memory: The Transformation of Tradition in American Culture* (New York: Knopf, 1991), pp. 220, 222.

51 See, for instance, 'The Burden of the New Immigration', *The World's Work* 6.3 (July 1903), pp. 3601, 3603.

52 See, for instance, Joyce Appleby, Lynn Hunt and Margaret Jacob, *Telling the Truth about History* (New York: Norton, 1994), pp. 108, 117.

53 See, for instance, Trachtenberg, *The Incorporation of America*, pp. 13–17.

54 See, for instance, Slotkin, *Gunfighter Nation*, pp. 51–2.

55 Ronald Takaki, *Iron Cages: Race and Culture in Nineteenth-Century America* (New York: Knopf, 1979), pp. 171–3, 175–6. For a particularly good analysis of the figure of Custer in early films, see Roberta Pearson, 'The Revenge of Rain-in-the-Face? Or, Custers and Indians on the Silent Screen', in Daniel Bernardi (ed), *The Birth of Whiteness: Race and the Emergence of U.S. Cinema* (New Brunswick: Rutgers University Press, 1996), pp. 273–99.

56 See Kammen, *Mystic Chords of Memory*, p. 186. About the same time, *Harper's* worked up a publicity campaign to popularise Frederic Remington's Western illustrations – see Kammen, *Mystic Chords of Memory*, pp. 395–6.

57 Robert Rydell presents this argument quite forcefully in his study of American world's fairs, *All the World's a Fair: Visions of Empire at American International Expositions, 1876–1916* (Chicago: University of Chicago Press, 1984). See also Michael Denning, *Mechanic Accents: Dime Novels and Working Class Culture in America* (London: Verso, 1987), pp. 205–6.

58 Owen Wister, 'The Evolution of the Cow-Puncher', *Harper's Monthly* 91 (September 1895), pp. 602–17. This essay was accompanied by five Frederic Remington illustrations. Wister, Remington and Roosevelt were Easterners, friends who had 'roughed it' in the Western mountains or plains in order to restore their sense of masculinity. This was a story of 'proven' regeneration which was sometimes told in films like Vitagraph's *The Easterner* (1907) – see 'Film Review', *VFI* (17 August 1907), p. 6.

59 See, for instance, Saxton, *The Rise and Fall of the White Republic*, pp. 341–2. Another example is Frederic Remington's short story, 'A Sergeant of the Orphan Troop', *Harper's Monthly* (August 1897), pp. 327–36.

60 See, for instance, W. Churchill Williams, 'Red Blood in Fiction', *The World's Work* (July 1903), pp. 3694–700, and Slotkin, *Gunfighter Nation*, pp. 156–7.

61 Frank Norris, 'The Frontier Gone at Last', *The World's Work* 3 (1902), reprinted in Donald Pizer (ed.), *The Literary Criticism of Frank Norris* (Austin: University of Texas Press, 1964), p. 111. Remington's words come from an 1893 letter to Wister, quoted in Saxton, *The Rise and Fall of the White Republic*, p. 344.

62 Eleanor Gates, 'A Round-Up in Central Park', *Saturday Evening Post* (6 August 1905), pp. 2–4. I found this story by chance when looking for articles, stories, and advertisements which could used as texts in a new course, 'The Emergence of Mass Culture', I was developing in the summer of 1994.

63 See Christine Bold, *Selling the Wild West: Popular Western Fiction, 1860–1960* (Bloomington: Indiana University Press, 1987), pp. 15–16.

64 Rydell, *All the World's a Fair*, p. 6.

65 See the Kalem ad in *MPW* (15 June 1907), p. 226.

66 See 'Reviews of Late Films', *NYDM* (11 July 1908), p. 7.

67 See 'Films of All Makers', *VFI* (25 July 1908), p. 11. A 35mm print of *The Renegade*, at the National Film and Television Archive, runs 778 feet.

68 See 'Reviews of New Films', *NYDM* (8 August 1908), p. 7. See also Lubin's *Western Romance*, in 'Reviews of Late Films', *NYDM* (18 July 1908), p. 7.

69 See 'Latest Films of All Makers', *VFI* (8 August 1908), p. 11; and 'Reviews of Late Films', *NYDM* (15 August 1908), p. 7.

70 'Latest Films of All Makers', *VFI* (12 September 1908), p. 11. There are no intertitles in the NFTVA print of *Cattle Rustlers* to identify the characters.

71 'Some Coming Headliners . . .', *MPW* (24 October 1908), p. 318.

72 See the Selig ad in *FI* (23 January 1909), p. 14; and 'Reviews of New Films', *NYDM* (23 January 1909), p. 7. Other cavalry films included Selig's *On the Warpath* and *Boots and Saddles* – see 'Reviews of New Films', *NYDM* (27 February 1909), p. 13, and (27 March 1909), p. 13.

73 See 'Reviews of Licensed Films', *NYDM* (4 December 1909), p. 17. Selig took the unusual step of advertising this film in *NYDM* (13 November 1909), p. 16.

74 See 'Films of the Week', *FI* (20 March 1909), p. 9.

75 See 'Comments on Film Subjects', *MPW* (3 April 1909), p. 494.

76 See the reluctant praise of this film, whose title character is named after a Walter Scott heroine, in 'Independent Reviews', *NYDM* (30 October 1909), p. 16.

77 See 'Comments on the Week's Films', *MPW* (13 November 1909), p. 683. See also 'Bison's *The Message of the Arrow*', in 'Comments on the Week's Films', *MPW* (18 December 1909), p. 882.

78 These specific phrases come from a review of Selig's *The Freebooters*, 'which smacks very strongly of the Wild West', in 'Comments on the Week's Films', *MPW* (25 September 1909), p. 415.

79 See 'Comments on the Week's Films', *MPW* (18 December 1909), p. 880.

80 'An American School of Moving Picture Drama', *MPW* (20 November 1909), p. 712.

81 The *World* first suggested this popularity early in 1909 – see 'Nemesis', *MPW* (27 March 1909), p. 366. See also the 'boy expert' cited in Louis Reeves Harrison, 'Stagecraft', *MPW* (14 May 1910), p. 774. And see the highly selective quotes from student essays in the San Francisco *Sunday Call* (15 May 1910), reprinted in 'A Little Child Shall Lead Them', *MPW* (4 June 1910), p. 936. A more authoritative survey of schoolchildren, done by the Child Welfare Committee of New York in late 1910, concluded that three-fourths of the boys liked 'Cowboys and Indians' best – see 'Pictures That Children Like', *FI* (21 January 1911), p. 3.

82 See Michael Kimmel, *Manhood in America: A Cultural History* (New York: Free Press, 1996), pp. 121–2. During the late 19th century, all kinds of middle-class fraternal organisations developed as 'masculinist alternatives' to these 'female-controlled' spaces – see Kimmel, *Manhood in America*, pp. 171–2. The attempt to 'masculinise' moving pictures through 'realist' narratives, and particularly Westerns, could be seen then as part of a push to transform the 'femininised' space of the nickelodeon into a juvenile or even young adult complement to fraternal organisations.

83 See Kimmel, *Manhood in America*, pp. 160–1.

84 'What is an American Subject?' *MPW* (22 January 1910), p. 82.

85 See Frank W. Blackmar, 'The Mastery of the Desert', *North American Review* 162 (May 1906) – quoted in Donald Worster, *Under Western Skies: Nature and History in the American West* (New York: Oxford University Press, 1992), p. 88. See also Albert Shaw, *The Outlook for the Average Man* (New York: Macmillan, 1907), p. 115. I borrow some language here from Kammen, *Mystic Chords of Memory*, p. 295.

86 James D. Law, 'Better Scenarios Demanded', *MPW* (29 August 1908), pp. 153–4.

87 Eileen Bowser even argues that 'Indian films' constituted a separate genre from 'Westerns' during these early years – see Bowser, *The Transformation of Cinema, 1907–1915* (New York: Scribner's, 1990), pp. 173–7. For an analysis of 'the function and traits' of Indian and Mexican characters in slightly later Westerns, see Peter Stanfield, 'The Western 1909–1914: A Cast of Villains', *Film History* 1,2 (1987), pp. 97–112.

88 'Moving Picture High Art', *Billboard* (19 October 1907), p. 20. See also the Kleine Optical ad in *MPW* (12 October 1907), p. 506.

89 See 'Reviews of New Films', *NYDM* (2 January 1909), p. 8.

90 See 'Comments on the Week's Films', *MPW* (14 August 1909), p. 226. Young Deer had performed with circuses like Barnum & Bailey and the 101 Ranch, worked briefly at Kalem (perhaps on *Red Cloud*), and then wrote, directed, and acted in Lubin Westerns, including *The Fallen Arrow* – see 'James Young Deer', *MPW* (6 May 1911), p. 999.

91 See also Gunning's analysis of compositional depth in the images of natural landscapes in *The Mended Lute*, in *D.W. Griffith*, pp. 209–10.

92 Probably the first reference to Young Deer and Red Wing comes in the announcement for *Half Breed's Treachery*, in 'Independent Films', *MPW* (21 August 1909), p. 267. See also the article reprinted from the *Los Angeles Examiner*, as 'Los Angeles Home of Three Film Companies', in *MPW* (19 February 1910), p. 256; and 'New York Motion Picture Company Notes', *MPW* (5 March 1910), p. 342. The company was also strong enough to attract Charles Inslee from Biograph to work in Bison films beginning in the summer of 1909. See Balshofer and Miller, *One Reel a Week*, pp. 28–9, 33, 40, 41, 54, 55.

93 See 'Comments on the Films', *MPW* (31 December 1909), p. 961, (22 January 1910), 92, and (26 February 1910), p. 300. The *Mirror* even found 'a credible attempt to give us a poetic story' in *The Rose of the Ranch* – see 'Reviews of Unlicensed Films', *NYDM* (19 March 1910), p. 18.

94 'Reviews of Late Films', *NYDM* (18 July 1908), p. 7. In *The Squawman's Daughter*, an Indian woman repays her 'cowboy sweetheart', who has saved her from 'a villainous desperado', by leading his friends on horseback to his rescue – see 'Comments on the Week's Films', *MPW* (7 March 1908), p. 195.

95 'Reviews of New Films', *NYDM* (7 November 1908), p. 8.

96 'Reviews of New Films', *NYDM* (8 August 1908), p. 7.

97 'Reviews of New Films', *NYDM* (26 September 1908), p. 9. This film, along with *The Heart of O Yama*, appeared in the first Biograph ad in the *Mirror* – see *NYDM* (19 September 1908), p. 9. See also *The Girl and the Outlaw* (released just one week before *Red Girl*), in which an 'Indian maiden' dies helping rescue a young white woman from outlaws. The 16mm print of *The Girl and the Outlaw*, in the Library of Congress paperprint collection, runs 315 feet.

98 See 'Film Reviews', *VFI* (8 August 1908), p. 10; and 'Reviews of Late Films', *NYDM* (15 August 1908), p. 7.

99 See, for instance, 'Reviews of New Films', *NYDM* (9 January 1909), p. 9; and 'Comments on the Week's Films', *MPW* (20 November 1909), p. 721. See also the review of Kalem's *Seminole's Revenge*, in 'Reviews of New Films', *NYDM* (20 March 1909), p. 13.

100 See the Biograph ad in *NYDM* (28 August 1909), 16; 'Reviews of New Films', *NYDM* (4 September 1909), p. 16; and 'Comments on the Week's Films', *MPW* (4 September 1909), p. 315. See also the *World's* criticism of Biograph's *Comata the Sioux*, which, in raising questions about historical accuracy, acknowledges with some reluctance that whites did force the Sioux to change their way of life and that perhaps that was worth representing in moving pictures – 'Comments on the Week's Films', *MPW* (2 October 1909), p. 450.

101 See 'Comments on Film Subjects', *MPW* (27 March 1909), p. 368, and 'Reviews of Late Films', *NYDM* (13 June 1909), p. 10.

102 See 'Comments on Film Subjects', *MPW* (29 May 1909), p. 714; 'Comments on the Week's Films', *MPW* (26 June 1909), p. 871, and (4 September 1909), p. 313; 'Reviews of New Films', *NYDM* (16 October 1909), pp. 17–18, and (23 October 1909), p. 15; and 'Comments on the Films', *MPW* (8 January 1910), p. 16. Young Deer and Red Wing also appeared in Vitagraph's *Red Wing's Gratitude* – see Bowser, *The Transformation of Cinema*, p. 173.

103 *A Mexican's Gratitude* was lauded for its 'true atmosphere', as one of 'Essanay's California series of sensational Western pictures' – 'Reviews of New Films', *NYDM* (15 May 1909), p. 15. The 35mm print of *A Mexican's Gratitude*, at the National Film and Television Archive, runs 876 feet.

104 See 'Comments on the Films', *MPW* (15 January 1910), p. 56, and (22 January 1910), p. 92; and 'Reviews of Licensed Films', *NYDM* (5 March 1910), p. 16.

105 A review of Lubin's *The White Chief*, for instance, begins with 'Indian pictures are the fashion' – see 'Reviews of New Films', *NYDM* (8 August 1908), p. 7.

106 George C. Jenks, 'Dime Novel Makers', *The Bookman* 20 (October 1904), p. 110.

107 See, for instance, Edmund Pearson, *Dime Novels* (Boston: Little, Brown, 1929), p. 218; and Bold, *Selling the West*, p. 15.

108 See, for instance, J. Edward Leithead and Edward T. Leblanc, '*Rough Rider Weekly* and the Ted Strong Saga', *Dime Novel Round-Up* 41,7 (July 1972), pp. 1–27.

109 Balshofer and Miller, *One Reel a Week*, p. 40.

110 See, for instance, Brian Dippie, *The Vanishing American: White Attitudes and U.S. Indian Policy* (Middletown: Wesleyan University Press, 1982), pp. 197–269; and Julie Schimmel, 'Inventing "the Indian"', in Truettner, *The West as America*, pp. 171–3. Rosaldo's concept is discussed in Ann Fabian, 'History for the Masses: Commercializing the Western Past', in Cronon et al., *Under an Open Sky*, pp. 232–3.

111 The felicitous phrase, 'thanatological tenderness', comes from Ella Shohat and Robert

Stam, *Unthinking Eurocentrism: Multiculturalism and the Media* (London: Routledge, 1994), p. 118. Fraser's 'End of the Trail' was first modelled in 1894 and then enlarged to monumental size for the Panama–Pacific Exposition in San Francisco, in 1915 – see Schimmel, 'Inventing "the Indian" ', pp. 172–4, 353.

112 Dippie, *The Vanishing American*, p. 207. Dippie cites Mary Alice Harriman, 'The Congress of American Aborigines at the Omaha Exposition', *Overland Monthly* 33 (June 1899), p. 508. See also Trachtenberg, The *Incorporation of America*, pp. 35–6.

113 See, for instance, Rydell, *All the World's a Fair*, pp. 167–78.

114 See, for instance, Trachtenberg, *The Incorporation of America*, pp. 33–4.

115 Slotkin, *Gunfighter Nation*, pp. 91–2.

116 This quote comes from the *State Sun*, as cited in Stanley Feldstein (ed.), *The Poisoned Tongue: A Documentary History of American Racism and Prejudice* (New York: Morrow, 1972), p. 258.

117 David M. Perry, *Proceedings of the NAM* (1903), quoted in Slotkin, *Gunfighter Nation*, p. 91.

118 Alex Nemerov, 'Doing the "Old America" ', in Truettner, *The West as America*, pp. 297–303.

119 Mary Heaton Vorse, 'Some Picture Show Audiences', *Outlook* 98 (24 June 1911), pp. 442–3, 445. Although her essay was probably written in the spring of 1911, it is very suggestive of how immigrant spectators responded to 'Indian and Western subjects'. The audience of this nickelodeon on Houston Street was Jewish, 'looking under-sized according to the Anglo-Saxon standard'.

120 See, for instance, Joseph Medill Patterson, 'The Nickelodeons, The Poor Man's Elementary Course in the Drama', *Saturday Evening Post* 180 (23 November 1907), pp. 10–11, 38; John Collier, 'Cheap Amusements', *Charities and the Commons* (11 April 1908), pp. 73–6; and Lewis E. Palmer, 'The World in Motion', *Survey* 22 (5 June 1909), pp. 355–65.

121 G. M. Anderson's Jewishness, which was not well known at the time (he had changed his name from Aaronson), offers an interesting corollary here for, as Essanay's Broncho Billy, this 'Yiddisher Cowboy' became, arguably, the first American film cowboy hero. In that Broncho Billy was frequently an outlaw who turned good, the figure offered a strikingly doubled model of assimilation. One of Bison's early releases had been a comic Western, *Yiddisher Cowboy* – see the Bison ad in *MPW* (14 August 1909), p. 229.

122 By 1910, 'one out of every five pictures produced by American companies ... was a Western' – see Anderson, 'The Role of the Western Film Genre', p. 25, n. 65.

123 In the conclusion of Pathé's *The Gold Prospectors*, for instance, the 'little son' of a miner killed by Indians gets to shoot the Indian chief in revenge – see 'Reviews of New Films', *NYDM* (8 May 1909), p. 16.

124 See, for instance, James McQuade, 'Pathé American Studio Announced by M. Berst', *FI* (9 April 1910), pp. 1, 3; 'Pathé Progress', *MPW* (9 April 1910), p. 557, 'New Pathé Studio', *NYDM* (9 April 1910), p. 18, 'Pathé's American Film', *FI* (14 May 1910), p. 5 and 'Reviews of Licensed Films', *NYDM* (25 June 1910), p. 20 and (30 July 1910), p. 27.

125 See the review of *The Girl from Arizona* in 'Reviews of Licensed Films', *NYDM* (28 May 1910), p. 20; and 'Pathé's American Company Makes Good', *MPW* (30 July 1910), p. 246. Pathé itself called *The Girl from Arizona* a 'sensational western drama' – see *Pathé Weekly Bulletin* (16 May 1910), n.p.

126 See, for instance, 'Reviews of Licensed Films', *NYDM* (28 May 1910), p. 20; and (25 June 1910), p. 20; and 'Comments on the Films', *MPW* (27 August 1910), p. 463.

127 See, for instance, Spencer, 'Notes on the Los Angeles Studios', p. 302; and 'James Young Deer', p. 999.

6 Dixie Cowboys and Blue Yodels: The Strange History of the Singing Cowboy
Peter Stanfield

By any measure, Gene Autry defines the singing cowboy. He had been working as a professional singer since the late 1920s. By the early 1930s he had a high profile on radio, on phonograph recordings and with product endorsements in Sears and Roebuck catalogues. At the time Autry made his first Western film in 1934 the idea of the cowboy strumming his guitar and yodelling across the high prairie may have been relatively novel to Western films, cowboy songs having been a staple element in the Western only since the transition to sound, whether humbly mumbled and sung by cowboys at the beginning of *The Virginian* (1929) or *Billy the Kid* (1930), around campfires or out on the open range, in saloons or in parlours. But precedents abounded within the tradition of vernacular American music that had its roots in the rural South. A history of the singing cowboy needs to look outside film and to take into account the commodification and exploitation of what was to become known as country music.

To understand Autry's role within country music and the Western film it is necessary to consider not only his films and star persona but also the cultural traditions and social context from which they were formed. The telling of this history takes us through medicine shows, blackface minstrelsy, the art of yodelling, the effects of the Great Depression on Autry's audience, country music's role in radio programming and product promotion for a rural audience, and the centrality of the female listener and filmgoer in Autry's recording, radio and film work.

Medicine Shows

For rural musicians, prior to the establishment of the recording and radio industries, there was little prospect of continuous employment unless they took to the road, either on their own or in the company of travelling road shows, which generally meant hooking up with some small-time medicine show huckster who needed an entertainer to draw the crowds necessary to ply his trade. Harmonica Frank Floyd worked as a medicine show performer during the 30s and 40s, and could blow his harmonica out of one side of his mouth and sing out the other. In the following extract from his 1953 recording of 'The Great Medical Menagerist', for Sun Records out of Memphis, he satirically evokes the tent show and sidewalk patter of these nineteenth- and early twentieth-century American tinkers, who sold 'health' tonics that promised to cure all except for the propensity to be a sucker. Success in selling their goods was secured through putting on a 'good' show, which was one of the few social forms of entertainment, other than revival meetings, for isolated rural communities.[1]

> Ladies and gentlemens, cough white dodgers and little rabbit twisters, step right around closely. . . . We have a wonderful soap right here on the market this afternoon, when we was here before a gentleman bought a bar of it, took a bath in it and found two suits of underwear he didn't even know he had. . . . Ladies, here's a wonderful tonic to give to your husbands, makes him tell everything he ever has done, not only that, but every-thing he intends to do. We also have a wonderful hair tonic here on the market this afternoon. It's guaranteed to grow hair on a doorknob in thirty minutes. Here's a letter from a gentleman up in Ohio, it reads, 'Dear Sir, after drinking two bottles of your hair tonic my hair is coming out very nicely. Time I drink two more I think it will all be out.'[2]

Central to the selling of the 'cure-all' was the image of the Indian on brands such as that produced by the Mohawk Indian Medicine Company and on bottles filled with Kickapoo Magic Snake Oil. The Indian carried connotations of the super-natural and knowledge of remedies outside the provenance of medical science. With Indians come cowboys and, arguably, it is through this type of show that large numbers of rural Southerners in the late 19th and early 20th centuries more fully acquainted themselves with the iconography of the West. The earliest known collection of cowboy songs was published by a producer of patent medicines, Clark Stanley, in 1897; the pamphlet placed the songs alongside advertisements for his wares.[3]

If the Indian gave credence to the powers of these 'elixirs of life', then it was the songs and performances of singers and entertainers like Harmonica Frank, who as often as not performed in blackface, that drew and held the audience long enough to sell them the stuff. White entertainers in the South were adept at adopting any number of personae to suit the tastes of their clientele, and invariably would find themselves cowboys or Indians during one performance, urbane balladeers or folksy men of the people in another, and in blackface.

The blackface tradition is deeply ingrained in the music and performance styles of Jimmie Rodgers and Gene Autry. Despite an advertisement for an early tribute to Rodgers that Gene Autry recorded, 'The Death of Jimmie Rodgers', which claimed he was a friend of the late singer, it is unlikely that Autry ever met the man who was the most significant influence on his formative years as a singer. If the two never shared a friendship, they did share a remarkably similar start in the entertainment business. Both worked for railroads, which allowed them to test and develop their talents in front of new audiences. But more pertinently, both roamed the South in the company of medicine shows and played in blackface.[4]

Blue Yodels

One of the great misconceptions that the singing cowboy brought to Western mythology is that yodelling and being a cowpoke go hand in hand. In a history of

African-Americans in the West, 'The Forgotten Cowboy' (BBC Radio, 1995), where the myth of the Anglo cowboy is contested, the programme still holds fast to another myth when it claimed that yodelling was developed by cowboys out on the range to calm the cattle as they settled down for the night. The actual history of yodelling in America is not quite so prosaic.

The hero in Owen Wister's *The Virginian* (1902) did not yodel; instead he sang blackface minstrel tunes:

'Yes, he'll be a missionary,' said the Virginian, conclusively; and he took to singing, or rather to whining, with his head tilted at an absurd angle upward at the sky:

'Dar is a big Car'lina nigger,
About de size of dis chile or p'raps a little bigger,
By de name of Jim Crow.
Dat what de white folks call him. . . .'[5]

But if the Virginian did yodel at the end of the verse it would have been in keeping with the minstrel form. Yodelling appears to have first gained a foothold in American arts when it was popularised by Tom Christian, a blackface minstrel who made his début in Chicago in 1847. David R. Roediger makes the point that blackface could work to efface and incorporate a diversity of European ethnic character types and musical styles (when it wasn't holding them up for ridicule), from Italian opera, Shakespeare, Irish songs to East European polkas and Alpine yodelling. The difficulty in trying to disentangle the origins of the yodel is that it is caught up in this ethnic confusion.[6] Emmett Miller, a 1920s blackface vaudeville artist, appears to have been the prime mover in popularising the blue yodel, an Americanised derivation of the Alpine yodel. In 1924 *Billboard* magazine, reporting on a show at the New York Hippodrome, noted that Miller's 'trick singing stunt' almost stopped the show, and won him 'encore after encore'.[7] Miller's influence on Jimmie Rodgers and on other seminal figures in country music such as Hank Williams has only recently been divined, though even a cursory listen to the way he contorts and plays with the middle vowels in 'love' and 'blues' on his 1928 recording 'Lovesick Blues' suggests how significant his influence was.[8]

In *Country: Living Legends and Dying Metaphors in America's Biggest Music*, Nick Tosches has excavated a host of non-cowboy and pre-Rodgers recorded yodelling performances, but he does not explain how yodelling moved from minstrelsy to cowboys.[9] The crossover probably occurred via medicine shows. Goebel Reeves, a contemporary and probable acquaintance of Jimmie Rodgers, also worked with medicine shows and his recorded body of songs shows the same plurality of personae that Rodgers concocted: drifter, rounder, mama's boy, soldier, blackface minstrel, hobo, father and cowboy. Jimmie Rodgers recorded around a hundred titles during his brief career from his recording début in 1927 to his last recording session in 1933, when shortly afterwards he succumbed to the ravages of tuberculosis. Only seven of these were cowboy songs, but he nevertheless found time to pose for publicity photographs in cowboy clothes. Reeves left twenty-six recorded titles, of which only two are cowboy songs. He yodels on both these tunes, but he also yodels on all the others, and on 'The Yodelling Teacher' he gives an object lesson into the history of the form by playing two 'black' characters:

98

'Hey boy, what in the world do you think you're doin'?'
'I'm yodelling. What do you think I'm doin'?'
'You doing what?'
'I said I was yodelling.'
'I heard it called "you-delling" '
'Well, you heard wrong, 'cause it's called "yodelling". That's what it is, I was doing it and I reckon I know.'
'What is that anyway?'
'Well, it's a musical thing that was discovered over in the Alps somewhere. Where the Swiss people live, you know, where they make that Swiss cheese.'
'Man, you know everything, don't you?'
'Well sure. I'd worked for the white folks, in a, in a tent one time. In a show, in a tent.'[10]

The performer who wanted to get ahead in the medicine show business had to learn to attract a crowd, and a long high yodel appears to have been the ultimate in vocal attractions. If, like Goebel Reeves, he could add a strange trilling to the front end of his yodel, then all the better.

If Roland Barthes had ever listened to country music from this period, he might have fashioned his ideas about *jouissance* on yodelling. Yodels come in many forms and carry many meanings, from the eerie, other-worldly sounds in Val and Pete's 'Yodel Blues Parts 1 and 2', wherein St Peter is called up and then summarily dismissed: 'I dreamt I went to heaven, Saw St Peter there. When St Peter stood up, I sat down in his chair. St Peter said, "I'm gonna tell you one more time, don't want a man around here with women on his mind," ' to the lonesome wail of Hank Williams looking for relief from life's torment, or the sound of pleasure and contentment in Gene Autry's later usage. At its best, as in Cliff Carlisle's 'Ash Can Blues', it gives voice to the ineffable. The singer tells of his bawdy life with a woman: 'Said, "I could haul her ashes better than any other man" – lord, lord – said, "I could sow my seed anytime in her ash can." ' In Jimmie Rodgers's first certifiable classic, 'Blue Yodel #1', the singer uses the yodel to both lighten and darken his tale of revenge on Thelma: 'that girl who made a wreck out of me'. Jimmie gets himself a pistol – 'as long as he is tall' – just to 'see poor Thelma jump and fall'. A short while later he gets himself a shotgun 'with a great long shiny barrel, I'm gonna shoot that rounder that stole away my girl'. The images of sex and violence that Rodgers conjures up in the words and the performance get little if any recognition in the general histories of Country. It is hardly fitting subject-matter for a music whose commercial exploiters from the early 30s onwards have striven to make respectable. But the dark stain of sex and violence in 'Blue Yodel #1' that draws its power from the synthesis of black and white musical forms is never that far under the surface of even the most bland and banal Country performance.[11]

The effect a well-modulated yodel can have on an audience is implicit in a contemporary account of a performance by Professor Aleck Smart given at the Georgia Old-Time Fiddlers' Convention in 1915. He was described as a 'quaint character ... who ... plays melodeon and sings ancient ballads, which end in a yodel that climbs clear out through the roof and wanders among the stars'.[12] But by the 30s the yodel had been co-opted by younger men who found Jimmie Rodgers's 'rounder' persona, as Mark Humphries explains, 'an appealing façade through which to vent sexual desire and aggression, stirrings which could be safely voiced in this new popular musical/poetic form, the blue yodel. At best, the yodel was more than a comic tag: it was a non-verbal statement of youthful bravado, a catharsis, Whitman's "barbaric yawp" '[13]

The South, Consumption and the Cowboy

'A Hill-Billie is a free and untrammelled white citizen of Alabama who lives in the hills, has no means to speak of, talks as he pleases, drinks whisky when he gets it, and fires off his revolver as the fancy takes him' (*New York Journal*, 23 April 1900).[14] This negative image of the poor white rural citizen of the South continued to hold sway and arguably became more pronounced by the 30s. W. J. Cash writing in *The Mind of the South* (1941) notes:

> the people of the towns [in the South] tended to develop a kind of supercilious contempt for all countrymen, including the yeoman himself. ... In some of the lowland areas of the South the terms 'farmer' and 'country jake' had got to be nearly equivalent to 'white trash', and fully surrogate for 'boor' and 'clown' – words not present in the ordinary Southern vocabulary.[15]

Before there was 'Country' music there was 'Country and Western', a term coined by *Billboard* in 1949 to head up its chart listing that had previously been 'Folk' and before that 'Hillbilly'. The changes had been brought about as one means among many to rid Southern vernacular music of its pejorative and negative connotations. The history of the singing cowboy is intimately tied up in this process of making Country music respectable and therefore marketable. It was the image and mythology of the cowboy that provided the most accessible means of repressing the vulgarity of Southern vernacular music, while simultaneously suggesting a classless and uncontroversial image of white supremacy. This move towards respectability while allowing rural audiences to maintain a sense of identity was driven on one level by the recording and radio industries, which throughout the 20s were establishing themselves as a permanent presence in people's lives, and on another by the rapid changes to rural lifestyles brought about by industrialisation and later by the traumas of dislocation, disenfranchisement and dispossession brought on by the Depression.

By the time American vernacular music confronted the possibility of broadening its appeal, the idea of the cowboy offered itself up for appropriation, allowing the hillbilly singer the means towards reinvention, while maintaining an identity that spoke to the needs and desires of a white rural audience. The significance of Jimmie Rodgers is that his success underscored the potential market for exploitation within this community, though his image was far too protean and coarse to appeal to a wider audience which, as it moved from the rural South into urban areas, had to contend with the prejudices of the established middle classes.[16]

This attitude was displayed in a 1926 edition of *Variety*, where a writer opined: 'Hillbillies have the intelligence of morons.'[17] Country stars such as Roy Acuff who more than anyone began to hone the Nashville image of the conservative strait-laced country star that we have today, overcame this prejudice by dropping the ribald songs, putting on a ten-gallon hat and changing his band's name from the Crazy Tennesseans to the rather milder Smoky Mountain Boys. By the early to mid-40s this trend was so firmly established that Hank (originally Hiram) Williams, dressed in cowboy duds, called his band the Drifting Cowboys, despite the fact that his music and words paid barely a passing reference to the Old West. Elvis Presley, in making his bid for wider acceptance through his TV appearances, had to suffer all kinds of indignities that were brought about as a direct result of his Southern working-class background. The most notable was in the *Steve Allen Show*, where Elvis was ridiculed by being costumed in tie and tails and made to sing to a hound-dog. It should then have come as no surprise, then as well as now, that his first film was a Western with a Civil War backdrop, *Love Me Tender* (1956), because by that date the process of the Southern musician ridding himself of any derogatory connotations through reinventing himself as a cowboy appeared totally unremarkable.

The dislocated rural Southerners brought with them connotations of poverty, class, overt racism, regionalism, anachronistic working practices and an absolute lack of sophistication. Southern vernacular music paradoxically confirmed this identity, yet it also displayed a remarkable ability to adapt and respond to a diversity of influences. Once Rodgers had established himself as a recording artist, he sought out all kinds of musicians to help him realise his ideas, the most notable being Louis Armstrong. Rodgers's music is American music, not caring much for musical or ethnic purity; he sings and plays the blues, jazz, old ballads, popular tunes, turning all into something unique to himself. But whatever form of music he played or whatever subject he sang about, or personae he adopted, he always addressed himself directly to a rural audience.

To say that Rodgers had a profound influence on Country musicians is to make only the most obvious of statements. Music critic and historian Peter Guarlnick likens his influence on a whole rural generation to be 'equalled only by such figures of contemporary myth as Babe Ruth and, later, Elvis Presley'.[18] Gene Autry's first forays on to disc (he made his recording début in 1929) are slavish imitations of his hero; between 1929 and 1932 he recorded twenty of Jimmie Rodgers's songs. By 1931 Autry had had his first sizeable hit with a maudlin tune, 'That Silver Haired Daddy of Mine'. There followed a number of sentimental songs within the mountain ballad genre, before he shifted both tone and subject-matter, and began billing himself as 'Oklahoma's Singing Cowboy' for regular and increasingly popular appearances on WLS radio's *National Barn Dance* out of Chicago. Chicago, up and until the mid-40s, was thought to hold the greatest concentration of country musicians.[19]

'Barn Dances as Showbiz' declared *Variety* in a front-page lead item in December 1934. Dan Goldberg writing from Chicago reported:

More than 10 years of steady audiences, more than 300,000 studio visitors for 140 consecutive weeks of shows to S.R.O. [Standing Room Only] business, the biggest mail-pulling strength in the history of advertising, the greatest box-office attraction in the smaller towns throughout the country, the most loyal audience ever assembled.
    That's the record of the radio barn dance, now the top attraction on some dozen of the major stations in the land. It's a story without precedent in show business, in radio or in the advertising and commercial world. A hillbilly twangs a guitar and yodels into a microphone that 'she'll be coming round the mountain' and hundreds of avid listeners rush out to buy some sponsor's work-shirt or fence-post.[20]

There is a certain amount of contrived disbelief and a deal of patronising guff from the writer on the potency of the barn dance phenomena, but his breakdown of the different barn dance formats from around the country is detailed, suggesting he recognises that this is more than just a passing fad. He also notes that the barn dance is absent from radio station programming in the East (that is, New York and New England) and has made little impact in the North-west. At this point in time stations ranked a particular programme's or performer's popularity from the amount of mail he or she pulled, and according to *Variety* the vast majority of listeners were from the rural regions, but what mail the stations did get from city audiences was almost wholly in response to the barn dances. It is safe to surmise that these urban listeners would have been recent migrants from the rural areas. From 1920 to 1930 the total urban population in the South increased by nearly 25 per cent.[21]

The products and implied sponsors mentioned in the article are clearly pitched at the rural working class – fence-posts and smoke-salts – and it is also clear that the radio stations had an active policy of not peddling patent medicines, leaving this to the barely legitimate radio stations that owned powerful transmitters just over the Texas border in Mexico. These stations were principally set up to get around the oligopoly that controlled radio licences in the States and as a forum for high-tech medicine show hucksters of the day who sold outrageous products such as cancer cures, potency revivers in the form of a goat gland transplant, and the rather less fraudulent Crazy Water Crystals, a laxative by any other name. Wrapped around these products and others such as glow-in-the-dark models of Jesus, 100 unsexed chicks, and prayer cloths, were occultists, astrologers, hillbilly musicians, singing cowboys and anyone else who could pull in the mail and weasel another dollar out of the listeners.[22]

During the mid-30s, exhibitors in the pages of *Motion Picture Herald* held an ongoing debate on whether radio was a poacher or provider of potential film audiences. The advertising manager of the Kerasotes Theatre in Springfield, Illinois, wrote a letter that expounded on the benefits of putting on a barn dance style show at his cinema that was then broadcast to outlying regions:

> This type of show is very popular in the Mid West, and we were able to run this show on our stage every Saturday night at seven for almost a year straight. This was a medium to reach rural sections and brought us a lot of new business in this particular field.[23]

Saturday night in cinemas that drew a rural audience was the prime slot for Gene Autry's Westerns, and though this kind of direct cinema and radio promotion may not have been widespread it nevertheless reveals how closely related film and radio audiences were for the singing cowboy.[24]

During the 30s WLS's *National Barn Dance* was America's number-one networked show of Country music. It would eventually be eclipsed by *The Grand Ole Opry*, which by 1940 had an estimated audience of 10 million.[25] Autry's popularity on WLS was recognised when he was given his own show, *Conqueror Record Time*. It was within this talk and sing format that he honed the amiable and sincere cowboy persona that would take him to Hollywood. WLS (World's Largest Store) was owned by Sears and Roebuck, which boosted the singer's reputation and its own sales through the promotion of mail-order 'Gene Autry' guitars, song books and other goods that he endorsed. Gene Autry was not just a singing cowboy. He was a singing merchandise store.

Autry was not the only Country musician to gain commercial backing. For Country groups, sponsorship was almost a prerequisite for turning professional. Western Swing outfits like the Swift Jewel Cowboys were formed for the sole purpose of promoting Jewel cooking products. The Aladdin Lamp Company sponsored the Aladdin Laddies, formed around Bob Wills, who changed their ridiculous name, when they shifted sponsors, to the equally implausible the Light Crust Doughboys in order to advertise Light Crust flour. These and a myriad other bands eventually found their audience through the powerful border radio stations and more legitimate broadcasting outlets.[26]

Throughout the 30s country music increasingly became one of the primary means by which manufacturers attracted consumers from the rural South. During the 20s Henry Ford had pioneered sponsorship of fiddle contests at his dealerships across the South which, as Charles K. Wolfe notes, were promoted as 'an antidote to the jazz music and "loose morals" that [Ford believed] were sweeping the country'.[27] As the use of rural music to promote goods grew, the need to present a respectable, uncontroversial, yet meaningful image became paramount. At the point at which commercial interests could search out a market within the South through the new mass medium of radio, rural communities were undergoing unprecedented changes brought about by the Depression and the increased industrialisation of agriculture. Early Southern vernacular recordings display an obsession with establishing regional identity and a sense of community, whether this was called up through a specific locale, either town or state, or in terms of home and family. This is particularly in evidence in the songs of the Carter Family, such as 'Clinch Mountain Home'. The Carter Family, often referred to as 'the first family of country', were contemporaries of Jimmie Rodgers. On the other hand, as the Depression took hold, the image of restlessness and rootlessness is endlessly foregrounded in, say, Jimmie Rodgers's or Goebel Reeves's songs of drifters and hoboes. As the 30s wore on, this tension between home and the road increasingly became displaced on to the image of the cowboy. The reason that, in the search for a popular yet respectable form of music to attract audiences to commercials, the radio stations should have chosen cowboy music was in part because the cowboy seemed to combine both a sense of regional identity, of roots, with a feeling of restlessness – neatly expressed in the title of one of the most famous cowboy songs, 'Home on the Range', a favourite tune of President Franklin D. Roosevelt.[28]

In his history of the Georgia Old-Time Fiddlers' Conventions which ran between 1913 and 1935, Wayne W. Daniel notes that at their height of popularity these shows could attract an audience of over 3000 to hear fiddlers battle it out for the title of state champion and a cash prize. As 'Old-Time' suggests, the songs and tunes performed at these conventions went back at least to the 19th century and in many cases could be traced back to the British Isles. The conventions' organisers, who saw themselves as guardians of an American tradition, made it clear that Tin Pan Alley tunes would not be tolerated, nor music that presumed to carry the haughty airs of opera. But by the mid-30s the conventions' popularity had waned, their audiences lost to radio, phonograph recordings and the cinema. In the face of these new technologies of entertainment, fiddlers' conventions must have appeared hopelessly anachronistic and parochial.[29]

In the 30s part of the cowboy's appeal was that he could be a figure who transcended a rural and industrial divide. Tied neither to a workbench in a factory nor to the seasonal vagaries of agriculture, he appeared to have freedom of movement, yet also a way of earning a living. The cowboy hero in 30s B Westerns is rarely a large landowner; he may aspire to own a small strip of land, but generally he spends his time helping to protect the heroine from being dispossessed of her land. Moreover, the cowboy carried none of the overt racist or class connotations of the hillbilly or his white-trash cousin, nor the parochialism implied in fiddlers' conventions, yet through deed and action the cowboy supported the concept of Anglo-Saxon superiority while also being incontestably of American origin. The cowboy was neither a Georgia Peckerwood nor an English gentleman. He was, as Walt Whitman claims for his ideal American in *Leaves of Grass*, beyond these divides:

> The vulgar and the refined, what you call sin and what you
> call goodness, to think how wide a difference,
> To think the difference will still continue to others, yet
> we lie beyond the difference.

The appropriation of the cowboy by white Southern musicians was partly brought about by that figure's commitment to a rural lifestyle, but also by his ability to confront and fend off the forces of modernity. In this sense the initial (or pre-filmic) popularisation of the cowboy was not only a response to the women's movement, as Jane Tompkins suggests in her book *West of Everything*, but also to industrialisation. Equally his uncontested Anglo-Saxon heritage met the fears aroused by the mass-migration of Latin and Eastern Europeans to America at the turn of the century.

The question of race as a crucial factor in understanding American popular music cannot be overstated. In 1949 when *Billboard* changed its 'Folk' chart to 'Country and Western' it also changed the 'Race' chart to 'Rhythm and Blues'. Both moves were an attempt to give a veneer of respectability to genres that at best (regardless of sales) were seen as marginal and at worse were seen as vulgar. But, whatever the name given to these charts and musical forms, the fact remains that a recording was marketed to either a black or a white audience. Yet, despite the industry's construction of racially separate forms of music and audiences, these divisions meant little to the musicians, who shared a common stock of influences that constantly challenges our idea of racial segregation in the South. The mutual influences on Blues and Country only furthered the industry's desire to keep them separate, an attempt to control racial boundaries through record marketing and distribution, radio programming, and the selection of records for jukeboxes.

The figure of the cowboy helped to suppress the black heritage apparent in so much of early Country music. When Elvis Presley in his Sun recordings overtly brought together black and white styles of performance it was, and still is to some extent, seen as a transgression. Yet Rodgers and his contemporaries took eagerly and unselfconsciously whatever they could from the Blues and jazz. And Bob Wills and his Texas Playboys fashioned a whole sub-genre – Western Swing – on mixing black and white forms, yet there was no criticism of him, Rodgers, or the myriad other Western Swing bands for having 'corrupted' white music and the minds and bodies of their audiences by importing into their performances the 'primitive sounds of Africa'. The cowboy carried with him such a transparent sense of white racial supremacy that his appearance in Country music transcended any critique of musical miscegenation.

The Origins of Cowboy Music

Interest in the cowboy's musical heritage first gained scholarly attention in the early part of the century with the publication of Nathan Howard (Jack) Thorp's *Songs of the Cowboys* in 1908[30] and with John Lomax's *Cowboy Songs and Other Frontier Ballads* in 1910. 'Cheyenne' (1906) was the first published Tin Pan Alley cowboy song.[31] These date-lines suggest that there was no widely recognised musical signifier for the cowboy until the early years of the 20th century. If this is so, it raises the question about what kind of music would have been played to accompany Wild West shows and theatrical Western melodramas. When Owen Wister adapted *The Virginian* for the stage in 1904 he wrote his own cowboy song, 'Ten Thousand Cattle Roaming', whereas in the novel, as previously noted, the Virginian sang a minstrel tune, as do the cowboys in Andy Adams's *Log of a Cowboy* (1903).[32] Interest in cowboy songs continued to grow throughout the 20s and early 30s. Tex Ritter, soon to be Grand National's first all-riding, all-singing sensation, was much in demand for lecture and song recitals in Eastern colleges. But as hillbilly musicians began systematically to appropriate and commercialise the image of the cowboy, interest waned among the intelligentsia and shifted to 'folk' music from the Appalachians and on to figures such as Bradley Kincaid, who, according to Bill Malone 'spoke disparagingly of hillybilly [*sic*] and bum songs', and extolled the mountain folk from whom he obtained his songs as 'a people in whose veins runs the purest strain of Anglo-Saxon blood'.

Kincaid's popularity with the intelligentsia would fade but in his place came performers like Woody Guthrie who wedded 'Folk' to 'protest':

> The urban folk movement's radical origins have always affected public perceptions of it, and the linking of 'protest' and 'folk song' has contributed to false impressions about the nature of the folk and the music they have made. Furthermore, a regrettable distinction between 'folk' and 'hillbilly' music developed in the popular mind. 'Folk' music, which had become largely the province of intellectuals and reformers, became increasingly removed from the folk, while 'hillbilly' music, the creation of the folk, developed in its own independent fashion.[33]

Malone's formulation helps explain how 'Folk music' took on the mantle of radicalism and authenticity, and 'Country music' that of commercialism and conservatism. But this opposition is to misread these two forms, as it is to see Country and Blues as two mutually exclusive genres; both are equally capable of criticising or supporting the *status quo*.

Following in the footsteps of those arch-American literary heroes such as Huckleberry Finn, who chose to withdraw from a repressive civilisation, Jimmie

Rodgers in 'Blue Yodel #8' rejects the workaday world: you won't see *his* initials on the back end of a mule. But in Gene Autry's 'Tumbling Tumbleweeds', or in other songs of drifting cowboys by him and others, the cowboy gives Rodgers's aimless wanderings and rejection of the work ethic a purpose. In effect, the cowboy transcends the banality of work that Rodgers so freely rejected, giving back to it a sense of purpose; in film and song Gene Autry always had an objective.

Furthermore, the cowboy's ascetic lifestyle as personified in the later stages of Owen Wister's *The Virginian*, in William S. Hart's reconfiguration of the Old Testament into the Wild West, or Tom Mix's juvenilisation of the cowboy, took the edge off the overt sexuality of Southern vernacular music. Early Country recordings can be splendidly coarse. The Prairie Ramblers cut a succession of *risqué* numbers under the name of the Sweet Violet Boys. In 'I Love My Fruit', the song starts with the singer telling of his delight in eating cherries in bed, and then works through every combination of fruit and sexual metaphor before ending up with bananas: 'I am always hungry for bananas (Ah Daddy!). So much so it almost seems a sin. That when I'm all through eating, I still like to nibble on the skin.' Early publicity photographs of Autry show him not as a cowboy but as a slicked-up guitar-picker in a suit, showing all the signs of a man desperately trying to escape the confines of his class. Where the suit failed him the Stetson saved him; as a cowboy Autry transcended any notion of class. Like Rodgers, Autry's early repertoire of songs ran the gamut of the sentimental and the downright obscene. In 'Do Right Daddy Blues' (1931), recorded before he became an actor, Autry sang 'You can feel of my legs, you can feel of my thighs. But if you feel my legs you got to ride me high.' In 1935 Tex Ritter recorded the cowboy's answer to this kind of ribaldry; in 'I'm a Do Right Cowboy' he sings: 'I'm a do right cowboy, top cowhand, I live away out there where the West began. Got a horse and a saddle and a ranch of my own, and I leave all the other men's women alone.' The song concludes: 'My biggest ambition is that I want to be the daddy of a great big family.'[34]

In his record and radio appearances Autry had systematically moved away from the plurality of personae that Rodgers and others had developed and concentrated solely on his Western identity. The cowboy allowed him to transcend any overt associations with a particular class, but allowed Autry to continue to appeal to a rural or new urban audience. His mode of address became increasingly sophisticated through production values, Tin Pan Alley-crafted songs, and a smoothing out of his vocal delivery. Outside the songs' subject-matter and steel guitar, his music by the end of the 30s owed more to popular song of the time than to regionalised vernacular American music-making, and eventually even the yodel would go. The blackface heritage was suppressed and the coarse and bawdy subject-matter of some of his earlier recordings was absolutely censored.

Gene Autry: The Lavender Cowboy

'This [*In Old Santa Fe*] is one of the best Westerns I've ever run. I highly recommend it to any fellow exhibitor that uses Westerns. Good story, plenty of thrills, comedy and some good music and singing by Gene Autry and his band. This is the kind of Western that pleases my patrons.' Played 21–2 December 1934, Sammie Jackson, Jackson Theatre, Flomaton, Alabama. Small-town and rural patronage.[35]

This was the first recommendation for *In Old Santa Fe* (1934), the Ken Maynard programmer that gave Gene Autry his first featured spot, to appear in *Motion Picture Herald*'s 'What the Picture Did for Me' column. The column acted as a post-board for independent exhibitors to flag up film hits and misses, as a space to moan about unfair distribution practices ('The real facts are we play Westerns because they make us money to pay for the clucks we're forced to run, against the better judgment of the wishes of our audience'),[36] and to publicise promotional events that had worked for them. Sammie Jackson's review was followed swiftly by a number of equally positive recommendations: 'Why, oh why, doesn't some company produce more Westerns like this one and give us small-town exhibitors something to make money on.'[37] 'At last they have learned how to make Westerns. Pulled and pleased 100%. More like this.'[38] 'No one could ask for a better Western.'[39] 'This one holds house record for this year. First musical Western I ever played.'[40] 'A good Western with plenty of music and fun. Not the usual shoot 'em up and drag out type, but just a good comical modern Western. Give us more of this type.'[41] 'Pleased many who are not Western fans.'[42] *In Old Santa Fe* was still getting favourable reviews and notices a year after its release.[43] The longer recommendations help to explain its success:

> One of the best bets you can make on Fri–Sat. It's above the average and will please not only Western fans, but others more sophisticated. The plot is good, it has historical glamor and some really delightful Gene Autry music to lift it out of the rut of the commonplace shooting and fighting which are alright as seasonings but why not make more Westerns like this and the O'Brien and Randolph Scott–Zane Grey stories? They have general appeal. Most folks (not decadent) like clean outdoor adventure, and with a little music and cowboy singing, Westerns go over well weekly in my town. And don't you ever think my Western fans don't know the difference between these two types of Westerns? The box office proves it conclusively.[44]

Autry's musical interlude and the light-hearted bits of comic business and dialogue coupled with the more formulaic episodes of fist-fights, shoot-em-ups and chases appeared to be pulling in a broader audience for the film. J. W. Noah, a regular contributor to the column and the proprietor of a small chain of independent cinemas, (New Liberty and Ideal Theatres, Fort Worth, Texas) which had a 'general patronage', wrote:

> The success we enjoyed with this picture [*In Old Santa Fe*] again proves the value of the exhibitor's reports. Had it not been for the glowing tributes paid to this film by fellow exhibitors we would have relegated this film to our 'B' house and then forgotten about it. However, after reading reports on it we made a radical departure from our almost set policy of playing everything except Westerns at our A house and booked it. It took some clever selling and the elimination of Maynard's name from the billing to put it over, but we stood them up and also received many compliments on the picture.[45]

What became clearer as the reviews of Autry's films continued to find space in the column was that he attracted a female audience and yet did not alienate the masculine crowd: 'Gene Autry is fast becoming one of our best box-office attractions, and our cashier has forgotten Gene Raymond in her admiration for Autry.'[46]

Gene Autry pictured during his Jimmie Rodgers phase.

The film is almost a blueprint for the formula Autry's Westerns would use for the rest of the 30s, except that here Autry is given the guest spot rather than the starring role, and the production values would rise along with Autry's popularity. His films would also make more of contemporary social concerns. The story of *In Old Santa Fe* is set in the contemporary West and is centred around a horse-race that a gang of 'city mugs' intends to fix. Chandler, alias Monte Korber (Kenneth Thompson), the lead villain, blackmails the owner of the dude ranch and demands half-shares in the ranch and the owner's daughter's hand in marriage, but his plans are foiled when one of his men betrays him and his attempted framing of Ken (Maynard) falls apart. There is plenty of fast-paced horse-riding and stunts, a fist-fight, a shoot-out, and chases after runaway horses and stagecoaches – 'I guess stopping runaways is my specialty today,' notes Ken, as he wheels Tarzan around to go after a driverless stagecoach. Disguises and mistaken identities, a chaste love affair, as well as comic interludes provided by Ken's partner, Cactus (George 'Gabby' Hayes), keep the story moving forward. But it is the six- or seven-minute musical interlude from Autry, supported by Smiley Burnette, that most of the exhibitors isolated for particular praise.

Autry and Burnette depart from musical interludes in earlier B Westerns in highlighting it as a distinct performance, rather than attempting to integrate it as a spontaneous singalong around the campfire or as an unobserved and private moment as the cowboy sings his song while riding high, wide and handsome across the lone prairie, or while he serenades his sweetheart. The scene begins with Autry leading the dudes in a dance which segues into 'Wyoming Waltz'; at the end Smiley pokes his head out and all but steals the show with his performance of 'Mama Don't Like Music' (a.k.a. 'Mama Don't Allow It'), trading instruments with the band and making his voice swoop up high and then drop down to his trademark frog impersonation. The interlude finishes with Autry singing and yodelling 'In Old Santa Fe', joined on the chorus by Smiley, and the audience of dudes on the final verse. Meanwhile, Ken is nervously making love to the owner's daughter, though she is doing much of the running after this 'sweet cowboy'.

The problem for Maynard was that he never was, nor could ever be, a 'sweet cowboy'. By 1935 his long affair with the bottle was showing, and he looks punchy and out of condition. Autry, on the other hand, had some years to go before he reached this physical stage, and when he sings he is so sweet he almost smells of lavender.

> I returned to Hollywood in 1935, to stay, and to strike paydirt in a movie called *Tumbling Tumbleweeds*. It was the first of a genre, the first Western plotted and sold around the main character's ability to sing. The Autry image was established in that film almost 100 per cent. It was tinkered with in minor ways. . . . But for the most part, the Autry of *Tumbling Tumbleweeds* was the Autry of 1947's *Robin Hood of Texas*.[47]

Autry's initial film contract with Mascot was transferred, after the studio's takeover, to the newly formed Republic headed by Herbert J. Yates (who was also the head of Autry's recording company, American Record Corporation). Yates, with radio, record and merchandising exposure to back him up, must have known he was on to a sure-fire bet with Autry, yodels and Westerns. Within two years of the release of *Tumbling Tumbleweeds*, Autry was Hollywood's number one Western star.

Tumbling Tumbleweeds's simple story of nesters verses ranchers has Autry, the son of the biggest landowner, rejected by his father when he fails to support the fight against the sod-busters. Five years pass and Autry returns to his home town of Gunstock in the company of a travelling medicine show and sets about solving the recent murder of his father. Arguably, the narrative functions purely as a device to serve up a number of songs and to trumpet Autry's star persona as recording and radio artist. Autry's first appearance in the film is heralded, off-screen, by him singing: 'And yodel my troubles away . . .'. The initial emphasis on his voice delays his entrance and plays with audience expectations, introducing him in a way they would have been familiar with through his radio appearances. Yet the narrative, as in all of Autry's 30s films, is also concerned with the plight of the small farmer.

The film begins by introducing itself as a historical recreation with a dramatic montage sequence and opening credits ('In the old west there was no law . . .'), the first and last time that a historical setting would be used in Autry's films. However, the electric lamp in the ranch-house, and later telephones and a phonograph playing Autry's first hit, 'That Silver Haired Daddy of Mine', finish off any notion of historical authenticity and fidelity. The dominant contemporary setting and the story of farmers versus corporate interests enables Autry to be set up as a champion of the common man in a way that overtly ties the film into the conflicts of the Depression. The film deals with the contradiction between past and present, not through any clever narrative device, but by simply avoiding the issue altogether.

> If one had to pick an example of the slice-of-life plots that tended to pop up in my films, *Guns and Guitars* would probably serve. I did not engage, for the most part, in such mundane activities as saving the old homestead or chasing bank bandits. While my solutions were a little less complex than those offered by FDR, and my methods a bit more direct, I played a kind of New Deal Cowboy who never hesitated to tackle many of the same problems: the dust bowl, unemployment, or the harnessing of power. This may have contributed to my popularity with the 1930s audiences.[48]

Indeed, Autry's ideal contemporary audience is interposed into the film through the attraction of 'Dr Parker's Phamous Purveyors Of Phun Phrolic and Painless Panaceas' medicine show, which, apart from the good doctor and Autry, contains a three-piece band and the tap-dancing minstrel Eightball (Eugene Jackson), wide-eyed and stupid. The townspeople of Gunstock, who gather to watch the show, are dressed in 30s work wear, and are bonded together via their participation in the medicine show and through their consumption of Gene Autry records. Apart from the heavies who taunt Autry by calling him a 'lavender cowboy', not one of the townsfolk is seen wearing a cowboy costume. The audience in Bottleneck are already familiar with Autry's recorded work and are offered the inducement of a free phonograph record with every bottle of dope they buy from Dr Parker.

At the outset, Autry's moral dilemma is whether to side with family ties or his conviction that the nesters 'Have just as much right to live as you and I. They have wives and children and they want homes.' Autry is strongly contrasted with his crippled and belligerent father. Autry: 'If you hadn't always been ready to fight at the drop of a hat you wouldn't be in that wheelchair. Listen, Dad, there must be some other way to handle the situation. Why not talk it over with the nesters?' If a peaceful solution is left open then Autry will take it; he prefers singing and talking to fighting, and as such he gives the lie (as does William S. Hart in films such

110

as *Hell's Hinges* [1916]) to the idea that the cowboy represents an unambiguous masculinity, as argued by Jane Tompkins. In his autobiography Autry points up the often central role given to women in his films:

> The leading ladies in Autry films were not there just for decoration or to point out which way the bad guys went. As written, they gave me a lot of anything-you-can-do-I-can-do-better sass, smoked a lot of Kools – that era's Virginia Slims – and, in general, played a thirties' version of waiting for Gloria [Steinem]. That may have been due, in no small part, to the presence of such screenwriters as Betty Burbridge, Luci Ward, and Connie Lee. We didn't exactly use them because they were experts on the West. Whatever their formula, those films were about the only ones in the B Western category, up to then, that had a mass appeal to women.[49]

At a number of points throughout his autobiography Autry argues that at least half his audience was made up of women. If this is so, then it begins to shed light on his films' concern with the domestic sphere, on his rejection of an absolute patriarchy, his dandyish appearance, sex replaced by an emphasis on friendship, and his 'motherly' concern and protection for his aberrant 'son'/sidekick.

Lizzie Francke, in her biographical history of women scriptwriters in Hollywood, devotes a section of her book to a discussion of the work of Betty Burbridge. It is offered to the reader as a curiosity, another example of women only being able to find work in 'low-grade stuff', given little value then or now: 'Burbridge's films may be forgotten now and no doubt for good reason.' Yet Autry clearly contradicts this reading, as do the number of women working in the genre. A survey of the filmography Francke provides reveals eighteen women who scripted Westerns between 1930 and 1941. This is not an insignificant number, even if it does pale against the number of male writers within the genre. Equally, these women had a significant profile in the production of singing Westerns. Francke takes great pleasure in pointing out Burbridge's lack of authenticity in the construction of her identity as a writer of Westerns, but this is to miss the point entirely, for an authentic construction of the Western was never a concern for these films and their audience.[50]

Autry's recognition of his female audience stemmed from his radio work. Pamela Grundy in an essay on Crazy Water Crystals and hillbilly music notes:

> Women made up a large and vocal segment of the hillbilly audience. Radio surveys of the 1930s showed that, despite the stories of farmers hurrying from their fields to listen to noontime shows, the major daytime audience comprised women and children. Women wrote more than two-thirds of the letters received by stations, sponsors, and performers in the period. . . . Perhaps more important, however, was the role of women in arranging personal appearances for hillbilly groups. Personal appearances provided the lion's share of most musicians' income. . . . Local (women's) organisations played an essential role in this system; in most cases they were the ones who rented a space, provided publicity, and handled the finances, dividing the profits with the musicians at the end of the performance.[51]

In *Colorado Sunset* (1939), which has a script co-written by Betty Burbridge, radio's female audience is highlighted. The story concerns the attempt by a 'Protection Association' to coerce local farmers, but their plans are foiled when the women use the radio to garner support for Autry's bid to become sheriff. In a montage sequence we see women cajole and badger their husbands into voting for Gene. Later they actively get into a mass fist-fight and help bring the association to book. The film foregrounds three female roles. One woman runs a restaurant and finally gets to form a couple with Frog Milhouse (Smiley Burnette) – a first, as far as I can make out, in giving Autry's sidekick a love interest, but you can tell he is far from happy in this situation. Another woman runs the radio station (indeed, having women operate and manage radio stations is a fairly common occurrence in Autry's films); she's wooed by Autry through action and in song. Lastly, there is a star cameo from Patsy Montana who performs a wonderful rendition of her million-seller 'I Wanna Be a Cowboy's Sweetheart'. The women are shown to be at the centre of the action and the absolute hub of the community. They are neither the harridans that plague the town of Tonto at the beginning of *Stagecoach* (1939), nor the kind of fallen woman played by Marlene Dietrich in *Destry Rides Again* (1939), nor are they fey and submissive housewives. The women in Autry's films cannot be made to conform to the stereotypes constructed in gender studies of the Western.

The female lead in the B Western occupies an ambivalent space, positioned initially as active, independent and in control of her own destiny, which, coupled with her responsibilities for her male kin, pushes her into a public arena and makes her visible and therefore vulnerable. It is at this point that the hero steps in to protect her, closing down her independence and activity, which has anyway been forestalled by the villain. But closure, with the villain vanquished and the hero and heroine in chaste embrace, is also ambivalent, and does not necessarily reinscribe traditional patriarchal constraints on female behaviour. Rather it leaves open the possibility of the woman being able to play out an independent role free from the threat of villainous entreaties.

'Our Hat's in the Ring with Westerns that Sing'

Gene Autry's success with *In Old Santa Fe* may have been the catalyst that led Warner Bros. to compete again in the Western market after dropping out in the early 30s, but it is just as likely that the studio was reacting to the growing popularity of cowboy music on the radio, as is apparent in this advertising copy:

> 'Our hat's in the ring with Westerns that sing.'
> Dick Foran 'The Singing Cowboy'
> Yessir, men, we've got the first new idea in Westerns since Broncho Billy Anderson learned to ride! All the rarin', tearin', ridin' and shootin' of the best of the old-time series – plus those *Cowboy Songs* the country's crazy over, featured in every release! That's why you'll have the edge on the other fellow if you'll grab Warner Bros. six Westerns presenting the screen's New-West star Dick Foran. *Moonlight on the Prairie*. [emphasis in original][52]

According to *Motion Picture Herald*'s listings of new films, *Moonlight on the Prairie* was ready for distribution on 2 November 1935; Gene Autry's *Tumbling Tumbleweeds* had a 9 November 1935 release date. But which film came first is not really the issue. Rather, it is the industry's recognition that there was a growing market to exploit. Columbia and Paramount both launched new Western series during this season: 'Paramount has not forgotten Sleepy Eye, Minnesota, Smackover, Arkansas, Red Lodge, Montana and 3500 other small towns where folks like red-blooded action in their moving pictures.'[53]

This was part of Paramount's advertising copy for its Zane Grey and Hopalong Cassidy series, and for a reissue of *The Virginian*. Columbia gave a new boost to Charles Starrett by starring him in *Gallant Defender*: 'Presenting the first of a new series ... thrilling romantic adventure stories ... in Western settings ... by Peter B. Kyne – millions of men and women – boys and girls – read his famous action yarns. His name is box office!'[54] RKO came up with the novelty of featuring Harry Carey, Hoot Gibson, Guinn 'Big Boy' Williams, Bob Steele and Tom Tyler in *Powder Smoke Range* – 'The Barnum and Bailey of Western shows'.[55] In early 1936 Paramount starred Bing Crosby in *Rhythm on the Range*, which featured Bing's big hit 'I'm an Old Cowhand'.[56] MGM put Jeanette MacDonald and Nelson Eddy in a wilderness setting for *Rose Marie/Indian Love Call*. And Poverty Row independent Grand National starred Tex Ritter in *Song of the Gringo*.

Dick Foran garnered far fewer recommendations from exhibitors than Gene Autry. His films, at least initially, had good production values and the narratives followed the predictable formula of rescuing a distressed maiden, but they are set in the historical West, not the contemporary West that Autry inhabits. His songs are also rather overblown compared with Autry's, lacking the intimacy, if not the bonhomie. There is also too great an emphasis on him as the star; in Autry's films a great deal of screen time is given over to the comic antics of Smiley Burnette, and there is always a featured performance by a musical guest star or stars who have made a name for themselves on the radio. Warner Bros. and Foran did not include cameos. They made only two seasons' worth of singing Westerns, twelve in all between 1935 and 1937.

According to the *Motion Picture Herald*'s poll of the top ten Western box-office stars Autry's greatest competition, until the arrival of Roy Rogers, came from Tex Ritter, but the competition did not amount to much. In its first year of polling, 1936, Autry came in at number three and Foran at six. In 1937 Autry had risen to the top of the poll (and would stay there until 1943 when he was deposed by Roy Rogers after Autry had enlisted in the armed forces), Foran had climbed to four and Ritter entered at six. In 1938 Ritter had slipped to nine and Foran to ten.[57] However, Ritter's films were hamstrung by meagre budgets, and while Autry could afford to showcase the talents of, say, Patsy Montana, the best that Ritter can do in *Arizona Days* (1937) is to give a spot to the harmonica talent of Salty Holmes, who plays a 'fox chase' replete with animal noises.

Conclusion

Film historians and critics have systematically ignored or vilified Autry. Robert Warshow in his classic essay on the Western writes: 'William S. Hart or Tom Mix, who in wooden absoluteness of their virtue represented little that an adult could take seriously; and doubtless such figures as Gene Autry or Roy Rogers are no better, though I confess I have seen none of their movies'.[58] Warshow's professed ignorance of the singing cowboy phenomenon at least displays honesty, but it is also an example of the bias against Autry in histories of the genre. Warshow knows that Autry's films are at odds with much that he celebrates; a perceived authenticity and a generic ideal that the singing cowboy evidently does not have a stake in. This is a concept of the Western that is carried over in Fenin and Everson's history of the genre:

> Although Autry's place in Western history is an important one, it is difficult to regard him as a serious Western star: he was a popular singer who had something new to offer to Westerns at a time when they were slipping back into the doldrums. A weak and colourless actor, and only a passable action performer, he could ride well, however, and with the help of Republic's overworked stunt men doubling for him, he won an enormous following overnight.[59]

Jon Tuska takes Autry to task not only for his lack of authenticity and for being an unwarranted digression from the Western ideal, but also because he does not embody a particular notion of masculinity:

> Prior to Autry's arrival on the screen, Western heroes were customarily portrayed as being strong, capable, occasionally austere men, believable frontier types who might actually have undertaken many of the heroic exploits attributed to them by the scenarios. In Autry's case this was not so because, physically and dramatically, it could not be so. So he had to be surrounded by a different kind of aura, if no less magical. He lived, it had to seem, a charmed life whereby, battling against frequently staggering odds, he invariably triumphed.[60]

Autry's particular image of masculinity clearly lies outside the 'ideal' as criticised by Jane Tompkins and here celebrated by Tuska.[61] As for authenticity, the problem appears to lie as much in Autry's propensity to solve problems through singing as within his films' refusal to be tied to critics' prescriptive historical placement of the Western in the latter part of the 19th century. On this latter point even Autry appears forced into a veiled apology. Writing in the foreword to Don Miller's *Hollywood Corral* he notes:

> The fact that most of my stories were set in the 'modern' West, employing cars, trains, airplanes, radio, and even television (long before that medium took hold), did not restrict the plots from including ecological and other problems that are more prevalent today than ever.[62]

Autry's concession that there is a 'problem' with his films' modern setting, and his defence that they might have a relevance to environmental issues of the 90s are not germane. However, it is indicative of how systematically his films have been denigrated for not complying to the Western ideal. Film critics often invite the reader to laugh at the apparent absurdity of Autry's plots and at specific moments isolated from the films. Tuska's work reveals this process as well as any other:

> In *Mexicali Rose*, Noah Beery Sr, playing a Mexican bandit, captures Autry and Burnette. Tied up at the campfire, Autry discovers that Beery has a secret passion. Not women, or liquor, or gambling; it's collecting Gene Autry records. When a member of the gang accidentally kicks over Beery's portable phonograph, on which he is playing Autry's rendition of the title song, smashing the record, before Beery can shoot the offender Gene takes up the song. Beery, thus learning Autry's identity, asks him to sing another song,

which Autry does. It brings tears to Beery's eyes and he resolves to reform and commits himself to helping Autry save an orphanage from the scheming of oil speculators.

The Autry fantasy said, in point of fact, that every human problem, every dislocation, every tragedy, could be dispelled, not with hard riding, not with straight shooting, but with the magic of song.[63]

This scenario is also repeated in Phil Hardy's entry under 'music' in *The BFI Companion to the Western*.[64] Tuska's blind dismissal of Autry's films simply misses the point: song in Autry's films is not a cure-all, it dispels nothing but the blues, and the scene described withholds the narrative context. Looked at from the perspective of Autry's career as a recording and radio star, an alternative view of the film becomes possible. The principal conflict in *Mexicali Rose* is established in the film's opening scenes. Gene Autry is a radio star sponsored by an oil company on a Texas/Mexico border station. His job is to sell stock in the company. Through the agency of a young woman we discover that the company is bogus. When this is brought to Autry's attention his credibility as an honest salesman is threatened. His objective now is to right the wrongs his sponsors have committed by bringing them to book. Autry and his screenwriters are addressing the consumers that listen to his radio shows and buy the products he promotes. Border radio by the late 1930s was notorious for selling spurious commodities. Through establishing an image of honesty, not just in *Mexicali Rose* but in all his films, Autry was confirming his (and radio's) credibility. By placing fraudulent stock at the centre of the narrative the film is addressing wider social and economic issues thrown up by the Depression. The Noah Beery character's 'secret passion' for collecting Autry's records is clearly marked within the film as a comic interlude – the audience is asked to laugh at Beery's character, but the scene also has the purpose of promoting the fact that Autry was not only a radio performer but also a recording star.

A less prejudiced view reveals that Autry's films were not just star vehicles, but also addressed the difficulties his audience confronted in making the socio-economic change from subsistence farming to a culture of consumption, from self-employment to industrial practices and wage dependency, from rural to urban living. Autry's films represent a confrontation, magnified by the Great Depression, with modernity. The films also show how broad the Western genre can be. Autry's films defy both stereotypical gender readings and the dominant conception of the Western as a frontier narrative. Autry's mutifaceted public persona as radio, recording and performing artist means that his films need to be understood as a syncretic operation that draws these activities together and makes them coherent.

Notes

1   See Brooks MacNamara, *Step Right Up: An Illustrated History of the Medicine Show* (Garden City, NY: Doubleday, 1976).
2   Harmonica Frank's 1950s recordings are collected on *The Great Original Recordings of Harmonica Frank* (Puritan Records, 3003, 1974).
3   Glen Ohrlin, *The Hell Bound Train: A Cowboy Songbook* (Urbana and Chicago: University of Illinois Press, 1989), p. xvii.

4 There is some controversy over these points. Alex Gordon, vice-president of Gene Autry's Flying A Pictures Inc., maintains in a letter to the author, 18 October 1995, that Autry never performed in blackface and that he did meet Jimmie Rodgers. This is contradicted by Douglas B. Green, who writes that Autry 'did blackface comedy' in the Fields Brothers Marvellous Medicine Show. See Packy Smith and Ed Hulse (eds), *Don Miller's Hollywood Corral: A Comprehensive B-Western Roundup* (Burbank: Riverwood Press, 1993), p. 336. Either way, Autry was familiar with minstrelsy; its legacy is there in the figure of Eightball in *Tumbling Tumbleweeds* (1935), and can also be seen in Smiley Burnette's blackface performance in *Round-Up Time in Texas* (1937). Nolan Porterfield in the booklet accompanying the Bear Family collection of Jimmie Rodgers's complete recordings writes: 'There is no evidence that Rodgers and Autry ever met.'

5 Owen Wister, *The Virginian: A Horseman of the Plains* (University of Nebraska Press, 1992; reprint of 1929 illustrated edition), p. 184.

6 David R. Roediger, *The Wages of Whiteness: Race and the Making of the American Working Class* (London: Verso, 1991), pp. 117–18.

7 Lawrence Cohen (ed.), *Nothing but the Blues: The Music and the Musicians* (New York: Abbeville Press, 1993), p. 252.

8 Emmett Miller – country music's Robert Johnson – can be heard to startling effect on *The Minstrel Man from Georgia* (Columbia Legacy, 483584 2, 1996). His 1928 recording 'Lovesick Blues' is also on *Okeh Western Swing* (Epic, EPC 22124, 1982), along with tracks by the Light Crust Dough Boys, the Sweet Violet Boys, Bob Wills and His Texas Playboys, and a host of others.

9 Published by Secker and Warburg, London, 1977, revised edition 1985.

10 The complete recorded works of Goebel Reeves are on *Hobo's Lullaby* (Bear Family, BCD 15680 AH, 1994).

11 On the diversity of styles displayed by Southern rural musicians (black and white) prior to attempts to standardise country music, listen to *Roots 'n' Blues: The Retrospective (1925–1950)* Columbia Legacy (C4k 47911, 1992). Also, *Before the Blues: The Early American Black Music Scene*, Volumes 1–3, Yazoo (2015/6/7), which despite its title contains both black and white recordings from the 20s and 30s – hardly 'before the blues', but great music none the less. A variety of non-cowboy yodelling styles, including many of those referred to in my text, can be found on *White Country Blues (1926–1938)* (Columbia Legacy, Col 472886 2, 1994); a truly stunning collection.

12 Quoted in Wayne W. Daniel, *Pickin' on Peachtree: A History of Country Music in Atlanta, Georgia* (Urbana and Chicago: University of Illlinois Press, 1990), p. 30.

13 Sleeve notes to Cliff Carlisle, *Blue Yodeler and Steel Guitar Wizard* (Arhoole, CD 7039, 1996).

14 Quoted in Colin Escott, *Hank Williams: The Biography* (New York: Little, Brown and Co., 1994), p. 15.

15 W. J. Cash, *The Mind of the South* (New York: Vintage Books, reprinted 1991), p. 283.

16 Nolan Porterfield, *Jimmie Rodgers: The Life and Times of America's Blue Yodeler* (Urbana and Chicago: University of Illinois Press, updated edition 1992). The complete recorded works of Jimmie Rodgers are found on *The Singing Breakman* (Bear Family, BCD 15540, 1992).

17 Quoted in P. Kingswood, and S. Costello (eds), *Country: The Music and Musicians* (New York: Abbeville Press, 2nd edn, 1994), p. 335.

18 Peter Guarlnick, *Lost Highways: Journeys and Arrivals of American Musicians* (New York: Harper & Row, 1989), p. 19.

19 Escott, p. 45.

20 *Variety*, 11 December 1934, vol. 116, no. 13, pp. 1, 52.

21 Cash, p. 262.

22 G. Fowler and B. Crawford, *Border Radio* (New York: Limelight Edition, 1990).

23 *Motion Picture Herald*, 22 February 1936, p. 99.

24 For more on the relationship between the major Hollywood studios and radio promotion see Michele Hilmes, 'The Ban That Never Was: Hollywood and the Broadcasting Industry in 1932', *The Velvet Light Trap*, no. 23, Spring 1989, pp. 39–49.

25 Escott, p. 105.

26 In a surviving transcription disc of a Light Crust Dough Boys radio programme (re-issued on Jambalaya, CW 207, France, 1990), the master of ceremonies announces that the Dough Boys are heading to Hollywood to appear in a Gene Autry film; the title isn't mentioned, but their performance can be seen in *Oh, Susanna* (1936).

27 Charles K. Wolfe, *Tennessee Strings: The Story of Country Music in Tennessee* (Knoxville: University of Tennessee Press, 1977), p. 56.

28 Bill C. Malone, *Singing Cowboys and Musical Mountaineers: Southern Culture and the Roots of Country Music* (Georgia: University of Georgia Press, 1993), p. 91.

29 Daniel, pp. 15–44.

30 Republished by University of Nebraska Press, Lincoln and London, 1984, with a fore-word by Guy Logsdon.

31 Guy Logsdon, Mary Rogers and William Jacobson, *Saddle Serenaders* (Salt Lake City: Gibbs & Smith, 1995), p. 9.

32 *The Log of A Cowboy: A Narrative of the Old Trail Days* (New York: Airmont Publishing Company, 1969 [1903]), p. 141:

> Two little niggers upstairs in bed,
> One turned ober to de oder an' said,
> 'How 'bout dat shortnin' bread,
> How 'bout dat shortnin' bread?'

I am grateful to Emily Kelley, who is researching nineteenth-century theatrical Westerns, for drawing my attention to Wister's song-writing talents.

33 Bill C. Malone, *Country Music USA* (Equation, 1985), p. 130.

34 A major survey of Gene Autry recordings are on *Sing, Cowboy, Sing: The Gene Autry Collection* (Rhino, 1997). *Yellow Rose of Texas* (Bear Family BDP 15204) collects RCA Victor recordings between 1929 and 1933; it contains many of Autry's more *risqué* per-formances and clearly shows the debt he owes to Rodgers. Tex Ritter's 1930s recordings are best heard on *Lady Killin' Cowboy*, which collects recordings made before his film work, and *Singing in the Saddle*, a collection of songs he included in his 1930s movies, Bear Family Records (BDP15209 and BDP 15231 respectively, 1986). See Guy Logsden, *The Whorehouse Bells Were Ringing* (Urbana and Chicago: University of Illinois, 1989) for the real low-down on dirty cowboy songs. Collections of pre-1940 recordings of cowboy songs on CD can be found on *Back in the Saddle Again* (New World Records NW314/315-2) and *Western Cowboy Ballads and Songs 1925–1939* (Frémeaux and Associés FA, 034). These double CD sets contain such classics of the genre as Harry McClintock's 'The Old Chisholm Trail', Carl T. Sprague's 'When the Work's All Done this Fall', Patsy Montana's 'I Want to be a Cowboy's Sweetheart', Tex Owens' 'Cattle Call', alongside early recordings by Autry, Sons of the Pioneers, Tex Ritter, Bob Wills, Jimmie Rodgers, and Ken Maynard giving his all on 'The Lone Star Trail' and 'Home on the Range'. However, neither of these sets can compete with *When I Was a Cowboy: Early American Songs of the West, Classic Recordings from the 1920s and 30s*, Volumes 1 and 2, Yazoo (2022 and 2023) 1996, which offer forty-six performances and includes Dick Devall's transcendent unaccompanied rendition of 'Tom Sherman's Barroom'.

35 *Motion Picture Herald*, 5 January 1935, p. 60.

36 P. A. McConnell, Emerson Theatre, Hartford, Ark., small-town and general pat. *Motion Picture Herald*, 13 April 1935.

37 M. S. Porter, Orpheum Theatre, Nelsonville, Ohio, small-town and rural pat. *Motion Picture Herald*, 16 February 1935, p. 72.

38 G. Carey, Strand Theatre, Paris, Ark., family pat. *Motion Picture Herald*, 23 February 1935, p. 80.

39 A. N. Miles, Eminence Theatre, Eminence, Ky., small-town pat. *Motion Picture Herald*, 21 September 1935, p. 53.

40 E. J. McClurg, Grand Theatre, Preston, Idaho, rural and small-town pat. *Motion Picture Herald*, 6 June 1935.

41 Charles T. Nelson, Fay Theatre, Jasper, Fla., small-town and rural pat. *Motion Picture Herald*, 7 September 1935, p. 59.

42 Walter Holifield, Elite Theatre, Greenleaf, Kan., small-town pat.

43 *Motion Picture Herald*, 1 February 1936, p. 55.

44 Mary Hayes Davis, Dixie Crewiston, Fla., small-town pat. *Motion Picture Herald*, 27 April 1935, p. 58.

45 *Motion Picture Herald*, 15 June 1935, p. 59.

46 J. W. Noah, New Liberty and Ideal Theaters, Fort Worth, Texas, general pat.

47 Gene Autry with M. Herskowitz, *Back in the Saddle Again* (New York: Doubleday and Co., 1978), p. 40.

48 Autry, p. 53.

49 Autry, p. 66.

50 Lizzie Francke, *Script Girls: Women Screenwriters in Hollywood* (London: BFI, 1994), pp. 74–5.

51 ' "We Always Tried to Be Good People": Respectability, Crazy Water Crystals, and Hillbilly Music on the Air, 1933–1935', *Journal of American History*, March 1995, vol. 81, no. 4, p. 1613. For a short but informed overview of women in country music see Ruth A. Banes, 'Dixie's Daughters: The Country Music Female', in Melton A. McLaurin and Richard A. Peterson (eds), *You Wrote My Life: Lyrical Themes in Country Music* (Philadelphia: Gordon and Breach, 1992), pp. 81–112.

52 *Motion Picture Herald*, 9 November 1935, p. 2.

53 *Motion Picture Herald*, 19 October 1935, pp. 47–51.

54 *Motion Picture Herald*, 7 December 1935, p. 67.

55 *Motion Picture Herald*, 5 October 1935, pp. 26–7.

56 Twenty-five of Bing Crosby's renditions of cowboy songs can be heard on *I'm An Old Cowhand, 1933–44*, Living Era (CD AJA 5160), 1996.

57 See Packy Smith and Ed Hulse (eds), *Don Miller's Hollywood Corral – A Comprehensive B Western Roundup* (Burbank: Riverwood Press, 1993) for complete listings of box office attractions, pp. 505–16.

58 'The Movie Chronicle: The Westerner', in *The Immediate Experience* (New York: Atheneum Books, 1970), p. 94.

59 George N. Fenin and William K. Everson, *The Western: From Silents to the Seventies* (London: Penguin, 1977), p. 214.

60 Jon Tuska, *The Vanishing Legion: A History of Mascot Pictures, 1927–35* (London: McFarland and Co., 1982), p. 162.

61 Jane Tompkins, *West of Everything: The Inner Life of Westerns* (Oxford: Oxford University Press, 1992).

62 Smith, p. xii.

63 Tuska, p. 165.

64 Edward Buscombe (ed.), *The BFI Companion to the Western* (London: BFI and André Deutsch, 1988), p. 194.

7 'Sixty Million Viewers Can't Be Wrong': The Rise and Fall of the Television Western

William Boddy

In December 1959 an American television executive boasted that 'a network that ran nothing but Westerns from 7 p.m. to midnight would, in time, capture the entire national viewing public'.[1] The casual hyperbole is testimony to the startling popularity of the new 'adult' television Western in late-50s America, the phenomenal success of which challenged many of the traditional commercial practices and critical assumptions of the US television industry. The precipitous rise of the television Western was both witness to and agent of the most thoroughgoing programming and economic changes in the network era of American commercial television. At the same time, the TV Western genre is also remarkable in its nearly total prime-time extinction by the mid-60s; unlike other television genres, from cop show to soap opera to sitcom, which exhibit long and fairly stable cycles of popularity, the TV Western has never recovered more than a faint echo of its commercial power in US prime time.

Because of the way in which the TV Western genre seemed both to precipitate fundamental changes in the modes of television programme production and to dominate discussions of the meaning of commercial television in the wider culture, debates over the enormously popular Western programmes in the late 50s and early 60s became entangled in wider commercial and ideological controversies within and outside the American television industry, including the relations between the Hollywood studios and the TV networks, the role of the television writer and critic, and the TV industry's place in US foreign policy and political life. The genre was also implicated in more general post-war cultural anxieties over violence, domesticity, and masculinity. In this essay, I should like to suggest a number of the historical factors behind the extraordinary rise and fall of the TV Western and discuss some of the meanings it provided for commentators in the wider culture at the time.

After the introduction of the first three so-called 'adult' television Westerns in 1955, the number of TV Westerns in network prime time grew to seven the following season, seventeen in the 1957–8 season and twenty-eight in the 1958–9 season, when they represented 26 per cent of total network prime time. In the 1957–8 season, four of television's five most popular programmes were Westerns, and the following season, despite widespread predictions of saturation, Westerns represented nine of TV's top eleven shows; the 570 hours of TV Westerns in the 1958–9 season were estimated to be the equivalent of 400 Hollywood features a year.[2] However, after cresting at thirty programmes in the 1959–60 TV season, the number of prime-time Westerns quickly declined to ten by the 1962–63 season, never to recover anything approaching their earlier programme hegemony.[3] The reasons behind the striking success and collapse of the genre can be found in historical circumstances both within and outside the television industry.

While the TV Westerns of the late 50s drew upon the historical figures, plot conventions and iconography of nearly a century of the Western genre in pulp literature, film and radio, the prime-time Western had more specific roots in television industry practices. It is important to note that the sudden appearance of the adult Western in network prime time in the mid-50s masks the fact that Western programming, in one form or another, had been a major presence in non-network fringe time for television stations from the beginning of commercial television in the late 1940s. A July 1947 business press article entitled 'Nickelodeon Days of Television' noted that, at a time when there were only twelve stations operating in the entire country and only 1000 sets in Los Angeles, and when networks were 'no more than a gleam in a broadcaster's eye', station operators exploited old Hollywood period films in order to avoid the dated costumes of old but non-period films; the result was a plethora of old B Westerns on local stations.[4] These Western features were syndicated to television on a market-by-market basis at widely varying prices, and CBS executive Frank Stanton told a group of advertising executives in 1948 that his network had no interest in pursuing such *ad hoc* deals.[5] Despite network resistance, the use of old Hollywood Western films was widespread in the early years of television, especially before the completion of the coaxial cable which carried live network programming; not only were Westerns inexpensive for individual station operators to acquire, but film programming required fewer station facilities and personnel than did live production. A recent oral history of television quotes the 'favourite sales pitch' of a syndicated film salesman to small-market station operators in the early 1950s: 'You can't stand in front of the camera and wave for less than we can sell you programming.'[6] Two contemporary observers noted that 'some new stations do 75 percent or more of their programming on film', and Dallas Smythe reported in 1953 that Westerns represented 7 per cent of the total programme output of New York City television stations.[7]

A handful of early entrepreneurs made substantial revenues from the television licensing of backlists of B Western features; most spectacular was the success of actor William Boyd, who had methodically acquired TV rights for the sixty-six low-budget Western features he appeared in between 1936 and 1948. By 1950 his re-edited *Hopalong Cassidy* episodes were appearing on fifty-seven television stations. More significant than the programme's ratings success, however, were the huge amounts of merchandising and ancillary revenues Boyd was able to leverage from the TV show. Indeed, while *Life* magazine in 1950 estimated Boyd's income from programme licence fees at $110,000, it estimated his total personal income for that year at $1,500,000; the TV spin-off revenues included $50,000 associated with the *Hopalong Cassidy* radio programme carried on 500 stations; $60,000 from records, comic books, and a comic strip which appeared in eighty US newspapers; $100,000 from personal appearances and Boyd's interest in a circus, and $125,000 from Paramount Pictures for a movie appearance with Bing Crosby. What the magazine described as Boyd's 'biggest bonanza', however, came from the

5 per cent royalties he collected from seventy-five manufacturers of Hoppy-related merchandise, including 'cowboy clothes, breakfast foods, blankets, towels, bedcovers, lamps, watches, bicycles, candy, soap, and even wallpaper'. The merchandising was promoted through *Hopalong Cassidy* fan clubs with an estimated two million members.[8]

It is clear that television's handling of Western material in the early 50s, both in the reuse of cheap Western features or the production of original programmes for non-network syndication, operated under severe financial and aesthetic constraints. Western feature films, which traditionally exploited the harsh visual contrasts and monumental scale of the Western landscape, probably suffered more than other Hollywood genres in their translation to the small screen. A 1950 *Sponsor* magazine article, 'How to Use TV Films Effectively', advised station managers and sponsors how to edit feature films for television use:

> Far from ruining a picture, expert editing can make it even better for TV. Obviously, twenty-five minutes hacked indiscriminately from any film will leave viewers confused and annoyed. How do you snip out thirty percent of a carefully made product and have it make sense? First eliminate all dark scenes that won't show up on a TV tube, and then all the long shots in which distant objects get lost.[9]

Unable to gain access to lucrative prime-time audiences and licence fees controlled by the networks, producers of early Western syndicated series like *The Cisco Kid, The Gene Autry Show, The Lone Ranger,* and *The Roy Rogers Show* were forced to shoot each thirty-minute episode in a few days on budgets that were modest even by the standards of Hollywood's Poverty Row studios. Cowboy star Gene Autry's Flying A telefilm company produced *Range Riders, Adventures of Champion, Buffalo Bill Jr* and *Annie Oakley*, all for syndication. In a 1952 trade press article, 'Producing a Western', Autry summarised his approach: 'I guess it can all be boiled down to: Keep it simple, keep it moving, keep it close and make it fast.' Autry told his readers that 'we try to use simple, straight-line plots with a minimum of counter-plot'. Regarding visual style, he advised: 'It's also a mistake to waste much film on long shots. . . . A medium shot is better than a long shot and a close shot is better than either.' Likewise, cinematography in the TV Western, according to Autry, should be guided by his experience that 'dead blacks or sharp whites simply do not come over properly on the television screen. Therefore, we keep our photography to the 'gray' or in-between shades, minimising or eliminating completely startling contrasts.'[10] Thus, the scale and dramatic visual contrasts of the feature Western were seldom part of an efficiently produced syndicated TV Western. Autry was similarly pragmatic in his treatment of violence in the TV Western; after noting his concern for his young audience, Autry explained that

> there's another reason for eliminating violence – it's expensive. If the hero shoots and kills the villain, the villain has to get paid extra for falling down, because the fall places him in the category of a stunt man. However, if the hero just wounds the villain, there's no extra pay. And if you kill off too many people in the first part of your story, that means you have to have a larger cast in order to finish the twenty-six minutes. So if we do have to kill somebody, we try to do the killing at the very end and limit it to one or two people at the most.[11]

Summarising the production constraints in the young television film business, radio and television producer-syndicator Frederick Ziv, who launched his company's efforts in television with *The Cisco Kid* in 1950, later recalled: 'In the early days of television, we had to produce these things cheap. There's just no question about it, and cheap is the word. Not inexpensive, but cheap.'[12]

Despite these constraints, the demonstration by *Hopalong Cassidy* of the power of a successful TV Western character to generate substantial merchandising revenues encouraged additional TV Western production. Boyd's merchandising success was replicated in early 1955, when Disney's limited-run series *Davy Crockett* on ABC sparked a seven-month, $300,000,000 merchandising frenzy of 300 licensed products, representing an estimated 10 per cent of total national expenditures on children's merchandise that year.[13] The success of Boyd and Disney in turning a juvenile TV Western hit into a merchandising gold-mine encouraged new entrants into the television Western market, while also provoking widespread social-scientific and popular press commentary on the power of the new television medium to shape young viewers and encourage consumerism.[14] The popular image of the TV Western as merely the lure for product tie-ins for the child market was antithetical to the prevailing high-culture notions of the autonomous artwork and disinterested spectator, and the adult television Western continued to labour under this critical aspersion through the 1950s.

The term 'adult' TV Western has been credited to TV programme executive James Aubrey, who helped develop the genre at ABC before becoming director of the CBS television network from the late 50s to the mid-60s. The adult label reflected an effort by producers and network executives to differentiate the new prime-time Westerns the networks hoped to sell to manufacturers of household products and cigarettes from the previous TV Westerns largely aimed at a juvenile audience in fringe time and sold to child-product advertisers. To this end, industry executives proposed a genealogy of the new adult TV Western rooted in the prestigious Western features *Stagecoach*, *Shane*, and *High Noon*; indeed, CBS premièred its long-running *Gunsmoke* (1955–75, CBS) in 1955 with an extended pre-credit introduction by Western feature film star John Wayne, who described the ensuing programme: 'It's honest; it's adult; it's realistic.'[15] However, at least some industry observers remained sceptical about the actual differences between the juvenile and so-called adult Westerns, and children under the age of sixteen remained an important target for prime-time Westerns, constituting an estimated one-third of the adult Western's audience.[16] This anxiety of influence within a shifting prime-time programme market is one aspect of the unsettled economic conditions in mid-50s American television, often involving changes which placed the new adult Western at the centre of controversy.

Alongside CBS's *Gunsmoke*, two new adult Westerns produced by Warner Bros. were launched by the ABC television network in the 1955–6 season, *The Life and Legend of Wyatt Earp* (1955–61, ABC) and *Cheyenne* (1955–63, ABC). Indeed, ABC became so closely identified with the subsequent proliferation of prime-time Westerns that the association threatened to obscure more fundamental changes in the television industry which encouraged the flourishing of the genre in the late 50s. While there is no doubt that ABC was uniquely situated and inclined to turn to Hollywood-filmed Westerns, the programme form

Gunsmoke: *(left to right) James Arness, Milburn Stone, Amanda Blake, Ken Curtis, (seated) Burt Reynolds.*

was quickly and enthusiastically adopted by the two larger networks jealous of ABC's success.

Although ABC programme director Thomas Moore explained the appeal of the TV Western to *Time* magazine in 1959 with the efficient rationale that 'the Western is just the neatest and quickest type of escapist entertainment, that's all', more considered network calculations guided ABC's interest in the genre.[17] Lacking the large affiliate rosters and advertising revenues of the other two networks, ABC throughout the mid-50s faced the mutually reinforcing handicaps of smaller sponsor time charges, pinched programme budgets, and meagre audience ratings. Furthermore, the sponsor-licensed programme structure inherited from network radio which prevailed in mid-50s television allowed the programme's sponsor to move any potential hit from ABC to one of the stronger networks. Perennial also-ran in the competition for revenues and ratings against the dominant CBS and NBC networks, ABC had not placed a single programme in TV's top ten until *Disneyland* in 1954, a hit substantial enough to make 1955 the network's first profitable year. ABC's strategy to address its competitive problems involved the network licensing of filmed programmes, thereby giving the network greater control of both affiliate clearances and its programme schedule for the first time. In testimony before a congressional subcommittee investigating television violence in 1961, ABC vice-president Thomas Moore argued that the principle of counter-programming had been fundamental to ABC's programme strategy since 1953; against the quiz programmes, live dramas and situation comedies of the other two networks, ABC introduced sixty-minute action adventure programmes produced in Hollywood: 'It was felt then that the public was being deprived of a very significant form of entertainment,' the executive told the senators.[18] The ABC TV Western strategy also targeted a specific demographic audience, designed to appeal to a distinct group of broadcast advertisers. ABC network head Oliver Treyz explained in 1959: 'We're after the post-war families, the big consumers of TV and of the products advertised on it.' The ABC sales promotion slogan was 'get them at the get age'. According to Treyz, the preferred television genre of the young post-war families was the action-adventure series. 'Television is a habit medium,' Treyz asserted, arguing that audiences preferred formulaic series to the one-off prestigious 'spectaculars' of the other networks. Reluctant to bid for high-priced comedians and singers used to anchor live variety programmes out of New York City, ABC made a virtue of the young, frequently unknown performers in its television Westerns: 'If you want to personify ABC, look at the ages of its stars – and the newness of them,' Treyz boasted.[19]

The 1955–6 season which marked the birth of the adult Western also witnessed the decade's greatest turnover in network prime-time programmes, including the beginning of the rapid extinction of live anthology drama, the prestigious programmes associated with American television's 'golden age'.[20] ABC cancelled all its quality live-drama programmes in the 1955–6 season, and the proportion of prime-time programming produced live on all three networks declined from 50 per cent in 1955 to 30 per cent the following year. The number of live drama programmes on all networks declined from fourteen in 1955–6 to seven in 1957–8, and to only one by 1959–60. A 1960 *Variety* article reported that the three networks planned not one regularly scheduled live prime-time programme for the new season.[21]

In place of its live programming, ABC introduced several prime-time Westerns in the next few seasons, and by the 1958–9 season three ABC Westerns were in television's top ten. The 1958–9 season witnessed the first genuine three-way network competition; the year ending in April 1959 saw ABC's overall audience rating rise from 26.6 to 31.2, with CBS at 36.4, less than a full rating point above second-place NBC.[22] ABC's earnings grew 49 per cent between 1958 and 1959, the largest percentage increase of all three networks, and at its spring 1960 affiliates meeting ABC executives claimed first place in ratings in markets served by all three networks. On a national basis, ABC executives claimed, it was the number-two network, first place in twenty of the possible fifty half-hour periods, compared with CBS's twenty-one and NBC's nine.[23]

ABC's rapid rise to full network competition in the late 50s through its barrage of Westerns and other action-adventure programmes provoked both imitation and irritation from leaders of the two dominant networks. Before a hearing of the Federal Communications Commission in 1960, NBC network head Robert Sarnoff blasted ABC as a 'narrow gauge network, . . . watering the stock of broadcasting'; at an NBC affiliates meeting later that year, Sarnoff accused ABC officials of manipulating ratings data and conducting other unethical business practices. However, industry and critical reaction to the Sarnoff attack was marked by a degree of cynicism: *Broadcasting* quoted one advertising executive who dismissed Sarnoff's complaints as 'sour grapes', and another executive who told the magazine, 'none of the networks is clean'.[24] Veteran television critic John Crosby criticised NBC's own wholehearted imitation of ABC's Western strategy, accused NBC of abandoning prestige drama, and wrote that 'NBC is a mess of colossal proportions.'[25] ABC network head Oliver Treyz responded to Sarnoff's criticism by lamenting the decisions of the two 'copycat' networks to imitate ABC's Western and action-adventure formula. 'Unfortunately,' Treyz told an industry group, 'in the wake of ABC's success, the old-line networks started to abandon their established areas of achievement in live drama, variety and comedy shows to attempt to parallel us.'[26] Indeed, after the 1959–60 season, when ABC and NBC each offered eleven prime-time Westerns (CBS offered eight), in each of the following two seasons NBC actually scheduled more Western series than did ABC.[27] Thus, while ABC may have pioneered the genre, by the end of the 1950s all three networks contributed equally to the extraordinary number of TV Westerns in network prime time.

The unanimity of the three networks' endorsement of the TV Western reflected a number of general conditions in the network television industry in the late 50s. The number of TV Westerns on all three networks grew from seven in 1956–7 to seventeen in 1957–8, and to twenty-five in 1958–9. One prominent boost to the growth of the TV Western which had nothing to do with ABC was the spectacular demise of an entire popular prime-time genre, the big-money quiz shows, in the face of public scandal over widespread coaching of contestants. A flood of imitators had followed the wild ratings success of CBS's *The $64,000 Question* (1955–8, CBS), introduced as a summer replacement in 1955, and at the height of their popularity eighteen months later there were twenty-four prime-time quiz programmes, all on CBS and NBC. However, between the tight-lipped CBS cancellation of *Dotto* in August 1958 and the spectacular confessions of celebrity contestant Charles Van Doren before packed congressional hearings in November 1959, both networks jettisoned all their prime-time quiz programmes, whether or not they were specifically tainted with accusation of rigging. With the precipitous end of the prime-time quiz show, Hollywood-produced episodic series, including a flood of TV Westerns on the ABC–Warner Bros. model, quickly filled the empty schedule slots on the two larger networks.[28]

The final factor encouraging the extraordinary number of prime-time Westerns at the end of the 50s relates to wider changes in the economics of network programme production and advertising. In the late 50s, all three networks encouraged a shift from the traditional practice of a television advertiser directly licensing a prime-time programme and acting as its sole sponsor in favour of the practice of network-licensed programmes sold to advertisers on a multiple-sponsorship basis. The networks sought the control over both individual programmes and its overall prime-time schedule that network licensing brought. At the same time, the networks were able to use their market power as oligopolistic buyers of prime-time programming to extract concessions from producers in the form of syndication and merchandising rights and profit shares to prime-time programmes. Such revenues increased exponentially with the growth of the domestic and international syndication markets for off-network reruns in the late 50s and 60s, and conventional wisdom in the TV industry saw action-adventure programming led by TV Westerns as the most lucrative genre in the syndication market.[29] Thus, all three networks had new incentives and new power to fashion their prime-time schedules in order to take advantage of the popularity of the new TV Westerns. A 1960 trade press article, 'The Swing to Network Control', reported that 80 per cent of prime-time shows for the 1960–1 season were network-licensed (the figure was 95 per cent at ABC) and estimated that the networks maintained profit participation in 62 per cent of prime-time shows.[30] In congressional testimony in 1961, network executives revealed the substantial creative control they exercised in the production process of the Hollywood programming. ABC maintained a full-time network employee at Warner Bros. whose duties included reading scripts, attending shoots, and viewing rough cuts; a CBS official described the work of that network's staff member assigned to each filmed series who

> was in constant contact conference with the producer on script development, rewrites and finalizing the shooting script. Occasionally, this CBS executive would make casting recommendations, he would approve or disapprove directors, attend screenings of the 'dailies', frequently ask for retakes on scenes that were unacceptable for one of many reasons – quality, storytelling values, matters of taste, considerations of scenes of violence, et cetera – he would attend all rough-cut screenings and again make recommendations for changes.[31]

The shift to network-licensed film programming sold to advertisers on a piecemeal basis was part of a fundamental shift in the composition and strategies of prime-time advertisers, who moved away from the goals of audience goodwill and corporate image advertising associated with single sponsorship of live prestige drama in favour of hard-sell marketing of small-ticket brand goods aimed at specific demographic segments within the television audience. This so-called 'formula buying' strategy of the mass-market makers of cigarettes, processed foods and household products encouraged the scheduling of continuing-character filmed series, which were believed to offer relative ratings and demographic predictability.

The shift in 1957 by Procter & Gamble, television's largest advertiser, to 'formula buying' with contractual demographic and cost-per-thousand targets encouraged other large TV advertisers to follow suit and increased pressure on networks and programme producers to produce high and consistent ratings. In a

November 1957 *Sponsor* magazine editorial entitled 'Ratings Madness', the trade journal noted that 'on the network level ratings worship has reached peak absurdity', and concluded that 'one day (soon, we hope) broadcast historians will look back on the rating madness of the mid-1950s as one of the oddest chapters in the development of a dynamic medium'.[32] Journalist Herman Land argued in 1958 that the new advertising and programme strategies had resulted in a new market segmentation of prime-time network programming between 'pulp, slick and quality', with the 'pulp' segment largely consisting of TV Westerns. At the same time, Land worried that, despite the high ratings of the new TV Westerns, 'endless repetition of a few basic legends must blur programme distinctions and vitiate the impact of even good shows. ... There is probably such a thing as too much exposure even for the hardiest of sagebrush myths.' Despite Land's warning that 'there are signs that buyers are becoming concerned lest they follow the action road to a dead end', the number of prime-time Westerns sold to sponsors the following season was even greater.[33]

Other observers of the rush of prime-time sponsors to the TV Western in the late 50s expressed specific concerns about the action-adventure genre as an advertising vehicle. The director of a marketing research company in 1958 outlined the appeal for the network advertiser of the TV Western, with its modest and stable time and talent costs, healthy audience ratings and low cancellation rates, and lower costs per thousand when compared with star-based network variety shows. 'When you can "buy" viewers of a Western for two-thirds of what it costs you to get exposure on a big variety show, the prospect appears very tempting,' he admitted. However, the researcher argued that in the case of 'tense' programming such as the TV Western, 'the factor which captures and holds the audience to the exciting programme is the very thing that is responsible for the diminution of advertising effectiveness'. The problem, according to the writer, was that the TV Western succeeded too well in involving the audience, drawing attention from the sponsor's commercial. This was especially the case for what the researcher termed the 'pleasant commercial', although he noted that 'products that emphasise relief from tension may not suffer from being in tense shows'. However, even this sceptic of the TV Western noted that for the large manufacturer of consumer goods, 'ultimately, efficiency becomes the guiding star of the mathematically oriented advertiser, with cost per thousand assuming almost fetish proportion'.[34] Recently deposed NBC network head Pat Weaver, closely associated with the earlier era of live prestige drama, in 1957 blamed formula buying for narrowing programme formats, and denounced the networks' new programming strategies that 'degrade everything to win ratings that count as equals moppets, morons and that fragment of our population that looks at anything'.[35]

The national economic recession of 1958–9 temporarily depressed network advertising expenditures by automobile and consumer-durable manufacturers, who were more likely to pursue corporate-image, 'goodwill' advertising strategies than were the makers of small-ticket consumer goods. Thus, despite the reservations of an assortment of industry observers, the new sponsorship philosophy with its emphasis on programme ratings prevailed, and the emerging model of television advertising encouraged the move to the TV Western. Indeed, Arbitron introduced moment-by-moment ratings from seven cities in the spring of 1958, and the detail, speed and importance of prime-time rating information only increased in the succeeding TV seasons, reinforcing the logic which encouraged action-adventure filmed programmes.[36]

While the general model of network-licensed prime-time Westerns pioneered by ABC was quickly adopted by the other networks, there were significant differences in the ways in which such programmes were produced by film companies in Hollywood. At one extreme was the attempt by Warner Bros. to exploit its access to ABC's prime-time schedule (by 1960 the studio supplied one-third of ABC's prime-time hours) in order to recreate the centralised, producer-unit system of the earlier Hollywood studio era.[37] Warner Bros. maintained tight ownership of all story material and restricted its relatively unknown actors and writers to long-term contracts at union scale, refusing the common industry practice of profit-sharing. Historian Christopher Anderson characterises the studio's television operation as 'the pathology of mass production', and Warner Bros. was relentless in its reuse of story material and its determination not to share its burgeoning television revenues with its star talent and writers. Warner Bros. never seemed to consider the television market in anything but a short-term manner; for example, each episode of weekly hour-long *Warner Bros. Presents*, a 1955–6 ABC series which alternated three story properties, including the successful Western *Cheyenne*, contained so much promotional footage tied to current Warner Bros. theatrical releases that the actual programmes were only forty minutes long, making them impossible to sell in the booming television syndication market. Likewise, when Warner Bros. moved to make its 750-film library of feature films available to the television market in 1956, it sold the entire package outright for a one-time fee of $21,000,000; within two years, the buyer had collected $30,000,000 in TV licensing revenues and resold the package for $35,000,000.[38]

Warner Bros. was likewise short-sighted in its dependence upon a single network customer, ABC, and upon a single genre, action adventure, for its television production; the strategy effectively tied the fortunes of the studio with those of a single network and television genre. More significant in determining the production budgets and aesthetic form of Warner Bros.' Western programmes was the studio's reluctance to embrace the principle of deficit financing, the strategy of investing in production budgets greater than the revenues provided by the programme's network licensing agreement, in anticipation that deficits would be recouped in syndication sales after network release. Warner Bros.' attempts to keep production budgets close to the network's $50,000 weekly licensing fee meant relentless cost-cutting pressures on programme producers, including extensive use of stock footage ('If you see more than two characters, it's stock footage,' was the industry observation quoted by historian Erik Barnouw), tight shooting schedules, and relentless reuse of story material across the growing roster of Warner Bros. Western and contemporary action-adventure programmes.[39] When a writers' strike interrupted the flow of new scripts in 1960, the studio merely shifted existing scripts between its sixty-minute Westerns and its contemporary crime dramas, such as *77 Sunset Strip* (1958–64, ABC) *Hawaiian Eye* (1959–63, ABC), and *Surfside 6* (1960–2, ABC). Warner Bros. revived the centralised producer-unit system of the classical Hollywood era for its TV operations, in place of the package-unit system more common in 50s feature film-making; the studio's below-line personnel worked on all its shows interchangeably and Warner Bros. centralised story editing under a single executive.[40] In the early seasons of Warner Bros.' television operation, writers and directors were hired on a freelance basis at salaries too low to attract established personnel, and TV production head William T. Orr noted at a 1961 congressional hearing that *Cheyenne* directors rarely had an opportunity to even look at rough cuts of episodes they directed, since they were usually too busy shooting subsequent episodes.[41]

The tight budgets, short production schedules and creative constraints of the Warner Bros.' TV Westerns caused significant discontent among its writers and actors, many of whom resented working under long-term, low-wage studio contracts. Warner Bros.' typical long-term, flat-fee contract with its Western stars required that the actors perform in any feature film projects the studio developed, took half the actors' personal appearance fees, and paid Screen Actors Guild minimums on all merchandising and syndication revenues.[42] *Cheyenne* star Clint Walker sat out the 1958–9 season in a contract dispute, though he returned the following season after the studio was able to maintain the series' popularity with a mixture of reruns and episodes featuring a new character and actor.

The single creative bright spot among the Warner Bros. Westerns was *Maverick* (1957–62), the only one of its programmes to win an Emmy Award, although the studio's relations with the programme's star, James Garner, and its producer and chief writer, Roy Huggins, were typically stormy. In *Maverick*'s first season, while noting that he only earned $500 a week for his work on the show, actor James Garner told *Time* magazine that the 'salary doesn't mean a cotton-picking thing to me'.[43] Two years and seventy-eight *Maverick* episodes later, however, Garner joked that his stand-in couldn't afford the pay cut to replace him, and he complained to *TV Guide* about working under the tight-fisted Warner Bros. studio contract: 'Contracts! They're completely one-sided affairs. Then, if you click, they own you – recording dates, publicity, merchandising, everything. . . . By the time you extricate yourself, you're either old and gray or so identified with the part that nobody will cast you in anything else.'[44] The following year Garner announced he would refuse to work on *Maverick*'s 1960–1 season, and sued the studio to get out of his long-term contract; the studio responded by introducing actor Roger Moore as the British cousin of Garner's character, hoping to repeat the studio's earlier successful response to Clint Walker's *Cheyenne* walkout. This time, however, the star's absence caused the series ratings to drop, and despite the studio's subsequent offer of the most lucrative talent contract in the history of Warner Bros. television, Garner refused to sign any contract involving exclusivity or a commitment to a weekly series. At the end of 1960 Garner won the court challenge to his Warner Bros. contract and he left the studio during the 1960–1 season. The same year, Warner Bros. also allowed *Maverick* creator Roy Huggins to leave; he quickly became vice-president in charge of television production at 20th Century-Fox.[45] The refusal of Warner Bros. to offer profit participation to its major actors and producers made it difficult to attract and retain the best talent in the television film industry. More seriously for the company, its decision to limit the studio's output to a single genre and a single network left the firm in weak condition when the fortunes of the TV Western and the ABC network changed in the early 60s.

Most other major television production companies of the late 50s and early 60s used a very different model from the centralised studio structure of Warner Bros. While 20th Century-Fox, United Artists, Metro-Goldwyn-Mayer, Columbia and Paramount all produced TV Westerns during this period, at the height of the genre's popularity in the 1958–9 season fifteen of the twenty-five Westerns were produced by only three firms: Warner Bros., Four Star Entertainment, and Revue Productions.[46] Four Star Entertainment began with a single show, *Four Star Playhouse* (1952–6, CBS), a thirty-minute filmed anthology series hosted by Dick Powell, and grew into a major independent producer with twenty series by 1958, including several Westerns. Four Star offered writers on one of its Western series an opportunity to develop other series; this was the case for Sam Peckinpah, who moved from being a writer on *The Rifleman* (1958–62, ABC) to the creator and producer of *The Westerner* (1960, NBC), and for Aaron Spelling, who moved from writing scripts for *Zane Grey Theater* (1956–62, CBS) to producing *Johnny Ringo* (1958–9, CBS).[47] Four Star's close relationship with talent agency powerhouse William Morris brought a number of major Hollywood actors, writers, and technicians to the Four Star Westerns, very different from the Warner Bros. model of casting unknown actors and less prominent writers and directors. Four Star also granted stars and writer-producers profit participation, unlike the practice of Warner Bros.

Revue Productions, a direct subsidiary of the other major Hollywood talent agency, MCA, began making television series in 1952, and by 1954 it was collecting more revenues from its television film business than from its talent agency; by 1957 its TV production represented 25 per cent of all television programming produced in Hollywood.[48] Revue's most significant Western series was *Wagon Train* (1957–62, NBC; 1962–5, CBS), with an emphasis on loosely linked episodes following a group of Western settlers led by wagon-master Ward Bond and scout Robert Horton. The programme's emphasis upon big-name guest stars was in part designed to provide writers greater flexibility and to relieve production pressures upon the lead actors of the five-day shooting schedules for each season's twenty-six episodes. The series was the most costly of TV Westerns of its era; *Time* estimated its weekly production budget between $90,000 and $120,000 in 1959, and *Newsweek* placed it at $140,000 in 1960.[49] Television historians Harry Castleman and Walter Podrazik argue that the quasi-anthology format and high production budgets of *Wagon Train* made the series 'more of a made-for-TV Western movie than a regular series'.[50] The series also featured the only television work of Western feature director John Ford in 'The Colter Craven Story', an episode aired on 23 November 1960. Like that of Four Star, the production structure of Revue Productions reflected its close ties to the Hollywood talent-agency business, and the company's strategy of big stars and high production values was very successful for *Wagon Train*, which was television's number one or number two rated programme for four seasons between 1958 and 1961. In general, independent producers or studios which embraced deficit financing, profit participation for stars and producers, and the production of series across several TV genres for more than one network, were more likely to survive the inevitable decline of a single prime-time genre like the Western.

The decline of the TV Western on all three networks after the 1959–60 season was swift, though partially obscured by the persistence of one or two sixty-minute

Westerns in television's top ten programmes into the 1970s. However, the extinction of the thirty-minute Western was nearly complete by 1961, and the genre increasingly survived in the form of genetic mutations and hybrids, such as the extremely successful domestic melodrama *Bonanza* (1959–73, NBC) and the extraordinarily long-lived and increasingly domestic-oriented *Gunsmoke*, which lasted twenty seasons until its cancellation in 1975. Other short-lived variations included a Western sitcom, *F Troop* (1965–7, ABC), a spy series *The Wild Wild West* (1965–9, CBS) and several largely unsuccessful series set among contemporary rodeo cowboys, ranchers and lawmen of the American West.

The general ratings slide of prime-time Westerns in the early 60s probably owed a great deal to simple saturation and audience exhaustion with the genre; however, the ways in which the TV Western became a critical shorthand for the wider changes and grievances in network television sometimes made it appear to become a pawn of external forces. After 1958, the Western became the most critically scorned of TV genres; in his 1960 dissertation on TV criticism, Frank Henry Jakes argued that 'the 1957–58 television season ... marked the outbreak of an open feud between representatives of the television industry and many of the critics – a feud that was to continue for many seasons'.[51] Critical discontent centred on the growing homogeneity of network schedules, the disappearance of live anthology drama, and the increased aversion to controversial programme content among advertisers and network operators.[52] Concerning the last complaint, Frank Pierson argued in the *New Republic* in 1959 that 'the adult television Western represents a flight from reality all right, but I suspect it is not the public fleeing so much as it is the creators. Television is fenced in by so many vexations in handling honest drama that its only solution is to make Westerns.'[53] As an example of the routine pressures exerted by network sponsors, the cigarette manufacturer of *The Virginian* (1962–70, NBC) prohibited all smoking by actors in the series rather than allow the depiction of cowboys rolling their own smokes in the era before filter cigarettes.[54]

TV Westerns were typically met with critical hostility or indifference, and were much less likely to be reviewed by the daily TV critics of the quality press than were the live anthology drama programmes they had displaced on network schedules. Recalling the happy match between the work of the television critic and the live anthology drama, influential New York TV critic John Crosby wrote in a 1958 column: 'I remember when there were ten or twelve hour-long drama shows on the air a week, and you could write a little essay, pointing out trends in dramatic themes, styles in acting and all sorts of other reasonably creative efforts.' On the other hand, Crosby admitted in another 1958 essay that 'after the first show, I don't know what to say about a Western or quiz show, and I don't know anybody else who does either'.[55] John W. Evans noted in 1962 that 'it is the Western, more often than even the soap opera or the quiz show, that is held up as the symbol of television's cultural bankruptcy'.[56]

Within the general climate of critical neglect and scorn, the TV Western was also linked to specific charges regarding social violence and the 'problem' of the public image of the United States abroad. The evidence for the anti-violence attack on the television Western included the frankly anecdotal, as in *Time* magazine's 1959 cover story describing 'a man in Pennsylvania, angered when his wife turned off *Have Gun, Will Travel* while he was watching it, ran for his revolver and took a shot at her. (He missed.)'[57] The anti-TV violence debate was largely framed by the alleged influence upon America's youth of dramatic television as cultural myth-maker; as John Crosby wrote in 1961: 'Today the storyteller function has been taken over entirely by television, and for the first time we have the totally irresponsible storyteller, the storyteller whose motive is not the welfare of the child but the profits of Warner Bros.'[58]

Public scrutiny of the effects of television violence, with the TV Western as a major target, reached a peak in an intermittent set of congressional hearings led by Senator Thomas Dodd between 1961 and 1964. Dodd's Juvenile Delinquency Subcommittee subpoenaed and made public hundreds of pages of proprietary production company and network documents concerning dozens of prime-time programmes, and the public testimony from industry officials, social scientists and public officials made frequent headlines in the daily press. While Dodd's investigation failed to produce any proposed legislative or regulatory reforms, the subpoenaed documents and public hearings provide valuable insight into programme decision-making and supplied a prominent platform for an assortment of critics of commercial television and the action-adventure genre. The public testimony included that of James Bennett, director of the US Bureau of Prisons, who reported that TV Westerns were some of the most popular programmes among incarcerated juvenile delinquents. Warner Bros. television head William Orr prefaced his testimony with a list of Warner Bros.' anti-Communist film-making efforts, including *I Was a Communist for the FBI*. Responding to the charge of excessive violence in Warner Bros.' *Cheyenne*, Orr told the subcommittee: 'As a matter of fact, I believe that a certain amount of violence, as it is portrayed on *Cheyenne*, has a good moral effect. The winning of the West was a victory for law and order. Such violence that is shown occurred because law and order were absent.' The subcommittee's chief counsel also led Orr through detailed public questioning that sought to determine which creative personnel were responsible for the specific treatment of a villain smashing another character's hand with a rock in a different *Cheyenne* episode, and the Warner Bros. executive was also interrogated about a third *Cheyenne* episode involving two thieves stranded in the middle of the desert; after one character suggested suicide, the other rejected the idea and was shot by the first. Pressed by the senators about the moral lessons of the scene, Orr responded: 'Well, possibly, the moral lesson could be that you should not take your own life; let somebody else kill you. I do not—'. At this point subcommittee chair Dodd interrupted his witness: 'I do not believe you think it is humorous, and I do not, certainly.'[59]

Despite its occasional absurd moments, the Dodd hearings provide a revealing snapshot of industry practices at the height of the TV Western's popularity; some in the industry also attributed to the hearings ABC's sudden firing of Oliver Treyz, who had directed the network's programming for the previous five years, shortly after the executive's unrepentant testimony before the hostile subcommittee in the spring of 1962. Fittingly, Treyz left ABC to become a vice-president at Warner Bros., though the company's television operations were in a precarious condition by that time. Although the studio had seven series on ABC in the 1961–2 season, only one of them was renewed the following season, and only one of its two new

ABC series lasted the entire 1962–3 season. Treyz arrived at Warner Bros. following a 25 per cent staff cut, and within a year had left the studio.[60]

More generally, although some observers pointed to the Dodd TV violence hearings as a major factor in the near-disappearance of the TV Western, the effects of the congressional hearings were probably marginal in relation to wider shifts in prime-time programming. The adverse publicity from the Dodd hearings was certainly unwelcome to the industry, and there is some evidence to suggest that the networks adjusted their selection of summer reruns and the specific handling of dramatic violence.[61] More importantly, the decline in the number of prime-time Westerns in the early 1960s reflected an earlier shift within the action-adventure genre from Westerns to contemporary crime series, and the fate of the Western was also linked to the more general shift to prime-time medical dramas, animated series, and, most significantly, situation comedies, including a string of popular rural sitcoms at CBS and a series of 'magic sitcoms' such as *My Favorite Martian* (1963–6, CBS), *Bewitched* (1964–72, ABC), *I Dream of Jeannie* (1965–70, NBC).

Beyond the charges concerning the influence of television violence on American youth, the TV Western became entangled in other disputes about American culture and politics, including the genre's role in constructing an image of American culture around the world. Reformist FCC Chair Newton Minow, in his famous 'vast wasteland' speech of 1961, asked his audience of broadcast executives:

> What will the people of other countries think of us when they see our Western badmen and good men punching each other in the jaw in between the shooting? What will the Latin American or African child learn of America from our greatest communications industry? We cannot permit television in its present form to be our voice overseas.[62]

Newton's evocation of the political responsibilities of America's global media firms in winning the hearts and minds of credulous Third World populations suggests the New Frontier inflection of Cold War ideology within which the TV Western was often debated.[63] Not surprisingly, conservative commentators contrarily argued for the usefulness of the same TV Westerns in the task of educating US foreign policy-makers and diplomats. Writing in the *American Mercury* in 1959, Donald Shea Teeple noted the 'silver lining' represented by the recent popularity of the TV Western in a medium the conservative Right still associated with a liberal intelligentsia:

> Many conservatives viewed with alarm the spread of television, recognizing the tremendous capabilities for political indoctrination from Washington. We know who controls the radio and television in America: to put it mildly, they could seldom be characterised as 'Conservative'. For years the American people have been fed a TV diet of sociological messages, 'arty' shows, many effeminate in character.[64]

Addressing the popular prime-time Westerns, Teeple asked his readers: 'Wouldn't it be a good idea for our diplomats and political leaders to watch these shows?' He proceeded to offer some of their geopolitical lessons: 'Would Wyatt Earp stop at the 38th Parallel, Korea, when the rustlers were escaping with his herd? Ridiculous! Would a Marshall Dillon refuse to allow his deputies to use shotguns for their own defense because of the terrible nature of the weapon itself?'[65]

Teeple's analogising of the TV Western sheriff's firearm with America's ultimate geopolitical military weapon was not unique; John D. Weaver evoked the recent Cuban missile crisis in his discussion of the TV Western in 1963:

> The form of the Western, with its clear-cut conflicts between the white hats and the black hats, is so deeply ingrained in the emotional mechanism of the American electorate that when the new lawman stood eyeball-to-eyeball with the Kremlin Kid over a parcel of missiles smuggled into the Cuban territory, the hands of the planet's clock seemed to meet at high noon on a dusty Western street, where Good was prepared to shoot it out with Evil, both armed with thermonuclear six-shooters.[66]

The TV Western's popularity could also be offered by conservative commentators as evidence for the public's nostalgia for a less complex moral universe; as Donald Shea Teeple argued, 'the American public, I think, wants to abandon the gray philosophies of fuzzy minds and return to the days when things were either black or white – right or wrong'.[67] William F. Rickenbacker, in a 1962 *National Review* article entitled '60,000,000 Western Viewers Can't Be Wrong', urged his readers: 'Don't let the intellectuals tell you it's a nasty subculture or an atavistic manifestation of the frontier days. These glorious shows, year in, year out, draw the greatest audience in the country, and that's because people would much rather live on the Old Frontier than the New one.'[68]

As the polemical appropriations of the popularity of the television Western raged in the popular press, social-scientific conventional wisdom of the 50s and 60s viewed the appeal of the TV Western as reactions to the generalised pressures of both the corporate workplace and suburban domesticity in post-war America. An article in the journal *Social Forces* in 1960 entitled 'Sociological Symbolism in the "Adult Western"' suggested the compensatory psychic appeal of the Western landscape: 'To the average city-dweller, confined to a neighborhood of row houses, a stretch of prairie or mountain range extending as far as the eye can see offers a transcending exhilaration.'[69] John Evans argued in a *Television Quarterly* article in 1962 that TV Westerns offer

> an almost perfect antidote to the alienated conditions of life in modern industrial society.... Through his vicarious participation in the powerful and final act of the gunfight, the factory worker or the organization man symbolically shoots down all the individual officials and impersonal forces that restrict, schedule, supervise, direct, frustrate and control his daily existence.[70]

For Evans, however, the appeal of the Western hero was wider than the alienated blue-collar worker; the Westerner 'presents an appealing contrast to the lives of the worker chained to an assembly line, the white-collar worker lost in the vastness of bureaucracy, and the alienated intellectual overwhelmed with his powerlessness to alter what he regards as an inevitable movement of events toward world disaster'.[71]

If the discussion of the meaning of the TV Western's popularity occasionally threatened to become lost in the hyperbole and abstraction typical of mid-century attitudes among American intellectuals towards popular culture generally, there seemed to be a consensus among these commentators that the Western spoke to the more specific pressures of post-war domesticity on the formation of socially sanctioned masculinity. During the first wave of juvenile TV Westerns, *Life* magazine in 1950 quoted anthropologist Margaret Mead on the appeal to post-war mothers of Hopalong Cassidy for their children: 'With fathers away from family life so much in modern times, mothers are afraid the boys will imitate them instead of their fathers, and turn into sissies; they encourage their little boys to copy the current play ideal of masculinity.'[72]

The appeal of the TV Western among adult male viewers was often linked to the psychic costs of defending an embattled masculinity, what critic John Cawelti has characterised as 'the sense of decaying masculine potency which has long afflicted American culture'.[73] Two researchers published in *Southwestern Social Science Quarterly* in 1963 saw the genre's attraction linked to the male viewer's desire to 'escape from the ambiguity of sex roles', a 'thorn in modern man's side', which they associated with increased numbers of women working outside the home, men performing housework, and the rise in egalitarian social activities outside the home.[74] The authors argued that

> modern man is cramped in the number of areas in which he can acceptably show his 'id'. He may participate in various sports in a 'do-it-yourself' fashion, or he may 'spectate' at boxing or other gladiatorial-type games. But the Western gives him the concreteness of an image of the way men were supposed to behave in a 'real' historical past and thus become something more than a mere game. The guns and wagons were in use at a time in the past when 'men were men'.[75]

Not surprisingly, some observers saw an aggressive aspect in the gendered appeal of the TV Western. Writing in *Commonweal* in 1957, John P. Sisk argued that the attraction of the Western hero, a man who refuses to be 'pushed around', was in fact 'a disguised admission that Americans these days let themselves get pushed around too much'; for Sisk, 'the Western Hero expresses for the modern American male his feeling that sex as he knows it, and is overwhelmingly assaulted by it, is a tyranny, and that women will unman him in proportion as her sexual function over-fascinates him'. 'Modern civilization', Sisk continued, 'has made a normal sex life so difficult that one is forced to counter it in fantasy with the idyll of a Man's World.'[76] Even the long-running family melodrama *Bonanza*, anchored in the domestic life of a widower and his three grown sons, seemed to operate via the expulsion of women; as the programme's producer, David Dortort, told *TV Guide* in 1960: 'We do not have any Moms built into our show – or for that matter, any women. We are, as it were, anti-Momism.'[77]

The TV Western's professed anti-Momism provides a link to other, sometimes incongruous, aspects of late 50s, early 60s American culture. 'When viewed from the general alienation perspective . . . ,' John W. Evans argued, 'the appeal of the Western is seen as of a piece with other apparently unrelated social phenomena. The "cool" behavior and the nihilist ideology of the beatnik, for example, may be regarded as just another type of response to feelings of powerlessness and meaninglessness.'[78] Sociologist Martin Nussbaum described the Western hero as 'a drifter; a vanishing symbol of individualism in an age of togetherness and conformity', and John W. Evans explained that 'unlike his contemporary counterpart who may feel tied down to a wife, children, monthly payments, and the daily routine of a job that is required to meet these family obligations, the Western hero is completely unfettered'.[79]

The resonance of the cowboy-hero as the last American individualist, the detached witness of human foibles and dispenser of justice, was clearly evident across the US mass media and survived the decline of the Western genre in the early 1960s. Likewise, the narrative structure of the TV Western, featuring the picaresque adventures of a wandering hero involved with a set of antagonists replenished weekly, was unusually well equipped to satisfy the balance of novelty and continuity demanded by episodic television. This narrative structure, like the Western hero, could be transplanted to other dramatic genres of television without great difficulty, and one can find continuities between the declining TV Westerns and the rise of new alienated, rootless heroes of 60s television series like *Route 66* (1960–4, CBS) and *The Fugitive* (1963–7, ABC). Veteran TV Western producer Roy Huggins later described how he developed *The Fugitive*:

'How can I do a show that has all the elements of a Western but in a modern setting?' . . . A Western hero . . . has no roots. He wanders on the next day . . . And I thought, 'How do you get this kind of utter irresponsibility and freedom in a contemporary setting?' And I decided that the only way you could get it was that it would have to be that the protagonist was wanted by the law – that he had to act that way.[80]

Despite the tendency of contemporaneous critics and social commentators to treat the genre monolithically, it is important to insist upon the formal and ideological diversity of the television Western programmes that appeared in the genre's years of greatest popularity. Indeed, what was seen as the growing narrative and psychological complexity of the TV Western caused at least a few critics to lament what they saw as the degeneration of the genre from its classical simplicity. Writing in *The New Yorker* in January 1958, James Lardner complained of 'the corrupting, and the potentially fatal, influence of the adult Western on the brave old Western-story form', and of Western plots which borrowed 'something from almost every page of a psychoanalyst's casebook'.[81] Another critic complained in 1957 that 'you've got to junk your Zane Grey and haul out your Sigmund Freud if you want to understand what's going on down there in Dodge or Silver Gulch nowadays'.[82] A critic writing in *Look* magazine in the summer of 1958 complained that 'each week, indecisive heroes and troubled villains work out tales laden with enough psychological conflict to last Tennessee Williams a lifetime'.[83] Indeed, in place of the simplified white-hat heroes of the critics' ideal form, the TV Western in the late 50s and early 60s presented a wide variety of cowardly, sardonic, mercenary, and reformist protagonists, from Roy Huggins's *Maverick*, Sam Peckinpah's *The Westerner*, actor Richard Boone's *Have Gun, Will Travel* (1957–63, CBS), Vincent Fennelly's *Wanted – Dead or Alive* (1958–61, CBS), and Rod Serling's *The Loner* (1965–6, CBS).

Finally, while a retrospective look at even a sample of the huge number of classic TV Westerns puts the lie to the conventional generalisations of critics and historians who have seen in the genre merely the expression of a quiescent and conformist 50s, the golden age of the TV Western continues to offer its ideological uses. While the history of the prime-time Western since the mid-60s consists largely of brave press releases linking the putative return of the genre variously to the box-office success of the occasional Western feature film, a resurgence of the appeal of Western-style fashions, or a new popularity of Country and Western music, the television Westerns of the late 50s have never left the syndicated television market.[84] By 1979, there were five ninety-minute TV Western series available in syndication, along with sixty-two hour-long shows, and sixty-eight half-hour shows; some of the individual series consisted of as many as 380 episodes, all offered for use by US stations in fringe time, for foreign syndication, and for sales to advertising-supported cable services. Several commentators in the 80s linked the strength of the syndicated classic TV Western to the conservative ideological climate of the Reagan era, and one critic in 1979 wrote of the appeal of the Western: 'In a disillusioned era, this return to simpler times without tricky moral complications is something for which the American public is hungry.'[85] A *Cue* magazine article from the same year suggests the cultural repositioning of the same Western TV series that had provoked public criticism of their violent content at the time of their original network release. The article quoted 'child psychologist and media expert Dr Don Comack [who] believes that of all the forms of literature adapted to television, the pure Western is the only one that is absolutely safe for children to view without parent supervision'. According to Comack, 'pure Westerns treat the subject of violence in a very healthy manner. . . . Good prevails almost always, and when it does not, the reason is fully explained – or else it wouldn't be an interesting story.'[86]

Indeed, the thousands of hours of TV Westerns from the late 50s and early 60s provided a central weapon of market differentiation for the Christian Broadcasting Network (CBN), an advertising-supported cable network founded by right-wing activist and former presidential candidate Pat Robertson. In 1986, fourteen of the top twenty live-action shows appearing on all advertising-supported cable channels consisted of Western reruns on CBN.[87] The irony of Pat Robertson's current cable network, the Family Channel, using a Sam Peckinpah-scripted *The Rifleman* as a commercial and ideological vehicle for the Christian Right in 1998, only points to the contingent and historically bound meanings and uses for any television text, including what remains one of television's alternatively most popular, disparaged and neglected genres, the TV Western.

I should like to thank Ron Simon at the Museum of Television and Radio in New York and the staffs at the CBS Reference Library and the NBC Records Administration for their research help, and Alison Griffiths and Edward Buscombe for their editorial assistance in the preparation of this essay.

Notes

1 Jack Scott, 'The Adult Gunslingers', *Cosmopolitan*, December 1957, p. 44.
2 John Reddy, 'TV Westerns: The Shots Heard Round the World', *Reader's Digest*, January 1959, p. 136; Donald Howe Kirkley, Jr, 'A Descriptive History of the Network Television Western During the Seasons 1955–56/1962–63' (PhD dissertation, Ohio University, 1967), p. 113.
3 Herman Land, 'After the Western – What?', *Television*, July 1958, p. 54; Kirkley, 'A History of the Network Television Western', p. 5; J. Fred MacDonald, *Who Shot the Sheriff? The Rise and Fall of the Television Western* (New York: Praeger, 1987), p. 56.
4 Philip Gustafson, 'Nickelodeon Days of Television', *Nation's Business*, July 1947, p. 38.

5 Frank Stanton, 'Cost of Today's Programmes', speech to Association of National Advertisers, New York, 26 October 1948, p. 4, Frank Stanton: Speeches/Statements, 1946–49 file, CBS Reference Library, New York.

6 Dalton Danon, former salesman for Motion Pictures for Television, quoted in Jeff Kisseloff, *The Box: An Oral History of Television, 1920–1961* (New York: Viking, 1995), p. 284.

7 William I. Kaufman and Robert S. Colodzin, *Your Career in Television* (New York: Merlin Press, 1950), p. 41; Dallas Smythe, 'Reality as Presented on Television', *Public Opinion Quarterly* 18: 2 (Summer 1954), p. 149.

8 Oliver Jensen, 'Hopalong Hits the Jackpot', *Life*, 12 June 1950, pp. 63–5.

9 'How to Use TV Films Effectively', *Sponsor*, 19 June 1950, p. 33.

10 Gene Autry, 'Producing a Western', *Television*, October 1952, pp. 25–6.

11 Ibid., p. 26.

12 Quoted in Morleen Getz Rouse, 'A History of the F. W. Ziv Radio and Television Syndication Companies, 1930–1960' (PhD dissertation, University of Michigan, 1976), p. 79; for oral history accounts of the production and marketing of film programming for television in the 1950s, see Kisseloff, *The Box*, pp. 270–98.

13 Margaret Jane King, 'The Davy Crockett Craze: A Case Study in Popular Culture' (PhD dissertation, University of Hawaii, 1976), pp. 2, 17.

14 Ibid., p. 17.

15 Christopher Anderson, *Hollywood TV: The Studio System in the Fifties* (Austin: University of Texas Press, 1994), p. 205.

16 Katherine Pedel, 'Can You Tell the Difference?', *TV Guide*, 21–7 September 1957, pp. 20–3; for demographic estimates of the audience for *The Life and Legend of Wyatt Earp*, see Marvin Barrett and Simon Bourgin, 'Just Wild about Westerns', *Newsweek*, 22 July 1957, p. 51; for *Maverick*, see J. P. Shanley, *America*, 3 November 1957, pp. 255–6; for a discussion of the demographics for *Cheyenne*, see US Congress, Senate, Committee on the Judiciary, Subcommittee to Investigate Juvenile Delinquency, *Hearings Part 10 Effects on Young People of Violence and Crime Portrayed on Television*, 87th Cong., 1st and 2d sess., June–July 1961; January, May 1962, p. 1742.

17 'Westerns', *Time*, 30 March 1959, p. 53.

18 US, Congress, *Hearings*, p. 1775.

19 'ABC-TV's Oliver Treyz: Daring Young Man with a Mission', *Printers' Ink*, 20 June 1958, p. 56; 'Strategy for a Programme Battle', *Broadcasting*, 17 August 1959, pp. 28, 30.

20 'TV's Fall Lineup: Fifty-five Changes Already', *Sponsor*, 27 June 1955, p. 29.

21 Martin Mayer, 'ABC: Portrait of a Network', *Show*, September 1961, p. 61; 'Sponsor Scope', *Sponsor*, 27 April 1957, p. 10; Frank Henry Jakes, 'A Study of Standards Imposed by Four Leading Television Critics With Respect to Live Television Drama' (PhD dissertation, Ohio State University, 1960), p. 9; ' "Live" TV: It Went Thataway', *Variety*, 4 May 1960, p. 23.

22 'Aubrey at CBS: A New Era Ahead', *Television*, September 1959, pp. 58–9.

23 'Income and Earnings Reach Record High', *Broadcasting*, 4 April 1960, pp. 76–7; 'Bulls on the Loose at ABC-TV', *Broadcasting*, 11 April 1960, p. 29. NBC officials denied ABC's claim to number-two status, and ABC's network revenues were still about half of the two larger networks at the time; see 'NBC-TV Fall Nighttime Plans', *Broadcasting*, 11 April 1960, p. 30.

24 'Sarnoff Buries the Hatchet – In ABC-TV', *Broadcasting*, 21 November 1960, pp. 89–90; 'Anyone Hurt by Sarnoff Blast?', *Broadcasting*, 28 November 1960, pp. 27–8.

25 'Crosby v. NBC', *Time*, 19 September 1960, p. 61; also see 'Critic in a Rage', *Newsweek*, 19 September 1960, p. 82.

26 'Treyz Attacks Copy-Cat Tactics of CBS and NBC', *Advertising Age*, 17 April 1961, p. 147; also see 'Are CBS-TV and NBC-TV Copycats?', *Broadcasting*, 17 April 1961, p. 46.

27 Kirkley, 'A History of the Network Television Western', p. 5.

28 For a discussion of the quiz show scandals, see William Boddy, 'The Seven Dwarfs and the Money Grubbers: The Television Quiz Show Scandals Revisited', in Pat Mellencamp (ed.), *Logics of Television: Essays in Cultural Criticism* (Bloomington: University of Indiana Press, 1990), pp. 98–116.

29 For discussion of the changes in prime-time programme production and sponsorship,

see William Boddy, *Fifties Television: The Industry and Its Critics* (Champaign-Urbana: University of Illinois Press, 1992), chapters 7, 9.

30 'The Swing to Network Control', *Broadcasting*, 16 May 1960, pp. 92–4; also see 'Are TV Nets Bullying Clients?', *Sponsor*, 4 June 1960, pp. 33–6; Murray Horowitz, 'Webs' Equity in Pix Shows', *Variety*, 19 April 1961, p. 31.

31 US Congress, *Hearings*, testimony of Thomas W. Moore, Vice-President, Programming and Talent, ABC, p. 1777; Oscar Katz, Vice-President, Network Programs, CBS, p. 1843.

32 'Ratings Madness – An Editorial', *Sponsor*, 30 November 1957, pp. 30–1.

33 Land, 'After the Western – What?,' pp. 55–7.

34 Horace S. Schwerin, 'Do Today's Programs Provide the Wrong Commercial Climate?', *Television*, September 1958, pp. 45–7.

35 Thomas E. Weakley, 'Pat Weaver Sounds Off on the Ad Business', *Printer's Ink*, 12 April 1957, p. 28.

36 'Instant Ratings Breakthrough?', *Sponsor*, 21 December 1957, p. 32.

37 Anderson, *Hollywood TV*, p. 257.

38 Ibid., pp. 221–2; see also 'Feature Films Spectacular Impact', *Sponsor*, 15 October 1956, pp. 27–8; Abby Mann, '2500 Films – How Will they Change TV?', *Television*, July 1956, p. 64; Leon Morse, 'TV Film: The Battle for Power', *Television*, May 1959, p. 92; Amy Schnapper, 'The Distribution of Theatrical Feature Films to Television' (PhD dissertation, University of Wisconsin, 1975), pp. 81–99; Michelle Hilmes, *Hollywood and Broadcasting: From Radio to Cable* (Urbana: University of Illinois Press, 1990), pp. 156–67.

39 Erik Barnouw, *The Image Empire: A History of Broadcasting in the United States vol. 3* (New York: Oxford University Press, 1970), p. 63.

40 Anderson, *Hollywood TV*, pp. 177–8.

41 US Congress, *Hearings*, p. 1755.

42 Anderson, *Hollywood TV*, pp. 238–9.

43 'Freewheeling Slick', *Time*, 30 December 1957, p. 37.

44 Dwight Whitney, 'The Cowboy's Lament', *TV Guide*, 21 November 1959, pp. 18–19.

45 Anderson, *Hollywood TV*, pp. 274–8.

46 Kirkley, 'A History of the Network Television Western', p. 113.

47 For Aaron Spelling's recollections of working for Four Star, see Richard Levinson and William Link, *Off Camera: Conversation with the Makers of Prime-Time Television* (New York: New American Library, 1986), pp. 224–35.

48 Anderson, *Hollywood TV*, pp. 262–4.

49 'Westerns', *Time*, 30 March 1959, pp. 58; 'Conquest of the West: Wagon Train,' *Newsweek*, 14 March 1960, p. 60.

50 Harry Castleman and Walter Podrazik, *Harry and Wally's Favorite TV Shows* (New York: Prentice Hall, 1989), p. 537.

51 Jakes, p. 11.

52 Stuart Lewis Long, 'The Development of the Television Network Oligopoly' (PhD dissertation, University of Illinois, 1974; New York: Arno Press, 1979), p. 120; Joseph R. Dominick and Millard C. Pearce, 'Trends in Network Prime-Time Programming, 1953–74', *Journal of Communication*, 26 (Winter 1976): pp. 76–7.

53 Frank Pierson, 'Go Western, Young Man', *New Republic*, 2 March 1959, p. 22.

54 Kay Gardella, 'It's No Smoking, Please, in a Two-fisted Western', *New York Daily News*, 9 August 1962, p. 72; for discussion of sponsor censorship pressures, see 'Sponsors Spell Out Their Do's, Don'ts', *Broadcasting*, 9 October 1961, p. 34; 'Two Views on Sponsor Control', *Broadcasting*, 2 October 1961, p. 24.

55 John Crosby, *Detroit Free Press*, 21 August 1958, p. 33; quoted in Jakes, p. 73; Crosby, *New York Herald-Tribune*, 6 July 1958; quoted in Jakes, p. 72.

56 John W. Evans, 'Modern Man and the Cowboy', *Television Quarterly*, May 1962, p. 31.

57 'Westerns', *Time*, pp. 53.

58 John Crosby, 'Cult of Toughness and Delinquency', *New York Herald Tribune*, 25 June 1961, n.p.

59 US Congress, *Hearings*, pp. 1737, 1748, 1750, 1753, 1761. For a discussion of the Dodd

hearings, see William Boddy, 'Senator Dodd Goes to Hollywood: Investigating Video Violence' in Lynn Spigel and Michael Curtin (eds), *The Revolution That Wasn't: Sixties Television and Social Context* (New York: Routledge, 1996).

60 'Treyz Gets Post at Warner Bros.', *Broadcasting*, 2 April 1962, pp. 74–4; Anderson, *Hollywood TV*, p. 284.

61 'Anti-Violence Binge Begins', *Variety*, 5 July 1961, p. 23.

62 The 'vast wasteland' speech is reprinted in Newton Minow, *Equal Time* (New York: Atheneum, 1964), p. 52.

63 For CBS defences of the export of TV Westerns, see Columbia Broadcasting System, *Annual Report* for year ending 3 January 1959 (New York: Columbia Broadcasting System, 1959), p. 20; Richard K. Doan, 'CBS President Defends Our TV Exports', *New York Tribune*, 4 May 1962, n.p.; for a discussion of the 1960s debates about US programme exports, see William Boddy, 'U.S. Television Abroad: Market Power and National Introspection', in *Quarterly Review of Film and Video* 15:2 (1994): pp. 45–55.

64 Donald Shea Teeple, 'TV Westerns Tell a Story', *American Mercury*, April 1958, p. 115.

65 Ibid., p. 116.

66 John D. Weaver, 'Destry Rides Again, and Again, and Again', *Holiday*, August 1963, pp. 78–9.

67 Teeple, 'TV Westerns Tell a Story', p. 117.

68 William F. Rickenbacker, '60,000,000 Western Viewers Can't Be Wrong', *National Review*, 23 October 1962, p. 325.

69 Martin Nussbaum, 'Sociological Symbolism in the "Adult Western"', *Social Forces*, October 1960, pp. 25–8.

70 Evans, 'Modern Man and the Cowboy', pp. 33, 36.

71 Ibid., p. 37.

72 Jensen, 'Hopalong Hits the Jackpot', p. 65.

73 John G. Cawelti, *The Six-Gun Mystique* (Bowling Green: Bowling Green University Popular Press, 1971), p. 58.

74 Bernice Goldstein and Robert Perrucci, 'The TV Western and the Modern American Spirit', *The Southwestern Social Science Quarterly*, 43: 4 (March 1963): pp. 362–3.

75 Ibid., pp. 362.

76 John P. Sisk, 'The Western Hero', *Commonweal*, 12 July 1957, p. 368.

77 *TV Guide*, 25 June 1960, p. 15, quoted in MacDonald, p. 75.

78 Evans, 'Modern Man and the Cowboy', p. 39.

79 Nussbaum, 'Sociological Symbolism in the "Adult Western"', p. 26; Evans, 'Modern Man and the Cowboy', p. 35.

80 Irv Broughton, *Producers on Producing: The Making of Film and Television* (Jefferson, NC: McFarland & Co., 1986), p. 165.

81 John Lardner, 'The Hybrid West (Continued)', *The New Yorker*, 25 January 1958, p. 64; John Lardner, 'The Hybrid West', *New Yorker*, 18 January 1958, p. 86.

82 John Sharnik, 'Cowpokes on the Couch', *House and Garden*, September 1957, p. 32.

83 George Eells, 'TV Western Craze: How Long Will It Last?', *Look*, 24 June 1958, p. 70.

84 For a sample of such hopeful announcements, see Ben Gross, 'Listen Pardner! Plenty of Horse Operas on Tap', *New York Daily News*, 4 May 1967, p. 77; Kay Gardella, 'Westerns in TV Comeback with "Sara" as First Entry', *New York Daily News*, 9 February 1976, p. 59; 'Interest in Western Garb Raises Speculation about Resurgence of TV Westerns', *Cue*, 7 June 1979, p. 8; Jefferson Graham, 'The Western Rides Back into TV City', *USA Today*, 8 August 1985, p. 10; Morrie Gelman, 'Westerns in Networks' Saddle Again', *Variety*, 2 December 1987, p. 39; Jerry Buck, 'Howdy Pardner Westerns Acomin' Back', *New York Post*, 20 June 1989, p. 82.

85 Douglas Netter, 'Re-birth of the Western', *Cue*, 7 June 1979, pp. 12–13; Brian Donlon, 'Westerns Ride Back into the Prime-time Lineup', *USA Today*, 19 March 1987, p. 30; Gelman, 'Westerns in Networks' Saddle Again', p. 39.

86 'Interest in Western Garb', pp. 11–12.

87 'Saddle Up – The Wild Westerns Ride Again', *New York Daily News*, 13 October 1986, p. 49; 'Interest in Western Garb', p. 8.

8 Finding a New *Heimat* in the Wild West: Karl May and the German Western of the 1960s

Tassilo Schneider

'The Greatest Moment of the West German Film'

Joe Hembus's *Western-Lexikon*, a German encyclopedia of the Western, employs a rating system, reminiscent of hotel and restaurant guides, which assigns the films it lists from zero to three stars, according to their perceived historical relevance to the genre.[1] One and a half decades after its last edition (Hembus died in 1985), the *Western-Lexikon* easily remains one of the most remarkable accomplishments of West German film criticism. It covers 1324 Westerns (presumably every one that was released in Germany theatrically, or broadcast on television since 1945) with reliable filmographic data, comprehensive synopses, and intelligent critical commentary. Hembus's historical perspective, as reflected in his ratings, is generally in line with the perceived wisdom on the genre, with the three-star category comprising the American canon from *The Great Train Robbery* (1903) to *The Shootist* (1976). Yet the *Western-Lexikon* features at least one three-star entry which is likely to be found nowhere else, and certainly not in the company of *Stagecoach* (1939), *Red River* (1947), or *Shane* (1952): *Der Schatz im Silbersee/Treasure of Silver Lake*, a West German film from 1962, based on a novel by Karl May, which was an overwhelming commercial success throughout Europe – so much so that it subsequently generated a whole series of Karl May adaptations (seventeen altogether between 1962 and 1968). *Der Schatz im Silbersee* is celebrated by Hembus as a singular achievement of the post-war German cinema:

> The greatest moment of the West German film in its generally misunderstood, and generally non-existent, quality as showbusiness, the successful synthesis of the most loved subgenre of German popular literature and the internationally most popular film genre, ... *Der Schatz im Silbersee* was the first continental post-war film that did not imitate the American Western but instead adapted it to a specific national heritage, here Karl May's romantic vision of the West (Hembus, p. 520).[2]

If Hembus's assessment of the film's historical significance is somewhat hyperbolic, it is undeniable that *Der Schatz im Silbersee* did indeed represent in several ways a singular achievement for a national cinema that, by the early 60s, was facing economic catastrophe. Thus far unable to arrest the disappearance of their domestic audience in the aftermath of television's initial impact, German films had also more or less completely failed in attempts to be significantly noticed abroad. The Karl May adaptation was a large-scale attempt to recapture a rapidly changing market with a new level of production values: with a budget of DM3.5 million the most expensive West German film to that date, *Der Schatz im Silbersee* depended on audience figures of a magnitude that, by 1962, had become extremely rare; according to Hembus and others, the film's producer, Horst Wendlandt, was considered a lunatic by the rest of the industry, and his production company, Hamburg-based Rialto, financially doomed (Hembus, p. 520; Barthel, p. 164; Kastner, p. 146).[3] The film also marked an unprecedented attempt to compete with Hollywood on generic terrain that was considered the latter's very own. Yet Wendlandt's gamble paid off and, although actual figures are not available, it seems reasonable to assume that *Der Schatz im Silbersee* played a significant part in postponing the demise of the commercial German cinema (it is worth recalling that 1962 was also the year the 'Oberhausen Manifesto' declared the 'old' German cinema dead). It became the most successful German production since the war, was distributed internationally (released in sixty countries), and did extremely well throughout Europe. It (temporarily) elevated the film's director, Harald Reinl, to the status of semi-auteur (*Cahiers du cinéma* advised readers to watch 'at least one Harald Reinl film every year' (Hembus, p. 521)), and its success was ultimately responsible for the avalanche of European (later mostly Italian) Westerns, some of which would eventually capture even the American market. Many 'spaghetti' Westerns were West German co-productions, including the first two films of Sergio Leone's 'Dollar Trilogy' (*Per un pugno di dollari/A Fistful of Dollars*, 1964 and *Per qualche dollaro in più/For a Few Dollars More*, 1965), and Leone himself has stated that it was the success of the German May adaptations that got Cinecittà interested in the genre. Several of the later May films were in turn co-produced by Italian companies (Frayling, p. 115).

But *Der Schatz im Silbersee* proved to be more than just a successful film. Together with sixteen more May adaptations in the wake of its popularity, it generated a pop-cultural phenomenon of wholly unprecedented dimensions in the West German context.[4] For the first time, the soundtrack of a German film was released on record. The film's title theme ('Old Shatterhand Melodie') topped the national singles charts for seventeen weeks, and May soundtracks sold altogether half a million copies (Kastner, p. 146). Soon there were board and card games, hundreds of toys, countless comics, coffee-table and drawing-books, even a cookbook, whole clothes ranges including socks, towels, glasses, shoes and a brand of cigarettes based on film motifs and characters. Since 1978, Karl May's name, as well as the names of his novels' (and the films') most popular characters, have been registered trademarks (Ueding, pp. 666–8).

Karl May (1842–1912) stands out as a unique figure in the German literary and cultural landscape. Enormously popular during the author's lifetime, May's novels have continued to attract a substantial audience ever since – an audience, in fact, substantial enough to keep in business a whole press (the Karl-May-Verlag) exclusively dedicated to the publication of ever new editions of May's *Gesammelte Werke* (Collected Works), currently comprising seventy-four volumes. By the time of May's death, the *Gesammelte Werke* had sold 1.5 million copies. By 1986, total sales of the Karl-May-Verlag alone, not including editions of May's works by other presses (which have proliferated since the original copyright protection expired in 1962), were estimated at 70 million (Ueding, p. 684). If correct, these figures would be significantly in excess of those by the most popular English-language Western novelist, Louis L'Amour, whose worldwide sales are estimated at 50 million (Buscombe, p. 174). In the wake of Rialto's film adaptations, May also became the most frequently translated German-language author; various sources have cited thirty-nine foreign-language editions, although the figure has generally been considered unreliable by German scholars (Schmiedt, *Karl May: Studien*, p. 1).[5]

Far and away the most widely read German-language author, May has traditionally been considered a dime novelist and his books 'trash literature' (*Schundliteratur*). As a result, author and texts have, until relatively recently, fallen outside the parameters of 'serious' literary scholarship. Since the 70s, however, there has been a remarkable surge of academic interest in May (Hans-Jürgen Syberberg's film collage *Karl May* (1974) can be seen as an early outgrowth of that development). A good deal of that interest has exhausted itself in attempts to reconstruct the author's biography, an extraordinarily distorted version of which had been perpetuated by May himself, who claimed that his adventure novels (variously set in the American Southwest, the Orient, and South America) were autobiographical in nature, whereas he had, in fact, never left the European continent until shortly before his death. A more analytical and textually oriented concern with May has long suffered from two major impediments: the inaccessibility of original text versions, and the ideological stigma that derived from Adolf Hitler's reported enthusiasm for May's writings.

Since the original editions of the texts comprising the *Gesammelte Werke* (1892–1912), the Karl-May-Verlag has re-edited virtually all of them and published successively more or less altered versions. The most radical editorial changes in the texts occurred between 1913 and 1939, a function partially of commercial considerations (manifested mostly in the 'modernisation' of language and literary style), but also of an ideological project that strove to streamline May's writings along the lines of a chauvinist, 'healthy' German literary tradition of 'people's authors' (*Volksschriftsteller*). Subsequent (i.e., post-war) commercial editions of the *Gesammelte Werke* have made no attempt to reverse the alterations, the result being that at least some of the novels contain passages that strike the reader as awkward at best, objectionable at worst.[6] The editorial history has presented May scholars with the arduous task of tracking down original manuscripts, although an increasing number of them has become available in reprints since the early 70s.

An extremely prolific author, May wrote 'village tales' (*Dorfgeschichten*), romances, comedies and historical novels, most of which originally appeared as serials in popular periodicals. His lasting popularity has been founded, however, mainly on the roughly two and a half dozen *Reiseerzählungen*, or 'travel tales', especially those (approximately half) among them set in the American West, in which May introduced his most popular characters: Winnetou, the 'last' chief of the Mescalero Apache, and Old Shatterhand, a German immigrant who becomes the Apache's 'blood brother'. Together (and with the help of various other 'supporting' characters, red and white), the two attempt to create understanding and mutual respect between Indians and white settlers, and to prevent white profiteers, ruthless land speculators, oil prospectors and gold-diggers, and railroad magnates from breaking the fragile peace between the races. The characterisations of Winnetou and Shatterhand as the archetypal 'noble savage' and the heroic, righteous (German) arbiter of justice (endowed with nearly superhuman strength) respectively, together with the anti-bourgeois, anti-capitalist, and anti-modernist currents that pervade the novels' universe, has led some critics to argue their fit with German imperialism in general, and Fascist ideology in particular. In the English-language context, Klaus Mann's assessment of May has remained, by and large, the last word on the subject. In an essay published in the United States in 1940, Mann, taking his cue from Hitler's self-avowed admiration for May's Western tales, called the author the 'cowboy mentor of the Führer', going so far as to suspect that May (through Hitler) 'influenced the course of world history' (p. 222).

Over the course of the past two decades, a somewhat more complex picture of the ideological implications of May's writings has emerged. Focusing on the historical context of the novels' production and initial reception, German May scholars have read them largely as collective wish-fulfilments (for author and audience) that provided imaginary resolutions to the violent contradictions experienced by society in turn-of-the-century Imperial Germany – a society simultaneously transformed by the effects of rapid urbanisation, industrialisation and cultural modernisation, and socially and politically immobilised by the constraints of an authoritarian, largely pre-urban, pre-industrial and pre-modern social structure. The response to this ideological crisis that emerges from May's writings is heterogeneous and highly contradictory: the contours of a Utopian counter-world which invariably remains confined within the ideological parameters of Imperial Germany. Thus, the emigrants in the Winnetou and Old Shatterhand tales are seen as fleeing the complexity, anonymity and social constraints of European civilisation and bourgeois society in pursuit of personal liberty and individualist ambition in a literally limitless exotic space, only to rapidly superimpose on that 'new' space the social positions and relations, the values and hierarchies of nineteenth-century Europe. The *Reiseerzählungen* almost obsessively speak an ethical discourse of pacifism, anti-racism, and anti-imperialism, yet their most violent, corrupt and immoral characters are invariably 'Yankees' (or the more gullible, corruptible Indians that have fallen under their influence), while heroes and, more generally, positive protagonists, if they are not Apache, are invariably German. Similarly, May's novels regularly celebrate the cultural achievements of Native American tribes, and bemoan the tragedy of their annihilation by European settlers; the tales' Indian characters are, on average, morally far superior to their 'palefaced' antagonists; yet one of the things Shatterhand admires most about Winnetou is the latter's 'European features', what initially wins his undying respect for the Apache chief is that he is familiar with the poetry of Longfellow, and when Winnetou dies (in *Winnetou III*) it is clearly a source of satisfaction (to Shatterhand, to May, and presumably to the historical reader) that he does so 'as a Christian'.

Recent scholarship has also attempted to place May more precisely within the context of nineteenth-century literary history, stressing the influences of eighteenth-century German historical romances about knights and robber barons

(*Ritterromane* and *Räuberromane*), and nineteenth-century adventure novelists (especially Alexandre Dumas). The most recognisable influence on May's Western novels, however, is clearly James Fenimore Cooper, who is explicitly referred to by Shatterhand in *Winnetou III*. The conservative critique of European civilisation, the idealisation of wild(er)ness, of nature and of American Indians, and the contradictory position of the white protagonist 'between two worlds' in Cooper's 'Leatherstocking' tales is clearly reflected in May (even though Shatterhand does not share Natty Bumppo's radical alienation, eccentricity and irascibility). The binary 'master opposition' which structures Cooper's 'Indian universe' (the hostility between the noble Mohicans and the debased Iroquois) reappears in May as the fundamental antagonism between Apache and Comanche, and the Winnetou–Shatterhand relationship appears as the obvious mirror-image of the friendship between Bumppo and Chingachgook. After Cooper, American Western literature bears little resemblance to May's *Reiseerzählungen*. When American popular literature 'moved westward' in the wake of Owen Wister's *The Virginian* (1902), introducing a new generic protagonist (the cowboy), and organising narrative action around new social and historical concerns, it moved into a narrative universe in which the notions of 'wilderness' and 'civilisation' took on altogether different ideological connotations and which, as a result, had little in common with the world of Cooper and May. In fact, the literature of Zane Grey and Max Brand bears a relation to May's novels that is even more remote than the links between the Hollywood Western and the German *Winnetou* films of the 1960s.[7]

'People Who Appreciate the Western'

While May's writings have, with some delay, succeeded in attracting the attention of literary scholars, their film adaptations – like the whole of (popular) German cinema during the 50s and 60s – have yet to become the subject of critical analysis. In Germany, aside from the entries in Hembus's *Western-Lexikon*, the literature on the May films has thus far been confined, virtually without exception, to fan publications, whose factual relevance is generally limited to information about the films' production history.[8] Occasionally, *Der Schatz im Silbersee* is mentioned in histories of the genre as a precursor to the Italian Westerns of Leone, Sergio Corbucci, Duccio Tessari and others (e.g., Seesslen and Weil, pp. 178–93). Within the context of English-language criticism, writing on the Western has produced some particularly grotesque outgrowths of the peculiar mixture of chauvinism and cultural parochialism that has traditionally informed certain sectors of popular culture studies. In American treatments of the genre, to be sure, it is usually the 'spaghetti Western' that is the object of derision, frequently ridiculed, as Christopher Frayling has documented, as a pitiful expression of 'the revenge of Europe on her bastard children who had succeeded (socially and economically) where Europe had failed' (p. 125). But quite commonly little effort is made to differentiate, and the 'spaghetti Western' is lumped together with the 'sauerkraut Western', and both are derided as impossibly inferior to the American product.

Similarities do, of course, link the Italian and German films. In fact, the most casual glance at *Der Schatz im Silbersee* will reveal its stylistic influence on the 'spaghetti Western'. The film exhibits several characteristics that would reappear (albeit not identically) in the Cinecittà productions of Leone and others, most recognisably a highly self-conscious referencing of American generic conventions. For example, Martin Böttcher's soundtracks to the May films significantly anticipate the operatic, hypertrophic quality that marks the musical scores of the most well-known Italian Westerns, especially Ennio Morricone's scores for Leone.

Like the 'Dollar Trilogy' shortly thereafter, *Der Schatz im Silbersee* visually and acoustically addresses itself to an audience assumed to be very familiar with the conventions of the genre.[9] The production design reinforces the generic 'self-consciousness' suggested by scores that sample and compile musical motifs recognisable as belonging to a particular generic 'universe', but adorn and exaggerate them in a 'baroque' manner. During its first five minutes or so, *Der Schatz im Silbersee* provides a virtual illustrated catalogue of recognisably 'Western' sets, costumes and props: from a colourfully adorned Indian chief and a white settler in trapper gear to arid mountain ranges and wide desert plains (complete with *cardón* cactuses which must have been specifically planted for the set) to a stagecoach and a frontier town. Even the visual design of the film's credit sequence, using playbill typeface and clearly taking its cue from Hollywood models (although it would no longer appear in such a 'generic' form in an American Western at this point in time), contributes to what is clearly a play on recognition values.

Despite the similarities, the ironic or even parodic quality that this generic 'self-consciousness' (or self-reflexivity) takes on in many Italian Westerns is missing from the May adaptations. While the 'spaghetti Western' might be said to 'deconstruct' the genre, the German films may be said to *reconstruct* it. If the Italian films might be said to be interested in 'demythologisation', the May adaptations seem to pursue the opposite objective: to construct, or reconstruct, a viable generic mythology. In fact, one of the striking paradoxes about the success of the German Westerns is that it occurs precisely at a time when the *American* Western appears to be running out of steam, presumably because its rigid, ideologically simplistic and ritualised formal and narrative conventions fail to speak to the cultural sensibilities of contemporary audiences. At the same time during which critics see the Hollywood Western move toward cynicism, self-deprecation and parody, and Cinecittà achieves international success with the genre's violent 'demythologisation', the German films commercially succeed with what appears to be the reincarnation of the most naïve, boyhood version of the 'classical' Western.

A 1965 *Films and Filming* review of *Winnetou I/Winnetou the Warrior* (1963) celebrates the film enthusiastically, precisely for what it perceives to be a return to 'classical' notions of the genre:

It's taken the Germans to really bring back the straight Western, unstunted by low budgets, the emphasis firmly on action and not on psychological overtones. . . . In a less self-conscious and pedantic way, [*Winnetou the Warrior*] has a DeMille-like grandeur about it. . . . [It] has obviously been made by people who appreciate the Western. . . . More than just exciting one, the film revives the legendary West in its magnificent natural setting. . . . There is respect, too, for traditional values: the corpse of an old warrior reverently raised on to the platform, bodies reclaimed during the night lull in a gun battle, the final ride into the sunset. (Eyles, p. 29–30)

Other reviewers comment on the German films' 'appreciation' and 'respect' for the genre, on a love and enthusiasm for it presumably missing in their American and European counterparts. The same year, the *Monthly Film Bulletin* notes about *Old Shatterhand/Apache's Last Battle* (1964) a 'Hawksian enthusiasm' (p. 94) and Robin Bean, in another *Films and Filming* article, favourably compares the May adaptations in general to their Hollywood contemporaries:

> It's ironical, but looking at recent American Westerns, it seems that maybe the Germans just have the edge on them. Whereas the Americans have become a little too slick, humorous, or message-conscious about the West, the Germans have taken the boyhood glamorous image where villains are villains and the good guys are supermen. (p. 51)

Thus it appears that, at least for critics, the appeal of the May Westerns resided in their restoration of the genre's classical mythology, their return to the representation of an ideologically unproblematic and deeply if simplistically moral universe. And the throwing into question of the social and ideological tenets of that universe, which was perceived by the early 1960s to have invaded the American Western, is in fact foreign to the German films – as is the ironic or benevolent treatment of the cynicism and hedonism that characterises the Djangos and 'Men with No Names' who populate the films of Corbucci and Leone. Yet the portrait of the May adaptations painted by these critics is misleading. While the German films have little in common with either 60s Hollywood's irony and 'message-consciousness', or Cinecittà's cynicism and 'demythologisations', they ultimately share just as little with those earlier, 'classical' 'legends' and 'traditions' of the American Western to which they are said to have 'returned'.

Blood Brothers in the Service of Humanity and Peace

A voice-over at the beginning of *Der Schatz im Silbersee* introduces the two protagonists, Old Shatterhand and Winnetou, as 'the white man who came across the great water to find a new home in the Wild West, and to accomplish deeds so heroic that they would bring him eternal fame, and the last chief of the Apache who never hesitates to risk his life in order to see justice done but over whom is already cast the shadow of the tragedy of his race rising one last time in a fight for survival'. The film's narrative depicts how the two help a young settler avenge the killing of his father by white bandits and prevent the latter's theft of an ancient Indian treasure.

Although it is the first film of the series, in terms of narrative chronology *Der Schatz im Silbersee* is preceded by *Winnetou I*, which centres around the first encounter of Shatterhand and Winnetou. As a worker for the Great Western Railroad, Shatterhand has to witness how his boss is corrupted by white bandits who convince him to steal land from the Apache. Initially mistaken by Winnetou as an adversary, Shatterhand eventually succeeds in convincing the Apache of his true allegiances, and the two become 'blood brothers' in a ritual which has them both slash their arms and press the wounds against each other. In *Winnetou II/ Last of the Renegades* (1964), *Old Shatterhand*, and *Winnetou III/ The Desperado Trail* (1965), the two have to contain the damage done by the machinations of oil prospectors, corrupt and racist cavalry officers, and land speculators, respectively, who are bent on igniting new Indian wars for financial gain. Winnetou dies at the end of *Winnetou III*, but subsequently reappears as a protagonist in six more films, all with narratives more or less identical to the pre-established pattern: the peace between Indian tribes and white settlers (and thus the chance of the former's survival) has to be defended against the sabotaging designs of white bandits and profiteers.

The May films' overriding narrative preoccupation with the 'tragedy' of the Indians' 'fight for survival' obviously sets them significantly apart from the overt ideological concerns that have traditionally dominated the American Western. More significantly, however, the diegetic universe is not structured in terms of the dichotomies between 'wilderness' and 'civilisation', or 'desert' and 'garden' that have been employed to account for the ideological oppositions of the Hollywood Western.

The Hollywood Western's use of landscape iconography has been seen as central to the genre's structuring oppositions, with John Cawelti and others asserting that the Western's setting does not only provide a picturesque context for violent and dramatic action.[10] Rather, it is argued, the visual dichotomies of the landscape – open range/enclosed landholding, familiar/hostile (white/Indian) territory, liberating/claustrophobic space, mountains/plains, savage/pastoral land – function themselves as displacements of ideological conflict. The German May adaptations, by contrast, not only lack, despite occasional geographical references to American cities or states, that characteristic 'sense of place' which Edward Buscombe has identified as one of the most salient characteristics of the genre, their settings are also devoid of the cultural and ideological charge that the Hollywood Western arguably derives from visual oppositions such as those enumerated above.

That the May adaptations lack a 'sense of place' is perhaps an inevitability, given the films' European locations. In search for stable weather conditions, cheap labour and a landscape that would at least resemble what a Hollywood-trained audience had come to expect from Western settings, Wendlandt found ideal conditions in Northern Yugoslavia. Yet their superficial similarity to North American landscapes already largely exhausts the narrative significance of the films' settings. As contradiction in a German Western is not one of ideology but always merely one of 'character' – i.e., a conflict of moral disposition rather than one of social organisation – the protagonists' environment remains largely devoid of narrative (and ideological) significance. The space in which narrative action unfolds often appears to be arbitrary. Thus, one of the pivotal episodes in *Der Schatz im Silbersee* takes place at a location called Butler's Farm where the Butler family keeps the second half of the map that describes the path to the ancient Indian treasure which is coveted by a gang of bandits led by 'the colonel'. Yet the Butler residence turns out to have little in common with a farm. There is no trace of cultivated land, of farm animals, or of agricultural equipment in sight. Instead, Butler's Farm strongly resembles a fort, located for no apparent reason in the middle of a vast arid plain. Why the 'farm' is fortified, however, remains just as unclear, as the Butlers are good friends with all the Indian tribes that reside in their vicinity. In fact, it is the Indians (led by Winnetou) who come to the rescue when the Butlers are attacked by the colonel's men – the obstruction of whose endeavour remains the only apparent *raison d'être* of the fortified 'farm'. Like obstacles in a board game, the settings in a German Western appear as an arbitrarily compiled series of tools whose only function is the intermittent delay and acceleration of narrative action.

In a May film, the landscape (of which the Indian, in the Hollywood Western, merely functions as an extension) is never a malignant, subversive force, to be subdued/conquered by the agents of a social order. In fact, what precisely constitutes such a social order (i.e., the 'desert'/'garden' antagonism in the 'classical' Western's ideological universe) is altogether hard to identify. White communities – farms, ranches, towns – play decidedly minor roles, and despite the prominence of Indian tribes and characters, there is little concern for their social organisation or the cultural and ideological structures that govern their existence. In a Winnetou film, protagonists and antagonists more often than not appear to simply 'pop up' somewhere in the landscape, ready to settle the narrative conflicts arising from the general, quasi-natural opposition between the forces of 'the good' and 'the evil' which determine the films' diegetic universe. In *Winnetou I*, a voice-over introduces the young Apache chief as 'the friend and protector of all the helpless and the merciless enemy of the unjust'; in *Winnetou III*, the hero articulates the simple, all-encompassing philosophy that governs his (and Shatterhand's) actions 'in the service of humanity and peace': 'Love everything that is good, and hate everything that is evil!'

Their simple, morally polarised universe also renders the May films resistant to the application of more complex, diachronic approaches to the genre, such as the one introduced in Will Wright's *Sixguns and Society*. Wright's model of analysis, which links the films he discusses to their sociological context based on the Western hero's relative position vis-à-vis the social order, cannot account for a variation of the genre in which the validity of an ideological and moral system is never at stake.[11]

That the landscape in the German Western is presented only as 'garden', never as 'desert', stems from the films' successful elimination of any heterogeneous forces that could throw the system into turmoil – above all, the threat posed by sexual difference. The Hollywood Western has generally been regarded as the most 'male' of all popular genres, given its obvious concerns with cultural notions of masculinity. Nevertheless, women have always played an important role in its system of signification. Female characters might appear subordinate in terms of the Western's overt narrative concerns, yet, from the blonde Eastern schoolteacher to the brunette saloon girl, they have clearly been central to the genre's ideological economy. In fact, the 'wilderness/civilisation' dichotomy so central to the genre's iconography can easily be read as a displacement of gender boundaries, the difficulty of delineating historical notions of masculinity, and the problem posed by sexual difference.

The May adaptations deal with this problem in a different fashion. Women in general, and heterosexual romance in particular, are virtually absent from the German films. Toward the end of *Winnetou I*, there is a hint of a developing romantic involvement between Shatterhand and Winnetou's sister, Nscho-Tschi, yet Nscho-Tschi is killed by bandits before as much as a kiss is exchanged between the two. At the beginning of *Winnetou II*, the young Apache becomes enamoured of Ribanna, daughter of the chief of the Assiniboins, but quickly and readily relinquishes her to a white cavalry officer in the interest of interracial understanding. It is as if the May films strive to protect their male protagonists from the threat of sexuality, and to keep them within the confines of a mythically pure, 'innocent', i.e., pre-/asexual boyhood universe. In fact, critics have suggested that the May novels' suppression of sexuality has been an integral part of their appeal to a largely adolescent male readership, in that it allows for an 'escape' from the problems experienced in the face of the contradiction between sexual desire and bourgeois moral codes (Schmiedt, *Karl May: Studien*, p. 236–7).

Yet May's novels practise a complete suppression of sexuality only at first glance. If never so much as a desiring glance is exchanged between a man and a woman, the novels' *male* characters display a strong affection for each other, with the explicitness of the bond between Shatterhand and Winnetou going far beyond the homoerotic subtext that is arguably at the heart of the Western genre as a whole. In *Winnetou I* the novel, even the hint of a romance between Shatterhand and Nscho-Tschi is missing. In fact, Shatterhand explicitly states that he has no interest whatsoever in his friend's sister. Winnetou, on the other hand, from the moment of his introduction, is described by Shatterhand (the novel is a first-person narrative) in romantic terms. Shatterhand recounts how he 'came to love' (*liebgewonnen*) his 'blood brother'. There are elaborate, admiring descriptions of 'my Winnetou', of the Apache's physical attributes, his hair, facial features, body and posture. (When Nscho-Tschi is introduced later on, Shatterhand's description of her looks hinges specifically on the physical resemblance to her brother.) At one point, Winnetou is described as looking at Shatterhand 'with the look of a woman' (p. 544), hugs and kisses are liberally exchanged between the two upon every encounter, and the sexual implications of the ritual that seals their 'blood brotherhood' (the exchange of body fluids) are hard to overlook.

The film adaptations significantly subdue these homoerotic implications, yet they clearly remain present. In a diegetic universe virtually without women, the physical presence of Winnetou and Shatterhand (played by the Frenchman Pierre Brice and the American ex-Tarzan Lex Barker, who have been referred to as 'the last dream couple of the German film' (Kastner, p. 16)) – both easily among the genre's most well-dressed and well-groomed protagonists – is insistently flaunted.[12] At certain moments in the films, their relationship is explicitly referred to in terms traditionally reserved for the discourse on heterosexual romance, as towards the end of *Winnetou III*, where Shatterhand is reunited with Winnetou after a long separation. His excitement at seeing his Apache friend (the two customarily address each other as 'my brother') is commented upon by one of his companions present at the scene: 'When he sees his "brother" he has no eyes for anybody else any more.' A comparison of the death scenes of Nscho-Tschi and Winnetou, at the end of *Winnetou I* and *Winnetou III* respectively, is instructive in this context. Fatally wounded by a bullet, both die in Shatterhand's arms, but Nscho-Tschi's death scene is far briefer. When the Apache himself lies fatally wounded in the arms of his white 'brother', the image dissolves into a lengthy flash-back montage, musically underscored, that recounts narratively significant episodes in Winnetou's and Shatterhand's relationship, from their first encounter to the sealing of their 'blood brotherhood' to various last-minute

150

rescues of the one by the other, in a sampling of scenes from all three films of the trilogy.

Helmut Schmiedt has described May's literary Western universe as a 'Utopian counter-image', a 'mythical world with its own life rules and norms', unrestrained by 'psychologies and probabilities' (Ueding, pp. 207, 209). In fact, May's Utopia functions on the basis of a radical suppression of the social and 'psychological' forces that would threaten to throw it into turmoil – specifically a suppression of the problems posed by sex, economics and national history. Even though Rialto's adaptations take significant liberties with the narratives of their literary sources (increasingly so as the series goes on), the central ideological parameters of May's 'Utopia' remain largely intact. Just as there is no place for women in this Utopia, any encroachment of economic designs poses a violent threat to it and has to be eliminated. There is never any question whether the ancient Indian treasure in *Der Schatz im Silbersee* or the gold and oil resources invariably coveted by 'Yankee' bandits in many of the succeeding films could benefit their rightful owners. These economic resources have to be destroyed, burnt, exploded, in order to eradicate the threat of ideological contamination they obviously pose to this 'mythical world', whose attraction resides in providing an unlimited, exotic, yet easily controllable space for male/masculine action in the service of 'the good'.

The film adaptations do *not* share with their literary sources the latter's emphasis on their characters' national identity. Most generally, the May Westerns, in their avoidance of domestic characters and settings, appear to signal a general 'move abroad' on the part of the commercial German cinema of the 60s. This 'move abroad' is manifested not only in the films' preference for foreign settings and characters, but also in their reliance on foreign generic sources, for although the May Westerns are based on German texts, as Westerns, books *and* films are heavily indebted to a non-German (American) literary tradition. At the same time, in May's *novels* it is of significant importance that many of their (positive) protagonists (including Shatterhand) are German. (*Winnetou I* devotes several pages to the history of Shatterhand's emigration from Germany.) The films, by contrast, refer only rarely to the precise origin of 'the white man who came across the great water'. Of course, the films' multinational cast, with Brice and Barker in the lead roles, lends additional impact to the obfuscation of national identity and ethnicity. While Barker was certainly known in Germany as an American actor (a fact that was obviously instrumental in his casting, since his appearance imported into the films an additional charge of 'Hollywood stature'), the actor's national identity might have easily been superseded in connotative significance by the fame he derived almost exclusively from his previous role as Tarzan. As the quintessential image of the primitive European 'abroad', condensed into a single figure, Barker's Tarzan image, rather than emphasising the genre's *American* heritage, and the films' *American* settings, arguably contributed further to the overall impression of a universal, a-historical realm of exotic adventures and timeless heroes in a land 'across the great water'.

Freed from the tensions generated by sex, economics and the problems of the nation, what remains in the German Western is a 'Utopia of the adventure,'[13] exotic and exciting, yet simple and uncomplicated – a long-drawn-out prepubescent boyhood fantasy uncomplicated by women and money. But the May

Westerns were the most successful films of the decade in Germany. How was this boyhood fantasy able to speak to an audience of tens of millions not composed entirely of pre-pubescent boys?[14]

Karl May *v.* Edgar Wallace: The Hegemony of the Genre System

The greatest paradox about the phenomenal success of the May Westerns in Germany in the 60s is arguably their simultaneous popularity with that of another genre. Three years before the release of *Der Schatz im Silbersee*, Rialto had launched a series of detective thrillers based on the novels of British pulp-fiction writer Edgar Wallace (1875–1932). The first, *Der Frosch mit der Maske/The Fellowship of the Frog* (1959), did well enough at the box office to generate a quickly accelerating wave of additional Wallace adaptations. In 1959 there were two, 1960 three, 1961 four, and 1963 five films based on Wallace novels released into German theatres within a single year. While the detective films were not box-office blockbusters of the magnitude of the May Westerns, their comparatively minuscule budgets allowed them to turn a sizeable profit none the less.[15] The result was a string of thirty-six Wallace adaptations (thirty-three of which were produced by Rialto, a few in co-production with British and Italian partners) that flooded German theatres during the 1960s and that, by the end of the decade, had sold 72 million tickets and grossed DM140 million in the domestic market alone (Dillmann-Kühn, p. 142; Bliersbach, p. 154). As far as the popular audience was concerned, the German cinema of the 60s belonged almost exclusively to Karl May and Edgar Wallace. At the end of 1963, of the five most successful domestic films of the year, two were May Westerns, the remaining three Wallace thrillers (with the May films also outperforming all Hollywood imports). The following year, the first three and seven out of the first thirteen top-grossing films belonged to one of the two categories.[16]

Together, the success of the May Westerns and Wallace thrillers marked a dramatic overhaul of the landscape of popular cinema in Germany. Within a brief period, the two series of adaptations displaced almost completely another genre, that of the *Heimatfilm* that had dominated German cinema throughout the 50s. Of the roughly 1100 German-language films produced between 1950 and 1960, 300 can be considered *Heimatfilme* (Höfig, p. 94). This translates into more than a quarter of the entire production – by far the greatest share of any genre during the period. During the genre's peak years in the middle of the decade, the share even amounted to more than a third of the industry's yearly output (Höfig, p. 166). Yet, starting in 1957, the commercial success of the genre had declined noticeably, and by the turn of the decade German theatre-owners showed little enthusiasm for *Heimatfilme* because, as they professed, the business had gone elsewhere (Höfig, pp. 135, 138, 142).

As it turned out, the *Heimatfilm*'s popularity had largely relied on an adult family audience (polls showed that the genre was particularly popular with female spectators (Berg-Ganschow, p. 27)). With its Westerns and detective films, Rialto partook in, and benefited from, a general transformation of the market. In the aftermath of the introduction of television, the family audience 'died out', and films relied for their success upon younger, and mostly male, spectators who, as audience surveys showed, preferred more action-oriented genres (Bartosch, pp. 839–40). But the change in the 'hierarchy of genres' can also be read in the light of the political, economic and social transformations West Germany underwent during the immediate post-war decades, and the violent ideological contradictions that resulted from them. While history cannot be simply 'read off' a series of texts, it is arguable that the shifts and transmutations of what Frank Krutnik has called the 'hegemony of the genre system as a whole' (p. 14), the moving in and out of popularity of particular genres, and the displacement of one genre by others at particular points in history, can give access to changes in the terms through which audiences related to and understood the social relations and positions that structured the environment in which they found themselves.

Always concerned with familial conflict, the narratives of the *Heimatfilm* are reminiscent of the Hollywood domestic melodrama of the 50s. *Heimatfilme* typically centre around domestic crises produced by generational conflicts, and they share with their American counterparts both a preoccupation with the crisis of patriarchal authority, and a privileging of female agency and of the point of view of women protagonists. Both narrative characteristics might be interpreted as symptomatic of the social upheaval of West German society in the aftermath of the Third Reich. After 1945, German men and fathers, those who had built, sustained and fought a war for a social and political system now discredited and destroyed, had become problematic figures and, as a result, traditional patriarchal structures proved increasingly unsustainable. The social space where this ideological crisis manifested itself most immediately and most urgently was the family, and virtually all *Heimatfilme*, with their weak, morally ambiguous father-figures, their strong and prominent women, and their troubled sons and daughters, are informed by the structuring oppositions characteristic of the domestic melodrama.

To a certain extent, the thematic preoccupations of the *Heimatfilm* – familial struggle, problems of parental authority/legitimacy, and generational conflict – persist into the detective films of the 60s. Radically distinguishing the former from the latter, however, is a significant realignment of narrative functions and positions along gender and class lines. The strong but wholesome farmer mothers and daughters, who in the *Heimatfilm* had generally occupied central and ideologically stabilising positions, often return in the Wallace films in the guise of sexually aggressive, revengeful and greedy female protagonists, while the *Heimatfilm*'s wealthy but socially conscious landowners reappear as ruthless speculators, power- and money-hungry entrepreneurs, and corrupt officials.

In the light of the 1950s *Heimatfilm*, the Wallace thrillers appear as a monstrous, concerted return of the repressed. Narratively, as well as stylistically, they are reminiscent of the American film noir of the 40s and 50s. Their plots figure all-encompassing criminal conspiracies driven by financial greed, powerful men with dark pasts, and unscrupulous *femmes fatales*, weakly opposed by the often ineffectual agents of the social order (the police, or a private investigator). They assault the spectator with incomprehensibly convoluted narratives, a barrage of 'suspicious' characters which often renders the innocent and the guilty indistinguishable, and an 'escalation' of stylistic means. Indeterminate and claustrophobic spaces, a proliferation of masks and disguises, and an almost exclusive reliance on night-time footage and artificial lighting emphasise a preoccupation with visibility and (mis)recognition. Low-key lighting patterns interact with costumes, make-up, camera angles and movements in creating the films' impression of a threatening environment, out of control and pervaded by dementia, insanity and violence. Crosslights, back- and underlighting distort settings and physiognomies. Oblique angles and rapid pans and zooms generate a pervasive atmosphere of panic and paranoia which is further reinforced by the soundtrack where gun shots and screams become part of the 'music', and shrill brass arrangements battle with electronic sound effects and distorted voices.

Perhaps in the radical reversal of iconographical conventions even more than in its displacement of generational conflict by sexual and class warfare, the supersession of the *Heimatfilm* by what might be called a German film noir can be read, symptomatically, in the light of the social context within which the films were produced and consumed. As West Germany entered the 1960s, the relatively stable social consensus that had marked the immediate post-war decade gave way to an ever more visible deepening of social divisions. With the country's 'economic miracle' (*Wirtschaftswunder*) in full swing, it became increasingly obvious that some social groups were benefiting from the *status quo* decidedly more than others, that a new social and economical élite was fast emerging with claims to a level of status and consumption that would remain beyond reach for the middle and working classes. Other gaps were widening, too: between the constraints of 'traditional' models of social organisation (aggressively promoted by a conservative government, an avalanche of 'family sociologists', and the churches) and the demands of a capitalist economy depending on social mobility and mass consumption; between a parent generation whose carefully reconstructed self-image relied on a sense of economic accomplishment and a selective memory of the past, and their children who were showing decreasing willingness to play along; and within the social, cultural and ideological economy of gender relations. German men and women suffered from contradictory ideological pressures: attempts to remove German women from prominent positions in the public sphere in general, and from the workplace in particular, which they had entered during and after the war; the demands of a capitalist consumer economy requiring cheap labour and solvent buyers; and a 'sexual revolution' that transported the image of Woman from private, domestic space into the public (commercial) one, in a move of simultaneous 'liberation' and instrumentalisation.

While the detective thrillers adapted from Wallace speak of these contradictions in their obsessive figuration of paranoid anxiety, and of the looming threat of social chaos, the May Westerns might be said to be symptomatic of the same ideological crisis, albeit in different ways. Aside from their preference for foreign settings, and their heavy reliance on male-centred plots, the two genres share what might be described as a general move from the 'internalised' (emotional) energy of the 50s *Heimatfilm* to narratives relying on 'external' (physical) action and movement. Yet recognisable similarities end here, as the German Western appears to represent rather the opposite of every thematic and formal characteristic that marks the Wallace adaptations. If the latter's guilt and revenge narratives are obsessed with the past, the former is only interested in the future. Narrative and characters in a May film have no prehistory. The past never impinges on the present, and is completely irrelevant to the future. Incessant, goal-oriented movement is of prime importance, and what critics have called the 'futuristic orientation of the narrative' in May's novels, in which narrative action unfolds in the form of an endless sequence of plan and realisation, is equally central to the films (Ueding, pp. 156–7).

The German detective films are narratives of epistemological confusion, of disempowerment (of the detective and of the spectator). By contrast, May's world is epistemologically straightforward, 'like that of the fairy tale, firmly dualistic ... separated into good and bad people, noble and sinister characters' (Klotz, p. 85). The moral, social and political allegiances of characters are instantly recognisable; there is never any 'middle ground' that can be taken between choices or alternatives; once introduced and ideologically demarcated, characters are not allowed to 'develop' or 'switch sides'. Where the detective films appeared to present violent but helpless expressions of paranoia, the German Western offers a neatly organised narrative and social Utopia where everything is out in the open, plain to see, and under control.

German critic Lothar Hack has attempted to conceive of the German crime and adventure films of the 1960s as two sides of the same coin, in an intriguing analogy:

> It is as if an observer is standing in a well, halfway between top and bottom: if he looks up, the contours against the sky are so sharp that everything appears to him in friendly, comforting clarity; if he looks down, he can hardly discern anything, and he gets the impression of a hopeless and terrifying chaos. What both perspectives have in common, however, is the faulty exposure (*Belichtung*). Because of the distorting light, a recognition of things at the top is as impossible as the recognition of what is at the bottom of the well. A rational attitude, which would require to approach the subject in its autonomy and multi-dimensionality, is present neither in the adventure film nor in the crime film. For rationalisation, even for simple thought processes there is no place in either type of film. (p. 351)

For Hack (who does not specifically mention the Wallace and May adaptations), the 'sociological content' of both the crime and adventure films represents a 'rigorous escape from reality' and an 'expression of a helpless swinging back and forth between fears and illusions, between insecurity toward everything and everybody on the one hand, and an obsessive clinging to everything that possesses the aura of unambiguity on the other' (p. 360).

The concept of 'escapism' can only partially address the significance and commercial success of the films in question (science-fiction films would have just as 'vigorously escaped' reality, yet there are virtually none in the German cinema of the 1960s). Yet Hack's analogy also implies a concern with the position of the spectator. The 'empowerment' of the (male) protagonist with which the May Western appears to 'answer' the noirish paranoia of the detective films is arguably accompanied by that of the audience. Whereas the Wallace films assault the spectator with violent aesthetic (and thematic) transgressions, subject him/her to an incessant barrage of shock effects, deceptions and surprises, and relegate him/her to narrative incompetence, the May Westerns offer a position of supreme control and confidence. Characters and narrative developments in a May film are reliable in their one-dimensionality and repetitiousness. The outcome of a narrative conflict is never in doubt. The spectator is presented with elaborate but unambiguous tableaux in which everything is open to his/her view, and where the main satisfaction offered is the one gained from having one's expectations confirmed, from finding out what one already knows, but wants to know again. The formal and stylistic strategies employed in the films, in a radical departure from the aesthetics of the Wallace adaptations, arguably support precisely such a 're-positioning' of the audience: 'epic' voice-over narration, omniscient point of view, wide-screen aspect ratio (*Old Shatterhand* was shot in 70mm, all other May adaptations used the CinemaScope format), and a reliance on long takes, slow pans and tracking shots, and static long shots (especially in panoramic landscape vistas).

Steve Neale has stressed the role of genre as a central regulatory system, operative in narrative cinema, through which 'the spectator . . . is maintained as subject in an economy of narration through the articulation of desire' (p. 49). Thus, individual genres differ not merely by means of their articulation of what Neale calls 'particular combinations of particular types or categories of discourse', but also in the ways in which they position the spectator (Neale, p. 20). By bringing into play 'specific variations of the interplay of codes, discursive structures and drives', genres are able to 'regulat[e] desire across a series of textual instances' (Neale, pp. 48, 55). But while individual genres employ different discursive strategies, which allow them to simultaneously speak to particular spectatorial concerns and interests, and reroute these concerns and interests along the signifying, but also ideological economy of the genre, each individual genre is in turn part of what we have previously called the 'hegemony of the genre system as a whole'. As Neale points out, like authorship, genre provides 'instances of repetition and difference' which function 'to produce regularised variety' (p. 48). Neale's emphasis here is on 'regularised', and the 'variety' produced by genre (as by authorship) is, in fact, necessarily limited (and contained). Yet it is precisely this variety which enables genre films to speak not only to different spectatorial (and ideological) concerns, but to the same concerns (and commercially exploit them) in different and multiple ways.

The simultaneous popularity of two and only two distinct genres in the German cinema of the 60s points to the mechanics of the system. *Der Schatz im Silbersee* was neither the first German Western, nor the first time May's novels were adapted to the screen. As early as the 20s, a Munich-based company under the name of Wildwest-Film & Co. had released films with titles like *Die Rache im Goldtal* (*Revenge in Gold Valley*), *Die Eisenbahnwüste* (*The Railroad Desert*), and *Der Todescowboy* (*Cowboy of Death*), all 1920. Shot on location on the shores of the Isar River, they came to be called 'Isar Westerns' (none of the films is known to have survived). Several German productions of the 1930s had also used Western settings for adventure narratives, as in *Der Kaiser von Kalifornien/The Emperor of California* (1936), *Sergeant Berry* (1938), and *Wasser für Canitoga/ Water for Canitoga* (1939). At the same time, the popularity of May's writings had already led to film adaptations (although before the 60s exclusively of the Orient novels) during the Silent period (six films based on May sources are on record between 1920 and 1959). It is the fact that none of these earlier adaptations had been significantly successful, which led to the notion that May was 'unadaptable' – and that Wendlandt's investment in 1962 was suicidal.

Yet the May films' sudden spectacular success in the 60s had quite possibly less to do with an individual producer's business acumen, or, for that matter, a particular director's creative ingenuity, than with the more general dynamics of genre cinema. The German Western of the 60s was obviously able to address successfully a large audience which it must have shared, at least in large part, with the German detective film. Like the latter, it appears to have provided more than a mere, undefined 'escape from reality'. By inviting its spectator to 'find a new home', like Old Shatterhand, 'in the Wild West', it offered, vis-à-vis the detective films, what might be called an alternative solution to the social and ideological concerns from which it allowed its audience to 'escape'. *Unlike* the Wallace adaptations, the German Western offered a 'new home' that was neat and clean; a home uncomplicated by personal and social positions and relations; a home unspoiled by sexual and economic threats; a home, above all, that had no past, but was all present comfort and future promise. *Like* the Wallace films, the German Western was not merely a cultural phenomenon overdetermined by textual, generic and social history (literary and cinematic genre histories in general, May's writings and the Hollywood Western in particular, political, economical and social conditions in post-war Germany, etc.), but ultimately a particular articulation – albeit the last: by the early 70s a German popular cinema had virtually ceased to exist – of a general economy of genre(s) which functions simultaneously to provide imaginary resolutions to ideological contradictions, and to exploit them commercially.

References

Barthel, Manfred, *So war es wirklich: Der deutsche Nachkriegsfilm* (Munich: Herbig, 1986).

Bartosch, Georg, 'Der Filmbesuch in der Bundesrepublik', *Film-Echo*, 22 July 1961, pp. 839–40.

Bean, Robin, 'Way out West in Yugoslavia', *Films and Filming*, September 1965, pp. 49–51.

Berg-Ganschow, Uta, 'Der Widerspenspenstigen Zähmung', *Frauen und Film* 35 (1983), pp. 24–8.

Bliersbach, Gerhard, *So grün war die Heide. . .: Der deutsche Nachkriegsfilm in neuer Sicht* (Weinheim: Beltz, 1985).

Buscombe, Edward (ed.), *The BFI Companion to the Western* (London: André Deutsch/BFI: 1988).

Cawelti, John G., *The Six-Gun Mystique*, 2nd edn (Bowling Green, Ohio: Bowling Green State University Popular Press, 1985).

Dillmann-Kühn, Claudia, *Artur Brauner und die CCC: Filmgeschäft, Produktionsalltag, Studiogeschichte 1946–1990* (Frankfurt/Main: Deutsches Filmmuseum, 1990).

Eyles, Allen, 'Winnetou the Warrior', *Films and Filming*, April 1965, pp. 29–30.

Feilitzsch, Heribert Frhr. v., 'Karl May: The "Wild West" as Seen in Germany', *Journal of Popular Culture* 27:3 (1993), pp. 173–89.

Frayling, Christopher, *Spaghetti Westerns: Cowboys and Europeans from Karl May to Sergio Leone* (London: Routledge, 1981).

Hack, Lothar, 'Soziologische Bemerkungen zum deutschen Gegenwartsfilm' in Wilfried Bredow and Rolf Zurek Bredow (eds), *Film und Gesellschaft in Deutschland* (Hamburg: Hoffmann und Campe, 1975), pp. 335–71.

Hembus, Joe, *Western Lexikon: 1324 Filme von 1894–1978* (Munich: Heyne, 1978).

Höfig, Willi, *Der deutsche Heimatfilm 1947–1960* (Stuttgart: Enke, 1973).

Kastner, Jörg, *Das große Karl May Buch: Sein Leben, seine Bücher, die Filme* (Bergisch Gladbach: Bastei-Lübbe, 1992).

Kitses, Jim, *Horizons West* (London: Secker and Warburg, 1969).

Klotz, Volker, 'Durch die Wüste und so weiter', in Schmiedt, *Karl May*, pp. 75–100.

Krutnik, Frank, *In a Lonely Street: Film Noir, Genre, Masculinity* (New York: Routledge, 1991).

McArthur, Colin, 'The Roots of the Western', *Cinema* (UK) 4 (1969), pp. 11–13.

Mann, Klaus, 'Cowboy Mentor of the Führer', *The Living Age* 359 (1940), pp. 217–22.

May, Karl, *Winnetou I–III*, 3 vols (Freiburg: Fehsenfeld, n.d. [1893]).

Neale, Stephen, *Genre* (London: British Film Institute, 1980).

'Old Shatterhand/Apache's Last Battle', *Monthly Film Bulletin*, June 1965, p. 94.

Pauer, Florian, *Die Edgar-Wallace-Filme* (Munich: Goldmann, 1982).

Schmiedt, Helmut, *Karl May: Studien zu Leben, Werk und Wirkung eines Erfolgsschriftstellers* (Königstein/Taunus: Hain, 1979).

— (ed.), *Karl May* (Frankfurt/Main: Suhrkamp, 1983).

Seesslen, Georg and Claudius Weil, *Western-Kino: Geschichte und Mythologie des Western-Films* (Reinbek/Hamburg: Rowohlt, 1979).

Ueding, Gerd (ed.), *Karl-May-Handbuch* (Stuttgart: Kröner, 1987).

Unucka, Christian (ed.), *Karl May im Film* (Hebertshausen: Vereinigte Verlagsgesellschaften Franke, 1980, 1991).

Wright, Will, *Sixguns and Society: A Structural Study of the Western* (Berkeley: University of California Press, 1975).

Notes

1 Although Hembus's editorial notes do not account for it, one single entry is actually awarded four stars: *The Searchers* (1956).

2 All translations from German-language sources are by the author.

3 Strictly speaking, *Der Schatz im Silbersee* was a West German–French–Yugoslavian co-production. Yet Rialto mustered the lion's share of the capital and, in addition to Wendlandt, virtually the entire principal staff of the film was German, including its director, cinematographer, screenwriter, composer, editor, and most of the principal cast. Rialto's French and Yugoslavian junior partners were SNC (Paris) and Yadran Film (Zagreb), respectively.

4 Of the 17 May adaptations released between 1962 and 1968, eleven are Westerns. Of the Westerns, all but two are Rialto productions. Wendlandt's main competitor (virtually the only one in the German cinema of the 1960s), Artur Brauner's Berlin-based CCC studios, attempted to compete with Rialto on the same terrain yet, after *Old Shatterhand/ Apache's Last Battle* (1964), had to content itself with adapting May's Orient and South America novels because Wendlandt had secured exclusive rights to the Westerns.

5 See also Ueding, pp. 646–50. In English-speaking countries, May has by and large remained unknown. A first attempt to publish (abridged) translations of the *Gesammelte Werke* was started by Seabury Press in 1977, but did not continue beyond the first seven volumes.

6 See Ueding pp. 138–42, where Jürgen Wehnert cites as an example several anti-Semitic passages in *Der Fremde aus Indien* (The Stranger from India) which became part of the *Gesammelte Werke* in a 1939 edition.

7 For helpful surveys of twentieth-century reception and recent literary scholarship on May, see the anthologies by Ueding and Schmiedt. For a recent English-language introduction to May's novels, see Feilitzsch.

8 See Kastner, but also Unucka.

9 Of course, like all the other May adaptations, *Der Schatz im Silbersee* could assume its audience to be familiar not only with the generic tradition to which it alludes, but, even more specifically, with characters and story motifs, since the novel from which it was

adapted was widely read – a fact to which the film's introductory voice-over is obviously referring when it introduces the protagonists: 'Now we *finally* meet them face to face: the *already almost legendary* blood brothers Winnetou and Old Shatterhand.'

10 For similar approaches, see Kitses and McArthur.

11 Frayling has demonstrated that Wright's methodology is also ill equipped to account for the Italian Western (pp. 27–9).

12 It is worth noting that the film adaptations are at pains to avoid the violence and brutality that sometimes characterises even the actions of the positive protagonists in May's novels, thus eliminating the sadist/masochist thrust that has often been regarded as muting the sexual implications of the male body on display in the American Western.

13 The term 'Utopia of the adventure' is employed by Hermann Wiegemann in an analysis of May's oriental adventure novels. See Ueding, p. 205.

14 The films' 'FSK 12' rating actually made them inaccessible to anyone under the age of twelve.

15 The films' budgets averaged DM1.4 million. Rarely more than ten weeks elapsed between the first day of any film's principal photography and its theatrical release. See Pauer, p. 20.

16 See *Film-Echo/Filmwoche*, 13 December 1964, p. 21, and 31 December 1965, p. 23, respectively.

9 John Ford and Monument Valley
Jean-Louis Leutrat and Suzanne Liandrat-Guigues

'Touch me: all these voices are alive in my musical stone' (Victor Segalen, 'Pierre musicale', *Stèles*).

John Ford chose Monument Valley as the location for seven of his sound Westerns: *Stagecoach* in 1939, *My Darling Clementine* in 1946, *Fort Apache* in 1948, *She Wore a Yellow Ribbon* in 1949, *The Searchers* in 1956, *Sergeant Rutledge* in 1960 and *Cheyenne Autumn* in 1964. In that series, only *She Wore a Yellow Ribbon* was shot entirely in Monument Valley. Nevertheless, all the others contain long sequences which unfold within the Valley's famous scenery. The audience can recognise shapes in the landscape which reappear from film to film. That Ford should choose to use the same locations time and time again has several implications which are all related to the notion of extended rhetoric in its widest sense.

If there is no impression of monotony and repetition, it is because Ford is a masterly director who knows how to use all the resources his practised eye and consummate craftsmanship place at his disposal. To present different fictions within a single setting means either that the setting is being given a strong symbolic value or that it is being granted an intensive function. Firstly, there may be a decorative intention (shapes as decorations), secondly, the locations in themselves might create an association between an image and an idea, and thirdly, these locations might occasionally trigger off or emphasise emotional mechanisms. Finally, the repeated use of a single space will create a place in the memory both for Ford to use personally and for everyone who goes to see his films.

Monument Valley is at the geographical centre of the Colorado plateau, straddling the border between two states, Utah to the north and Arizona to the south. Its rocks have been eroded into fantastic shapes. It is a landscape made up of impressive mesas, aiguilles or jagged peaks, massive buttes, rocks sculpted by the passage of time, sand, sparse vegetation, the occasional water-hole or stream, and where the dominant colours are orange and red. In Ford's seven films, the Valley appears in the ways listed below. Four of the settings are in the north, and appear in virtually all the films. The others are in the south, and appear less often.

1. A very large area to the north-west containing the rock formations near Butte Wash, Rock Door Mesa, the land between Rock Door Mesa and Mitchell Butte (this is where Ford locates Tombstone in *My Darling Clementine*, and where a certain number of chase sequences in *Fort Apache* and *She Wore a Yellow Ribbon* occur; it is also where the patrol escorting the two women in *She Wore a Yellow*

Monument Valley in Once Upon a Time in the West.

Ribbon strays before reaching Fort Starke), and stretching westward as far as the river which is crossed by the characters in *She Wore a Yellow Ribbon, The Searchers* and *Sergeant Rutledge*.

2. The north-eastern mesas and buttes (Eagle Mesa, Setting Hen, Saddleback, King-on-his-Throne, Stagecoach, Bear and Rabbit, Castle Rock and Big Chief) generally appear entirely or partially as a frieze on the horizon.

3. Sentinel Mesa and the three buttes West Mitten, East Mitten and Merrick Butte make up the most famous landscape, which appears in *Stagecoach*.

4. Mitchell Mesa, flanked by Mitchell Butte and Gray Whiskers, appears notably at the beginning of *The Searchers*.

5. The buttes surrounding North Window (Elephant Butte, Cly Butte and Camel Butte, together with The Thumb) make up the space where the cow massacred by the Comanches is discovered at the beginning of *The Searchers*.

6. The panoramic shot taken from what has become known as John Ford's Point and which shows East Mitten, Merrick, West Mitten, a part of Sentinel Mesa with the outlines of Castle Rock and Big Chief in the background, and the foothills of Elephant Butte and the rocky plateau overlooking the San Juan River in the foreground, is used twice to show characters on the look-out, in *The Searchers* (at the end, when Ethan looks down on the Indian encampment) and in *Cheyenne Autumn*.

7. The group comprising Three Sisters which stands out from the extreme edge of Mitchell Mesa is used above all in *Sergeant Rutledge*.

8. To the south of the Valley, Totem Pole and Yei Bi Chei, sometimes with Rooster

Rock and Meridian Butte in frame, is the place reserved for the Indians, from *Fort Apache* onwards. It is here that the Comanche and Cheyenne encampments are found in *The Searchers* and *Cheyenne Autumn*.

9. Not far from Totem Pole, Big Chair and Thunderbird Mesa, together with Sand Springs, is the place where Debbie meets Ethan and Martin in *The Searchers*. In the same area the little butte known as The Hub is to be found. The Comanche pass in front of this as they pursue Ethan and Martin.

The groupings we have listed stand out from the rest. Sometimes Ford chooses only to show a part of the north-western buttes, or to isolate Sentinel Mesa or West Mitten. Sometimes he films the rocks in long-shot, transforming them into a frieze on the horizon, at others he uses them to establish a contrast between them and the human dimension: the 'monuments' may stand out sharply in long-shot, with minuscule human beings at their feet, or the latter may be in close-up with the 'monuments' reduced to a blurred background which cannot be identified. It is above all the use of different camera angles which provides diversity, to such a point that we sometimes get the impression of being in different places. Head on, West Mitten appears as an impressive mass of rock; from the side, it appears relatively slender. Sometimes Yei Bi Chei and Totem Pole seem to form a single block, at others they appear separate. The Thumb looks quite different when seen from the front or the back. The spatial relationships between one butte and another modify according to the point of view. Colours, lighting, the presence or absence of clouds – these are all meteorological parameters which can bring their influence to bear. Their variety creates the idea of a vast multiform space. Ford sometimes uses the commonplace cinematic device of editing to link different places together for a specific sequence (the battle at the end of *Fort Apache*, for example), or to create the impression that his characters are travelling long distances (as they are in the fiction) when in fact the actors are moving within very limited parameters (as in *The Searchers* or *Cheyenne Autumn*). Conversely, however, with a single camera movement he can bring places which seemed quite distant close together (*She Wore a Yellow Ribbon*). By choosing to limit himself to one single setting, the director is forced to draw upon the resources of a rhetoric, in the sense of a 'technique'; in other words, technical skills involving an advanced use of formal craftsmanship and cinematic devices.

If these procedures make it possible to present a precise space in a variety of ways, the space itself also appears as a system of rhetorical figures. The names of the various places within it have either a commemorative function (Mitchell and Merrick were former soldiers of Kit Carson who were killed by Indians while prospecting for gold) or derive from the specific shapes of the 'monuments' (Pole, Big Chief, Three Sisters). In the latter case, it is a question of simile (a rock which looks like an elephant or a dromedary), in the former, we are required to remember someone. In both instances we are directed towards rhetoric, either via figurative style or via a mnemonic procedure which reminds us that the art of memory is one of the five categories of rhetoric.

It is inconceivable that Ford was unaware that one of the northern massifs is called Stagecoach. In the most famous poster for the eponymous film we see the stagecoach in close-up going from right to left (in the film the setting is identical, but the coach is travelling in the opposite direction) against the background of the frieze of monuments, with Stagecoach and Big Chief in the centre of the photograph. In *She Wore a Yellow Ribbon* Fort Starke is at the foot of Sentinel Mesa. The same location is used in *Stagecoach* when Lieutenant Blanchard says goodbye to Mrs Mallory as she leaves the protection of the army in the stagecoach. At another moment in *She Wore a Yellow Ribbon* the positioning of Elephant Butte behind Nathan Brittles marks him out as 'a lonely old man'. In *Stagecoach* the word 'mitten' suggests the pointing forefinger of one of the Indians watching the stagecoach pass by West Mitten. Thus the mimicking of the rock formations can function in relation to the characters in the films in a number of ways. In *Sergeant Rutledge* one shot shows the hero by the river wearing a hat whose shape seems to be reproduced by the summit of a chimney of rock behind him. There is a shot in *She Wore a Yellow Ribbon* where an ensemble of three buttes (West Mitten, East Mitten and Merrick) mimics or is mimicked by a group of three Indians (when the detachment leaves Fort Starke). There is a similar shot in *The Searchers* with the three figures of Ethan, Clayton and Martin as they prepare to attack the Indian camp at the end of the film. When similar elements are to be found in a single shot it would appear that the spectator is faced with a process of identification rather than with a simile. To use the distinction made by Gérard Genette, identification can be motivated or non-motivated. The members of the audience who know that the butte behind Nathan Brittles is called Elephant Butte will mentally identify him as 'a lonely old man'. Those members of the audience who do not have this knowledge (the majority) will interpret the in-shot juxtaposition by a formula such as 'he is as solid as a rock'. We may find other procedures preferable to in-shot juxtapositions, superimposition for example (via a dissolve) or substitution (via a camera movement). The dissolve, for example, functions as a procedure which associates two terms (rather like the 'as' in a simile). It is not so much an identification as a simile where the term of comparison is explicit. In *The Searchers*, a dissolve associates Martha and Debbie – mother and daughter – with West Mitten, which is made up of a large shape and a smaller one.

The most remarkable feature of Monument Valley is the architectural metaphor contained in its name, which Ford exemplifies in his use of both the frieze (the skyline) and the stele, which are linked in so far as the monuments rise like steles in relation to a horizontal space. This 'stelar' space (as Jean-Pierre Richard might put it) is characterised by verticality, frontality, immobility and sharpness of outline. This verticality has an arrogance which suggests depth and burial while at the same time commemorating disappearance and absence. Inlaid into the sky, the stele's flat, unchanging form imposes the presence of an image, but also it implies something hidden from view, be it the other side of the stone, or the part which penetrates the earth as into the depths of memory. From *My Darling Clementine* onwards, Ford's perception of Monument Valley is as a place of funerals. There are no Indians in *My Darling Clementine*, yet in *Stagecoach* the north-western fringes of the Valley where the action takes place had been presented as Redskin territory. The horizon beyond Tombstone is encircled with monuments to absence (the only Indian in the town in thrown out at the beginning of the film). The very name Tombstone, and the gravestone of Wyatt Earp's brother in its setting of the frieze comprising Castle, King-on-his-Throne and

Saddleback, underline the gradual association between the rocky massifs and steles. In *Fort Apache*, Owen Thursday and his men are literally submerged by the tide of Indian horsemen who themselves are buried in a cloud of dust. In *She Wore a Yellow Ribbon* and *The Searchers*, the graves, which are generally linked to West Mitten, belong to white women who have disappeared. In *The Searchers* the body of an Indian is lying on a flat stone, prefiguring the scene of the Indian chief's funeral in *Cheyenne Autumn*.

As the example of West Mitten shows, the same 'monument' can refer to different (but not necessarily contradictory) signifieds. In *She Wore a Yellow Ribbon* there is a conversation about cyclamen flowers during which two similes/identifications are juxtaposed: either rabbits' ears or flaming arrows. As it happens, Genette's examples of stylistic analogy are of love and a flaming arrow. In this scene it is therefore left to the audience to deduce the idea of love from a series of culturally coded associations (the flame, the arrow), but also from the colour purple in which the entire setting is bathed, from the presence of Olivia Dandridge, from the proximity of the grave of Nathan Brittles's wife and the association already established in Nathan's mind between his wife's appearance and that of the young woman (who has brought the flowers). The effort required of the audience is not always an easy one. Three Sisters appears several times in *Sergeant Rutledge*, and the image the massif presents is not so much that of three sisters (with the most slender of them in the middle), but rather that of a prisoner flanked by his warders. Sometimes we are presented with a veritable rebus. King-on-his-Throne is in the north of the Valley, Big Chair in the south. Ford does not establish any direct relations between these two places. In a scene in *The Searchers*, Debbie finds Ethan and Martin near a river; Big Chair rises in the background. In fact, this scene illustrates the words of the theme song of the Fordian community (used twice in the film), 'Shall We Gather at the River?':

> Yes, we'll gather at the river,
> The beautiful, beautiful river,
> Gather with the saints at the river
> That flows from the throne of God.

Of course, the throne of God is a reference to Big Chair, but God sits on his throne like a king.

Totem Pole is a fairly good example of the various ways Ford transforms each place in Monument Valley into a pool of rhetorical figures. The aiguille rises into the sky like a totem pole, hence its name. But we know that a totem stands for an animal which is both the ancestor and protector of a clan. Totem Pole immediately conjures up the Indians. The Comanche and Cheyenne camps in *The Searchers* and *Cheyenne Autumn* are situated here, where Yei Bi Chei (the daughter of the Navajo dancers) is also to be found: in both cases the Indians are seen lining up. Previously, in *Fort Apache*, as Kirby York approaches Geronimo's camp, we see him with Totem Pole and Yei Bi Chei in the background. In *The Searchers* the aiguille of Totem Pole dominates the scene when Chief Scar meets Ethan and Martin, appearing behind each of their faces respectively. This clearly signifies that despite their racial differences, they share the same totem, they belong to the same clan. There is a moment in *Sergeant Rutledge* when Totem Pole appears in the background behind the Ninth Cavalry, recalling the great missing person, the black sergeant himself: indeed, he belongs to the same clan as the soldiers of that regiment and Totem Pole applies strictly to him since, watching over it and protecting it as he does, he too is the 'totem' of the regiment. By locating *Sergeant Rutledge* in the Valley, Ford associates blacks with Indians: while his men sing 'Captain Buffalo', the sergeant is presented like a living statue. The credit sequence for *Cheyenne Autumn* is built around Remington's statue of an Indian. Thus Monument Valley can be understood as a topos, a place, or rather, to use the appropriate rhetorical terminology, a system of places.

> Why 'place'? Because, as Aristotle says, to remember things all we need is to recognise the places where they are to be found (a place is therefore the element in an association of ideas, a conditioning, a dressage, a mnemonic); thus places are not arguments in themselves but the pigeonholes in which we classify those arguments. Hence every image brings together the idea of a space, a storehouse, a localisation and an extraction: a *region* (where arguments are to be found), a *vein of a certain mineral*, a *circle*, a *sphere*, a *spring*, a *well*, an *arsenal*, a *treasure*. ... Thus places form this very particular storehouse ... a corpus of forms devoid of meaning in themselves, but converging on meaning by selection, organisation, actualisation.[1]

It has been suggested that Ford's *inventio* is more discovery than invention. The reverse is true. Monument Valley is certainly a real space; but it is Ford who has progressively constructed this space as a topos, in the sense of a stock of stereotypes. Only after his visits and the shooting of seven films there did Monument Valley become this topos. There was a potential treasure there, but a different kind of treasure from that which obsessed Mitchell and Merrick (they died of their obsession). This alternative treasure had to be made to exist.

With *Stagecoach* Ford appropriates a place. He invests it. It is notable that he uses it sparingly at first, just three buttes (West Mitten, East Mitten and Merrick) and the skyline. At the beginning of the film, and principally during the credit sequence, we see Mitchell Butte and Gray Whiskers as well as The Capitan and an adjacent space. Monument Valley represents the untamed space contained between two towns, the domain of the Indians. For the whites who turn round and round within it, it is above all a labyrinth. *My Darling Clementine* starts in the middle of the three buttes and concludes on The Capitan, which reminds us of the previous film whose opening scene contains the same monument. Apart from that, most of the action takes place in the north-west, where Ford had located Tombstone, with its haunting skyline. A new space appears which also belongs to the north-western area, in an extension of Mitchell Butte. This is where Wyatt Earp catches up with the stagecoach carrying Doc Holliday, and where parts of several chase sequences in *Fort Apache* and *She Wore a Yellow Ribbon* were filmed. But the Indian attack on the stagecoach in *Stagecoach* was shot somewhere else (Lucerne Dry Lake, California), which is perhaps an indication that at that point Ford was not yet fully aware of the Valley's potential. *Fort Apache* uses all the locations already mentioned. During the credit sequence West Mitten is placed symbolically, towering above the silhouetted profile of a soldier blowing his bugle, another statue. *Rio Grande* retains the silhouette but eliminates West Mitten; while it belongs to the cycle of films about the cavalry, it is not part of the Monument

Valley cycle. Like *My Darling Clementine*, *Fort Apache* introduces a new location, this time more to the south: Totem Pole with its Indian and labyrinthine associations. Before meeting Cochise again, Kirby York and his companion are seen on the edge of a canyon in whose bowels a river bends and meanders far below. This canyon is not actually in the Valley (in fact it is several hundred miles away). Therefore Ford has included the shot purely for the metaphorical value of the river, which appears to double back on itself.

From *Stagecoach* to *Fort Apache*, Ford's procedure has been composed of repetitions and additions. *She Wore a Yellow Ribbon* marks a turning-point in his use of the Valley. To begin with, no new places are added, but instead Totem Pole is subtracted and there is a withdrawal to the north of the Valley, which is systematically exploited. West Mitten appears as a focal point which is constantly returned to; the idea of the labyrinth is replaced by that of a magnetic pole. For the first time Ford seems to conceive of the site as a place of memory. The opening sequence is like a condensed version of the three previous films: the stagecoach and the telegraph refer to *Stagecoach* (even the theme music for the stagecoach itself is quoted fleetingly); the houses where the Pony Express and the stagecoach stop are in the location used for Tombstone (*My Darling Clementine*); whereas in *Fort Apache* General Custer appears in the guise of Owen Thursday, here he is given his real name. Thus, *She Wore a Yellow Ribbon* follows on chronologically from *Fort Apache* (1876), which itself was a chronological continuation of *Stagecoach* (1875). The action of *My Darling Clementine* takes place in 1882, so it stands apart from this series (it contains no Indians). *She Wore a Yellow Ribbon* is also characterised by at least five panoramic shots which refer back to the previous films. The last of these follows Nathan Brittles as he retreats from Fort Starke. One after the other we see East and West Mitten, Merrick, Elephant, Camel (with Spearhead Mesa in the background), Mitchell Mesa, Gray Whiskers and Mitchell Butte. This is an exceptional camera movement in that in all the other films these locations are always shown disconnectedly, as can be seen in *Stagecoach* or *The Searchers*, for example. Ford is not attempting to reconstruct Monument Valley as a real place, but rather to establish a recapitulation. He dissolves into the next shot, which continues to follow Nathan Brittles as he rides towards the frieze made up of King-on-his-Throne, Saddleback, Setting Hen and Eagle Mesa. The two shots must be read as a single unit. The journey they describe runs like a spiral over the map of the Valley and brings together all the places Nathan Brittles has been involved with. Thus the recapitulation is specific to him, but also to the audience, as is shown by the film's opening shots: using the vision of the Valley offered by *She Wore a Yellow Ribbon*, the audience is invited to evoke the films which have gone before.

Seven years later Ford returned to Monument Valley to make *The Searchers*. One of the wonderful things about this film is the way the location is used. The two buttes of Gray Whiskers and Mitchell which appear almost at the end of the previous film are now presented right from the start. They fulfil a similar function to that of West Mitten in *She Wore a Yellow Ribbon*. The Edwardes' farm is at the foot of Sentinel Mesa with the two buttes on the horizon. Brad Jorgensen's death takes place not far from there, and the Jorgensens' farm is situated at the foot of Mitchell Butte. West Mitten also appears; as in the previous film, its associations are that of a stele. The photos of Nathan Brittles's wife and two daughters are in three frames which are echoed by the three gravestones and the three buttes (West, East and Merrick). In *The Searchers* West Mitten dominates the Edwardes' little family cemetery. In this film the north of the Valley is used, but the south is not totally neglected. The location for Chief Scar's camp in New Mexico is near Totem Pole and Yei Bi Chei. New places are introduced: The Thumb, Big Chair and The Hub. In the next two films there is an increasing displacement towards the south of the Valley. The credit sequence in *Sergeant Rutledge* begins with the northern skyline, then shows Three Sisters, a new setting which will appear several times in the film (whereas West Mitten, East Mitten and Merrick are absent) and also in *Cheyenne Autumn*. This is the last work Ford shot in the Valley. It is dedicated to the Indians, and Totem Pole is one of its most majestic features. The northern landscapes make an appearance. There is one panoramic shot which encompasses Camel, Cly Butte, Elephant, East Mitten, West Mitten and Merrick. Most significantly, a night shot in the last part of the film (it could be footage from *She Wore a Yellow Ribbon*) shows a line of cavalry soldiers passing between Gray Whiskers and Mitchell Butte. This is what is shown in the third shot of the credit sequence in *Stagecoach*; Ford ends where he began and, all things considered, the two buttes (Gray Whiskers and Mitchell Butte) emerge as a place of major importance since they are also the link between *She Wore a Yellow Ribbon* and *The Searchers*. *The Searchers*, *Sergeant Rutledge* and *Cheyenne Autumn* are linked by Totem Pole, just as the first four films are linked by West Mitten, East Mitten and Mitchell Butte.

It is self-evident that Ford made use of Monument Valley with loving care and exemplary rigour. He saw in it a place of memory, or more exactly a theatre of memory, of the kind which characterises the Renaissance (and indeed the name John Ford has Renaissance connotations), that is, a stage with its entrances, a circumscribed space with an inside and an outside, an assembly of monuments intended to facilitate remembrance of something, providing the order in which they appear is adhered to. In this landscape Ford erected three statues inscribed with what he considered to be the essential features of the American experience (with the exception of Lincoln, who is nevertheless referred to in *Sergeant Rutledge* and *Cheyenne Autumn*; Rutledge was the surname of Lincoln's fiancée): the allegorical journey from the city of moral order to the city of vice via the experience of Nature untamed, the establishment of the rule of law (as in the story of the OK Corral), the constitution of the legend, Wyatt Earp and Custer, the anonymous hero (Nathan Brittles), the north–south divide, racial conflicts, the line which cuts all human beings into two like the invisible frontier which divides the Valley between Utah and Arizona (we may imagine that the panoramic shot which follows Nathan Brittles's departure was taken with the camera actually placed on this frontier). Like the lazy line in Navajo weaving, this line, which is the principal motif of *The Searchers*, is always found within the same motif or colour; it is a constituent of the divisions of the American experience.[2] It is also more of a symptom or an effect than something already formed and measurable. The reference to woven cloth comes from Ford's work itself. Its flat extensions contradict the coldness of their stone. People are divided among themselves, like light through a prism, and this divide is a place of difference whence intensity springs forth and where the well-ordered mechanisms of rhetoric are abandoned, allowing the landscape to emerge in all its strange power and glory.

Monument Valley is a theatre of memory in another way. It contains the memories of the films for which Ford used it as a location – and which, by association, can recall other films which are not part of the series. Not only is every sector of the Valley redolent with all the sequences shot there, but the audience finds itself in the same position as the Proustian narrator in relation to the steeples of Martinville and the trees of Carqueville. This experience is both in the nature of a metaphor and something totally different:

> The essential thing about involuntary memory is not similarity, or even identity, which are merely conditions. *What is essential is internalised difference which has become immanent.* It is in this sense that remembrance is analogous to art, and involuntary memory is analogous to a metaphor: it takes 'two different objects', the madeleine and its flavour, Combray with its qualities of colour and temperature; it enfolds the one within the other, and makes the relation between them something internalised.[3]

Ford's strength is that he associated Monument Valley and his own work so intimately that the one is enfolded within the other. Just as his vision of the Valley becomes progressively clearer, so does his vision of his own work. What we have here is nothing less than a series of seven films which constitute a unit of image-time. We could say of the monuments of the Valley what Victor Segalen wrote in his book *Stèles* about certain steles which

> designate the quintessential place, the milieu. Like upturned slabs of stone or vaults engraved on an invisible surface, they offer their signs to the earth while stamping it with a seal. They are decrees from another empire, a strange empire. We submit to them or we challenge them, silently and without unnecessary discussion; and moreover without ever confronting the real text: merely the footprints we steal from it.

Filmographic Note

Monument Valley was not unknown to nineteenth-century travellers and photographers. There was John Strong Newberry, for example, and Frederick I. Monsen (author of *With a Kodak in the Land of the Navajo*, 1909). Zane Grey discovered Monument Valley as early as 1913. He went back in 1922 with Jesse L. Lasky and Lucien Hubbard, and this gave him the idea for *The Vanishing American*, which he wrote soon after. George B. Seitz adapted it for the screen in 1925; Ford certainly knew this film, which opens and closes with a shot of the Valley with the following intertitles: 'In a Western state, far from the present haunts of men, there is a stately valley of great monuments of stone', and 'Then – stillness again – the hush of the ages, for men come and live their hour and go away, but the mighty stage remains'. Monument Valley clearly appears both as something associated with the Indians (the film begins with a fairly lengthy prologue which traces the history of the successive peoples of this region in northern Arizona) and as a cathedral in stone which was already there before the coming of man and which will still be there when man has disappeared. Like *Cheyenne Autumn*, but forty years before it, the film commemorates 'a disappearing race', and like *Cheyenne Autumn* its credit sequence is built around the statue of an Indian (James Earle Fraser's *End of the Trail*, 1915).

Seven of Ford's sound Westerns were shot in the Valley, seven were not. In the latter group we should also include 'The Colter Craven Story', an episode in the television series *Wagon Train*, and the sequence in *How the West Was Won* which deals with the Civil War. The other films are *Wagon Master* and *Rio Grande, Drums along the Mohawk* (1939) and *The Horse Soldiers* (1959), which could not have been made in the Valley for obvious geographical reasons; *3 Godfathers* (1948), which was a remake of *Marked Men* (1919) and a homage to the silent actor Harry Carey, 'bright star of the early Western sky', who belonged to a period before Ford knew the Valley; *Two Rode Together* (1961), with similar subject-matter to *The Searchers*, which doubtless Ford did not wish to evoke by filming in the Valley; and *The Man Who Shot Liberty Valance* (1962), which was not shot there because the character of Ransom Stoddard is an Easterner, and cannot easily be associated with Monument Valley (this film uses the theme music from *Young Mr Lincoln*).

Not many directors dared to film in the Valley during Ford's lifetime. Nevertheless, George B. Seitz filmed *Kit Carson* there in 1940 and David Miller made *Billy the Kid* there in 1941. Walt Disney's 1953 production *The Living Desert* was shot in the Valley, as was George Marshall's episode for *How the West Was Won* (1962). After the end of the 60s films using this prestigious setting became more numerous: a sequence in *2001: A Space Odyssey* (1968); another in Leone's 1969 homage to Ford, *Once Upon a Time in the West* (1968) – as in *Stagecoach*, the characters make a circular journey; Frank Laughlin's *The Trial of Billy Jack* (1973); William A. Fraker's *The Legend of the Lone Ranger* (1980); not to mention various advertisements for Marlboro, Chanel No. 5, etc. The landscape of Monument Valley has become a cliché, a stereotype, an empty signifier which can accommodate any number of signifieds.

Notes

1 Roland Barthes, 'L'ancienne rhétorique', *Communications*, no. 16, p. 206.
2 See Jean-Louis Leutrat, *John Ford: La Prisonnière du désert – une tapisserie navajo* (Paris: Editions Adam Biro, 1990). [Editors' note]
3 Gilles Deleuze, *Proust et les signes* (Paris: Presses Universitaires de France, 1976), p. 75.

10   Magazine Advertising and the Western
Colin McArthur

Advertising was quick to exploit the popularity of the Western, with its apparently wholesome values and instant recognisability, and advertising using a variety of visual motifs from Western films and other sources was well established by the end of the Second World War. The gold rush, the Pony Express, the wagon trains of emigrants, the building of the railroads and the Indian Wars were motifs frequently drawn on to sell a wide range of consumer goods and other products, including breakfast cereals, tobacco, cars, life insurance and, later, television sets. In the 30s, 40s and 50s especially, as the Western established itself as Hollywood's dominant genre, advertising made full use of its familiar iconography and its ready acceptability to the American public.

I have selected four typical examples, all taken from the *Saturday Evening Post*. They also provide an indirect visual commentary on several of the essays in this book. In the first advertisement (Plate 1), from 1932, Custer's Last Stand is invoked, reproducing once again the archetypal figure of the blonde, long-haired general going down fighting against hopeless odds, an image established and perpetuated, as Roberta Pearson shows, in countless films both fictional and documentary. In this case, the selling-point is not an analogy ('be like Custer!') but instead a contrast: nature, as in the Wild West, is raw; Lucky Strikes are mild. But presumably there is all the same a kind of association intended between Custer's heroism and smoking the right cigarettes. At least, if Custer were not universally accepted as a hero the advertisement would not work. It's hard to imagine such an advertisement being used today except in an ironic mode.

The second advertisement (Plate 2) dates from 1942 and is an excellent example of the way in which merchandising was from an early age an important element in the commercial success of film heroes such as Gene Autry. It is also an indication of how Autry's image was wholesome enough to sell to children; the creation of a more respectable Western version of the rural music of the South, a process defined by Peter Stanfield in his essay, was already paying dividends.

In the third advertisement (Plate 3), taken from a series in the *Post* in 1952, the Santa Fe Railroad promotes its trains with an image of a Pueblo Indian. As Edward Buscombe describes in his essay 'Photographing Indians', the Santa Fe and the Harvey Company (the ad reads: 'that wonderful Fred Harvey food is all you've heard about') played a major role in constructing an image of the South-west that combined exoticism and reassurance to produce the ideal tourist environment. For once it is an image of the West that derives not from Hollywood but from the promotion of South-west Indian arts and crafts that ran counter to the stereotype of the mounted warrior of the plains.

"*Nature in the Raw is seldom MILD*"

—and raw tobaccos have no place in cigarettes

They are *not* present in Luckies ... the *mildest* cigarette you ever smoked

WE buy the finest, the very finest tobaccos in all the world — but that does not explain why folks everywhere regard Lucky Strike as the mildest cigarette. The fact is, we never overlook the truth that "Nature in the Raw is Seldom

Mild"—so these fine tobaccos, after proper aging and mellowing, are then given the benefit of that Lucky Strike purifying process, described by the words—"It's toasted". That's why folks in every city, town and hamlet say that Luckies are such mild cigarettes.

"It's toasted"
That package of mild Luckies

LUCKY STRIKE
"IT'S TOASTED"
CIGARETTES

Copr., 1932. The American Tobacco Co.

"*If a man write a better book, preach a better sermon, or make a better mouse-trap than his neighbor, tho he build his house in the woods, the world will make a beaten path to his door.*"—RALPH WALDO EMERSON. Does not this explain the world-wide acceptance and approval of Lucky Strike?

PLATE 1

Plate 2

![Santa Fe advertisement]

Santa Fe

something new to
remember
every magic mile

Maybe it's one of the many colorful sights you see in the Indian country along the Santa Fe.

Maybe it's the friendly train crew or some new feature of your Santa Fe train . . . an added comfort . . . or an extra service.

Whatever it may be, you'll find something new to remember every magic mile when you travel Santa Fe between Chicago and California. Five famous trains each day, each way. For reservations, just see your local ticket agent or travel agent.

YOU CAN HARDLY WAIT for mealtime . . . that wonderful Fred Harvey food is all you've heard about it.

Zuni Drummer painted by a Pueblo Indian

Super Chief · Chief · El Capitan · Grand Canyon · California Ltd.

Texas Chief between Chicago-Texas · Kansas City Chief between Chicago-Kansas City

R. T. Anderson, General Passenger Traffic Manager, Santa Fe System Lines, Chicago 4, Illinois

PLATE 3

Year after year after year...

Only the most enduring things can be indifferent to the passing years.

All Lincoln automobiles are built to fight the ravages of *time*—to keep their distinctive beauty, their superlative performance and their incomparable comfort for many more years than you will ever drive one.

Lincoln's superb "inVincible 8" engine is not assembled by the multi-thousands, it is slowly and painstakingly produced—with a jeweler's patience and precision. It is designed to give you more trouble-free miles than you can ever use.

And the faultless work of master craftsmen builds many years of comfort into the Lincoln ride. The cushions stay luxuriously soft. The mechanics of the springing and the steering are as satin-smooth in action as the workings of a fine watch.

See the 1951 Lincoln and the magnificent Lincoln Cosmopolitan at your dealer's showroom. Discover how much less they cost than you imagine. Take one out for a drive over the route of your choice and understand what proud owners mean when they say...*Nothing could be Finer.*

LINCOLN DIVISION · FORD MOTOR COMPANY

Standard equipment, accessories, and trim illustrated are subject to change without notice.

Nothing could be finer — Lincoln for 1951

PLATE 4

The final image (Plate 4), from 1951, demonstrates that by this time Monument Valley had already achieved an iconic significance that was associated both with quality ('Nothing could be Finer') and with a kind of permanence ('Only the most enduring things can be indifferent to the passing years'). The essay by Jean-Louis Leutrat and Suzanne Liandrat-Guigues is largely focused on the use made of this location by John Ford. But this advertisement is an early example of how easily a signification achieved within the cinema can be extended into other media. Today, the frequency with which Monument Valley is used in TV and other commercials threatens to reduce its resonance to an empty banality which may eventually undermine even the power of Ford's films.

11 The Fantasy of Authenticity in Western Costume
Jane Marie Gaines and Charlotte Cornelia Herzog

In the American Western, costume is the place where nature flows into culture like the Missouri runs into the Mississippi. The point is that somewhere, at some juncture, the two become indistinguishable. Just as the motion-picture cowboy seems to have grown out of the Western landscape, his Western wear seems to have magically grown out of and on to his body, so ideally are his clothes and gear suited and proportioned to the functions he effortlessly performs in the taming of the wilderness. From the heel of his spurred boot to the brim of his high-domed J. B. Stetson hat, the cowboy is a creature of the desert and the plains, a creature whose biological evolution and genetic adaptation historically ensured his day-to-day survival. Even the Colt revolver in his holster, the most cultural of his natural gear, is camouflaged as part of the hip, contributing to the ideology that a great gunfighter is 'born' a good shot.

If it is difficult if not impossible to tell where nature leaves off and culture begins in the Westerner's body, this tells us that the authentic is perhaps closer to the mythic than we may have imagined. In asserting this we are going upstream against the current of common sense which gives us the familiar and intransigent oppositions: reality/fiction, authentic/inauthentic, nature/culture, and actuality/myth. The cowboy is one of those places in mass culture where common sense always wants to see the mythic as estranged from the authentic, as having either lost sight of or wantonly abandoned an original moment or a genuine article.[1] Not surprisingly, then, it is an especially popular exercise within the discourse on Western costume to compare real historical cowboys with their motion-picture representations. (Did 'real' cowboys wear belts or braces? Did they wear wool trousers or Levis like movie cowboys wear?) Rather than fall into this particular trap, we propose to see instead the interdependence of the mythic and the authentic which, although seemingly distant and unrelated (in common sense), are merged in what we are calling the 'fantasy of authenticity', our attempt to indicate the impossibility of ever knowing but all-the-while-reaching-for the 'real' West. We are enabled in this argument, not only by the conditions of the post-structuralist critique of popular culture but also because of a relatively recent postmodern reception of the Western film as genre. To put this another way: while we are sceptical post-structuralists about the possibility of ever retrieving or ever knowing the real American cowboy, we are post-modern consumers in relation to the inextricability of the myth and the reality. In this American genre perhaps more than any other, the image has *become* the historical reality, only one indication of which is the temporal difference between the short-lived reality and the long-lived myth. While the Wild West may only have existed in reality for less than a quarter of a century, and for barely a century as a culture, North Americans have been living the myth as consumers. Significantly, this long-lived myth has been nurtured by a craze for ready-wear Western clothes as much as by a cycle of Western genre fiction. Far from fleeting as most crazes, the rage for Western wear seems to have continued almost unabated into the present since the earliest hey-day period for vintage Western wear and collectables that began in the 1920s with Western-wear mail-order catalogues. This extended rage peaked between 1930 and about 1970, experienced another surge in 1985 around the time of the release of *Silverado*, and has continued without losing momentum into the 1990s.[2]

Cycles of Realism

The historical image has become historical reality as much in the act of putting on and taking off our Western-wear boots (pretending to be cowboys and cowgirls) as through any cataclysmic shift in the culture. One might say that the image supplants the reality as the one fills out what is missing or unknown about the other. In the end, all that matters is the fantasy of authenticity which is part of the cultural pastime of reinvention of which Western wear is such an important part. And we have a deep need to periodically reinvent that reality, for the Western reality-myth is that myth that narrates for Euro-American culture its relation to the indigenous Other as well as to the virginal land, that tells us whether we once were (and by implication continue to be) benevolent rulers or ruthless imperialists.

If nothing else, this understanding of image as our historical reality should alert us to the highly ideological function of the notion of authenticity, which in theatrical costuming as in other encoding practices always provides the justification for the introduction of any novel elements. As has been argued before, Hollywood must periodically renew its lease on realism, pressing creative personnel to raid the historical records for more and more fresh signs of authenticity.[3] These fresh signs work to bolster a new Western mythos that is ostensibly more true to the old reality, best defined as whatever it is that we so obsessively strive to retrieve. A Western film must announce in the first few scenes that this, finally, is the real West, all other Westerns going before having been but pale imitations. So every Western aspires to the condition of unimpeachable authenticity and strives to be the final word and even the last of its kind, as seen in the critical pronouncements of the 'end of the genre', a pattern that established itself in the critical reception of Sam Peckinpah's 1962 *Ride the High Country*.

Shifts in the genre have historically been signalled by the costume or prop detail that produces, in Roland Barthes's terms, the 'effect of the real', not reality itself, of course, but the sense of realness that is ultimately all that is called for in the classical text.[4] This tell-tale detail will signify 'the real West' by looking as though it was found 'growing' in the wild, that is, looking as though it escaped the cultural manipulation to which theatrical signs are conventionally submitted. The pattern begins as early as the teens and the films of William S. Hart, who used Native

173

Americans and working cowboys as extras to produce the 'reality effect'.[5] Forty years later, initiating another cycle of realism, Howard Hawks's *Red River* (1947) announced itself as committed to a new standard of realism signified by authentic costume detail, from the use of rubber slickers to buckskin jackets. In this gritty black-and-white film, screen realism contributes to the film's overall project, underwriting the justification of a new version of the great cattle drives and the 1851 settlement of Texas as an Oedipal struggle between fathers and sons, as John Wayne's order is overthrown and replaced by that of Montgomery Clift. Initiating a cycle of more politically sensitive Westerns, Marlon Brando as Rio in *One-Eyed Jacks* (1960) dares to wear a sombrero and the laced-pant of the vaquero, signifying his anti-hero status and looking ahead to the ambiguity of Clint Eastwood's unnamed serape-wearing hippie in the Sergio Leone trilogy (*A Fistful of Dollars*, 1964; *For a Few Dollars More*, 1965; *The Good, the Bad and the Ugly*, 1966). Without any intention of fully becoming Mexican, these Westerners restore order in the Third World across the border, signalling identification with the oppressed which stops short of a tribute to the ingenuity of the vaquero, an issue we shall revisit later. In 1972, *The Culpepper Cattle Co.* used lush detail and close attention to the texture of leather and cotton to reinforce the idea that it was one of a new breed of Western that would not flinch at the 'truth' about the horrors of violence in the old West. Directed by former cinematographer Dick Richards, the narrative is experienced through the eyes of a young boy who yearns to be a cowboy with his own gun and ends up the centre of senseless slaughter. In the 90s, the television series *Lonesome Dove*, staking out the terrain as the new multicultural Western, was promoted in terms of its costume authenticity, signified most prominently by the high-domed 'Montana Peak' hats, but also by the use of braces and collarless shirts on the male characters. Only fidelity to the historical record can explain the use of this exaggeratedly high hat which, if we hadn't been told was 'true to life', might seem instead to be a comic caricature of the 'real' cowboy whose silhouette is defined in our recent memory by the flatter, creased top and lowered brim as seen on the ideal cowboy hero, John Wayne. At every juncture, the recourse to costume realism has enabled a new version of the 'truth' about the way it was on the frontier. And we are reminded once again that popular culture is never about genuine knowledge of our historical past. *The way it was* always underwrites *the way things are*. In the lapse of our historical memory, familiarity gets overcoded as verisimilitude.[6]

Thus it is that each wave or cycle of realism in the Western is measured against every earlier Western in addition to an imagined 'real' West, a double measure on two parallel tracks that will eventually converge. Tom Mix's 'Montana peak' Stetson and elaborately embroidered satin shirts, once signifiers of realism in the early days of cinema, became progressively relegated to the dustbin of Western costume codes and were eventually discounted as fabrication (even though the early cowboy costume did have a real historical relationship to the performing cowboy, beginning with Buffalo Bill Cody's Wild West show).[7] The fact that the culture has now come to think of the show cowboy as exceedingly distant from the real historical range-rider is humorously indicated in Robert Altman's parodic *Buffalo Bill and the Indians* (1976) in the moment when the ineffectual Bill (Paul Newman) rifles his closet for his 'real' jacket before he rides off in a fruitless attempt to find and return the missing Sitting Bull.

The Return of the Duster

One of the most interesting cases of this phenomenon of cyclical rediscovery is that of the duster, an article of Western clothing seemingly forgotten in the teens that makes a comeback as authentic detail in the 40s, again in the 70s, and continues to reappear into the 90s. Certainly the return of the duster to the big screen is an important signifier of that 'authentic' West towards which every new film has aspired in the long transition from the Wild West fantasy cowboy to the contemporary 'reality' cowboy (a cowboy soon to be replaced by another, more real cowboy).

The case of the duster confirms that the real West is nothing more than source material, food for the voracious myth of the 'real' West. In addition, however, the reappearance of the duster on the screen also tells us something about the degree to which the studios in their heyday emphasised costume research, research based on photographs and paintings more than any other type of source. To find dusters, one only has to look at the easily available work of Western genre painters Charles Russell and Frederic Remington, both of whom represented the Westerner wearing the long linen coat.[8] Such research, an attempt to 'raid the historical record' for new detail, might have turned up the forerunner of the Western duster in the Civil War medical coat or the coachman's coat of the 19th century.[9] Here, in fact, we find the long linen coat worn over the standard costume of the cattleman, a cover that essentially worked as a protection against the thick dust stirred up in the cattle drive. But as important as the retrieval of an item of clothing that has produced a major contemporary alteration in the basic silhouette of the Westerner is the understanding of the functionality of the duster, functionality being an aspect of screen realism that goes beyond the two-dimensional iconography of the painting or the photograph and points to the fact that costume research involves the study of material culture as well as historical representations.

There is, then, the realism of the material object, the museum relic of the old West, to which we would add the related realism of the contemporary reincarnation of the duster. The reincarnation in turn invites a corollary realism of actually wearing the long, flying coat *as though one were* a Westerner. At some point, then, contemporary clothing practice gets imagined back on to the historical period, producing the new rage as the historical authentic, or reinforcing the unknown or vaguely recollected with the familiar, even with the fashionable. But it is never as though the coat can be exactly 'traced back' to the Western frontier. Like other aspects of popular culture, Western costume has a mixed paternity so that its sources may not necessarily be the rugged West but may even be the urbanised East. The duster cover-all that we think of as so exclusively Western, in vogue between 1890 and 1930, came into its own with the advent of the open-air roadster as protection from soot, and made a significant contribution to the evolution of the light coat with large pockets worn over a suit of clothes.[10] And it is this hybrid coat that has recently reappeared in the pages of the J. Peterman catalogue where the following copy draws on the collective memory of the West: 'Classic horseman's duster protects you, your rump, your saddle and your legs down to the ankles.' Still other variations are pictured in the Hammacher Schlemmer catalogue and represented by the long yellow coat worn by the

Wearing dusters in Pale Rider.

'Marlboro man' in contemporary cigarette advertisements. This waterproof coat
has more in common with the black rubber slicker that was used in *Red River* in
the interest of 'bringing back Western realism', although the same coat can be seen
on screen over thirty years before in John Ford's early Western *Straight Shooting*
(1917), along with the high-domed Stetson (although on the supporting cast and
not on the hero, Harry Carey). Curiously, the charm of the contemporary versions
of period clothing is in direct proportion to the degree of atrophy of the more
utilitarian aspects of this clothing. It is not only that the contemporary wearer of
the J. Peterman coat does not need the extra coat length to protect his or her legs
while riding but that he or she certainly doesn't need the slit up the back together
with the 'pron' or flap that was meant to cover the 'cantle' on the back end of the
saddle.[11]

Over the last decade the duster has produced a new Western silhouette, the look
of a more business-like gunfighter who, with coat flapping around him in the
wind, has just weathered the desert storms. This is not the lean and tight figure of
earlier periods, the figure whose motives could be easily 'read' in his body, it is a
more mysterious and covered Westerner, unpredictable and inscrutable. Consider,
in this regard, the rule that in contemporary Westerns the virtuous hero still does
not flamboyantly wear a duster. More often, it is the villain or the lawbreaking
hero who is thus covered up. That the duster is relegated to the job of signifying
malevolence as well as 'realism' is explicitly signalled in the scene in *The Great
Northfield Minnesota Raid* (1972), where Cole Younger tells his gang to disguise
themselves in dusters in preparation for the fatal bank hold-up, suggesting not

176

only that dusters are associated with cattle buyers but that they are also indicators of duplicity. The hated Pinkerton guards wear dusters in *Pale Rider* (1985) and Henry Fonda's brutal gang members disguise themselves in dusters in an attempt to blame their crime on the 'good guys' in *Once Upon a Time in the West* (1968). The fact that the Younger and James brothers wear dusters again in *The Long Riders* (1980), accentuated in a telephoto shot as they ride into town, coats billowing, suggests the degree to which the duster silhouette has become attached to the Jesse James legend. Earlier appearances of the duster also suggest the connotations of aberration in, for instance, the medical coat on Ward Bond's 'Reverend' character in *The Searchers* (1956) and Clint Eastwood's long leather coat in *The Good, the Bad and the Ugly* (1966).

The culmination of the association between the flamboyant duster and aberrant heroism comes, however, with Sharon Stone's gunfighter in *The Quick and the Dead* (1996). Wearing a stiff sienna-coloured duster that appears to be suede or pigskin, vintage wire-rimmed sunglasses, long paisley silk neckerchiefs and thick cotton shirts, Stone is a J. Peterman catalogue fashion-plate in every scene, looking exquisitely windblown as she stands down the unscrupulous Gene Hackman character in a series of bloody duels. It could be that films such as this one as well as *Wild Bill* (1996) signal the beginning of the fashion-plate Western in which inordinate close-up attention is lavished on the iconographic trappings of the West – on elaborately decorated guns and tooled leather in addition to the many changes of costume. (The Western movie hero of the 1930s through to the 1980s never changed his clothes at all.) Today, the object is to feature the perfection of the reproduction of the material culture of the West, the West of the museum imagination and the nostalgia catalogue.

The Multicultural West

Although film history and theory have treated the 40s film noir tough guy as having evolved from the 30s motion picture gangster and literary hard-boiled detective, the Western hero has been understood as fully formed by the time he first appeared on the screen. However, this understanding of the Western hero as somehow 'pure' with no antecedents unfortunately contributes to a misunderstanding of the cultural commingling that has produced the very American popular culture we know and love, a production that both precedes and succeeds the Westerner in his heyday. We propose in place of the fully formed Western an understanding of the hybrid nature of the iconography of the Western hero which can be grasped by artificially separating the figure into his component parts: Indian brave, Mexican *vaquero*, Civil War soldier, US cavalryman, cattleman, horse wrangler, and gambler. In this exercise, costume signifiers are not the remnants of lost cultural connection, rather they are signs that keep this connection alive, that work against the repression of origins because they are so undeniably present. Furthermore, what this example reveals is that, more than anything, it is the custom and costume of the Mexican *vaquero* that provide the outline of the earliest Westerner. Like the linguistic connections to the Spanish language (*la riata* to *lariata* to *lariat*), these Mexican costume signs have undergone the kind of historical alteration that has essentially buried the trail back to the *vaquero*, whose expertise with the cow (*vaco* means 'cow' in Spanish) as well as the horse was emulated by the early South-western frontiersman. The evidence, however, is still visible in the ties under the cowboy hat, the pommel in the saddle design, the width of the chaps (originally *chaparejos*), the wide brim of the Western hat, and certainly the design of the tooling on leather belt, boot, and cotton shirt. It has been said that if John B. Stetson hadn't given his name to the wide-brimmed Western hat, it might still be called the sombrero.[12] In and of itself, this may not be remarkable, yet the continuance of the figure with these features intact means that the evidence of hybridisation is constantly in front of us, constantly available. A comparison between cultural miscegenation and interracial mixing may be apt here in the controversial denial or suppression of origins and the desire to assert the thorough Anglicisation of the West. It would also seem here that, in comparison with the Mexican, the native American paternity is much more clearly foregrounded, especially if we look to the iconography of the buckskinned theatrical Westerners, beginning with Buffalo Bill Cody and continuing with such screen figures as Alan Ladd's Shane, Gene Autry, Roy Rogers, Buck Jones, Tim McCoy, and the fifty-odd films featuring versions of the historical Wild Bill Hickok.

In the American fantasy of the frontier, the native American is despised and eradicated at the same time that he is revered and emulated. Testimony to this emulation is the degree to which the Westerner absorbed some aspects of the Indian mode of dress into his own, perhaps best exemplified by the incorporation of fringed buckskin. The remarkable multi-purpose long fringe could be broken off in pieces and used as ties or, extended down the arm, it worked to shoo away flies. As this utilitarian function of the fringed shirt and trousers eroded, the Westerner was left with what appeared to be a shirt with a fringe trim across the front and sometimes under the sleeves. Thus it is that utility becomes decoration as the native heritage in American culture gradually recedes.

Male Sexuality in the Western

In its commitment to authenticity, costuming always adheres to the dominant ideology or reigning fantasy, thus deferring to one historical moment's preferred version of another. But in its simultaneous dedication to legend, it gives it all away, telling us not only that it is a deep ideological indicator but that it is also only an embellishment on the surface. As we have been arguing, in the body of the Westerner it is difficult to tell where nature leaves off and culture begins, and it may be that it is the proportion of nature to culture, of biology in relation to society, that, as Judith Butler tells us, is the tell-tale ratio.[13] But whereas Butler's insight has the advantage for feminism of a more comprehensive theorisation of the relationship between female biological reproduction and, say, the cultural construction of motherhood, the same insight applied to the male biological would seem to do nothing more than confirm old assumptions about the male 'sex drive'.

Setting aside the problem of the beauty of the Western male body for any conservative argument about the naturalness of sexuality, we want to look instead at the way naturalisation works to re-eroticise the sensuality of the Western scenario, particularly for a gay male pornographic fantasy. Due to the harmony between the Westerner and his environment, as a figure he makes an irresistible argument for the inevitability and irreversibility of male sexual expression as rough and tough. Undeniable in the Westerner's costume is the super-naturalisation of the favourite props of the Victorian fetishist, with the functionality of whips and spurred boots having been demonstrated in countless incidents in thousands of narratives of survival. Lest this functionality is taken for granted, we want to stress the absolute perfection of the economy of the Westerner's 'rig', as his outfitting was called. (As the Kevin Kline character remarks in *Silverado*, he does everything with 'what he's got'.) The high-heeled boot had its origin in the need to dig heels into the ground to secure the wrangler in the process of roping steers, but has its flip erotic side in the exquisite torture of the sado-masochist's fantasy.[14] The cowboy chaps had their essential function in the protection of the front part of the leg but took flight in fantasy as they framed the crotch area, going on to enter the realm of the baroque in the extreme bat-winged chap or the sheepskin or angora goat-hide chap with silver-concho trim as seen on Tom Mix and other showmen cowboys. This dialectic between economy and excess is further exemplified by the problem of how to hold up the Westerner's trousers, the place where the trajectory from historical function to sexual fantasy is so straightforward. If the original cowboy preferred heavy wool trousers (as opposed to Levis), inevitably held up with wide braces (legacy of the military uniform) and if belt loops did not appear historically until 1922, what explains the proliferation of belts on the Westerner's body, even John Wayne's use of braces in addition to the double belt (trousers and gun belt)?[15] Here we would want to look to the ritual function of the various belts, the strapping on and off of the gun belt as sexually charged and the echoes of these ritual acts in the pornographic imagination.

It is difficult to imagine a male costume that lends itself more to eroticisation than that of the Western gunfighter, and it is not surprising that the iconography of the low-slung, skin-tight trousers and the cocked hat, the texturing of raw and smooth cowhide, is one of the favourite costume repertoires of gay male pornography, lending itself to fantasies of soft flesh concealed and protected by leather. But even more relevant in motion-picture history is the tradition of early cinema exhibitionism to which the Western movie hero belongs, since he defines himself through remarkable action – through bulldogging the steer, breaking in and cinching up the bucking horse, trick riding and shooting, wrestling the outlaw to the ground, kicking him in the gut with pointed toe, and punching him with gloved fist. Although early cinema, characterised by frenetic movement for movement's sake, might not be seen as synonymous with the erotic, given our more contemporary idea of the sensuality of the tight shot and elongated hold, it did lay the groundwork for an erotica of Western action. Here, the gunfight itself is a masterful example of the ritualisation of sexual tension and release, the elongation of anticipation in the cross-cutting between two men faced off against one another, exposing their weapons, cupping trigger-ready hands, opening the coat, readying for what viewers and diegetic onlookers know will be short ejaculations of fire. It often seems in the heat of the gunfight that the two figures 'come' together.

At the same time it is clear that the Western scene is the homosocial scene *par excellence*, the corollary to this homoerotica is an auto-eroticism of the self-sufficient loner. The elusive Westerner needs and wants no man, preferring the company of his horse. His animal sexuality is exhibited against the backdrop of the wilderness that demands the peak performance for which he is so casually out-fitted. If the Westerner wants no man, he is equally indifferent if not hostile to women, and this indifference is nowhere more apparent than in the Westerner's practice of having sexual relations with his clothes on (some examples include *Pat Garrett and Billy the Kid*, 1973, and *Unforgiven*, 1994). The range rider who not only sleeps but screws with his boots on defines the ideal of casual, noncommit-tal sexual relations, best undertaken with the occasional whore, an ideal of inter-mittent and interrupted sex that complements his itinerant existence. But, in addition, the cowboy hero proves his worth as a man of action in his adherence to the code of sexual expediency. The Western man is always hard and always ready.

There is, then, no nudity in the Western. The Western gives us sexuality com-pletely without nudity. Although it has been noted that the man in the bathtub is a recurring motif in the Western, most certainly a civilising ritual, it is just as sig-nificant that he will often keep his hat on or conceal his gun beneath the bath water.[16] When he strips to swim (and sometimes even to bathe), it is often down only as far as his long johns. And it is the long john that gives us the insight into the Westerner's sexuality. As has been argued earlier, 'The prickliness of the one-piece long john suggests the vulnerability and sensitivity of the untoughened white flesh beneath, which no Western woman would ever touch.'[17] The Westerner is never represented as nude because no woman can ever put a hand on him. The exception to this rule is found in what might be called the 'gone native' subgenre of the Western (*A Man Called Horse*, 1970, and *Dances with Wolves*, 1990), where the Richard Harris and Kevin Costner characters are both shown naked in sequences prefacing their integration into Native American life and ritual.

Even this question of the nudity of the Western male is tied up with the fantasy of authenticity as we speculate about how many baths he took per year. In order to feed our appetite for the genuine West, Hollywood's elaborate authenticity machinery went into gear. The work of the costume department for the period Western involved the production of the illusion of time and toil. The effects of the brutal frontier existence were produced on Western costume often by the use of sandpaper, fuller's earth, and even blowtorches. Mineral oil was used to simulate sweat on the band of his hat, with the incremental effects of the desert heat pro-duced on different hats representing different times of the day. John Wayne was said to have had as many as eight identical shirts prepared for him on a single film, each marked by the appropriate degree of wear to which it had supposedly been submitted in the narrative.[18] If at any point we doubt the constructedness of reality in the classical narrative, we need only look to the behind-the-scenes labours of the costume department and the dedication there to the task of satis-fying the fantasy needs supplied by authenticity.

Notes

1 We are using common sense here as almost interchangeable with the notion of ideology. For perhaps the best explication of the way common sense works in popular culture, see Richard Dyer, 'Introduction', in Richard Dyer, Christine Geraghty, Marion Jordan, Terry Lovell, Richard Patterson and John Stewart (eds), *Coronation Street* (London: British Film Institute, 1981). For an illuminating discussion of the way 'real' and 'imaginary' may come to have a new relationship to one another in the post-modern era, see Hayden White, 'The Modernist Event', in Vivian Sobchack (ed.), *The Persistence of History* (New York and London: Routledge, 1996).

2 Tyler Beard, *100 Years of Western Wear* (Salt Lake City: Gibbs-Smith Publisher, 1993), pp. 30, 112, 126.

3 Edward Buscombe (ed.), *The BFI Companion to the Western* (London: BFI/André Deutsch, 1988), p. 99.

4 Roland Barthes, 'The Reality Effect', in Roland Barthes, *The Rustle of Language*, trans. Richard Howard (New York: Hill and Wang, 1986).

5 Beard, *100 Years of Western Wear*, p. 20.

6 On the proximity between *verisimilitude* and a certain cultural familiarity, see Roland Barthes, 'The Sequences of Actions', in *The Semiotic Challenge*, trans. Richard Howard (New York: Hill and Wang, 1988).

7 Ibid., p. 21; William Everson, *A Pictorial History of the Western Film* (Secaucus, New Jersey: Citadel Press, 1969), pp. 185–6.

8 See Edward Buscombe, 'Painting the Legend: Frederic Remington and the Western', *Cinema Journal*, vol. 23, no. 4 (Summer 1984).

9 Michael and Ariane Batterberry, *Mirror, Mirror: A Social History of Fashion* (New York: Holt Rinehard & Winston, 1977), p. 266.

10 Beard, *100 Years of Western Wear*, p. 18.

11 Beard, *100 Years of Western Wear*, p. 11.

12 Paul Fees, *Frontier America: Art and Treasures of the Old West from the Buffalo Bill Historical Society* (New York: Harry N. Abrams, Inc., 1988), p. 113.

13 Judith Butler, *Bodies that Matter* (New York and London: Routledge, 1993).

14 Beard, *100 Years of Western Wear*, pp. 17–18.

15 Ibid., pp. 16–18.

16 Buscombe, *Companion to the Western*, p. 64.

17 Jane Gaines, 'Costume', in Buscombe, p. 99.

18 Ibid., p. 100.

12　The New Western American Historiography and the Emergence of the New American Westerns

Rick Worland and Edward Countryman

Like Western films, the history of the American West rises and falls in fashion. The most influential single piece of academic American historiography is still the Ur-text for the whole subject of Western history, Frederick Jackson Turner's 'The Significance of the Frontier in American History'. 'The Turner Thesis' is a mere essay, written in 1893 for the American Historical Association's convention in Chicago. Disdaining footnotes and evidence, Turner inscribed a prose-poem that hymned Westering whites. 'Stand at Cumberland Gap', he wrote, 'and watch the procession of civilization, marching single file – the buffalo following the trail to the salt springs, the Indian, the fur-trader and hunter, the cattle raiser, the pioneer farmer – and the frontier has passed by' (Turner, 1961, p. 44).

Turner set the terms for professional study. Serious Western historians would disdain mere adventure and romance. They would deal with the land and its disposition, with developing social forces, and with how free land and social development created a distinct, even unique, American nation and character. They would confront 'the problem of the West' (the title of another of Turner's essays) in its relation to the whole problem of what is distinctive about American history.[1]

Land, social forces and problems defined in academic terms: these do not offer promising material for Hollywood screenplays. How far Western historiography and Western movies diverged during the Western's classic age can be seen in the work of Turner's heirs. The foremost single volume in Turner's tradition, a vast undergraduate-level text called *Westward Expansion*, pays only the slightest note to many of the film genre's great icons. The bandit tradition gets particularly short shrift, with no mention at all in more than 800 pages for either Jesse James or Billy the Kid. The conflict of whites and Indians is harder to ignore. But only two chapters of *Westward Expansion* make it their prime theme. One, at the beginning of the book, is called 'The Land and its People', effectively reducing Indians to just one element in the natural landscape. The other, near the very end, discusses 'The Indian Barrier', likening the First Nations to such other barriers to white expansion as the Appalachians, the Rockies, and the wide Missouri. All were there to be overcome. General George Armstrong Custer, who stands in Hollywood and popular cultural terms for the whole encounter of whites and Indians, gets only three citations in *Westward Expansion*'s index (Billington and Ridge, 1982, pp. 15–28; 591–610). The dominant mid-century graduate seminar, run at Cornell by

Paul Wallace Gates, worked in the same tradition. Gates's vast scholarly output deals with the disposition of land, from his earliest study of the colonisation work of the Illinois Central Railroad to a volume produced nearly sixty years later on land issues in California.[2] His many doctoral students have worked almost entirely in the same vein.[3]

At first glance the divergence between film and history is surprising. Westerns are 'about' history and many claim to reconstruct it. The American West has been immensely fertile as a source both of symbolism and iconography (for films and fiction) and of problems of formal understanding (for historians). One of the foremost contemporary Western historians, Richard White of the University of Washington, puts his finger on why the two have failed almost completely to intersect. White notes that the American Historical Association meeting of 1893 took place at the World's Columbian Exhibition, held to mark four hundred years of the European presence in the western hemisphere. The exhibition was much more than a scholarly gathering. Crowds and celebrities poured into Chicago to visit this 'Great Fair', which celebrated its host city, the surrounding 'Great West', and the whole enterprise that Columbus had begun. Among the celebrities was Colonel William F. Cody, who was there to entertain the crowds with 'Buffalo Bill's Wild West and Congress of Rough Riders of the World'.

Like Turner, Cody had a vision of the West's past. Unlike Turner's, it did not consist of advancing stages of civilisation, from trappers and traders through farmers until it culminated in city folk. Again unlike Turner's vision, the process that made Cody's West was not essentially peaceful. As White notes, the prime tool of Cody's version of westward expansion was the bullet, not the plough. The great conflict that Buffalo Bill and his troupe enacted was between Indians and whites, not between abstract stages of civilisation. Cody's performances brought to the arena real figures who had taken part in the Plains Wars, including Cody himself and, for a time, Sitting Bull. Whatever else might be said about the handling of Indians by Cody and his many successors, they at least possess enormous vitality. In Turner and the work that he inspired they figure hardly at all.

By the time of the Chicago exhibition Sitting Bull was three years dead, killed by Indian policemen acting under white command. The year 1890, the year Sitting Bull died, marked the complete surrender of the plains nations. It also marked the point at which, according to Turner, the frontier disappeared. For Turner, however, what signified the frontier's end was not the end of armed Indian resistance (which in any case was effectively over well before Wounded Knee). It was the disappearance of what he called 'free land', meaning extended contiguous territory with a population density of less than two persons per square mile.

For all their gaudy showmanship, as White notes, Cody's spectacles recognised the fundamental truth that the land had never been free. Turner never visited Cody's Wild West during his own time at the Great Fair.[4] His ideas have had their moments, however, in Westerns. There is a point in George Stevens's *Shane* (1952) when two characters argue out the terms of what the historian had to say. Significantly, though, that part of the script was the work of the Pulitzer Prize-winning novelist and academic A. B. Guthrie Jr, who had been hired in by Stevens from his professorship at the University of Kentucky. For the most part Cody's framework of understanding, not Turner's, has ruled.[5]

During the fifteen years between *The Outlaw Josey Wales* (1976) and *Dances with Wolves* (1990), when the Western was lying more or less fallow, a new group of historians was attempting a wholly different understanding of the Western American past. Two of the foremost among them, White and Patricia Nelson Limerick of the University of Colorado, attempted for a time to completely abandon the notion of the 'frontier'. To both, it had become so intellectually meaningless and ideologically laden that it simply obscured understanding. It deserved dismissal as the 'f-word'. White produced an entire textbook of Western history without ever employing the word, and Limerick has described her own contorted efforts to teach undergraduates in the same terms.[6] The effort proved impossible. As Limerick puts the issue with reference to Disneyland:

> If professional Western American historians find themselves conceptually without anchor when they visit Frontierland, the reason is clear: with the possible exception of [Disneyland's current] suggestion that environmental carelessness produced the settler's cabin fire [formerly blamed on Indians], the work of academic historians has had virtually no impact either on Disneyland's vision of the frontier or on the thinking of Disneyland's visitors. That cheerful and complete indifference to the work of frontier historians may in truth be the secret of the place's success. (Limerick, 1994, p. 72)

Despite ourselves, we return to Turner, or at least his terminology. In very recent historiography, the attempt to abandon the term 'frontier' might as well never have been made at all.[7]

The non-encounter of Turner and Cody in 1893 points to the larger problem of professional historiography in relation to American popular culture. It is not enough to fall back on an easy distinction between 'myth' (Cody) and 'history' (Turner). Cody and Turner both had stories to tell. Each story had and still has its truth. It is the academics' loss (in terms of both money and cultural influence) if their version of the Western story has been discounted for public consumption. *How the West Was Won* (1962), a self-consciously epic attempt to draw the whole genre together, drew on the amateur historian Theodore Roosevelt's *Winning of the West*, not on the professional historian Turner's 'Significance of the Frontier'.[8] However, during the same fifteen years (1976–91) when the Western seemed practically dead, a new intellectual current was emerging among historians. If the 1990s Westerns are more than just a commercial cycle, that current may offer real possibilities for a revived Western genre, able to discuss the United States as seriously yet just as much in popular terms as the great run of films that extended from *Stagecoach* (1939) to *The Outlaw Josey Wales*.

In the late 20th century, it is no longer possible to write American history in terms of simple triumph. This is not because of mere 'political correctness' or pressure from interest groups. The 'new Western history', associated with White, Limerick and a growing number of others, is part of a larger enterprise that has aimed at 'recovering the diversity of the American past'.[9] The enterprise has real artistic possibilities. Framed in historical terms, it is nothing other than what Walt Whitman attempted in his magnificent nineteenth-century poetic effort to capture his people, history and culture, 'Song of Myself'.[10] In page after page of free verse, Whitman exalted men and women, Northerners and Southerners, Easterners and Westerners, red, black and white, free and slave: the whole huge canvas of American experience. In monograph after monograph, contemporary historians have been recovering all those people, and trying to see how their lives fitted together into some sort of coherent, distinctively American picture. We may have reached the point where the monographs, with all their many narratives and actors, do unite into a single story.[11]

Central to the (newest) 'new Western history' is an appreciation of two qualities. One is that there never was empty, virgin, free land that was just there for the taking. The 'national domain' was created when the United States made peace with Britain in 1783. It was extended by the Louisiana Purchase (1803), the Florida Purchase (1819), the Mexican cession (1846), the agreement with Britain that drew the western boundary ('frontier') with Canada at forty-nine degrees north latitude (1846), and the Gadsden Purchase defining the present border between Mexico and New Mexico/Arizona (1853). If that land seemed 'free' it was because white Americans did not have to pay the price of its purchase. That price instead was borne by Indians and by conquered South-western Hispanics.[12] The second great truth is that the land had always been occupied, by Indians for millennia and by Hispanics for centuries.

At one level this is a mere truism. The film genre's conventional imagery of displaced Indians whose way of life was going or gone and of ageing, decaying South-western Hispanic architecture and communities has always recognised it. What is just receiving serious scholarly attention is how complex were the terms on which the Indians, the British, the French and Hispanic white conqueror-settlers, the mixed-race *métis* and a surprising number of black Americans dealt with one another. At least part of the artistic strength of the film genre in its great days was the simplicity of its iconography, its remarkably limited number of themes and images. The genre's power grew from how film-makers used that simple repertoire to express ideas that could be very complicated. In that sense, at least, the tradition that film-makers extrapolated from Cody resonated with the enormous body of academic writing that grew out of Turner. For more than eight decades Western films and Western historiography alike made complex use of what began with a very simple point.

Newer historiography is more complex, both socially and morally. So are newer Westerns, and that is where intersection between the two streams of understanding finally appears to be possible. One of the central themes in the past two decades' historical work is the destruction of the hoary notion that Indians were simply and inexorably pushed back. What historians have seen instead is summed up by White's concept of a 'middle ground' on which empires, European colonies and Indian republics intersected, mingled and co-existed. White himself writes about the *pays d'en haut* surrounding the Great Lakes, where, in his view, the middle ground lasted from roughly 1650 to as late as 1820. During that time 'the West' was a bloody and violent place, but it was also stable according to its own terms. The 'westward advance' of English-speaking settlers stalled at roughly the crest of the Appalachian chain of mountains, to be advanced by neither the bullet nor the plough.[13]

Though White has stated the issue most clearly, many other historians have worked and are working within this understanding. Whether we consider Catawbas, Cherokees, Creeks, Choctaws or Iroquois, we now understand Indians as active agents within the large structure of colonial, revolutionary and early republican America. Not at all 'outsiders', the tribes east of the Mississippi were entirely surrounded by three great arcs of European settlement by 1770. One stretched along the Gulf Coast, another up the Mississippi and east along the Great Lakes and St Lawrence, and a third the length of the Atlantic coast.[14] Historian Jay Gitlin sums it up by noting that 'French merchants in St Louis were reading Voltaire while, far to the east, Daniel Boone was "trailblazing" in the supposedly unmarked wilderness' (Gitlin, 1992, p. 72).[15] In principle, the same situation held west of the Mississippi as east of it.[16]

Consider one historical figure who has a minor position in the Western film genre. William Johnson was an Irish immigrant to New York who climbed the imperial ladder, became superintendent of Indian affairs in the northern colonies, acquired a baronetcy and made himself *de facto* lord of the Mohawk Valley. Though the film never mentions him, his presence looms over John Ford's *Drums Along the Mohawk* (1939) and he appears powerfully in the novel from which the film is drawn. Johnson does appear briefly in *Northwest Passage* (1940), portrayed as a foppish English gentleman who stands in the way of Rogers' Rangers' historic mission of destroying Indians wherever they go. In the most recent historian's account he is much more a denizen of the middle ground. Like his Mohawk counterpart, the 'emperor' known as Hendrick, Johnson shuttled back and forth between the white and Indian worlds, and was almost equally at home in each. Even the self-display of both men consciously mingled Indian and white modes.[17]

Johnson always remained deeply British and Hendrick never ceased to be a Mohawk. None the less, modern understanding of both men as deeply liminal is not far at all from Kevin Costner's Lt John Dunbar in *Dances with Wolves*. It is even closer to the portrayal of Indian–white relations in Michael Mann's *The Last of the Mohicans* (1992) and the Canadian/Australian co-production *Black Robe* (1991). Like *Dances with Wolves*, both films enjoyed serious co-operation from modern-day descendants of the historic Indians they portray. The Mohawks of *Black Robe* and Wes Studi's Magua of *Mohicans* may be forest horrors of the sort that viewers of older Westerns know only too well. But in both cases there is explanation for what they do, rather than mere assertion that they are evil by their very nature. In each film, they are located historically, and in relation to other Indians who, like them, have complex motivations and serious choices to make. This new complexity has come to the Western motion picture though – however grudgingly and incompletely – after nearly two decades of hibernation in which new films and film-makers working continuously in the form were not its principal source of inspiration and example.

If, as Patricia Limerick only half-jokingly suggests, frontier mythology in popular culture succeeds precisely because it ignores developments in professional historiography, historians as much as film-makers still occupy the same cultural time and place as their readers and audiences, each group responding in its own way to larger social currents. As various commentators have observed, the decline and 'death' of the Western in the mid-70s paralleled the political turmoil and social schism engendered by the Vietnam War. The shattering of the ideological consensus that had governed the post-Second World War era reverberated throughout the realm of popular culture, but was especially acute in the transformation of

Hollywood's most traditionally reliable genre. The issue largely turned on two factors: the Western's depiction of American Indians, and the centrality of violence in the genre. What had long been taken for granted in countless movie and TV Westerns before the late 60s – that Indians were irreconcilable savages whose destruction was perhaps unfortunate but in any case unavoidable – was now completely inverted until 'the Western suddenly stood for everything imperialistic and genocidal about America' (Clarens, 1980, pp. 13–14).

The growing equation of the Vietnamese with Indians, particularly after My Lai, compounded by anguish over the decade's political assassinations, and violent racial and anti-war protests and riots, had the subsidiary effect of tainting the Western, where most issues are ultimately settled by gunplay, as both symptom and cause of a uniquely violent strain endemic to American culture itself. Add to this the increasing presence of John Wayne as Vietnam War champion and self-appointed spokesman for 'Americanism', and the reception of the Western – which had actually used genre language to speak in complex ways about the war – inseparably mingled with the bile of Vietnam. Films such as *The Green Berets* (1968), *Soldier Blue* (1970) and *Ulzana's Raid* (1972) finally collapsed Vietnam and the Western into a single scenario we might call 'Drums Along the Mekong'. This strangled the genre's commercial viability until the 'post-Vietnam Western' meant virtually no Westerns at all.[18]

Ironically, on-screen and off, then, 'history' doomed the Western. Historian Richard Slotkin argues that the partial replacement of the Western by science fiction in the 70s (led by the *Star Trek/Star Wars* phenomenon) succeeded because the latter genre 'presented ... alternatives to the historicized spaces of the Western' which could 'purchase imaginative freedom ... by keeping real historical referents at a distance' (Slotkin, 1992, p. 636). Remarkably, since the 1991 Oscar sweep by *Dances with Wolves*, a feat repeated by Clint Eastwood's *Unforgiven* in 1993, the Western film has enjoyed a minor resurgence. The number of new Westerns that followed Kevin Costner's directorial début, while small by comparison with the Vietnam period, let alone the Hollywood studio era, is significant in relation to the dearth of genre entries produced since the mid-70s. Seven years after *Dances with Wolves*, even with a number of new Westerns released, we cannot describe this renewed interest as anything but a commercial cycle rather than a full-blown genre renaissance. But film cycles, such as the anti-Communist films of the 50s or the disaster movies of the 70s, often indicate the presence of topical socio-political trends or anxieties distinctive to their historical moment.

Westerns of the 1990s seem self-conscious of history in two senses: that of the 'new', essentially *popularised* history of the American west vis-à-vis treatment and image of the Indian particularly; and secondly, the history of the genre itself, especially its rich period in the Vietnam era. These new film-makers confront an intriguing dilemma. Their immediate genre antecedents were often disillusioned, determinedly revisionist films whose greatest and often most popular works loudly declared the final closing of the frontier, both literal and metaphorical, and proceeded to work out implications of that theme that typically left their protagonists dead or pathetic vestiges of a vanished time, i.e. the twenty-year period whose milestones range from *The Man Who Shot Liberty Valance* (1962) through *The Wild Bunch* (1969) to *Heaven's Gate* (1980). How to begin again from this point? Refusing the by now well-worn paths of embittered revisionism or callow parody, the films of the 90s may describe a distinct 'post-Cold War Western' that attempts to balance a range of issues both historic and generic. Among these are attempts to assimilate the past (primarily the Vietnam War period and the acute racial consciousness fostered and reinforced by the civil rights movement); and an inescapable awareness of the genre's complex heritage in the films of Ford, Peckinpah and Leone especially. Combined, these two sub-texts suggest new efforts to move forward without ignoring or simply inverting the formal and ideological styles of earlier films.

Unforgiven establishes its contemporary scepticism towards popular Western lore by including the Eastern dime-novelist character Beauchamp (Sol Rubinek), who has breathlessly detailed the exploits of gunfighter 'English Bob' (Richard Harris) until the sordid facts behind the killer's legend are explained to him by Gene Hackman's spiteful sheriff. Yet the film advances its themes on the physical and psychic costs of violence primarily through the figure of Clint Eastwood himself. For two generations of moviegoers, Eastwood's weathered William Munny floats uneasily between the cynical 'Man with No Name' who helped explode genre clichés in Sergio Leone's Marxist anti-Westerns of the 60s, and the rightist avenger 'Dirty Harry' Callahan of the 70s and 80s whose aura was eventually embraced by Ronald Reagan. A powerful ambivalence about Munny's motives and actions results in a suggestively open-ended conclusion uncommon in post-*Star Wars* Hollywood.

Since Costner's film, a number of Westerns including *Son of the Morning Star* (ABC-TV, 1991), *The Last of the Mohicans* and *Geronimo: An American Legend* (1993) have tackled Indian war scenarios, the very trope over which the form evaporated after Vietnam. In the American frontier myth created and refined by whites over three centuries, Indians, despite their historically and narratively central role, seldom represent themselves in any sense; rather, the Indian is foremost a *metaphor* manipulated to address in narratively conventionalised terms the shifting historical circumstances, problems and values of dominant white culture. For years, Hollywood Westerns have periodically taken an apologetic, 'pro-Indian' stance – often taken as evidence of a new level of 'maturity', 'balance' and 'realism' – that typically proves short-lived. From *The Vanishing American* (1925) to *Broken Arrow* (1950), *Cheyenne Autumn* (1964) and beyond, such films are traditionally lauded then rather quickly forgotten often because of their loudly self-proclaimed importance.

Regarding the new Westerns more positively, however, authentic Indian discourse is present to a greater degree now than in films of the past. Native Americans were enlisted as technical advisers on the specific Indian cultures represented in these films. All speaking parts are played by Native American actors, who are at last permitted to speak in authentic cultural languages, related through subtitles. At last it appears that the day of Rock Hudson, Charles Bronson, Jennifer Jones et al. in 'red-face', mouthing white-invented babble, has been permanently banished. This new level of cultural respect was touted as central to the matured revisionism of *Dances with Wolves* – a minor victory that at least opens up the possibility of more open popular dialogue on the West in American history.

Depicting the aftermath of a Civil War clash in which Lt John Dunbar

(Costner) is badly wounded, then attempts suicide on the battlefield to avoid amputation of his leg, *Dances with Wolves* begins by imagining white American society as wholly bent on self-destruction. From this *guignol* opening, white society will be steadily denigrated until it is identified almost solely and literally with excrement – from the decadent, incontinent officer who dispatches Dunbar to the distant frontier outpost, to the brutish cavalry troopers who use pages from the journal of his life with the Sioux for toilet paper. The Sioux nation is soon posited as an alternative, indeed superior society – the human incarnation of the frontier landscape that completes Dunbar's physical and spiritual regeneration, as the Indian serves in the traditional Romantic role as 'noble savage'.

Upon reaching the mysteriously deserted army outpost Dunbar's revulsion at discovering a fetid deer carcass in the water-hole completes the image of white society as in all ways sick and unclean. Amplifying the film's alliance with environ-mental concerns, a consistent counter-cultural theme, Dunbar had knowingly intoned that he must see the frontier 'before it's gone'. During his time with the Sioux we witness the hungry Indians' incomprehension of white barbarism when they come upon a field of slaughtered buffalo massacred for the commercial exploitation of tongues and hides, the vital meat left to rot. This trope alone starkly contrasts the 'progressive' ideals of exploitative, go-getter capitalism with the harmonious integration of people and land that the Sioux represent.[19]

The Sioux buffalo hunt and its aftermath are key scenes. After Dunbar shoots a wounded bull just before it tramples a young Indian boy, he is called upon to tell and retell the story around the campfire that night as the tribe celebrates its good fortune. At this moment, however, a potentially divisive conflict erupts: a Sioux man wearing Dunbar's lost cavalry hat refuses to return it. Dunbar's friend Wind-In-His-Hair (Rodney Grant) negotiates a settlement that reconciles Sioux ways ('I found it on the prairie, it's mine') and Dunbar's property rights. The threat of individualist claims to disrupt a communal feast is averted by compromise when the Indian is prompted by the group to trade something to Dunbar in exchange for the hat, which the Sioux retains.

What is so appealing about this vision of Indian culture is that it seems to reflect foremost a just society where individual accomplishments are rewarded and private property rights respected, *as well as* a co-operative communitarian circle where no one is left to fend for him/herself psychologically or materially (e.g. Kicking Bird has adopted the white captive Stands-With-Fist as his daugh-ter). Sioux life seems to effect a grand reconciliation between liberal capitalist individualism and tribal 'socialism'. Hollywood has a long history of 'solving' implacable socio-political conflicts through such fantasy compromises, yet the film's lack of condescension in its portrayal of the Sioux, added to the great popu-lar response it generated, suggests a broad yearning for a history in which the past is neither romanticised and exalted for its own sake nor completely rejected as corrupt and shameful.

As with any popular text, particularly one as rich in structuring binarism as the frontier myth, there is a double-edged implication to the increased culturally pro-tective creative input by Indians. The casting of Sioux activist Russell Means, one of the founders of the militant American Indian Movement and participant (later defendant) in the Wounded Knee incidents of the mid-1970s, as Chingachgook in

The Last of the Mohicans strikes an ambiguous note. The presence of a frequently outspoken Indian activist injects a note of conscience and integrity to the film, but may also imply a subtle endorsement of the film's perpetuation of the fundamental good Indian/bad Indian dichotomy that Fenimore Cooper, Buffalo Bill and John Wayne have long popularised. Indeed, Russell Means's appearance in the film might be considered a contemporary version of the rhetorical inclusion of 'original participants' such as Sitting Bull in Buffalo Bill's Wild West shows, spectacles that presented commercial mass entertainment at the turn of the century as edifying lessons in living history (Slotkin, 1992, pp. 66–9). It is impossible to say what portion of the audience was aware of Means's political biography but the crucial, albeit indirect, reference here is to the politically and morally charged period of crisis that hastened the decline of the Hollywood Western.[20]

As contemporary biographies of famous frontier figures, both *Son of the Morning Star* and *Geronimo: An American Legend* discursively present themselves as 'historical' narratives in ways that purely fictional genre pieces like *Dances with Wolves* and *The Last of the Mohicans* do not. Of course, while these recent incarnations of General George A. Custer and the Chiricahua Apache chief Geronimo are qualitatively different from movies of the past, both these legendary figures have appeared in dozens of invented dime-novel adventures and Hollywood movies, bearing little relationship to their historical characters and actions. Indeed, both films contain the usual mixture of historical fact and dramatic licence. Still, as mythical icons, Custer and Geronimo offer particular insights into popular perceptions of the frontier past in the early 1990s.

Starring Gary Cole as Custer, *Son of the Morning Star*, based on the best-selling 1984 non-fiction book of the same title by Evan S. Connell, was aired as a network television mini-series in February 1991. Though riding the Western revival prompted by *Dances with Wolves*, the series must be understood in relation to both the long legend of the 'Boy General' as well as the evolution of the Western genre in the Vietnam era. As with historical accounts of the Little Big Horn itself, a complete review of the changing image of General Custer in popular culture is impossible due to the sheer volume of material accumulating practically from the moment the fighting ended.[21] One authority estimates there are more than a thousand canvases of 'Custer's Last Stand', probably making it the single most frequently rendered historical scene in American painting (Russell, 1968, pp. 3–5). The most popular of these was a lithograph issued by the Anheuser-Busch Brewing Company in 1896, an icon and staple of American bar-room décor for decades. *Son of the Morning Star* is but the most recent of Custer movies that began with a William Selig three-reeler in 1909. Before the Vietnam period, the definitive film was Warner Bros.' *They Died with their Boots On* (1941), starring Errol Flynn as the epitome of the gallant, exemplary Custer.

Virtually the last film treatment before the ABC mini-series was the raving, genocidal caricature created by Richard Mulligan in the central episode of Arthur Penn's *Little Big Man* in 1970, which used absurdist comedy to expose and ridicule practically the entire catalogue of frontier mythology. Mulligan's delusional Custer bellowing 'No prisoners!' as his troops drop dead around him seemed to forestall any further attempts at balance let alone celebration of an Indian-killing militarist. Time and Connell's book, however, partially rehabilitated Custer's reputation (Hutton, 1992, p. 517). Gary Cole's flawed but recognisably human Custer in *Son of the Morning Star*, lying part way between Errol Flynn's saintly superman and Richard Mulligan's deranged parody, assumed a new aura of 'realism' and authenticity by virtue of its moderation alone. Yet as a cultural symbol, the ideological meaning of 'Custer's Last Stand' will remain for ever in contention.

Later in the same year that the Custer telefilm was aired, the name of the storied Montana ground on which he died was officially changed (December 1991) from Custer Battlefield National Monument to Little Bighorn Battlefield National Monument, with the addition of memorials to the Sioux and Cheyenne warriors slain there. Moreover, at the time, the park superintendent was Barbara Booher, a Cherokee/Ute Indian woman (Welch, 1994, p. 106; Dippie, 1994, p. xii). In accordance with such popular and official post-60s currents to expand and open the dialogue on American history to multiple voices and cultural perspectives, *Son of the Morning Star* tackles the controversial tale principally through the device of conflicting opinions of the general both spoken and visualised within the narrative. According to an opening title the series was based on Connell's book as well as 'other historical sources'. Unique among the many macho Custer films, *Son of the Morning Star* is the only one scripted by a woman, Melissa Mathison. This is entirely fitting, however, because Mrs Elizabeth ('Libby') Bacon Custer was a prominent author of the Custer mystique and keeper of the flame in three books of memoirs written after her husband's death.[22]

The series is in fact narrated by two women, Libby Custer (Rosanna Arquette) and Kate Big Head (voice by the Indian activist and singer Buffy Sainte-Marie), a Southern Cheyenne woman who witnessed the Little Bighorn fight after having the misfortune of being present at the Washita battle in 1868 in which Custer's cavalry annihilated her village, killing mostly women and children. Drawing on the published narratives of Elizabeth Custer and Kate Big Head, the script gives dichotomous perspectives on the Boy General in the name of both balance and complexity. However, it does so in a way that tends to favour Kate's view of events as authentic history while Libby's glowing account increasingly becomes the romanticised, and thus unreliable, version.

Presentation of the women's disparate summations of the Washita massacre is telling. While we see images of the bloody aftermath, Libby speaks of it in voice-over as a great victory with 'one hundred-three warriors killed'; Kate immediately rejoins: 'Eleven warriors died and we remember their names; the rest of our dead were women and children.' This scene is crucial for our interpretation, because the self-serving Custer is presumably the source of Libby's information whereas we are actually shown young Kate watching in horror as soldiers surprise the sleeping village and shoot down helpless Indians, including a woman fleeing with her baby. The Cheyenne woman's authority is cemented by her eventual presence in Sitting Bull's encampment on the fateful day in June 1876.

Walter Hill's *Geronimo: An American Legend* is also a self-conscious film not only in relation to the genre history woven into it in certain ways, but foremost in its looser, more fragmented narrative point of view that resists the central authority of a single protagonist, the most common narrative device of the classical Hollywood style. As with *Son of the Morning Star*, the film's very structure acknowledges that historical reality is too complex to be reducible to any single interpretation, personal or otherwise. What is significantly missing from *Geronimo* is a Natty Bumppo or 'John Wayne' – the traditional white male hero who becomes both moral centre and primary shaper of events.

Tacitly acknowledging the mythic west, *Geronimo* includes both variations of the central frontier myth figure Richard Slotkin calls 'The Man Who Knows Indians' – the sagacious frontiersman who respects them, Lt Charles Gatewood (Jason Patric) and the racist Indian-killer embodied by grizzled scout Al Sieber (Robert Duvall). Gatewood and Sieber have strikingly different scenes of individual battle with Indians. Gatewood faces an Apache warrior in single combat in full view of their respective groups, invoking a chivalrous joust, while Sieber later chases down two Indians on horseback, shooting one in the back without concern. The film features a third important voice among the whites: a voice-over narration in the form of journal entries by Lt Britton Davis (Kevin Damon), a young officer newly arrived on the frontier, a figure who seems meant to observe and thus mediate our perceptions of Lt Gatewood, Al Sieber and, through them, Geronimo.[23] Despite the title, the Apache chief is but one voice in a film that might really have been called 'The Men Who Chased Geronimo'.

The film's narrative structure is reminiscent of Hollywood's epic reconstructions of pivotal Second World War battles produced in the 60s and 70s – films such as *The Longest Day* (1962) and *Tora! Tora! Tora!* (1970) whose viewpoints shift around constantly on the thread of a documentary-historical narrative chronology, telling 'both sides of the story' in the name of historical accuracy and 'balance', and implicitly contrasting themselves to the heightened emotionalism and propaganda of the war years. The style assumes that sufficient time has passed so that the once-hated adversary can now be conceived as a human being with his own needs and motives. *Geronimo* contains a remarkable scene in which an Apache band surrounds a group of white miners. The one miner who angrily 'debates' with the chief on the rightness of their place on his traditional lands (economic development and exploitation of its rich resources versus the Indians' lack of interest in such things) is spared by Geronimo for his bravery when the others are shot down. This brief cultural/ideological argument in the midst of a traditional genre 'massacre' gives Indian 'atrocities' context and rationale usually entirely lacking.[24]

Wes Studi's fine portrayal of Geronimo draws on a certain intertextual reference to his roles as the bloodthirsty Pawnee leader in *Dances with Wolves* and the snarling Magua in *Last of the Mohicans*. If we come to respect Geronimo, it is only after getting past Studi's coiled physical rage in the earlier films, vehemence which seems entirely justified here. The way the film gives us glimpses of the mystic visions that guide Geronimo allows him to be both 'Other' in some ways as well as knowable too, a great man essentially at the mercy of larger historical forces, finally unable to be either a victorious warrior or a comfortably assimilated political leader. As frontier heroes often do, the white protagonists recognise that the end of the Indians' way of life is the end of theirs too. Sieber, the 'wildest' of the white men, feels this most acutely and in fact dies, ironically, in a gunfight protecting an Apache scout from vicious white scalp-hunters.

This latter episode, though affording Robert Duvall a bravura death scene, is wholly fictionalised. Referring to Geronimo's saga as 'an American legend' allows the film-makers to contrast traditional genre experiences with more contemporary outlooks on frontier history. The scene in which Lt Gatewood duels with the Indian in single combat within view of their respective comrades, for example, may have been inspired by the semi-legendary event of Buffalo Bill's clash with the Cheyenne leader Yellowhand. The incident became the foundation of Cody's heroic persona and was eventually included in a theatrical precursor of the Wild West (Dippie, 1994, pp. 90–1). Indeed, Walter Hill's staging of Gatewood's fight visually recalls Western artist Charlie Russell's painting 'Buffalo Bill's Duel with Yellowhand' (1917). Gatewood and Sieber's dissimilar bouts with Apaches are important not only because they contrast knight with brutal pragmatist but because they set notions of myth and history against each other in the story.

The films' oblique references to genre sources and imagery of the past (Cody, Russell, Ford, etc.) are counterpointed by Hill's carefully arranged re-creation of a famous series of photographs of General George Crook (Gene Hackman) and Geronimo made during a peace negotiation in Mexico in 1883, 'the only known photographs ever taken of the American Indian as an enemy in the field', according to Lt Davis's voice-over. Hill's studied attention to historical detail includes not only the frozen tableaux but shots of the photographer taking them, yet the re-creations notably eschew reverting to the period authenticity of black and white film stock. Myth and history tug at each other throughout the film.

In the end, 'history' wins. Against the dominant tradition of the frontier myth, *Geronimo* is not climaxed by a decisive 'savage war' or 'last stand' (Slotkin, 1992, pp. 10–16). Instead, the film emphasises the centrality of the reservation system in mediating the one-sided relationship between white America and Native Americans, in which a politicised bureaucracy functions as a reflection of national politics beyond the control of any individual. The temperate General Crook is replaced by the hard-line General Nelson Miles but for the Indians the results are unchanged. Before departing to negotiate Geronimo's final surrender Lt Gatewood admonishes Davis to 'stay noble'. Yet as the film's dismal conclusion makes clear, the Indian scouts regiment is humiliatingly disbanded and arrested, and with chilling parallel to the Nazi Holocaust the Apaches are bundled into box-cars and shipped to imprisonment in Florida – traditional frontier heroes like Gatewood and Davis may retain their 'nobility' in spite of, and not because of, 'the winning of the West'.

Of the films discussed here, however, *Geronimo* died at the box office. The lack of a central psychological perspective may have been an important factor (Walter Hill is an accomplished director, and it was a well-made film with popular stars) though this marks the film's thematic sophistication. While a narrative style built on an ensemble cast and multiple points of view embedded in a chronology of 'actual events' is no more radical than TV-movie versions of sensational headline cases, Hill's film failed to find an audience. Since the action-adventure blockbuster replaced the Western in the late 70s, Hollywood has trained a new generation of young film-goers – who still make up the core theatrical audience and came of age largely without experience of, or interest in, this 'obsolete' genre – to expect an invincible hero violently opposing the forces of a powerful villain in ideologically stark and simple terms, an experience *Geronimo* pointedly avoids.

Genre largely depends on a shared assumption of key beliefs and values within the form itself and among the larger community of producers and spectators. The tentative reappearance of the Western theoretically implies that some new consensus has been negotiated. Yet for a society that currently finds more fragmentation than coalition in the term 'multi-culturalism', it remains unlikely that the genre will ever return to the broad cultural prominence it once assumed. Tellingly, since the late 70s a steady trickle of Westerns have been produced as made-for-television movies or mini-series (*Kenny Rogers as The Gambler* (CBS 1980ff.); *Gunsmoke: Return to Dodge* (CBS, 1987); *Stolen Women, Captured Hearts* (CBS, 1997), etc.), airing on the three original networks whose audiences have grown steadily smaller and older in the last fifteen years.

The impact of the new historiography is felt perhaps most noticeably in nonfiction film explorations of Western history, which often employ professional consultants. Films such as *Last Stand at Little Bighorn* (Paul Stekler, 1992) and documentary series including *How the West Was Lost* (Chris Wheeler, 1993) and *The Way West/The Wild West* (Ric Burns, 1995) aim to present untold or neglected stories, often with sharply revisionist tones contemptuous of traditional frontier lore. Yet the major theme of Patricia Nelson Limerick's *The Legacy of Conquest* stresses the unbroken *continuity* of issues and conflicts in the history of the American West that extend to the present. The divisive Vietnam era and 'identity politics' aside, the Western was never wholly unmindful of the dialectic of history and mythology. The genre always promised to vibrantly address the history of American society. To the degree that cultural definition is broadened, the Western's promise is not broken but fulfilled.

References

Billington, Ray Allen with Martin Ridge, *Westward Expansion: A History of the American Frontier* (New York: Macmillan, 1949); fifth edn 1982.
Clarens, Carlos, *Crime Movies: An Illustrated History* (New York: W. W. Norton, 1980).
Davis, Britton, *The Truth about Geronimo* (New Haven: Yale University Press, 1929).
Dippie, Brian W., *Custer's Last Stand: The Anatomy of an American Myth* (Lincoln: University of Nebraska Press, 1994).
Gitlin, Jay, 'On the Boundaries of Empire: Connecting the West to its Imperial Past', in William Cronon, George Miles and Jay Gitlin (eds), *Under an Open Sky: Rethinking America's Western Past* (New York: W. W. Norton, 1992).
Hutton, Paul Andrew, ' "Correct in Every Detail": General Custer in Hollywood', in Hutton (ed.), *The Custer Reader* (Lincoln: University of Nebraska Press, 1992).
Limerick, Patricia Nelson, *The Legacy of Conquest: The Unbroken Past of the American West* (New York: W. W. Norton, 1987).
Limerick, Patricia Nelson, 'The Adventures of the Frontier in the Twentieth Century', in Richard White et al. (eds), *The Frontier in American Culture: An Exhibition at the Newberry Library, August 26 1994–January 7 1995* (Chicago: The Newberry Library; Berkeley: University of California Press, 1994).
Limerick, Patricia Nelson, Clyde A. Milner II and Charles E. Rankin (eds), *Trails: Toward a New Western History* (Lawrence: University Press of Kansas, 1991).
Russell, Don, *Custer's Last* (Fort Worth: Amon Carter Museum of Western Art, 1968).
Slotkin, Richard, *Gunfighter Nation: The Myth of the Frontier in Twentieth-Century America* (New York: Atheneum, 1992).
Turner, Frederick Jackson, 'The Significance of the Frontier in American History' (1893), in

Turner, *Frontier and Section: Selected Essays* (ed.) Ray Allen Billington (Englewood Cliffs, NJ: Prentice-Hall, 1961).

Utley, Robert M., *Cavalier in Buckskin: George Armstrong Custer and the Western Military Frontier* (Norman: University of Oklahoma Press, 1988).

Welch, James with Paul Jeffrey Stekler, *Killing Custer: The Battle of the Little Bighorn and the Fate of the Plains Indians* (New York: W. W. Norton, 1994).

Notes

1 Frederick Jackson Turner, 'The Problem of the West' (1896), in *Frontier and Section*, pp. 63–76.

2 Paul Wallace Gates, *The Illinois Central Railroad and its Colonization Work* (Cambridge: Harvard University Press, 1934); and *Land and Law in California: Essays on Land Policies* (Ames: Iowa State University Press, 1991).

3 See the *Festschrift* produced in Gates's honour when he retired from the Cornell faculty: David Maldwyn Ellis (ed.), *The Frontier in American Development* (Ithaca: Cornell University Press, 1969).

4 Richard White, 'Frederick Jackson Turner and Buffalo Bill', in James R. Grossman (ed.), *The Frontier in American Culture* (Berkeley and Los Angeles: University of Calfornia Press, 1994), pp. 7–65. For discussion of the Exhibition, see William Cronon, *Nature's Metropolis: Chicago and the West* (New York: W. W. Norton, 1991), pp. 341–70.

5 See the development of the *Shane* script from Guthrie's original version to the final release dialogue text, George Stevens Papers, Margaret Herrick Library, Academy of Motion Picture Arts and Sciences, Beverly Hills, California. Given Turner's own dismissal of Indians, it is appropriate that in this most 'Turnerian' of Westerns their only mention is an offhand reference by the rancher Riker (Emile Meyer) to a 'Cheyenne arrowhead' that he still carries.

6 Richard White, *It's Your Misfortune and None of My Own: A New History of the American West* (Norman: University of Oklahoma Press, 1991); Patricia Nelson Limerick, 'The Adventures of the Frontier in the Twentieth Century', in Grossman (ed.), *The Frontier in American Culture*, pp. 67–102.

7 See, for example, David J. Weber, *The Spanish Frontier in North America* (New Haven: Yale University Press, 1992).

8 Theodore Roosevelt, *The Winning of the West*. Seven volumes. (New York: G. P. Putnam's Sons, 1907).

9 Joyce Oldham Appleby, 'Recovering America's Historic Diversity: Beyond Exceptionalism', *Journal of American History*, LXXIX (1992), pp. 419–31.

10 Walt Whitman, 'Song of Myself' in his *Leaves of Grass* (New York: New American Library, 1955 [1881]), pp. 49–96.

11 For an attempt to bring this scholarship together, see Edward Countryman, *Americans: A Collision of Histories* (New York: Hill & Wang, 1996).

12 See John Chavez, *The Lost Land: The Chicano Image of the Southwest* (Albuquerque: University of New Mexico Press, 1984).

13 Richard White, *The Middle Ground: Indians, Empires and Republics in the Great Lakes Region 1650–1815* (Cambridge: Cambridge University Press, 1991).

14 See John Mack Faragher, *Daniel Boone: The Life and Legend of an American Pioneer* (New York: Henry Holt, 1992); Francis Jennings, *The Ambiguous Iroquois Empire: The Covenant Chain Federation of Indian Tribes with English Colonies from its Beginnings to the Lancaster Treaty of 1744* (New York: W. W. Norton, 1984); and *Empire of Fortune: Crowns, Colonies and Tribes in the Seven-Years' War in America* (New York: W. W. Norton, 1988); James H. Merrell, *The Indians' New World: Catawbas and their Neighbors from European Contact through the Era of Removal* (Chapel Hill: University of North Carolina Press, 1989); William G. McLoughlin, *Cherokee Renascence in the New Republic* (Princeton: Princeton University Press, 1986); Daniel K. Richter, *The Ordeal of the Longhouse: The Peoples of the Iroquois League in the Era of European Colonization*

(Chapel Hill: University of North Carolina Press, 1992); Daniel H. Usner Jr, *Indians, Settlers and Slaves in a Frontier Exchange Economy: The Lower Mississippi Valley before 1783* (Chapel Hill: University of North Carolina Press, 1992); Peter H. Wood et al. (eds), *Powhatan's Mantle: Indians in the Colonial Southwest* (Lincoln: University of Nebraska Press, 1989).

15 For a more extended summary, see Edward Countryman, 'Indians, the Colonial Order, and the Social Significance of the American Revolution', in *William and Mary Quarterly*, 3rd ser., LIII (1996), pp. 342–62.

16 See Weber, *Spanish Frontier* and Richard White, *Roots of Dependency: Subsistence, Environment and Social Change among the Choctaws, Pawnees and Navajos* (Lincoln: University of Nebraska Press, 1983).

17 Timothy J. Shannon, 'Dressing for Success: Hendrick, William Johnson and the Indian fashion', in *William and Mary Quarterly*, 3rd ser., LIII (1996), pp. 13–42.

18 For thorough analysis of Vietnam's ideological impact on the Frontier Myth and cultural reception of the Western genre, see Slotkin, pp. 441f.

19 Costner's title role in Lawrence Kasdan's *Wyatt Earp* (1994) includes a brief scene in which young Earp is employed in a squalid buffalo-skinning job, in which he drives a horse hitched to drag the hides off carcasses. The scene is otherwise unremarked in the film except perhaps to contrast this dissolute episode with Earp's eventual destiny as noble 'town-tamer'. Both Kasdan's film and its more cynical rival *Tombstone* (1993) demystify the Earp clan somewhat by stressing its selfish economic motives as against the idealism portrayed most famously in *My Darling Clementine* (1946). Both Earp biographies primarily tap contemporary anxiety about violent crime which the films answer with the harshest, vigilante-style solutions.

20 Means, for example, as leader of the American Indian Movement led a protest at the centennial observance of the Little Big Horn battle in June 1976 (Utley, p. 11).

21 For an introduction to the vast Custer literature see, for example, Paul Andrew Hutton (ed.), *The Custer Reader*; Brian W. Dippie, *Custer's Last Stand: The Anatomy of an American Myth*; and Robert M. Utley, *Cavalier in Buckskin: George Armstrong Custer and the Western Military Frontier*.

22 Mathison is actually the first woman to receive screen credit as principal writer. Leonore Coffee was assigned 'to punch-up the romantic scenes between George and Elizabeth' for *They Died with their Boots On*. Coffee rebelled against the many historical inaccuracies in the script and was ultimately denied credit. The Warner Bros./Flynn film was also the first to draw on Elizabeth Custer's writings (Hutton, pp. 499–501).

23 Davis's role as the diarist–narrator evokes a similar character and rhetorical strategy in Sam Peckinpah's cavalry epic *Major Dundee* (1964), which also involves an American army incursion into Mexico in pursuit of an Apache chief modelled on Geronimo.

24 The real Britton Davis summed up this interpretation in 1929: 'In treachery, broken pledges on the part of high officials, lies, thievery, slaughter of defenceless women and children, and every crime in the catalogue of man's inhumanity to man the Indian was a mere amateur compared to the "noble white man". His crimes were retail, ours wholesale' (David, p. 114).

13   The Twelve Custers, or, Video History
Roberta E. Pearson

It is a blisteringly hot afternoon on the plains of Montana. Thousands of scream-
ing, weapon-brandishing Indians surround a cluster of dismounted cavalry
troopers. At the centre of the ever-diminishing circle stand a cavalry guidon and
a Stars and Stripes. Next to the flags, a bearded, long-haired man in buckskins rapidly fires his six-shooters. Hit by arrows or bullets or both, he collapses and dies.
The Indians overwhelm the last few gallant soldiers. The scene fades to black.

There we have it: the Custer's Last Stand of legend, memory and cinema and
television screens. Although probably bearing little resemblance to the actual
events of 25 June 1876, the image of the beleaguered white men, their dashing
leader and their barbarous foes has imprinted itself upon the consciousness of
generations of Euro-Americans. Generations of Native Americans have, of course,
recognised the image's ideologically loaded message: white civilisation attacked by
the savage hordes. But to write only of a binary opposition between the white and
Indian versions of Custer's Last Stand would be to gravely oversimplify the complex diachronic and synchronic undulations of the representation of the Battle of
the Little Big Horn. I have elsewhere addressed the issue of diachronic variation.[1]
This essay addresses synchronic variation by comparing twelve texts from the
1990s that deal in whole or in part with Custer and his final battle. I shall argue
that all twelve texts, be they 'fiction' or 'non-fiction', employ similar strategies of
historical representation, although variations among them can be partially
explained in terms of the different discursive formations that produced and
received them. I shall also argue that the same explanation can partially account
for the significant variations among the texts' narrative structures. Both strategies
of historical representation and narrative structures attest to the fit between producer and audience that Pierre Bourdieu speaks of in *Distinction*: textual signifiers
match the lifestyle, social class or what Bourdieu would term *habitus* of the
implied viewer.[2]

This attempt at correlating screen histories with discursive formations is
intended to contribute to the ongoing debate concerning the cinematic and tele-
visual representation of the past. The interminable and not very interesting
debates about historical accuracy in which historians were wont to engage still
continue,[3] but now many historians and film historians writing about screen histories agree that such texts always speak more to the present than of the past; they
can more fruitfully be analysed in terms of the era that produced them than in
terms of the era they purport to depict. This position shifts rather than resolves
the underlying epistemological dilemma of a text's relationship to history: instead

Dustin Farnum as Custer in The Flaming Frontier *(1926).*

Errol Flynn as Custer in They Died with their Boots On *(1941).*

of matching a text's signifiers to the era that it purports to represent, scholars now seek a match between textual signification and the historical conditions of production and reception.

Most scholars who have attempted to connect textual signification to historical conditions of production have tended to focus on a few well-known texts. Leger Grindon, Michael Rogin, Roger Rosenstone and Pierre Sorlin take this approach to produce admirably illuminating analyses of even over-familiar texts. Rogin's essay on *The Birth of a Nation*, for example, connects the film's construction of the Reconstruction era to contemporary debates about immigration and American national identity, making clear the resonance that the film's title may have had in 1915[4]. But what of the myriad other films produced to celebrate the Civil War's sesquicentennial (1911–15)? Griffith had himself directed several Civil War-themed Biograph films which, together with those produced by his counterparts at other studios, contributed to a major genre of the cinema's second decade. The analysis of a single text, such as *The Birth of A Nation*, may reveal how a particular construction of the Civil War and Reconstruction related to contemporary debates about race, but an analysis of several texts all representing the same periods might reveal interesting contradictions and complexities. At any particular historical moment the representation of a prior historical moment or historical figure can be appropriated by different discursive formations for widely differing ideological agendas.[5]

The essays in this volume have addressed texts dealing with a historical period at least as central to American national identity and American racial politics as the Civil War; the westward expansion of the post-war years. This final essay discusses one of the most famous Westerners of all, George Armstrong Custer, a 'popular hero' who has served as a floating signifier, capable of myriad and often conflicting meanings. Custer's death at the Battle of the Little Big Horn, an encounter of military insignificance but great symbolic resonance among both Euro-Americans and Native Americans, assured his lasting fame. The initial news of the defeat of the crack 7th Cavalry and the death of the 'Boy General', famous for his dashing Civil War exploits, hit the newspapers just as the country celebrated its centenary on 4 July 1876. From that moment on the name of Custer became inextricably associated with the epic saga of westward expansion that has formed a central component of American popular culture. Native Americans still celebrate this encounter between the famous Indian fighter and some of their most renowned leaders, Sitting Bull and Crazy Horse among them. Their defeat of the 7th Cavalry was the greatest but also the last Indian victory of the Plains Wars; an outraged American government and military stepped up a programme of extermination that led to the final white–Indian 'battle', the Wounded Knee massacre of 1890.

Several of the texts studied for this essay assert the importance of the Little Big Horn Battle. A promo for the Turner Network Television docu-drama, *Crazy Horse*, boasts, 'From TNT, the best movie studio on television, the greatest battle of the American West'. The prologue to Episode 3 of Ric Burns's documentary *The Way West*[6] speaks in melodramatic terms of 'a struggle for the soul of the continent' that culminated at the Little Big Horn:

As the European vision of America took hold, Crazy Horse, Sitting Bull and a handful of other Native Americans would rise up as never before against the white man's destiny, determined at all costs to hold on to their own way of life. In the fateful summer of 1876, as the Republic prepared to celebrate its first hundred years, three decades of rapid expansion and strife would come to a violent climax on the windswept plains of southern Montana. What happened there would haunt for ever the imagination of the American people and define the character of the American nation for centuries to come.

Judging by production patterns, several others in the television and video industries share Ted Turner's and Ric Burns's assessment of the importance of Custer and his final battle. The first half of the 1990s witnessed a veritable Custer boom, related to a general resurgence of interest in all things Western. I have already written about the American ABC network's Custer mini-series *Son of the Morning Star* and about five documentaries aired on American television in 1992 and 1993 that deal in whole or in part with Custer: *Crossed Sabers* (a history of the United States Cavalry), Arts and Entertainment Network; *Last Stand at Little Big Horn*, an episode of the PBS *American Experience* series; 'Indians' and 'Soldiers', two episodes of the ten-hour mini-series *The Wild West*, distributed by Warner Bros. Domestic Television Distribution; *Custer and the Seventh Cavalry*, an episode of the Arts and Entertainment Network's *Real West* series; and *A Good Day to Die*, an episode of the Discovery Network's *How the West Was Lost* series about Native Americans.[7]

For this essay, I have viewed three fictional programmes, one docu-drama and eight non-fictional programmes. The three fictional programmes are single episodes of ongoing series: *Dr Quinn, Medicine Woman*, produced for the American CBS television network and now airing on the Disney Channel in the UK; *Legend*, a brief-lived series on the Paramount Network in the United States; and *The Lazarus Man*, a Turner-produced series airing on Sky One in the UK. All three series are focused around fictional protagonists: the eponymous Dr Quinn, a female doctor in the Old West; a journalist turned dime novelist who has taken on the persona of his fictional creation; and an amnesiac who wanders the West in search of his past. By contrast with these fictional texts, the programme that I have dubbed a 'docu-drama', Turner Network Television's *Crazy Horse*, tells the story of a 'real' historical character, the famous Oglala Lakota war chief, but fills in historical lacunae with invented incidents. The eight non-fictional programmes are: *The Way West* (directed by Ric Burns and aired on the Public Broadcasting Network in the USA); the American CBS network's history of Native Americans, *500 Nations*; *Touring the Little Big Horn Battlefield* produced by the Old Army Press; 'Boy Generals', an episode of the American Arts and Entertainment Network's series *Civil War Journal*; the Turner Broadcasting Station's history of Native Americans, *The Native Americans*; *Paha Sapa: The Struggle for the Black Hills*, the story of the Lakota nation's fight to regain its sacred territory; and two low-end, inexpensive compilations produced by Scimitar Video, *The Legend of Custer* and *The Indian Wars*.

All the texts under consideration, be they 'fiction' or 'non-fiction', make 'truth claims' regarding their representation of the past. In all three fictional programmes, the protagonists' interactions with a real historical character constitute a truth claim: Custer functions as a guarantor of the text's relationship to a 'real' historical period. Some truth claims are more overt. The episode of *Dr Quinn*,

Medicine Woman is a fictionalised recounting of the Washita massacre/battle; in the winter of 1868 Custer and his troops attacked a sleeping Cheyenne village at dawn, killing few warriors but many women and children. At the conclusion of the episode, Dr Quinn goes to her woman reporter friend, saying she wants to tell her about her Cheyenne friends: 'who they are and what's happened to them'. The reporter responds, 'You tell me the truth ... and I'll print it.' It seems that the viewer is meant to conclude that the programme's representation constitutes the 'truth'. Even a text that flagrantly violates academic notions of historical accuracy by relying upon Hollywood fictions begins with a truth claim. At the beginning of *The Indian Wars* the announcer states: 'For over a century historians have recounted numerous colourful tales of ... fierce conflict between Indian nations and white settlers. Many of these stories have been greatly embellished over the years, embellished to such an extent that the true stories of the Indian wars may be lost for all time.' It seems that the viewers are meant to conclude that they will now be shown the 'true story'.

More generally, a historical text, be it 'fiction' or 'non-fiction', makes truth claims by employing authenticating strategies that conform to the culture's inter-textual representation of a historical period or a historical figure. The deployment of these authenticating strategies results in a representation of the past that the text's audiences accept as verisimilar since it conforms to other familiar historical representations. By referring to the accumulated intertextual frame at the moment of production rather than to the text's 'real' historical referent, this for-mulation acknowledges that history can be accessed only through textual repre-sentations, that there is no objective and unmediated past. Hence, even when referring to 'real' historical events or characters, I shall speak of a text's conform-ity to the historical archive; one can assert that a particular screen Custer matches pictorial or verbal descriptions of the historical figure without asserting that the historical figure himself matched those descriptions.

The accumulation of 'correct' details in the text's image and soundtracks helps to construct this historical verisimilitude, which in this sense resembles what Steve Neale has dubbed 'generic verisimilitude'.[8] Indeed, for the Western genre, the same aural details work to produce historical and generic verisimilitude: gunshots; Indian war whoops; horses galloping and neighing. These aural details appear in the three fictional programmes and the docu-drama, as might be expected, since all can roughly be said to conform to the Western genre. But all the non-fictional pro-grammes, which might more properly be considered documentaries than Westerns, incorporate these details into their soundtracks as well. Many of these texts 'restage' battles with rostrum-animated photographs or drawings accompanied by a 'realis-tic' soundtrack, the aforementioned gunshots, war whoops and horse sounds. The non-fiction texts also share with their fictional counterparts the use of period music to enhance both verisimilitude and emotional affect. Custer's 'theme song', the 7th Cavalry's marching tune, 'Garry Owen', can be played on period instruments (fifes and drums or military brass bands) to add verisimilitude, played at a fast, jaunty tempo over paintings of charging cavalry or, as in *The Way West*, played at a slow, dirge-like pace over photographs of men soon to die at the Little Big Horn.

The spoken word also contributes to historical verisimilitude. Quotations from historical figures are one of the markers of the historical documentary and abound in the non-fictional texts under consideration, but fictional texts also employ this authenticating strategy. Sometimes the quotes are so familiar that they might be termed historical sound-bites. In *Crazy Horse* a young, unidentified cavalry officer boasts, 'With eighty men I can ride through the whole Sioux nation.' He then leads his troop into a deadly ambush, as did the quote's historical originator, Captain William J. Fetterman. The words' unwarranted hubris have made them a scriptwriter's favourite. Sometimes, however, the quotes are relatively obscure. In the *Lazarus Man* episode, Custer tells the hero: 'During the last six months of the war, I captured ten thousand prisoners, including seven generals, and during that time I never lost a colour, never lost a gun, and certainly was never defeated.' This is a paraphrase of the historical Custer's farewell message to his Civil War regiment, the 3rd Cavalry Division:

> During the past six months ... you have captured from the enemy, in open battle, one hundred and eleven pieces of field artillery, sixty-five battle-flags, and upwards of ten thousand prisoners of war, including seven general officers. ... You have never lost a gun, never lost a colour, and have never been defeated.

The scriptwriter probably employed the paraphrase to define the Custer character as arrogant and unsympathetic, but, for those well versed in the historical archive, it also serves to strengthen the text's historical verisimilitude, or at least to signal that some degree of research has gone into the production.

Soundtracks now convey what seems to late twentieth-century viewers a more 'authentic Indianness' than that of previous texts. Indian chants, flutes and drums, often performed by Native Americans, substitute for the 'dum, dum, dum, dum' drum beats and 'Indian' themes of the classical Hollywood Western. The success of *Dances with Wolves* has even made it possible for Indians occasionally to speak their own language, although television programmes mostly eschew the subtitles employed in that film. At the beginning of *Crazy Horse*, in the framing story that surrounds the flashback of the war chief's life, the titular hero and his small band of followers arrive at an army fort to surrender. For the first few minutes they converse in Lakota but quickly switch to English when their dialogue begins to convey narrative information. Towards the end, a crucial plot point turns upon a mistranslation: Crazy Horse speaks Lakota, correctly translated to the audience by subtitles and incorrectly translated to his white interlocutors by a treacherous Indian. The contemporary Indians who feature as 'talking heads' and voice-overs in the documentaries may not speak their ancestral languages but they do speak an 'Indian'-accented English. And both fictional and non-fictional texts quote historical Indians almost as much as they do historical whites. In *Crazy Horse*, the Red Cloud character paraphrases his historical progenitor's reaction to a trip to the white man's capital. 'I rode the iron horse to Washington. For five days I rode through their towns, their cities. There is no end to them. In Washington I saw things you can't even imagine. Our way of life is finished. There is only the white man's way and we will learn it or we will all die.' *The Way West* begins with a quote from Sarah Winnemucca, a Paiute Indian who learned to speak and write fluent English. 'My father told of a fearful dream. I dreamt I saw the greatest immigration that has yet been through our country. ... I heard a great weeping. I saw women crying and my men shot down by the white people.'

Like the soundtracks, the visual tracks of all the analysed texts have more in common than one might expect; all seek to include as much visual 'evidence' as possible, ranging from period photographs to contemporary re-enactments. This speaks to the demands of the documentary genre, which has staked its truth claims largely upon Western culture's obsession with the visual: 'seeing is believing'. Such is the desperation for the moving image that the producers often 'cheat', using footage shot during the 1890s or 1900s to illustrate events that occurred several decades earlier. The most blatant example of this is the use of 'phantom rides', footage taken from the front of a train's engine, usually dating from the cinema's first decade. *The Way West*, for example, uses such footage to accompany discussion of the building of the transcontinental railroad (completed 1869), while several programmes use it as a general illustration of the post-Civil War westward movement. Since nitrate decomposition and multiple duplication signify filmic antiquity, many in the audience may believe that the images were taken during the period being discussed rather than several decades later. The gunshots, horses' hooves and other noises that accompany the rostrum-animated battles further attest to this valorisation of the visual. Documentary producers who reject certain techniques, such as re-enactments, as overly 'fictional' seemingly have no qualms about accompanying 'authentic' period photographs and Indian pictograms with totally fabricated soundtracks. The visual track contains period images: the aural track contains recreated sounds. The visual track provides the evidence: the soundtrack provides the 'effects'.

Producers of historical documentaries set in the post-cinematic era can draw upon the filmic archives, permitting their audiences literally to 'see', if not always to hear, the past. The producers of documentaries about the West are not as fortunate: Frederick Jackson Turner proclaimed the close of the frontier in 1893, a year before the Edison Company began commercial distribution of the Kinetoscope. But still photography, period paintings and Indian pictographs can legitimately be incorporated; all the non-fictional texts rely extensively upon such images, some employed so frequently that they constitute the visual equivalent of the sound-bite quotations. Even here, however, verisimilitude rather than historical accuracy remains the goal, with producers following the convention established by Ken Burns in the very successful *The Civil War*. Burns explained that he looked for

an equivalent – that is, an image that may not be what an expert would certify as belonging to the precise moment I'm describing, but that combines with the narration to make a synthesis that's good history, so that you say, 'My God, I hear that. I know what they must have felt.'

Here and elsewhere Burns points to the importance of what might be termed a dramatic realism or verisimilitude that the visual enhances:

Film goes directly to the emotions without translation. . . . Film has the power to reach profound levels of emotions, and I can't be interested in a piece of history unless there's something I can loosely describe as emotional about it. I think the ordinary person feels that way too. I think that in allowing history to be defined and presented exclusively by the academy, we've bled it of its powerful emotional aspect.[9]

Burns established the practice, followed by subsequent documentarians, his brother Ric among them, of using what might be termed generally illustrative images. *The Civil War* sequence that went 'most directly to the emotions', judging by public response, dealt with Major Sullivan Ballou, who wrote to his wife shortly before his death telling her that even were he to fall in battle he would be with her always in spirit. As the narrator read Ballou's letter, the image track showed a photograph of a Union soldier. It was not Ballou – no photograph had been found. Many of the texts I analysed employed a similar tactic, using a photograph of a generic Indian when talking about Crazy Horse, who never permitted his photograph to be taken. When the text fails to identify their provenance, the photographs that serve these general illustrative purposes 'cheat' just as much as the phantom rides or the fabricated soundtracks. A general audience may not know when film was invented or that Crazy Horse was never photographed, but do 'know' that documentaries tell 'the truth' and may quite reasonably assume that the photograph is of Ballou or Crazy Horse or whichever historical figure, event or location the soundtrack discusses. I point to this practice not necessarily to criticise it, but further to reveal the fuzziness of the boundaries between 'fact' and 'fiction' in the historical documentary.

Although period images constitute a 'truth claim', producers seem to believe that cinematic images better convey a sense of dramatic verisimilitude; camera movement renders still images cinematic. The camera pans over battle scenes, zooms into a portrait's eyes, roams around panoramic landscapes, singles out telling details of an Indian pictograph. The search for historical and dramatic verisimilitude also leads to the incorporation of twentieth-century moving images that evoke or even attempt to replicate the 19th century. Many of the documentaries include contemporary footage of historical locations: battlefields, Indian homelands, buildings and so forth. As with the still images, cinematic techniques enhance emotional impact. Helicopter tracking-shots reveal the rugged beauty of the sacred Black Hills; point-of-view shots represent the perspectives of historical protagonists; shaky tracking-shots and disjointed editing convey the fear and panic of battle. But such tactics do not satisfy the demand for moving images: all the non-fictional texts incorporate fictional sequences – contemporary restagings of historical events. Sepia, black and white, slow motion and soft-focus all signify 'pastness' but some of the texts include more straightforward re-enactments, a practice eschewed by the Ken Burns school of documentarians.[10] *Touring the Little Big Horn Battlefield* contains shots of an 'Indian' village occupied by present-day Native Americans in their ancestors' dress, while the battle sequences in the episode of *Civil War Journal* feature Civil War re-enactors (perhaps also in their ancestors' dress).

The (non)inclusion of fictional sequences most clearly distinguishes the texts and links them to their discursive formations. Cinematic genres, be they classed as fiction or non-fiction, are constrained by audience expectations; producers may stretch or even violate genre conventions in the name of novelty, but too wholehearted abandonment risks confusing or alienating the audience. The visual evidence provided by re-enactment footage might buttress a historical documentary's truth claims, but might also undermine them with particular audiences. If perceived as overly fictional, these sequences may threaten the text's claim to documentary status and hence to the didactic and uplifting associations that the documentary genre has enjoyed since the actualities of the late 19th century appealed to a middle-class Victorian audience that looked with suspicion upon the merely entertaining. In the United States, the Public Broadcasting Service, which began life as National Educational Television, depends for its continued government funding upon serving a didactic function. *The Way West,* broadcast on PBS, includes a few re-enactments, but the shooting style presents these sequences as metaphoric or evocative rather than direct windows on the past, as in, for example, a sepia-tinted, slow-motion close-up of wagon wheels to illustrate pioneers moving westward. Other programmes, distributed through outlets dependent upon advertiser revenue or audience subscription and needing to appeal to a more disparate audience than that for PBS, must to some degree contest the documentary's potentially off-putting didactic associations. These programmes retain and even heighten the documentary's commitment to visual evidence through more extended use of re-enactments. *The Native Americans,* aired on the Turner Broadcasting Station, a so-called 'super-channel' based in Atlanta, illustrates a discussion of the Civil War with footage of re-enactors staging a battle and illustrates a discussion of white–Indian conflicts with brief excerpts of mounted Indians and cavalry troopers taken from Hollywood Westerns. The two video compilations, *The Legend of Custer* and *The Indian Wars,* produced by a company directly dependent upon retail sales and repeat custom, consist almost entirely of often lengthy clips from Hollywood feature films.

The culturally coded distinctions between 'fiction' and 'documentary' grant greater dramatic licence to the former even when dealing with 'real' historical characters or events. The texts must none the less accord with the culture's intertextual representations of historical periods and characters through the inclusion of the correct visual details. In previous eras, Custers wore long hair and fringed buckskins; now they accord more closely with portraits of the historical Custer. In *Legend, Lazarus Man* and *Dr Quinn,* Custer has long, blond, curly hair and an imperial beard and wears a costume consisting of knee-high cavalry boots, light-blue cavalry trousers, leather gauntlets, a sailor shirt (single stars on either side of the broad, flat collar), a non-regulation military tunic (with more braid than strictly required) and a red cravat or scarf. The Crazy Horses of previous eras usually had more in common with the standard Hollywood Indian than they did with the historical archive concerning the historical figure. Now they ride into battle with white spots of hail painted on their bodies and a white streak of lighting painted on their face, the warpaint adorning the warrior in Crazy Horse's boyhood vision. This move to signs of a greater 'authenticity' is in keeping with the trend noted by Gaines and Herzog in this volume: 'These fresh signs work to bolster a new Western mythos that is ostensibly more true to the old reality.' Visual guarantors of 'authenticity' are not confined to costume and décor but include physical actions. In *Dr Quinn,* the heroine attends a formal dinner hosted by the general, at which he feeds his wolfhounds from the table. The historical archive reveals that Custer doted on his dogs and kept wolfhounds.

The visual and aural signifiers discussed to this point combine to convey historical verisimilitude but also combine to create a narrative structure that endows the same historical events with particular and distinctive meanings. As do the signifiers of historical verisimilitude, the narrative structure varies according to the discursive formation that produced and received the texts. The choice of the narrator who provides the voice-over tying the visual and aural signifiers together often clearly signals the intended audience. *The Way West*, produced by noted documentarist Ric Burns, airing on the prestigious Public Broadcasting Network, employs as narrator Russell Baker. Baker, well-known columnist for the *New York Times* and the replacement for Alistair Cooke as host of the respectable, middlebrow PBS anthology series of British television, *Masterpiece Theatre*, speaks in patrician, mid-Atlantic tones well suited to the up-market audience the producers must have envisioned. Gregory Harrison, once the attractive young co-star of a medical series who now appears in made-for-television films, narrates the CBS network's *500 Nations*. Again, narrator suits audience: Harrison, and his middle-American accent, would be relatively well known to network television viewers. *Touring the Little Big Horn Battlefield*, a video sold to Battlefield tourists and produced by the Old Army Press, features an un-credited narrator whose authoritative, Voice of God delivery directs the punters how to organise their tour. The low-rent, low-production values *Legend of Custer*, which consists almost entirely of excerpts from Hollywood films, features an inexperienced narrator who consistently confuses cavalry with Calvary, a confusion, it must be admitted, not that uncommon among Americans. Those who watch PBS get Russell Baker while those who purchase cheap, knock-off videos get a narrator who cannot pronounce cavalry.

The narrative structure is more overtly ideological, seeking to position the viewer with the Native Americans, with the Euro-Americans or with what I call the 'official' perspective. These are not mutually exclusive; different parts of the same text can take the Euro-American, the Native American or the official perspective. By the official perspective, I refer to the dominant representation of Native American/Euro-American conflicts that now seems central to a US national identity predicated upon the heroism and sacrifices of both sides. This is not to deny the constant challenge to dominant representations but rather to acknowledge that, at a particular historical moment, the dominance by a specific set of representations erases the signs of contestation. The naturalised and widely accepted dominant representations temporarily halt history, establishing a set of static and abstracted 'facts' that play a crucial role in the construction of a dominant national identity. As the Popular Memory Group argues about activities of the British National Heritage organisations:

> it is as if a strange and obliterating glaciation is being drawn across the entire surface of social life, as if history is being frozen over, arrested and in this sense 'stopped'. National Heritage appears to involve nothing less than the abolition of all contradiction in the name of a national culture. . . . History appears not as necessity, struggle or transformation but as 'our' National Heritage.[11]

In the case of the Plains Indian Wars, the abolition of contradiction establishes a national culture, or what I term the official perspective, that equally valorises the heroism and sacrifice of both sides. This is in keeping with Tzvetan Todorov's formulation of the available positions vis-à-vis an ethnic or racial Other. In *The Conquest of America*, Todorov argues that one can either consider the Other as

206

unequal and thereby clearly inferior, or project one's own values on to the other, in the process eradicating difference. 'Difference is corrupted into inequality, equality into identity.'[12] As a result, 'What is denied is the existence of a human substance truly Other, something capable of being not merely an imperfect state of oneself.'[13]

In 1990 and again in 1991 the US House of Representatives debated changing the name of the Custer Battlefield National Monument to the Little Big Horn Battlefield National Monument. Examination of the debates reveals how the corruption of equality into identity establishes the official perspective that elides contradictions. Representative Rhodes asserted that the legislation was intended to 'honor the Cheyenne, Sioux and other Indian Nations who gave their lives to defend their families, life-style, culture and their lands',[14] the implication, of course, being that any right-thinking individual would have behaved in precisely the same manner. Representative Burns made this sentiment more explicit: 'These people fought to save what they believed was theirs and rightfully theirs. They did what any of us would have done to save and protect our own families and homeland.'[15] These statements cast the Indians as the heroes, but, at least as far as the United States Congress is concerned, this does not necessitate casting their white opponents as the villains. The official perspective on the Little Big Horn represents both sides as equally valorous. Representative Ben Nighthorse Campbell, the Native American who originally introduced the legislation, said, 'The Indians fought valiantly for their way of life, their families, as they knew their very survival was at stake. . . . The soldiers fought bravely, too, believing that their battles would make the West safe for settlers, miners, trappers, and others who sought fortunes and their futures during our nation's westward expansion.'[16] Beneath this rhetorical equality that eradicates difference lurks the assimilationist agenda that has shaped United States Indian policy since colonial times. Indians and whites may have exhibited similar heroism and sacrifice in defence of similar ideals, but only one side could win. The official perspective implicitly posits the inevitability of the defeat of the indigenous peoples by a 'superior' white civilisation, but assuages their descendants through the construction of a national identity predicated upon a multiculturalism to which both sides, Euro-Americans and Native Americans, have made acknowledged contributions. The eventual renaming of the Custer Battlefield National Monument as the Little Big Horn Battlefield National Monument elides the contradiction at the heart of the official perspective posed by the often impoverished descendants of the Plains Indians: their lives may be blighted by abnormally high rates of infant mortality, disease, alcoholism and unemployment but their most hated opponent has been at least partially symbolically eradicated.

As might be expected in a video sold in a National Parks bookshop to visitors and prospective visitors, *Touring the Little Big Horn Battlefield* takes the official perspective. After set-up shots of the cemetery, the video shows the ceremonial reburial of the bodies of thirty-one cavalry troopers who died in the Little Big Horn Battle. We see a park ranger and a war-bonneted Indian shaking hands while an army officer looks on. The narrator intones, 'Once the scene of deadly combat, all races mix proudly here.' The next shot shows a war-bonneted Indian colour guard carrying the Stars and Stripes, while 'Garry Owen' plays on the soundtrack.

The narrator says, 'To the Native American, this is the scene of his last great victory over the white invader. The white Americans that visit the scene are also proud. No cowards died here.' As the video tour continues, it reaches the 'area of Reno's retreat' where there are three stone markers. 'One is for the 7th Cavalry's part-Indian officer, Lt Macintosh. And the newest marker is for the only black man with the 7th, the interpreter Isaiah Dorman.' Macintosh's and Dorman's markers concretely embody the official perspective, reminding tourists that men of all races have made the ultimate sacrifice for American national identity.

The episode of *Dr Quinn, Medicine Woman* is a fictionalised interpretation of the Washita battle/massacre at which Custer, portrayed as a bloodthirsty glory-hunter, causes the death of Cheyenne Indians sympathetically portrayed in this and previous episodes as friends of the series' central protagonists. It none the less depends upon the official perspective for the plot's emotional resolution, the event that causes Dr Quinn to turn from despair and bitterness to hope for her Cheyenne friends and the country's future. Dr Quinn and her Indian shaman friend Cloud Dancing had discovered a Cheyenne baby hidden under his dead mother at the massacre site. The child was given into the care of first a white wet nurse and then a childless African-American couple. At the episode's conclusion Cloud Dancing plans to return the baby to his Cheyenne people. The African-American woman hands the baby to the Native American man, saying, 'You must always remember how a Negro couple took care of you and a white woman nursed you at her breast. Now you grow up to be part of a brave and proud people.' Cloud Dancing rides away carrying the baby, whom he says will be called 'Lives in Hope'. Presumably the child lives in the hope of the multicultural America of the late 20th century, a country that erects battlefield monuments to part-Indian cavalry officers, African-American interpreters and their Cheyenne and Lakota foes, these symbolic acts contributing to the construction of a national identity that obscures both present-day racial inequalities and the nation's legacy of genocide.

The docu-drama *Crazy Horse*, produced as part of Ted Turner's series of documentaries and television films on Native American history and celebrating the life of one of the most honoured of Native American leaders, rather curiously espouses the official perspective. The first title states, 'In 1865 the Civil War ended. As the flow of settlers heading westward increased, so did the disputes between the government, the settlers and the Indians. Conflict was inevitable.' Crazy Horse's rallying cry to his braves at the Battle of the Little Big Horn – 'It's a good day to fight, it's a good day to die!' – retrospectively confirms the logic of his own defeat and death and of the destruction of his people's way of life. The scriptwriter's failure to imagine a peaceful and just resolution to the conflict between Euro- and Native Americans typifies the 'strange and obliterating glaciation' that official histories perform in the construction of national identity. An alternative history in which whites did not seek brutally to eradicate Indian culture literally becomes unthinkable. Such an alternative history implies an alternative present, and the maintenance of a hegemonic order requires the suppression of such alternatives.

Such suppression can never totally succeed and some programmes do hint at alternatives to the official view of noble self-sacrifice on both sides; these can be characterised as taking the Native American perspective. This is not to claim that an 'authentic' representation of Native American culture can ever appear on the screen; since the first white man set foot in the 'New World,' the voice of the Native American has been refracted through a Euro-American communication medium, be it speech, writing or the screen. But some texts produced with the white man's tools do permit more scope for self-representation than others. *Paha Sapa: The Struggle for the Black Hills* falls into this category. While not explicitly constructing an alternative history, the programme suggests its possibility. The narrator describes the programme as 'The story of the theft and desecration of the Indians' ancestral lands ... and the struggle to regain them.' As the image track shows shots of sky, mountains and wildlife, the narrator, accompanied by native flute music, speaks of the importance of the Black Hills to the Lakotas' 'spiritual power and identity as a people'. A warning klaxon interrupts this rural idyll as the image track shows first a sign saying 'Black Hills – Holy Land', then mining equipment shifting soil. Just as the bulldozer tears holes in the earth, the programme tears holes in the frozen glacier of the official perspective to reveal the ongoing consequences of the Euro/Native American conflict of over a century ago. Had not the white man triumphed that bulldozer might not now be defiling the sacred landscape. Nor should the white man's triumph be posited as inevitable; rather, it resulted from deliberate and not terribly noble or self-sacrificing machinations. A Native American interviewee states, 'Crazy Horse and Sitting Bull, two of the greatest leaders of the Lakota nation, were killed, were politically assassinated. They were the two greatest leaders that could pose the most resistance to the taking of our sacred homelands.' Had Crazy Horse and Sitting Bull survived, the statement implies, not only the past but the present might well have been very different.

None of the other programmes that provides the Indian perspective hints at an alternative present, but many do contrast historical Indian cultures to a white 'civilisation' whose customs many Native Americans found baffling. The TBS series, *The Native Americans*, spends the first hour portraying life in North America before the coming of the white man, the period known to the Indians as the 'dog days', since they had not yet acquired the horse from the Spanish. Through voice-over narration and interviews with several Native Americans, the programme details the Indians' spiritual beliefs, tribal organisation and hunting/gathering techniques. Such expressions of regard for Native American culture can, however, veer perilously close to a new-ageish appropriation, as in the episode of *Dr Quinn, Medicine Woman*. After the Washita massacre at which he loses his family, Cloud Dancing insists on conveying the Cheyenne's knowledge of what might be termed holistic medicine to his white friend. The acquisition of the other's knowledge serves as part of the healing process that enables Dr Quinn to confront her grief over her Indian friends' deaths and to relate their story to the reporter at the episode's conclusion. Respect is granted the other's culture, but primarily in so far as it benefits the white heroine.

The most challenging native American rebuttal to the official multicultural they-were-all-brave-noble-and-self-sacrificing perspective questions the hallowed image of the gallant Last Stand, soldiers in an ever-dwindling circle, steadfastly fighting to the last man. Native American oral histories and archaeological evidence from the battlefield suggest that the overwhelming numbers of Indians caused the rapid disintegration of morale and discipline among the cavalry troopers. The Little Big Horn segment of *The Way West* presents this relatively new view of the battle. Historian Robert Utley states,

> In my own mind it is simply one enormous chaos with virtually no organisation on either side. . . . It is just a whole lot of Indians all over the place killing soldiers. I believe that discipline and command broke down on the military side and, as one Indian characterized it, it was just like chasing a lot of buffalo to be killed.

At this point, the camera dramatises the narrator's account of the action by taking the point of view of first the troopers and then the Indians. Over a rapid tracking shot to Last Stand Hill the narrator says, 'They were only a few yards to the top of the rise when they were hit with a final horrifying surprise. Over the crest came Crazy Horse and a thousand Oglala and Cheyenne warriors.' Over a rapid out-of-focus tracking shot back down the hill past the markers for the fallen troopers the narrator says, 'Crazy Horse and his men swept down the ridge crushing everything before them.' The camera then takes the perspective of an individual Indian warrior. Over a shaky, low-angle, black-and-white tracking shot of brush and trees, as if one were creeping through the cover towards one's foes, an Indian-accented voice quotes the warrior Standing Bear:

> I could see warriors flying all around me like shadows. And the noise of the hoofs and the guns and the cries was so loud it seemed quiet in there. And the voices seemed to be on top of the cloud. There were so many of us that I think we did not need guns. Just the hooves would have been enough.

Another warrior is quoted as saying, 'The soldiers became foolish, many throwing away their guns and raising their hands saying, "Sioux, pity us, take us prisoner." '

A white historian and then the narrator confirm that the terrified soldiers did not, contra countless depictions of the Last Stand, rally around the flag and fight to the last man. Says historian Steven Ambrose: 'No, not like we envision it. . . . Because of the Indian accounts. The soldiers broke and ran. Their knees hit their chins they ran so hard. . . . Not a last stand.' Says the narrator: 'Some of Custer's men fought valiantly to the end. Some panicked and were cut to pieces as they ran. Some may have killed themselves to avoid torture and mutilation.' Cowardice, panic and suicide clash radically with what the United States military considers its glorious history and, with the exception of *Little Big Man* (1970), film-makers have been reluctant to depict such behaviour. As became apparent with regard to the Gulf War protests, criticism of politicians and the military command may be tolerated, but criticism of individual soldiers is taboo even, it seems, if they died over a century ago. Some descendants of the Indian warriors who fought at the Little Big Horn, however, must take pleasure in finally seeing their ancestors' accounts considered as reputable historical sources. At the conclusion of *The Way West*'s account of the battle, Native American Michael Her Many Horses says:

> I think I would have liked to have been at Little Big Horn to see all of the Lakota people and their allies together. And to see the finest that the United States had in terms of a fighting machine come rolling over those hills trying to attack us and our reaction to it. It was suicide for them to do that and it . . . reinforced a lot of ideas we had about non-Indians – that they were mentally inferior. . . . I would like to have been there to have

seen American arrogance stamped out. That little forty-five minutes that it took to do them all in. I think that would have given me a lot of satisfaction.

Michael Her Many Horses radically undermines an official perspective that obscures the lasting resentments of a conquered people; rarely do the white man's media permit Native Americans to express satisfaction at the defeat of their foes. Even rarer, however, are white expressions of hostility to Native Americans, permitted only when they serve to shore up rather than undermine the official perspective. In the *Dr Quinn, Medicine Woman* episode, three bearded, unkempt and doubtless smelly men lounge round the general store while the proprietor reads an account of an Indian attack. Says one of the layabouts, 'Them bloodthirsty Indians was looking to scalp us all.' Given the source of these sentiments, it is unlikely that viewers would wish to endorse them. While such outright antagonism is *verboten*, however, many of the texts under consideration do present what might be characterised as the white perspective. *Touring the Little Big Horn Battlefield*, referred to above as the exemplar of the official perspective, literally presents a white perspective by asking the viewer to put him/herself in the place of the beleaguered troopers in Reno and Benteen's command. Says the narrator, 'Imagine lying in these shallow depressions with bullets everywhere, with the cries of the wounded, the acrid smell of gunpowder and the merciless sun beating down on you.' This programme, unlike *The Way West*, does not alternate between white and Indian viewpoints. The account of the battle all but ignores the Indian perspective; it follows the actions of the white soldiers, mentions the Indians only as the attacking foe and does not draw on Native American oral histories. *500 Nations* attests to the remarkable persistence of the white perspective even in texts that purport sympathy for the Native American. This programme's version of the Little Big Horn battle presents 'classic' pictures of the Last Stand – a whirling circle of Indians picking off an ever-dwindling group of whites – balancing this representation only with a sole Indian pictogram.

What, then, can we conclude about the connections between narrative structure and discursive formation? Direct correlations cannot be drawn since, as noted above, many of the programmes incorporate more than one of the three possible perspectives – official, Native American or Euro-American. The various texts do, however, provide some suggestive evidence as to the ways in which specific producers and audiences narrativise the Battle of the Little Big Horn. *Touring the Little Big Horn Battlefield*, produced by the Old Army Press and sold at the official museum shop, begins with a powerful formulation of the official perspective and then recounts the actual events of the battle mostly from the white perspective. *Dr Quinn, Medicine Woman* and *Crazy Horse*, broadcast to the mass, mainstream audiences that watch the CBS network and the TBS superstation, have narratives that sympathetically portray their Indian protagonists and yet ultimately espouse the official perspective. *The Way West*, broadcast to a smaller, more up-market audience on a network that regularly comes under attack for its left-leaning tendencies, concerns what the narrator refers to as 'incompatible visions of America, the promise and the sorrow of the American dream'. The text gives Native Americans the space to put forward their perspective on the battle, while at the same time giving accounts of white self-sacrifice and heroism, but refrains from the obscuration of the official perspective. *Paha Sapa: The Struggle for the Black Hills*, produced by and sold at the bookshop of the Museum of the American Indian, most radically contests the official perspective by pointing to the ongoing consequences of the distant events of 25 June 1876. The two texts at either end of the spectrum, *Touring the Little Big Horn Battlefield* and *Paha Sapa: The Struggle for the Black Hills,* are both distributed at sites of official memory, owned and maintained by the United States government, a fact that points to the complexities of historical representation.

Notes

1 ' "Custer's Still the Hero": Textual Stability and Transformation', *Journal of Film and Video* (Spring/Fall, 1995), pp. 82–97. This article argues against the rather simplistic notion that changing ideological context is the sole determinant of textual content by comparing the 1941 Warners film, *They Died with their Boots On*, to the 1991 ABC mini-series *Son of the Morning Star.* See also my article comparing several silent Custer films, 'The Revenge of Rain-in-the-Face, or Custers and Indians on the Silent Screen', in Daniel Bernardi (ed.), *The Birth of Whiteness: Race and the Emergence of US Cinema* (New Brunswick: Rutgers University Press, 1996), pp. 273–99. The reader interested in representations of Custer might also wish to look at my article on the short-lived television series, 'White Network/Red Power: ABC's *Custer*', in Lynn Spigel and Michael Curtin (eds), *The Revolution That Wasn't: Sixties Television and Social Context* (New York: Routledge, 1996).

2 Pierre Bourdieu, *Distinction: A Social Critique of the Judgment of Taste* (Cambridge: Harvard University Press, 1984). The concept of *habitus* is considerably more complicated than lifestyle or social class, but this is not the proper venue to explicate Bourdieu. However, this is not necessarily to argue that the audiences for these texts are mutually exclusive. Custer buffs, or those more generally interested in the Old West, may, like me, want to see them all.

3 I suspect, however, that historians will never entirely abandon the desire for accuracy. Many of the contributors to *Past Imperfect: History According to the Movies* judge films in terms of their conformance to some supposedly objective historical record (Mark C. Carnes (ed.), *Past Imperfect: History According to the Movies* (New York: Henry Holt and Company, 1995)).

4 Leger Grindon, *Shadows on the Past: Studies in the Historical Fiction Film* (Philadelphia: Temple University Press, 1994); ' "The Sword Becomes a Flashing Vision": D. W. Griffith's *The Birth of a Nation*' in Michael Rogin, *Ronald Reagan, The Movie and Other Episodes in Political Demonology* (Berkeley: University of California Press, 1987); Roger A. Rosenstone, *Visions of the Past: The Challenge of Film to Our Idea of History* (Cambridge: Harvard University Press, 1995), and Pierre Sorlin, *The Film in History: Restaging the Past* (Totowa, NJ: Barnes and Noble Books, 1980). On cinema and history see also Vivian Sobchack (ed.), *The Persistence of History: Cinema, Television and the Modern Event* (New York and London: Routledge, 1996).

5 On this point see William Uricchio and Roberta E. Pearson, *Reframing Culture: The Case of the Vitagraph Quality Films* (Princeton: Princeton University Press, 1993), particularly Chapter 4.

6 Called *The Way West* when broadcast in the United States, the programme was retitled *The Wild West* for transmission by Channel 4 in the United Kingdom.

7 See ' "Custer's Still the Hero": Textual Stability and Transformation', and 'Custer Loses Again: The Contestation Over Commodified Public Memory' in Dan Ben-Amon and Liliane Weissberg (eds), *Cultural Memory and the Construction of Identity* (Detroit: Wayne State University Press, 1998).

8 Steve Neale, 'Questions of Genre', *Screen*, vol. 31, no. 3 (Spring, 1990), pp. 45–51.

9 Bernard A. Weisberger, 'The Great Arrogance of the Present is to Forget the Intelligence of the Past: An Interview with Ken Burns', *American Heritage*, Sept./Oct. 1990, pp. 99, 100.

10 Said Burns: 'We have ground rules – no re-creations, for instance; no overweight folks in Reeboks and uniforms charging across the fields. That's fun when you're there, but it's no way to pass on information about the Civil War, it would be violating a trust' (Weisberger, p. 99).

11 See Richard Johnson, Gregor McLennan, Bill Schwarz and David Sutton (eds), *Making Histories: Studies in History-writing and Politics* (London: Hutchinson, 1982), p. 265.

12 Tzvetan Todorov, *The Conquest of America: The Question of the Other* (New York: Harper Torch Books, 1987), p. 146.

13 Todorov, p. 42.

14 'House approves monument for Indians who killed Custer', *Detroit Free Press*, 18 September 1990, p. 5A.

15 *Congressional Record*, vol. 136, no. 92, 18 July 1990.

16 *Congressional Record*, vol. 137, no. 98, 24 June 1991.

Index